THE POWER OF WORDS

THE POWER OF WORDS

ALEXANDER JAMES HARIZ

Dedication

*To all members of the Wordplay-L list who have generously contributed to the discussions and provided literary fodder for lively debates and informative exchanges. To all those who are still with us and those who have since passed on.
I am infinitely indebted to Rollo Ross who managed the technical side of the mailing list and insured its smooth operation during his afterhours.*

Also by Alexander James Hariz
A Way with Words

Contents

Foreword ix

1	Philosophical perspectives on language	1
2	Vocabulary	11
3	Etymology	76
4	Grammar	131
5	Style and Syntax	154
6	Pronunciation	180
7	Language Oddities	206
8	Greek, Latin, and other languages	258
9	Foreign Phrases	273
10	Errors of Literary Logic	279
11	Colloquial English	291
12	Weird but Logical	339
13	Language Jokes	381
14	Word Games and Puzzles	408
15	Soliloquies from Michael	441

References 447
About the Wordplay List 449

Foreword

This book – the second in the series is entirely inspired by the proceedings of an online forum on words and their use in the English language, which I convened early in 1995. Back then they were called distribution lists, and were managed by listservs. I have always had a fascination with words and the turn of phrases that goes way back to my teenage year and my early formation in French, before I even learnt a single word of English. I was pleasantly surprised to find English just a s rich and just as replete with subtle nuances and depth of meaning.

I am forever indebted to the contributions of all list members from around the world who showered us with their abundant knowledge, wit and wisdom over the seven years the forum was in existence. The list was called Wordplay-L, and I was often asked when I am going to summarise the content into some book of best of wordplay or some such. Life had its priorities, and it wasn't until I retired from my day job that I found the time to go back and look at the idea seriously.

The idea of founding the internet forum was inspired by earlier works on the machinations of the English language such as those and Richard Lederer, William Sapphire, or Steven Pinker etc. The internet was in its infancy, when discussion groups popped up all over with list servers quickly catching up to the requisite technology. I then set out to pen down the description and charter of the forum. I submitted it to the list of lists, and voila! The rest is history.

Discussion groups being experimental at the time, it wasn't long before I found a host server which could manage the traffic for free – provided manned intervention is not required. I was not technically savvy when it comes to server software, so I turned to my colleague Rollo Ross to help me manage the list traffic remotely. He has a great deal of experience in managing the university computer centre, and particularly academic discussion groups through email. It was just as well that I requested this assistance, as the various tedious problems with excessive traffic that surfaced later on proved critical.

Within days from the launch, we were flooded with new subscription and contributions. Advertising the forum on the list of lists server turned to be pivotal in giving it adequate exposure. The email traffic was so hectic that we resorted to scheduling the deliveries in digest forms instead of single messages. Then it evolved to two digests a day. The contributors were spread evenly among the English-speaking countries, with odd ones from countries with English as a second language.

The membership comprised a varied background, but primarily teachers, copy editors, reviewers, programmers, and librarians. This mix made up for very educational discussions laced with wit humour, and at times down-right laughter.

This book (volume 2) aims to synthesise, summarise, and collate the contributions made in the second half of 1995 into focussed themes to fit in a book about language, usage, and the evolution thereof with time.

Proceeds from the book sales, after production costs, will be donated entirely to charities working in children education in disadvantaged communities. The publication of this book is wholly motivated by the desire for public education and sharing the gift of language.

Copyright © 2025 by Alexander James Hariz
All rights reserved. No part of this book may be reproduced in any manner whatsoever without written permission except in the case of brief quotations embodied in critical articles and reviews.
First Printing, 2025

1

Philosophical perspectives on language

Evolution of language: *"the language is a complex dynamic adaptive system -- the act of playing the game has a way of changing the rules."*

Lomond in Sacramento pondered:
Starting Over - If we were to start over with the words and punctuation marks that we now have in the English language:

Would it be better to pronounce words the way they are spelled or change the spelling to reflect the way they are pronounced?

In other words, would it be better to write the way we speak or speak the way we write?

To which, Sara in Boston opined: "Write the way we speak, or speak the way we write?" My two cents:
It would be nice if we could speak the way we write, but I don't think that will ever be feasible. Likewise, writing the way we speak could probably lead to a lot more misunderstanding. Speaking usually requires more on-the-spot thinking, because while you can change something you've written (especially on a PC!), you can't unsay something you've said. I think that even if we started the language again

from scratch (and I wonder where *that* particular phrase came from), we would find that speaking and writing would tend to differ. Then again, maybe I'm just full of it. You decide.

Then Heath in San Antonio followed up with:
As to speaking and writing, a fine book I read suggested folks should write more as they speak (with less pretentiousness, among other points), and speak more as they write (with better grammar, et al).

As a coach of debate, and an amateur rhetorician, I tend to agree. But writing and speaking are separate arts, with separate virtues. Speaking allows the use of paralanguage and nonverbal communication. These must be approximated with UNGAINLY and *d*i*s*t*r*a*c*t*i*n*g* _typographical_ tricks and emoticons.

At the same time, writing gives leisure for rereading, allowing concise and poetic expression, which may be mulled over at leisure.

Which reminds me of the discussion on writing, reading, and associated danger. I recall the Catholic Church opposing the translation of the Bible from Latin, for fear that common folks being able to read it, might jeopardize their authority.

Toni of Minneapolis, MN observed:
I was re-reading Feynman's autobiographical '"Surely You're Joking, Mr. Feynman!" Adventures of a Curious Character' (yes, there are quotation marks in the book's title), in one chapter he discusses how he got involved in a conference to discuss "the ethics of equality". During the reading of one of the papers that had been written by a sociologist, he decided that he would read _one sentence_ slowly to try to figure out what it meant. The sentence went something like:

"The individual member of the social community often receives his information via visual, symbolic channels."

After several readings and "translations", he reduced it to two words; "people read".

I often wish that someone would do that with legalese.

--

Patrick of Collegeville, MN said in a discussion about the inclusion of "under God" in the pledge of allegiance:
Wordplay isn't just innocent amusement; it can be and regularly is a sinister, destructive tool for those who have and want power. George Orwell's essay on "Politics and Language" is the best treatment of this kind of word play that I know. Misinformation by using emotionally laden ambiguous terms is one kind of such word play--e.g., the general, ambiguous, usually misapplied "Judaeo-Christian." Many of America's founding fathers, BTW – Franklin, Jefferson, Madison, Monroe, Charles Carroll among them – would be appalled by the suggestion that they in any way consulted "Judaeo-Christian" religion or ethics when composing or approving the Declaration or the Constitution (and Carroll was a devout Christian); but it's unlikely that those who voted to insert "under God" into the Pledge and those who labor to have church and state cozy up with one another had and have the deist's "Nature's God" in mind.

--

Bob in Chicago responded to Heath in San Antonio who said: "The formal principle of distributive justice, as articulated by Aristotle and others: to treat equals equally and unequals unequally, in proportion to their relevant differences."

In my opinion this all boils down to the "Golden Rule" which is often quoted as "Do unto others as you would have them do unto you" but which, to be truly fair, ought to be stated: "Do unto others as THEY would have you do unto them" or "in a manner in which THEY would rather be done unto".

To which Dean observed in jest:
As I recall, there is a level of hell reserved for those who thought it was "Do others if they'll do you."

--

On the topic of language and theology, John of Keel, UK wrote:
Fine-sounding language can be too high a price to pay, especially for something heard only once [like a bible reading in a service] as op-

posed to a liturgy, which is by definition repeated, permitting growth of understanding. Some of us quite like the theology of the BCP, too...

To which K in Rochester, NY responded:
Actually, most of the time I like the theology, too. And when I'm wearing my grew-up-in-the-sixties-liberal-feminist hat, I heartily approve of all efforts to remove discriminatory patriarchal language. I really do believe that language shapes thought and that children should be raised on liturgy that frees them from outdated stereotypes. I just wish that 'correct' language weren't so damned DULL. That's all.
--

Bill from Columbia, CT opined on the role of the dictionary:
The dictionary is not the source of word precision. The dictionary reflects verbal occurrences. It is not the authority for the purity of usage. You can find anything in the dictionary (dict = say, speak, word; tion = state of; ary = pertaining to, which translates to "pertaining to the state of speaking."). "Ain't" is in the dictionary. Any grammatical precision is resolved in the books written by the grammarians.

Here are a few examples of some words that I have heard over the last few weeks - words that are not the same in definition. We allow too many words to end up meaning the same thing.

 recur - to happen repeatedly
 reoccur - to happen once again
 impel - to encourage
 compel - to force
 wiggle - quick jerky movements, movement of body parts
 Wriggle - slow twisting and turning
 census - number
 consensus - opinion
 toothy - prominent teeth
 toothsome - delicious
 imminent - will happen
 eminent - respected
 persuade - get to act

convince - get to act with conviction
exalt - praise or raise
exult - rejoice
Blatant - obvious and innocent
flagrant - obvious and malicious
official - in authority
officious - pushy
Etc.

The dictionary is a good place to seek definition and suggested ways to spell words but as a place to determine the accuracy of usage, it is woefully inadequate.

--

On the subject of nerds, dorks, geeks, bugs, Alex in Adelaide, AU pointed us to Steven Pinker, author of the brilliant _The Language Instinct_ who wrote an interesting article in Time magazine recently on computer jargon. Here are a couple of excerpts:
"RAM, ROM, MIPS, FLOPS, CPUS, IRQs, asynchronous floating-point multitasking initialization delimiters- why do computers breed so much godawful jargon? Is it all a bunch of incarnations muttered by the wireheads to intimidate new users (or, as they call us 'lusers')? Will digital argot corrupt the English language, leading future generations to mumble in the acronym-clotted gobbledygook of computer manuals?"

"...A hacker is a member of an unofficial meritocracy whose members are distinguished by their ability to program quickly and enthusiastically. They do not fit the stereotype of the pasty-faced, polyester-clad, pocket-protected need-a-life's. Rather, they are literate, articulate quasi-hippies, and their culture esteems precise, witty wordplay."

"...By analogy to a typo, absentminded hackers can make a 'thinko' or a 'braino'. Exiting a window on the screen is 'defenestrating; leaving off the page numbers at the foot of a printed document is 'depeditating' it. A poorly designed program might be 'barfulous' or display a high degree of 'bogosity'..."

He goes on to defend jargon to some extent in the benefit of brevity and conciseness, or as he put it: "Clarity and conciseness trade off; you can be either clear and verbose or concise and opaque."

Recommended reading!

--

Phil of Salt Lake City, UT expressed his concern about increasing vulgarity in the forum exchanges:
Until a month or two ago, the ubiquitous "F-word" had not been seen on this list. Since then, it seems to be seen more and more frequently. Its appearance, particularly on this list, disappoints and saddens me. Why particularly here? Perhaps I can best explain that with reference to a definition I once heard: "Profanity (we could add 'vulgarity') is nothing more than the attempt of a feeble mind to express itself forcefully." I think there is a lot of truth in that, but let me comment right away that I don't think for a moment that I am in the midst of a group of feeble minds. Quite the contrary.

I think this list comprises people who love language, who delight in the many nuances and twists which can enlighten, instruct, and amuse. You are people of great intelligence, culture, and erudition. It is particularly here that I look for people who have the ability and will make the effort to make language rise to the heights of which it is capable, not allow it to descend to gutter level. I like the statement made to Eliza by Henry Higgins in the first scene of "My Fair Lady":

"Remember that you are a human being with a soul and the divine gift of articulate speech. Remember that yours is the language of Shakespeare, and Milton, and the Bible."

For me that applies to our situation as well as to Eliza's. I like the philosophy of the man who said "I generally try to use the best language I can command". I think that is a good goal.

If the above definition does not explain the use of vulgarity, what does? In some cases, laziness, perhaps -- not taking the time to think of powerful words that are not offensive. In some cases, a desire to shock, although vulgarity has become so commonplace as to remove much of the shock value. What then is left?

I realize that many uses of vulgarity on this list pertain to "clever" double meanings, or "funny" twists. But is "cleverness" the supreme value? Not everything that is or appears (to some) to be funny, needs to be said, particularly when saying it risks offending others. How many hundreds of unseen others do we address on this list? Do we always know why some disappear?

I love language! It has the capacity to enlighten, to amuse, to comfort, to delight, to ennoble. It also has the capacity to cheapen and degrade. Significantly, it has these effects upon the user, perhaps even more than upon the reader. It is in our hands what we do with it.

One last point: This list is to me a particularly choice group of people, people who quickly express concern for one another, who are consistently aware of the sensitivities of gender, race, ethnicity, and nationality. It seems paradoxical, then, that we should not also be sensitive to the sensibilities of others regarding coarse language. Yes, there are some of us left who find it objectionable.

I am also painfully aware of my own imperfections, and I realize that I may also have inadvertently offended, perhaps in trying to amuse. Let me here sincerely apologize to any so offended. Some may also be offended at this effort. What I have written is admittedly strongly worded, but let me assure you that this is not written as a flame, but with all good will, pure friendship and yes, even love. If I did not think this could improve and deepen our friendships, I would not write it. Because I value this association, I am willing to risk offense in the attempt to improve it. I have done so in the gentlest way I know how.

--

Sara in Boston responded to Phil thus:
On obscenities in general: you make some interesting points. Apparently, you didn't realize that the appearance of the "f word" was hardly

a new phenomenon here; it's circulated in and out since the list began. Every now and again someone is offended by it, or comments on it. I'd say we can certainly use asterisks if people feel it's necessary, but who doesn't say the word to themselves when seeing that anyway? I think it's certainly true that the shock value of so-called swear words has diminished considerably, as they can be heard in common use in many grade-school playgrounds these days. I also agree that common occurrence is no reason to condone it, necessarily.

I appreciate your viewpoint, and your suggestions; this is not meant as a personal attack, nor am I trying to start a flame war, either.

Ah, nuts. This is starting to sound way too formal. Let's just say that opinions differ; if people want to use the asterisks to soothe sensibilities, certainly they should. They should not, however, have to worry about being chastised if they do not. Fair enough?

Hugs to everybody; "you guys" are great!

--

David of Glendale, CA added to the subject of the use of vulgarity:

A word is only a symbol, but sometimes the symbol and the reality get blurred, and words (especially those that now have the legal appellation of art, "fighting words") can do more than offend, they can hurt... Hence, the differences of opinion over the relative value of some euphemisms.

Since words have meanings pinned to our individual experiences, each of us has a different perspective on what is personally acceptable. Some level of offense is inevitable on any usage -- in the early days of this list I was taken to task when I suggested that German is structured for precision (e.g., agglutination, tacking on explanatory details within the word to clarify the meaning). I pointed out another general principle: that words ending in "chen" are affectionate diminutives, childlike, and their tendency to be neuter is a very neat and precise understanding of the relationship of adult to child. A subscriber wrote, pretty angrily, that this was a foolish exercise in national stereotyping.

Well, of course, I had been foolish. I had used an example without stating that general principle. The example: that the word for "boy" is masculine (as is the word for "man"), while the word for girl (unlike the word for "woman") is neuter. I made a wordplay that obviously misfired: the boy's masculinity is apparent (in several senses), but the madchen is by definition a virgin, therefore untested. Privately and in a minor way listwise, all aitch-ee-double-toothpick broke loose.

What I am getting at with all this pedantry is this: I appreciate the gentle and moderated tone of Phil's post and especially his implied invitation that we think about where our own personal lines are drawn.

My contribution to this thinking is that we might explore what there is in our own individual backgrounds that puts a word on this side or that side of the line we draw for ourselves. ... No fair attributing to others, just why our own individual lines get drawn there. Maybe a little serious word analysis, discreetly slipped in among the delightful funny stuff might make our light wordplay even more enjoyable.

When I get my act together, I'll post a couple of paragraphs about my own take on this, and I hope that I'll see the occasional post from others -- I really want to know more about what makes us virtual friends so interestingly individual!

Apologies for the bandwidth usage, but English is a rich and difficult language, wonderful for expressing direct either/or stuff, but requiring a lot of verbiage to express shades of grey. Do other languages have sayings like, "My country right or wrong", "You're either with me or against me", "You're either part of the solution or you're part of the problem", "It's gotta be this or that", "Help or get out of the way". Or is that another thread?

--

Bill in Mobile, AL continued in the same theme:

Shakespeare is wild with sexual references that I wouldn't necessarily classify as obscene. Just because a four-letter word is used doesn't make it obscene if it depicts an insight and reality that might elevate the reader's consciousness to a better outlook on life. Violence for the sake of violence is obscene; however, the observation of violence that creates a repulsion for physical exploitation and a quest for sensitivity and caring is not obscene.

I guess my point involves the loose use of the word "obscenity" that often leads to the public's thundering for censorship. I've seen too many instructive books dropped from the high-school curriculum because of some mild references to the realities of life.

2

Vocabulary

Choosing adequate words for precise communications cannot be over emphasized. Here is an exchange among the participants:

Kristofer in College Station, TX asked:
Please enlighten us neophytes (myself being one in the true sense of the word!) with a more exact explanation of the "forgo" line.

Maria in Austin, TX responded:
My Webster's, though based on the discredited Third New International, lists (one meaning of) forego as a variant of forgo, both meaning to abstain from, renounce. The first meaning is 'precede'. I take this to mean you are wrong only when you write forgo to indicate going before.

Brian in London follows up:
What this means, I'm afraid, is that a dictionary simply isn't the right beast to help you sort out a problem like this (despite popular impression to the contrary!). If it gives "forego" as a variant of "forgo", it is saying that some people use "forego" when they mean "forgo". This, of course, was exactly my point! What we need to help us here is a study of the etymology or use by careful people, or a usage or style guide, or some thoughts on the form of the words and similar words. (We have had the last discussed neatly and clearly by our resident proof-reader in a former posting.)

This is not a criticism of dictionaries, of course: if you are trying to divine someone's meaning (the true use of a dictionary), it is helpful to be told that by "forego" he could well mean "forgo". And as for "writ[ing] forgo to indicate going before": be assured that if we did, this (mis)use would soon find its way into any good dictionary too!

Jack in London, introduced us to a new word:
I think this should be rodomontade, which Collins defines as: Literary. n. 1. a. boastful words or behaviour; bragging. b. (as modifier): rodomontade behaviour. vb. 2. (intr.) to boast, bluster, or rant.

[C17: from French, from Italian rodomonte a boaster, from Rodomonte the name of a braggart king of Algiers in epic poems by Boiardo and Ariosto]

Jeff in Edinburgh, UK challenged us: What do the following words have in common:
aspirin, linoleum, yo-yo, cellophane, lanolin, celluloid, dry ice, escalator, kerosene, and zipper?

Varda in Portland, ME answered: (Let me guess, Jeff -- you and I are both on another mailing list which has recently been discussing trademarks?)

Words which were once trademark names but have now become generic terms?

Jeff continued:
On brand names: btw, did you know that the words (and conditions) "pyorrhea" and "halitosis" were invented by Listerine, "Athlete's foot" by Absorbine Jr. "fallen stomach", "dandruff" "vitamin deficiency" and "scabby toes" were all invented by manufactures who, miraculously, sold products that alleviated said disorders.

Still on the topic of trademarks, Lee in Sacramento observed:
How many people talk about "xeroxing" something, when they mean photocopying? and they don't even capitalize with an X. Same thing with Kleenex and definitely Cellophane. And who among us ever thinks of that little super TM?

David in Glendale, CA followed up with:

They are all horrible examples of what happens when they allow words like Kleenex (tm) and Scotch (tm) brand tape to appear in public without initial capitalization, the little (tm) dingbat, and (though slightly more optional) without the word "brand" or a nearby statement that such are trademarks owned by X Corporation.

I think it is almost too late to protect the brand name Scotch (tm) in France, where there is a lower-case verb in frequent use: scotcher (to plaster with any kind of sticky tape, including duct). The real mark of their defeat was a bright red warning not to "descotcher" a strip of electrician's tape protecting a temporary cable across the floor of the stage of the Paris Bastille Opera House... It's too late for 3M company to growl at M 'n' Ms, either.

Bob in Tokyo asked:

What is 'fronton'? This was included in a list of sports in some teaching materials we have. I vaguely recall reading about this in the sports pages a few years ago. I think it said that fronton is a racquet sport similar to squash that is popular in Asia. Does anyone on the list know what this is?

David in Glendale answered:

Hereabouts, in a provincial nation north of Baja California, the fronton is the court in which is played Jai Alai. There is a resemblance between racquetball and Jai Alai, but, then, there is a resemblance between a firecracker and a blockbuster, too. The action is enhanced by an arc-shaped wicker-like extension to the hand and arm of the player.

Maria in Austin, enlightened us further:

A fronton is the location within which the game of Hai-lai is played. The players (two) each have a paddle-type thing strapped to their arms. It is strapped to their forearms for leverage, and the part extending past the hand, and about 18 inches long, bends like a huge artificial nail. The ball is caught with and then propelled by these claws at close to bullet speed, making the game highly dangerous. Like dog and cock fighting, the game seems to exist for the benefit of the betting spectators, and the players are heroes according to their skill. The fronton itself consists of an auditorium where the bettors sit, and a stage where the action takes place. Miami has several frontons, I believe, and about eighteen years ago one opened in Bridgeport, Connecticut. I don't know if it is still extant.

Jim in Philadelphia wrote: Somehow, I don't even want to know what a goat-sucker is...

Richard in Boulder, CO chimed in:

Sorry Jim, Goatsuckers are not even vaguely debauched. It is the generic name for a series of nocturnal insect eating night birds often named for their call. Common examples in America are Nighthawk (well maybe we are a little debauched here) and Whip-poor-will.

When Whip-poor-wills call,
And evening is neigh,
I hurry to my blue Heaven!

Kristofer in College Station, TX also commented:

Goat-Sucker is another name for a Nighthawk. As I've seen it written, there is no hyphen, so my Goatsucker may not be your Goat-Sucker! The Nighthawk is a nocturnal bird, black with distinguishing white spots on the belly and white bars across the underside of the stretched-out wing, that is fairly common in most of the United States. Usually, it can be found around dusk, circling the lights in parking lots, feasting on the many bugs that gather in these areas. It is further distinguishable from its high pitched "kree" call, and its flight pattern, which consists of circling high into the night sky and then rapidly diving - hence its name: Nighthawk. (Wow! I could actually contribute something that is more than questions!)

Jeff in Edinburgh drew comparisons between UK and US English: A pilliwinks was an instrument of torture used for squeezing fingers. re: rocket scientist: still unheard in the UK (guess we've never been at the forefront of rocket science, and anyway, shouldn't it now be "shuttle or HOTOL scientist?". We still say "brain surgeon".

On a completely different tip, I've noticed some often bizarre differences between US and UK English. I suspect this may have been mentioned before?

Anyone know of a (humorous) dictionary along these lines, e.g.:
You say; I say
booger; bogie
snicker; snigger (the chocolate + peanuts bar, which must be a laugh a minute, we called "Marathon" until a couple of years ago)
bum; tramp
fanny; bum
?(pudendum); fanny
purse; handbag
?(female wallet); purse
and the obvious ones, like sidewalk (pavement); faucet (tap)

My favourite synonyms are digleberries, clinkers, fartleberries, bumtags.

Oh, yes, and while I'm still in the gutter, the word "avocado" came from the Aztec word for "testicle", because of the resemblance.

And on the subject of prozzie synonyms:
quean; baggage, cat, cockatrice, cony, courtesan, doxy, drab, driggle-draggle, flirt-gill, hackney, harlot, hiren, hobby horse, laced mutton, limber, loon, minx, mort, mutton, public woman, pucelle, punk, stale, stew, street-walker, strumpet, tomboy, wagtail (all 16th century);
buttock, cousin, crack, customer, fireship, flap, lady of pleasure, marmalade madam, night walker, nymph, pug, strum, tomrig, town-woman, vizard, waistcoater (all from the 17th century);
demi-rep, fille de joie, lady of easy virtue, rake, woman of the town (18th century);
buer, chippy, cocotte, demi-mondaine, fallen woman, flagger, flapper, hooker, horizontal horse-breaker (my fave), pick-up, scarlet woman, tart, unfortunate (19th century);
brass nail, broad, call girl, demi-vierge, demi-virgin, hostess, hump,

lay, make, model, muff, pavement princess, scrub, scrubber, and finally slag.

Have I missed one?

p.s. : can anyone tell me what the practice of "bagpiping" is?

p.p.s : did someone mention hangovers: I've just emerged from a 24 hour one.

p.p.p.s : does "on on" mean anything to anybody?

Ken in Victoria, BC challenged us:
MATCH THE PHOBIA'S - From the Agoraphic Foundation of Canada's newsletter.

Acrophobia	fear of crowds
Apiphobia	fear of germs
Blennophobia	fear of fire
Katagelophobia	fear of being alone
Cynophobia	fear of slime
Claustrophobia	fear of bees
Gynophobia	fear of dogs
Spermophobia	fear of women
Eremophobia	fear of heights
Pyrophobia	fear of ridicule
Ochlophobia	fear of fire

Terrence in Bermuda responded to John:

John asked if breathing in to a paper bag to slow breathing in a panic attack has a real physiological basis. It does indeed. This is an effective cure for hyperventilation, a condition wherein one breathes to quickly/deeply so that too much carbon dioxide is exhaled, lowering the acidity of the blood. Unfortunately, hyperventilation frequently accompanies panic or anxiety, while the symptoms of lowered blood acidity tend to make one even more anxious (and ex-hale, to throw in some wordplay)! By breathing into a bag, exhaled carbon dioxide is inhaled again, raising the blood acidity and alleviating these symptoms. This manoeuvre in the absence of hyperventilation, however, will have no beneficial effect on a panic state per se, unless one considers hypoxic loss of consciousness beneficial.

I have one more thing to say about phobias:
Medectophobia: fear that the bulge of one's penis will be visible through one's clothing.

Frightening that this must be common enough to have a word for it. Who would have such a phobia (other than men with small members and tight pants, of course)?

David in Glendale, CA picked up on the "cleaver" discussion:
How clever of Alyssa to point out that "cleaver" proteins cut away (actually, I suppose, envelop) receptors of viral invasions! However, I'll bet there is a whole generation of folks in the USA who never saw a real cleaver, and some of them think it has no meaning outside of "Leave It to Beaver" [USA TV show some time back].

How/What-ever, "cleave" is a very confusing word, being actually two different verbs currently in conjunction. For the linguistic moment, they are not only homonyms, but they are also spelled identically, while of almost diametrically opposed meanings: to cut/split and to adhere/stick. It's fascinating to me to see them start as different words (I think they still are different in some languages, e.g., "klieven"/"kleven") and then to come together in current English (and to separate in the future?)

A lot of people don't connect cleave/cut with cloven (as with hoof). You'd think that "clove" (of garlic) and "clove" (the spice) were connected, too, but they're a different breed of pups. Funny, though, that "clover"'s ancestor-words are close to "cleave"'s; they took a route only a little different from the "cleave"s ("klaver" instead of "klieven" or "kleven").

...But back to the old/new rope thread. Does anyone know why there is a difference between "hung" (suspended) and "hanged" (suspended from a noose) even though they both are a version of the same verb? (...not to mention the colloquial compliment: "well [and truly] hung" – although I suppose the referent could be called a complement, without which the owner would be truly incomplete, and can't we let Abelard lie -- not lay, of course -- in peace, if, perhaps, in pieces)

Mike in Brisbane wished to clarify:
I've always understood that "hanged" was expressly to differentiate from "hung". i.e. we can talk about an artist being hung in a particular gallery, meaning his pictures are hung on the walls thereof. This is a bit different from the same artist being hanged.

Which reminds me of several things - the story of the chap who was doing some genealogical research, and discovered an entry in a family bible relating to a great-uncle, which said: "Fell off a platform at a public gathering and broke his neck." Sure enough, further research elicited the fact that the gentleman had been hanged.

Toni in Minnesota brought up the issue of word confusion:
This complaint from a sports-related mailing lists that I receive:

The most confusing word in the English language, especially with respect to sports, is "resign". If I see the headline "Charles Haley Re-signs", what am I supposed to think? Of course, if they throw in "with" or "from", then it is clearer, but geesh. There should not be words that essentially have opposite meanings like that!

I tend to try to avoid the confusion by using "re-signs" if it is at all ambiguous in context. Is that proper?

Which started me to wondering ... what other commonly used pairs of words suffer from this confusion? (Methinks "pair" in plural should be "pair", but that didn't sound right in the above context.)

Brian in London answered:
Why, yes! And it causes problems for compositors when splitting words across lines: "resigns" cannot be split, as it would have to become "re-signs" which would be ambiguous (or plain wrong). The examples in Hart's Rules [for Compositors and Readers at the University

Press, Oxford] - based on the work of Horace Hart, who was Printer to the University around the turn of the century - include:

An old umbrella needs to be re-covered, but a lost one recovered. An exacting director is a demanding one, but an ex-acting director has given up his own stage career.

Some words, e.g. "legend", cannot be split, as "leg-end" looks altogether silly.

Terrence in Bermuda also weighed in:
Toni Morgan pointed out the ambiguity in the headline about the athlete who RESIGNS, and asked for any other such word.
If a racecar driver RETIRES his car, is he resigning or re-signing?

Andy in Chichester, UK said:
Kristofer has asked a number of questions to which he has received no response. Just for you Kris, I had a look into the origins of dawdle:

Though giving no etymology as such, the Concise Oxford suggests the reader compare it with the dialect words daddle and doddle. Daddle is not listed, even as a variant of doddle. The only definition of doddle given is as a noun (easy task - it was a doddle). It goes as far as to say that, perhaps, doddle may be a variant or cognate of toddle. Toddle (as a child learning to walk) it says is found in 16th c. Scots and northern English but is of unknown origin.

IMHO: From toddle pronounced with a Scots accent to dawdle does not seem an unreasonable step to me. And the change in sense from someone walking like a baby to someone wasting time (often literally walking aimlessly) seems equally plausible. Why the Oxford took me via doddle I have no idea.

Hoke picked up on Dean's assertion that said: <In the last episode Ruth mentioned that delightful term "pixilated". The word enjoyed a brief revival in computing circles referring to scanning an image. More recently, photorealistic image manipulation has added a new dimension to political satire.>

I always thought that if you were pixilated, you had been afflicted or "touched" by a pixi, or were acting like a pixi, and hence were ornery and difficult to deal with. Are you sure you're not talking about "pixelated"?

Mike in Brisbane responded to Slades, who wrote: <In the US, Seagrams is referred to as Whiskey. Although Scotch is technically a whiskey, Scotch whiskey is distilled using malts. Scotch is sold in the US in either single or double malt. Personal favourite: Johnny >Walker Black Label.>

Nope, Scotch is a whisky, with no "e". Whiskeys, when spelt that way, with an "e", refer to Irish Whiskey, bourbon, and rye. Scotch Whisky is made from malted barley, and the top of the line are the single malts, such as Glen Fiddich, which are the product of a single malt. Most of the cheaper scotches are blended from the products of a number of distilleries.

Patrick in Collegeville, MN followed up with:
On the thus-far-short aquae-vitae thread, begun by Hans, Jeff remarks that Seagram's is called whiskey in the US. Here in Minnesota, we call whiskey made in Canada Canadian, and think of Seagram's primarily as Canadian, although they do import Scotch and make gin. Canadian is, I believe, a rye blend. I've never heard of a straight Canadian rye, although such there have to be, even if they're not marketed retail. To a Heartlander the quintessential American whiskey is bourbon, a corn whiskey named for Bourbon County, Kentucky, distilled mostly in that state, Indiana, Illinois, and Tennessee. New Jersey has its applejack, Pennsylvania and Maryland have their rye; but nothing equals the perfume of a bourbon highball after a strenuous day.

Patrick continued:
On the hard-stuff thread, whether it's whiskey or whisky depends on who's spelling it where. To the Brits, Scotch and Irish and Canadian and Bourbon are all whiskies; to the Irish and Americans, they're all whiskeys. Simply variant regional spellings, like curb/kerb, tire/tyre.

To generalize, the spelling whisky, remembering the Irish exception (they always have been mavericks, haven't they), pretty well coincides with driving on the wrong side of the road. The word itself comes from the Irish uisce beathadh and the Scots uisge beatha (both second words often transliterated baugh), Celtic for aqua vitae, eau de vie, akvavit, water of life.

--

Frank in Ottawa contributed few items on the toponymical food thread:
>Irish Stew
>Spanish Onions
>Welsh Rarebit (not Rabbit)
>Yorkshire Pudding
>Melton Mowbray Pie
>Lancashire Hot Pot

Janet in Calgary also pitched in:
On the food thread, I once ended up having dinner with an American backpacker at the youth hostel in Namur, Belgium one night. When her meal arrived, she looked at her plate in amazement and said "Brussels Sprouts? I didn't know they had those over here".

Gerry in Ottawa added to toponymical food topic:
It also seems to be fact of life that none of the foods named after countries or localities are known by that name in that country or locality. French Toast is certainly a mystery to the French, Russian Dressing to the Russians and, so far as I know, Boston Lettuce to the folks in Boston which, incidentally, is in England and surrounded by fields of the stuff.

Brian, in London said:
Use of place names to describe objects that may not hail from those places is one circumstance in which those proper names do not take capital letters: scotch whisky, French windows, venetian blinds, rugby football, plaster of Paris, Picardy third, port from Portugal, Turkish delight.

Mike in Brisbane asked: Anyone got any thoughts on why we say:
> Dutch Courage
> French leave
> Scot free

And what is it that the French refer to as "The English Disease(?)" Something to do with corporal punishment/homosexuality?

Also Jeff in Edinburgh observed:

I spent three weeks in Denmark ten years ago, and found no evidence there of what we Americans refer to as "danish".

Janet responded:

The last time I was in Denmark, you couldn't get any other kind of pastry for breakfast other than what we call a danish. Who knows what the Danes call them, but they're there in copious numbers. I found it fascinating to discover that the Germans call them "Copenhageners". Once again, we see the English tendency to name things in a broad sense, while German narrows it down to specifics.

Pat in Collegeville retorted:

The Danes call it Wienerbrod, Viennese bread. The story I heard from a Copenhagener is that it was introduced by Austrian bakers, but I can't remember why they came to Denmark. Were they imported, perhaps, by the Bernadottes, or does the introduction of the pastry go back further?

--

Katherine in Oakland, CA interjected on Welsh Rarebit:

No, no--it _is_ Rabbit; Rarebit is a back-formed attempt to make sense of what probably started as an ethnic slur.

From Brewer's Dictionary of Phrase and Fable (and I think I've seen it put better in a cookbook, but can't find that source any more): 'Welsh rabbit: Cheese melted with butter, milk, Worcester sauce, etc., spread on buttered toast. _Rabbit_ is not a corruption of _rare-bit_; the term is on a par with "mock-turtle", "Bombay duck", etc.'

She continued on topic:
My favourite is, of course "Dutch Treat". And perhaps (to join this thread to another one), Dutch Courage (for strong liquor)?

Andy in Chichester, UK agreed:
For all of you still confused by references to Welsh rabbit/rarebit, it's basically another name for cheese on toast.

Gerry in New York also had a take on this:
With respect to the listing of foods, let me note a disagreement with the view that it's Welsh "rarebit" and not "rabbit". That is to say, I think that the opposite is true.
In support of the above I offer the following quotes from The American Heritage Dictionary:
Welsh rabbit: noun, a dish made of melted cheese, milk or cream, seasonings, and sometimes ale, served hot over toast or crackers.
I guess that the early diners on this cheese etc., dish (a) thought that it tasted like rabbit or (b) wanted to pass it off as a meat dish.

Ted in San Diego added to this theme:
I just tuned in to read about Welsh Rabbit. Everyone seems to know what it is, but not how it got its name. According to my "Great Dinners from Life" cookbook the answer is as follows.
"The dish is ancient and a couple of centuries ago some cooks began calling it 'rarebit,' apparently because this sounded more refined. The name is actually a culinary joke. When a hunter's bag was poor, a Welsh housewife cooked cheese instead of rabbit."

Patrick in Collegeville, MN weighed in:
There are probably as many recipes for Welsh rabbit as there are thrifty English cooks. The version I know is a sauce of cheddar-cheese scraps melted in beer and whipped with some mustard powder and a dash of cayenne pepper. You spread it on toast and can run it under the boiler to bubble and brown a little if you like. It was originally, I think, a pretty humble high-tea dish, but became one of those late-night chafing-dish productions that bon-vivants whipped up early in a seduction production. It makes a fine lunch, brunch, or supper if

you have no problems with cholesterol or triglycerides, and no scruples about the way more and more cattle are treated to produce the amount of milk our national diet demands.

--

On beer additives, Allan in Brandon, Manitoba wrote:
In Alberta it was (any maybe still is) called 'red eye'. The tomato juice is usually added to a glass of draft beer, and the proportion would certainly be very much less than 'half and half'. I have known people who added a touch of salt to it.

Drinks, like words, have innumerable regional variations.

--

Varda in Portland, ME wrote:
And here in Philly (home of *the* definitive hoagie!), "grinders" are hoagies which have been grilled under the broiler!

To which Mike in Aurora, IL responded:
In Chicago we call a steak and cheese sandwich a Philly steak and cheese. Do Philadelphians call a steak and cheese sandwich a grinder or a steak and cheese?

--

Katherine in Oakland observed:
in the seventeenth century, syphilis was:
> to the English, "the French disease"
> to the French, the Italian malady,
> to the Italians, the Spanish (something-or-other)...

Someone enquired about the texting term: ROFLMAOWTIME Translation? I came in late on these and while I can figure out easy ones like LOL, I feel I'm missing something in the greater scheme of things. Could somebody post a quick user's guide to these things, and consider it the same as translating foreign sentences for the uniliterate?

Radmilla in Georgia responded:
The one above means Rolling On Floor Laughing My Ass Off With

Tears In My Eyes.
Some other useful ones are:
- BRB -- Be Right Back
- OIC -- Oh I See
- FLK -- Funny Looking Kid
- IPT -- In Poor Taste
- GMTA -- Great Minds Think Alike
- BTW -- By The Way
- AFK -- Away From Keyboard
- BAK -- Back At Keyboard
- IMHO -- In My Humble (NOT!) Opinion
- WTG -- Way To Go
- WB -- Welcome Back
- PWT -- Poor White Trash
- YOYO -- You're On Your Own
- SPL -- Serum Porcelain Level (i.e. a crock)

Catie in Arlington, VA gave us the whole spread:

IMO - In My Opinion: Innocent enough, the author is expressing an opinion about the subject at hand.

IMHO - In My Humble Opinion: Not quite so innocent, the author is expressing an opinion that s/he believes handed down from God. Sometimes, the user is actually offering a humble opinion, if there is any doubt, assume that the person is indeed being humble.

IMNSHO - In My Not So Humble Opinion: Back to innocent. The person is being arrogant, but with a touch of wit, and at least recognizes the arrogance. Sometimes referenced as IMAO, or In My Arrogant Opinion. It means the same thing.

FYI - For Your Information: Trying to impose a fact or an opinion taken as fact on the other party.

BTW - By the Way: The comment the author is about to make is marginally connected to the topic at hand, but it will be placed in this message anyway. See message header.

OOTC - Obligatory on Topic Comment: The author felt that there should be at least a portion of her/his message that pertains in some slight way to the usenet newsgroup that the message appears in. Since this is misc.kids, and children must live in the world, all messages are on topic, so you may not see this one much. (#include <sarcasm.h>)

YMMV - Your Mileage May Vary: Like cars, what works for one person will probably work differently for another. Usually said after true anecdotal information.

IMPE - In My Personal/Previous Experience: The aforementioned true anecdotal information.

FWIW - For What It's Worth: Usually related to the previously mentioned true anecdotal information, but may also be related to IM(H)O or YMMV.

DIY - Do It Yourself: What you wish your three-year-old would do, when you know that s/he can.

DIM - Do It Myself: What your three-year-old insists on doing, when they really aren't ready to do so yet.

YKYATP - You Know you're a Tired Parent: The author is about to relate something s/he did that is really silly, but if you will be honest with yourself, you've done equally silly things. Laugh with us. (A variant is YKYAPW, apparently not tired. I haven't met a parent who wasn't tired. This one appears in headers a lot)

RL - Real Life: A mythical concept, unknown to this author.

FAQ - Frequently asked questions: Rather than have the same questions asked over and over again, people have volunteered to keep updated copies of the answers to those questions and send them out to people asking for them. Cuts down on traffic. This is contrasted with:

Flame Bait - Frequently argued questions. Rather than admit you could be wrong about something, couch your beliefs in absolutes. "Mothers who work outside the home are irreparably damaging their children.", "All boys should be circumcised.", "Ferber is a saint!", "Ferber is the devil incarnate!" etc, etc, ad nauseum. Causes: Kill files - a device allowing you to opt out of said flame wars. There is a FAQ on these too, but I don't know where to find it.   Warning, these can grow to enormous proportions.

FOAF - Friend of A Friend: Mythical creature, like the griffin. This is the person who:

- found a finger in a can of tomatoes
- found a mouse in a coke bottle
- had their girl (it's always a girl) kidnapped at Disney[land, world] and then they shut the park down and found the girl, drugged, boys haircut, boys clothing, and being hustled out of the park.
- has time at the end of the day to sew all his/her children's clothes, volunteer at PTA, etc.

SIL - sister-in-law

BIL - brother-in-law

MIL - mother-in-law

FIL - father-in-law: Relatively speaking, these are easy to decipher. Sometimes it may seem that some of these are out-laws rather than in-laws. Usually your spouses.

ROFL - Rolling on Floor Laughing: (Also ROTFL, Rolling on The Floor Laughing). What you said was very funny.

ROFLOL - Rolling on Floor Laughing Out Loud: What you said was extremely funny, and in fact people at work are looking at me weird. Has also been referenced as ROFLMAO, the derivation of which is left to the gentle reader.

IOAS - It's Only a Soap: The author is expressing amusement that something so inane could be happening. In other words, it's like a soap opera.

CTTS - Cute Things They Say: One of those precious and wonderful things that they come up with, showing you once again that the world is a wonderful place to someone just starting out. By transference, it becomes a wonderful place to you to.

CTTD - Cute Things They Do: More touching, funny, silly, smart, etc. things that they do to make us glad we know them.

CU - See you: All-purpose close to an e-mail letter, even when the party has no intention of ever actually seeing you, and in fact may not even be on the same continent with you. A variation is CUL8R, meaning see you later.

TTUL - Talk to you later: Similar to CU, also seen as TTYL.

OTOH - On the Other Hand: Hold on folks, I can see more than one side to this!

DFM - Don't Flame Me: This really happened, or I really want to know, or I was just asking a hypothetical question, etc. I really don't want to wade through pages of vitriol. (I know, there are those who can't resist, but don't be one of them, ok?)

GTG- Got To Go: If I spend any more time typing to my misc.kids friends, I'm going to lose my net access, job, car, home, etc. I will log back on when the boss isn't around.

YGGM - Your Guess is as Good as Mine: I don't have a clue. Some of the things kids come up with completely defy adult logic.

:-) - Previous was meant in jest: Well, maybe. Usually true. But once in a while, this is rather like the "just kidding" in spoken American English. "God you're fat! Just kidding." Apparently some folk think you are allowed to say anything you like, as long as you say "just kidding" afterwards, or post anything you like with a smiley.

- (Lack of "smiley"): Previous was absolutely serious, no matter how sarcastic or tongue-in-cheek it may have sounded. In fact, the more in jest the remark sounds the more seriously it should be taken. Should always be replied to with searing flames, and, later, with "Well, the original poster couldn't have been kidding, because there was no smiley in the message". This is heavily used by the sarcasm or humor impaired.

Jan added: ACRONYMS--Don't forget,

WYSIWYG (pronounced "wizzy wig") -- "What You See Is What You Get" and

GIGO -- "Garbage In, Garbage Out."

--

Caleb in Albany, NY answered Mike who enquired about "sic'em":
And for "sic", Webster's has thus: " sic or sick \' sik\ \' sikt\ vt or sicced or sicked; or sic. cing; or sick. ing [alter. of seek] 1: CHASE, ATTACK - usu. Used as an imperative esp. to a dog {~ 'em} 2: to incite or urge to an attack, pursuit, or harassment: SET "
No word on the origin.

--

Katherine in Oakland answered Caleb who asked: [how many 5-letter words can you wordplayers find which start and end with "k"?]
"Hmm...knock, knack, kayak, kapok, kopek? Kodak? ...klick..."
Matt in Minneapolis added to this:
I'll throw in kiosk, kulak (rich Czarist-Russian peasant), and kyack (AmHer: a packsack that hangs on either side of a packsaddle).

On the topic of slang, Mike in Brisbane asked:
Anybody know the definition and derivation of the somewhat pejorative term "prat"? And does it have any connection with the vaudeville term "pratfall"?
Jan answered:
According to The World Book Dictionary, both "prat" (buttocks) and "pratfall" (a fall on the backside as part of a "slapstick" routine) are U.S. SLANG, of unknown origin. BTW, the word "slapstick" is also American Slang--from the long narrow sticks, fastened together so as to make a loud slapping noise when a clown hits something or someone with them.

--

Gerry in Ottawa observed:
Finally, just for lagniappe - a lovely word - you should all know that the South African term for traffic light is "robot." Logical, I guess, but a bit disconcerting at first when you're told to turn right at the first robot.

--

Hans wrote:
There are just a few Dutch (or rather South-African?) words in English that I'm aware of: Apartheid and Aardvark.

Mike in Brisbane noted:
One that Australians are unlikely to forget is "Springbok"! Of course, there's always aasvogel, too. (Not that I use it a lot!)

--

Ken in Victoria, Canada recalled a book by an advertising person in which the author claimed that "'teenagers' didn't exist as a distinct group until the early 50's. The concept was born out of Madison Ave. looking for a whole new market to create and supply." He then asks, does anyone remember if a 'teenage' distinct group existed before this time?"

Jim in Tacoma, WA answered:
Yes, apparently the concept of TEENAGE as a distinct phase of life had shown up by 1920, when the word TEENAGE first appeared in print. But the concept may not have saturated the popular consciousness until somewhat later, perhaps with the help of advertising.

--

Alex in Adelaide observed:
Someone mentioned words that momentarily (is this adv used correctly?) come into vogue then disappear from daily use. This reminds me of seasonal words and phrases that come back cyclically with the event such as election lingo where not only the terms disappear after the event, but many of us forget their meaning the next time around. To wit _electoral colleges_, delegates, line-item veto, New Hampshire primaries, and so on...

Bill in Lexington, KY observed:
As far as I'm concerned it is. Until I was in my thirties, I never heard "momentarily" used to mean anything but "for a moment". Then I heard a radio announcer say something like "The President will be on the platform momentarily." I thought that that wouldn't be enough time to make a speech. It took me a while to realize that he meant "in

a moment". I've heard it used that way many times since, but it always sounds wrong.

Marilyn in San Francisco followed up:
According to THE MILLSTEIN, a style manual used by NBC News for many years (and maybe still, I haven't worked there in 10 years), "momentarily" does mean "for a moment". The example quoted in the manual is "The plane will depart momentarily" This means the plane will depart for a moment and then come back, not that it will depart soon.

--

Paul Young wondered:
I am looking for another, specific word for popular adages such as:
    Don't cry over spilt milk.
    Wild horses couldn't drag me away.
    Butterfingers
...and similar phrases. I am looking for something different besides aphorism, cliche', maxim.

Any help would be greatly appreciated.

--

Jeff in San Diego wondered:
What is it about Australians and Wordplay?! This new word is the subject of an article, out of Australia, in one of my journals: "stiction."

You know... when something sticks due to friction? Like the black rubber part of the plunger in a syringe.

Heath in San Antonio, TX informed us:
The term adolescent was used centuries ago to describe a teenager, and the concept garnered much attention at the turn of the century in the USA. Folks began referring to teenagers in the 1920's, but the concept had already been used.

Some people suggest that the notions of adolescence and teenagers are invented by societies who have the luxury of developing people between childhood and adulthood. Those people are called inventionists (imagine that). Madison Avenue did not create the group, they merely capitalized on it.

I guess my hours and dollars were not wasted in that seemingly silly Adolescent Development class I had to take to keep my job.

In the same vein, Bob in Chicago followed up:
It is my understanding that certain historians believe that prior to about the year 1500 children were considered to be merely a smaller version of an adult and were treated about the same. Supposedly it was the invention of the printing press and the rapid spread of knowledge as a result that placed childhood in a separate category for the purpose of learning. Unfortunately to this very day there are still many places on earth that children begin working for a living before they enter their teens.

--

Gerry in Ottawa picked up on another theme:
Just to catch up, yes, "coney" or "cony" is an English word, though not one that you often hear around the old water cooler. Its main use now is in heraldry as a term for rabbit. The Conesby family's coat of arms, for example, is blazoned "Gules, three conies sejant within a bordure engrailed sable." Incidentally, it s called a "canting charge" when the object shown is a pun on the family name.

The names of the officers at the College of Arms in London are equally obscure. A friend of ours once served as secretary to Rouge Dragon Pursuivant. "What on earth do you call him when you're alone in the office?" I asked. "Sam?" "Heavens, no," she replied huffily. "He's always called Rouge Dragon." Which conjured up a picture of some fascinating conversations. "Sorry about that, Rouge Dragon. We seem to be all out of dairy creamer."

I couldn't agree more with Frank's complaints about "paradigm" and "egregious." One thing they have in common is that, more often than not, they're used incorrectly which I suppose is inevitable once a word becomes fashionable and people who've never heard it before try to pick it up. The current ones seem to be "cusp" which at least is shorter than the previous "cutting edge" and "anal-retentive," a rather disgusting term which seems to have started out as a substitute for "neatness freak" and now appears to be used as a general pejorative for anyone you don't much like.

--

Katherine Oakland, CA was reminded on some obscure terms:
Did we already talk about the horrid canting arms of the family Peché? The book from which I started learning heraldry gave that as the worst example.

On "anal retentive": Not just neatness freak--as I understand the term, it refers to the obsessive-compulsive type: somebody who wants control over everything, and is fanatically neat, and obsesses about details...I remember a character in an otherwise uninteresting novel who had all the foods in the pantry arranged in the alphabetical order of their names; she'd probably qualify.

--

On a different note, Jim in Schenectady, NY asked:
Q.: What adjective aptly and accurately stands as the direct antonym of the word 'muggy'?

In my house we use the word 'zeer' which is an Anglicization of the Greek xeros (from which Xerox) meaning dry. Arid and dry don't accurately describe a summer air mass, or a summer day, which is not plagued with steamy, humid air. "Muggy" is such a great word for oppressive humidity. Our "zeer" connotates a fresh, dry, not-hazy summer sky, summer day, air mass, etc. For example-- "Yesterday it was very hot and humid, but an overnight thunderstorm cleared the air, and now we can look forward to a few zeer days before the humidity builds up again." Comments?

Caleb in Albany, NY bud in:
Is "sere" a close relative of "zeer"? Yes. "sere" refers to the same concept of very dry, from 'xerus'. BTW, "Xerox" is also from that word because that corporation first marketed the dry-copier concept in its machines.

Catie in Arlington, VA also chipped in:
Love the term "zeer"! In the mid-Atlantic region (I'm in the Washington DC area) we have too many hot humid days. The weathermen have taken to quoting the "heat index" which is like the chill factor in reverse, using the percent humidity.

For example: the temperature is 95, but with the heat index, it will feel more like 110. Other weathermen call it the "humiture". Now I've entered zeer into my vocabulary -- something to long for on those high humiture days!

--

Someone enquired:
What exactly is a "synesthete?" And since I'm a policy analyst in the health >area, would that make me a "sanesthete?" Any other titles for your wordplayers out there?

Michael in Mesa, AZ answered:
It's a "sufferer" of synesthesia: a neurological condition by which one experiences perceptions in one of the senses in response the stimulus of another sense. Read "The Man Who Tasted Shapes" by Dr. Richard Cytowic. It's a really weird kind of perception that, to just about everyone who does not have it, seems to be a real burden to those who do. Thus, the tongue-in-cheek use of "sufferer." I suppose, for those who see more colours than I do, it's a lot like living on acid, but if you've never known anything else, it seems perfectly normal. To lose it would be like going blind or deaf. Sorry, no wordplay, with the possible exception of reducing those whose synesthesia is limited to smells to the status of sinusthete.

--

Terrence in Bermuda added to the topic of Brewing, Worts, Ale:
Doppel Bock - A lager made with darker roasted grains and a more highly concentrated wort (wort= beer before it ferments.)

Some other beer terms:
>	barley + water & heat = MALT
>	malt + milling = GRIST

grist + hot water = MASH
mash is composed of solids = RETURNS
liquid = WORT

One might like to wish a brewer "many hoppy returns", but hops aren't involved, unfortunately, until the next step.

Terrence also picked up on another theme:
I always caution my residents when they say "pussy" (PUH-see) as an adjective for pus, and advise them to use the medical term purulent. For while the meaning is clear in speech, "The patient had a pussy discharge" doesn't look so good in print on the chart.

Mike in Brisbane observed:
I leave beck section to the Kiwis, but a choko is known in the Americas, where it is a native, , as a "chayote" it's a green pear-shaped vegetable that grows on a vine, doesn't have a lot of taste, but is a great ingredient in stir-fries, curries, or served with a cheese sauce.

Mike in Brisbane cringed at a certain metaphor:
An expression that's becoming vogual (note neologism), which I don't particularly care for is "ramping up". Heard it eight times yesterday at a staff meeting.

Jim in Schenectady, NY introduced yet another clanger:
The second thing is a word I coined to mean the opposite of pandemonium (Gk. all devils) which is pangelium (all angels). It refers to an ecstatic state, or a place full of joy, music, beauty, love...you know, like Grand Central Station at 5 pm on a humid Friday afternoon... well, seriously folks, it's a nice synonym for euphoria.

Someone brought up a term obscure to many, and Katherine in Oakland shed some light on it:
My guess would be that "crippleware" refers to sample programs, some

portion of whose functioning has been deliberately disabled so that the user will be interested in paying (more) money to get the whole thing.

And John in Keele approved:
Quite right about crippleware, whoever that was: sometimes the whole functionality is reduced, sometimes it's just printing that's disabled, often there's a cutoff date after which the package won't work any longer. And a "nag screen" is the display that tells you how to register the shareware package, often with a certain amount of carrot-and-stick by-play: programmers will be starving in the streets if not paid for their work... and besides, if you register, you actually get a copy of the manual etc. etc.

--

Gerry in Ottawa weighed in on "berm" brought up by Marilyn:
From our days in Canberra, I can certainly confirm the universal use of "nature strip" for the patch of grass between the road and the pavement. In Canada, however, to the extent that it's used at all, it means the it means the bank of a canal opposite the tow path.

NOW I know where I've heard the word Berm. Peter Sellers in his role as a French police inspector (Insp. Clouseau or something similar). "Careful, it may be a berm about to explode."

Kat in Providence, RI provideed a more formal description:
According to my dictionary, it comes from the French: _berme_. Paraphrased from AHD3:

> Berm n.
> 1a. a narrow ledge or shelf
> 1b. the shoulder of a road
> 1c. a raised bank or path

I think this is the one that applies to the road feature I've always called the median strip. It also shows up in glossaries of civil engineering textbooks.

> 2. a terrace formed by wave action on a beach
> 3. a mound or bank of earth placed against a wall

4. a ledge between the parapet and the fortification's moat

Dave in Carey, NC had another take:
A berm is a very small hill, an earthen wall. Motocross racers (off-road motorcycles) uses berms in their turns to turn more quickly. They'll ride up on the berm to use it as banking.

Patrick in Collegeville, MN remarked:
I've never heard berm in Minnesota, although I've seen in on notices from the state DOT. When I was a kid in northeastern Hoosierland, it was the shoulder of the road, especially where it broadened out on the outside of a curve or made a stopping area. My hand-dictionary traces it to the Dutch berm, strip of ground along the top of a dike, akin to Middle English brimme, which means verge.

Lee in Sacramento was amused by one definition of a berm:
Hm-m. Nature strip--a new "special" from ecxydeseists (sp?), sometimes known as "exotic dancers"?

Hans in the Netherlands added to Patrick's take:
Adding some Dutch flavour to the conversation: berm is a Dutch word for a grass strip next to the road. Some roadsigns say "Pas op, zachte berm".

We even have "bermlampen" on the cars. Some people like to practice "bermtoerisme" (picknicking by the roadside). Wonder where the name "Bermuda" came from...

--

Mike in Brisbane asked:
Could someone please explain about biscuits? In Australia, biscuits are things you buy in packets at the store, or bake in your own oven. They are the things that Cookie Monster likes so much.

Kat in Providence answered:
Chapter 72 from the British/American Translation Dictionary:
British 'biscuit' = American 'cookie'
American 'biscuit' = British 'scone'
(Disclaimer: ain't no such thang as an EXACT translation!)

Brian in London added:
The British term "biscuit" includes both the sweet things - that I understand to be the American "cookie" - and the savoury things one eats with cheese or whatever that I believe to be American "crackers".

--

Someone enquired:
It sounds as though insure/ensure are almost interchangeable, but I guess they're not, right??

Steve in Austin, TX answered:
According to the Army, they were. But (and I have actually seen a directive stating this!) 'ensure' is preferable in order to avoid the connotation of a financial transaction. (???!!). If we include (enclude?) an attachment with a letter, we must refer to it as an inclosure, as an enclosure refers to a boundaried area or a tactical battlefield action.

As they say, there are three ways to do things: The right way, the wrong way and the Army's way!

--

Dave in Glendale burst on the scene with:
Gotta share a joyous word from today's Wordsmith list:
The opposite of calligraphy is cacography. Wonderful, what with the number of other concepts cac- has come to be associated with these days...

ca.cog.ra.phy n (1580)
1: bad spelling--compare orthography
2: bad handwriting--compare calligraphy -- caco.graph.i.cal adj

--

John in Palo Alto, Ca posed:
Okay. How about the only English word that has the 5 vowels, each occurring once, in alphabetical order?

And Katherine in Oakland corrected him:
Which one? Facetious or abstemious?

--

Susan in Cheney, WA brought up a new word:
Youse guys on AWAD list know about our recent word "mussitation" meaning murmuring and grumbling. Excellent word for this group, especially those of us outside the cat thread.

Another fine specimen from AWAD was the today's "funambulism" meaning a show of mental agility, another classic for this group.

--

John in Keele, UK answered Jack in Pine Bluff, AZ:
People who shoe horses, of either gender, are called farriers.

--

Bob on Chicago in a discussion on hair products, reminisced:
When I was a boy (and Hector was a pup) every good housewife used to have lace "doilies" pinned to the arms and the headrests of all upholstered furniture to protect them from greasy hair products. They were referred to as "antimacassars" and were named for macassar oil which at one time was a popular and widely used hair dressing product. I think that many "over 45ers" will remember antimacassars from visits to their grandmother's house.

--

Patrick in Collegeville responded to Mike in Brisbane who asked what the opposite of anachronism might be.
Haven't looked it up, but I suggest katachronism. Mike also mentions hearing the expression "to out the light." I believe that that is Pennsylvania Dutch idiom, too.

Pat also responded to John who is in astonishment over the phrase "visit with":
In American idiom, to visit can mean to chat or converse, and, like those two verbs, takes "with" when it does. So, visit me and visit with me haven't quite the same meaning.

--

David in Glendale instructed us:
About labels in general, including those things you slap on a package to indicate destination or fragility ... in Latinate European languages,

the word for them is some version of "etiquette," even when the term refers to labels on bottles of whiskey or packages of coffee (e.g., "etiquette noire" -- black label, a mark of quality in both fields). The meaning of "etiquette" related to protocol, which is the only one I know of in English, is strictly secondary.

My question: does anyone know the connection between these two meanings? Apart from a couple of guesses (labels of rank having something to do with the polite way to treat a person, for example), I haven't a clue ...

--

Gerry in Ottawa aired an annoyance:
While I have you here, however, I'd like to add another pet peeve to the list and that's the increasing use of "exit" for "leave." I've just finished a mystery novel in which the hero time and again exited his house, his office, his car and innumerable restaurants. It wasn't a bad book but my reading rhythm was constantly being thrown off by the use of a word that I'd never have used myself in that particular context. What's wrong with good old "left?"

American Express. Don't exit home without it.

--

Rich in Ridge, NH said apropos Caleb's sardine thread:
Would anyone like to address the New England fish delicacy called "scrod?" It's served all the time in restaurants in this part of the world yet I've never known a fisherman to catch even a single scrod.

--

Brian in London on British vs American:
By the time the concert has finished, the pedestrian tunnel has been locked up for the night. Many are the evenings when I see some confused soul at the tunnel entrance reading the notice that sets out the "Subway opening times". I make some friendly overture, and when I detect the American accent, I can safely reassure them that although the British English "subway" (= pedestrian tunnel) is closed, the American English "subway" (= underground railway) is still very much open.

Jesse in Sunnyvale, CA wrote:
Following on from the "beaver thread," does any one know the origin of the term "Spanish Fly?" For those that don't know, this is a (mythical?) aphrodisiac of great strength. I'm just curious where the term comes from. Anyone have any clues?

Mike in Brisbane answered:
Yep, it really exists, it's the ground-up remains of the cantharides beetle - and what it does is irritate the urinary tracts in both males and females. The urge to relieve this itch is apparently unbearable and leads to tumescence in the male and I dunno-what in the female - I can't believe it could be a pleasant experience.

Allan in Brandon, Manitoba informed us:
The active ingredient of Spanish Fly as I recall was something called cantharidin, or cantharis, and it used to be prepared by crushing up an insect known as a blister beetle (also known as Spanish Fly), Cantharis or Lytta vesicatoria. Apparently, these beetles were found in great abundance in Spain, and the country was the major source for the drug. The compound was widely used as a counter-irritant and a diuretic in ancient medical practice since the days of Hippocrates, and was listed for these uses in the British Pharmacopeia as late as the 1920s. Its supposed aphrodisiacal properties stemmed from its irritant effect on the lining of the bladder and urethra. It was well known to the ancient physicians as a cause of haematuria (blood in the urine) when used or prescribed in excess.

I believe that some cantharidin containing compounds for specialised dermatologic use are available in the US (Canthacur, Cantharone).

Zeno in Minneapolis, MN responded to a query "What's the rhetorical device that refers to using a part (of a person) to refer to the

whole? Litotes or something like that?"
Synecdoche (pronounced sin NECK doe key)
--

Bill in Columbia, CT introduced a related device:
A litotes is a figure of speech consisting of an understatement in which an affirmative is expressed by negating its opposite. "Not bad" is an example of a litotes. If somebody is not unwelcome, he or she is welcome. A synecdoche is a part to denote the whole. Twenty sails were seen on the horizon. (Sail is part for the whole boat.)

Someone illustrated thus:
Chair is a perfectly good use of synecdoche, in the same vein as using "crown" >>to represent the British royal personage. No opposition from me.

Allan in Sydney, NS objected:
Plenty of opposition from me, for one. Aside from the fact that using 'the Crown' as a substitute for the monarchy is far more a form of metonymy than synecdoche, when we speak of the Crown we invariably are referring to the institution rather the individual, e.g. the Crown will appeal the verdict. When referring to the actual monarch, we usually talk about the queen, or the king (not capitalised).

However, when we use the currently popular and politically correct substitute for the individual in charge of a committee, the chair, we invariably, and without exception are talking about the individual who occupies the position, NOT the committee headed by the man or woman under discussion, nor the piece of furniture on which they sit.

Call a chairman or a chairwomen a chair if it makes you happy. The table objects, and the desk abstains. The insistence on genderless or gender-neutral terms however ridiculous seems to be very much in vogue in the US and Canada, though I believe that there is considerably more resistance to the terms in the UK. As noted by the Oxford Companion to the English Language, many such non-sexist alternatives are controversial and unstable.

Phil in Salt Lake City, UT acquiesced:
I agree with you. I think the negation of a negative (not really a "double negative") is much stronger. If you boil both forms of expression down to the essentials, they mean the same thing, but what you lose is nuance and flavor, which is where the stronger statement comes from. It has more punch. I remember a couple of years ago, after a particularly scandal-ridden period for the royal family, Queen Elizabeth II made the statement: "This has not been a year of undiluted pleasure." Classy. Real classy.

Gerry in Ottawa added to this:
According to my handy-dandy Oxford Companion to the English Language, a litote isn't a case of using a part for a whole but refers to "a positive and often emphatic statement made by denying something negative." Examples given are "in no small measure" and "by no means negligible." If I read this definition right, it would seem to support me in a running argument I've been having with a friend who claims that phrases like "Your suggestion is welcome" and "Your suggestion is not unwelcome" mean exactly the same thing. It's my contention that they don't, that the latter in fact is a stronger statement since, by first establishing a negative and then setting up a contrast, one accentuates the positive, so to speak. What do you all think?

Katherine had a slight disagreement:
Hmm....I think I tend to read/hear litotes in the opposite way. "Your suggestion is not unwelcome" comes across to me as something like, "Well, it was useful, so I can't say it was unwelcome exactly, BUT..."

On the other hand, "his appetite by no means being a small one" means he asked for eight eggs and eleven slices of buttered toast for breakfast [sorry, example from a story I heard last night]. Maybe I don't use or hear this form consistently.

Kat in Rochester, NY agreed:
I agree. In fact, the second construction always seems to include an implied "but...".

Carol in Indianapolis IN, said:

On the spam thing, the following is from Patrick Crispen's Roadmap to the Internet, an online introduction in a series of lessons.

The introduction to the "map" on Spamming and Urban Legends - "Well there's egg and bacon; egg, sausage and bacon; egg and spam; bacon and spam; egg, bacon, sausage and spam; spam, bacon, sausage and spam; spam, egg, spam, spam, bacon and spam; spam, spam, spam, egg and spam; spam, spam, spam, spam, spam, spam, baked beans, spam, spam, spam and spam; or lobster thermidor aux crevettes with a mornay sauce garnished with truffle pate', brandy and a fried egg on top of spam." --Monty Python's Flying Circus.

I hope that clears things up.

--

Barb in Stephenville, TX suggested a correction:

To Hans....whose sig line stated ARM: Elegance is Power... Do you think Eloquence would be more powerful than Elegance?

Jody in St Paul, MN was inspired:

Having just viewed a spectacular full moon rise over the horizon of Trout Lake in northern Minnesota, a group of us began discussing the different phases and types of moons. During this discussion, a question arose to which no one had an answer. Perhaps members of WordPlay could answer. Why is a second full moon during a single month referred to as a "blue moon?" Apologies in advance if this group already covered this topic before I began lurking.

--

Guy in Cupertino, CA posed a question on leaving:

Can anyone here authoritatively explain why, though American enclosures (such as subway stations) have signs marking the EXIT, the signs in British ones mark the "WAY OUT"?

Brian in London answered:

Yes, British signs for normal exits often say "way out", but safety-related ones (e.g. the always-lit signs in public buildings, theatres, concert halls, etc.) usually say "exit". And it would always be "fire exit" and "emergency exit", never "fire way out" or "emergency way out" (though in this building these signs have recently turned into pictograms). My guess is that London Transport and the like have decided to be a bit plainer and less classical - and perhaps more grammatically correct.

--

John in Keele responded to a query from Katherine:
"Temporary threshold shift" refers to the phenomenon of loss of hearing sensitivity for a while after listening to loud noise. Down in the former location for the Research Students' Club, in the basement of the old manorial Keele Hall, bands tended to play in the room adjoining the bar. With the communicating door closed they often sounded quite respectable...from the bar...

Before I forget, could someone enlighten me about the relative familiarity of the word "clobber" to non-UNIX-speaking Americans? A representative of NATO with a pronounced North American accent was to be heard on the radio recently telling us that the intention was to "clobber the Serbian army" and suchlike [the verb was used more than once in different combinations]. Is this everyday usage, comprehensible but unusual, totally weird or what? To me it just sounds "very English", but I admit that precisely this sense of the word occurs in a feature of the UNIX operating system, which originated in the U.S. Perhaps I haven't listened to enough standard American usage!

Lee in Sacramento answered:
Yes John--even us non-unix speakers know from "clobber." A very respectable word for beating the (I was about to use the "S" word) tar out of something or someone.

Phil in Salt Lake City, UT also had a take on this:
Glad to oblige. "Clobber" is common usage, understood by everyone in the US. Having stretched my neck this far, I should now go home and see if my teenagers know the word. Every now and then I use a word that was in common usage when I was a kid, and *my* kids stare uncomprehendingly. Or maybe they understand from the context, but

are silently asking: "Where did he get *that* word?" But I am digressing. My Webster's defines clobber as "1. (slang) to pound mercilessly, and 2. (slang) to defeat overwhelmingly."

The use of slang in computer languages is, I suppose, common practice. DBASE used the command "ZAP" to erase all records in a file.

Mike in Perth, AU gave us his usage version:

Down under, "clobber" is also a slang term for clothes or more particularly for an outfit -- something like "Geez, mate. Where d'ja get the flash clobber? Been raidin' the St. Vinnie's bin again, 'ave ya?" (Translation: "Good heavens, friend! Where did you get the smart looking outfit? Have you been taking stuff from the St Vincent de Paul used clothes bin again?"

Mike in Brisbane followed up:

I bet my clobber's daggier than yours – I got mine from the Sallies. Look about as flash as a rat with a gold tooth.

--

Martin in Los Angeles wondered:

The word "rational", when "e" is appended, does not do the standard "silent-e" shtick. Is there a reason for this (perhaps "rationale" is from French?), and are there other words like this?

--

Toni in Minnesota was puzzled:

I had an appointment to have my hair done yesterday evening. My hairdresser is in a section of the Twin Cities called "Uptown". I've always thought it was oddly named, because it is south of downtown, and everyone knows that north, not south, is up. Anyway, it got me to wondering not only about the "Uptown" name, which is not really relevant to this list, but also about the derivation of "downtown", which is a more universally applicable word. Any ideas?

Mike in Brisbane added another complexity: Ups and Downs

In Oz, where there are two railway tracks running side by side, they are referred to as the "up side" and the "down side". Regardless of compass direction, the "up side" always refers to the track which goes towards the state capital, and the "down side" refers to the track on which trains travel away from the capital. Hence in Newcastle, which is north of Sydney, one travels by train "Up to Sydney". I guess it's a way of being consistent and avoiding confusion if you're a railway despatcher or signalman or fettler or whatever. Is this convention used in the US?

Steven in Atlanta answered to Mike, then to Toni:
Not that I've ever heard, particularly since we've been dismantling our rail network for decades. But it is used around Tokyo: "nobori" (upward) trains go toward the Imperial Palace (and Tokyo Station) at the center of the city, and "kudari" (downward) trains go out.

Re uptown and downtown, I always thought that it had something to do with street numbering where the harbor/heights dichotomy isn't as important, as in New York. Tokyo has no "uptown," but the old section along what was once the edge of the bay is still called "shitamachi" (lower town).

--

Jesse in Sunnyvale, CA suggested:
I suppose my favorite word I'd love to make in Scrabble (but I don't think there are enough blanks, Y's, and Z's) is "zyzzyva" which can actually be found in a surprising number of dictionaries. For those without one (a dictionary, not a zyzzyva, silly!) handy, a zyzzyva is a small bug that eats cotton.

"Zarf" is another good Scrabble word.

--

CJ proposed to come up with a few "STAND" phrases..
    STAND by
    can't STAND it
    STAND in
    STAND tall
    STANDING ovation (OK, I'm starting to stretch it)
    getting STOOD up

--

Bill in Lexington was puzzled:
"Awful". "Full of awe". Somehow those two don't seem to go together. Or has the meaning of "awe" changed?

--

Pat in Collegeville, MN wrote:
Ken used salmagundi as subject heading to a posting on various unrelated topics. Can we expect, Ken, a farrago, an olio, a hodge-podge or hotch-potch, a pastiche, a potpourri or olla podrida, a stew or ragout, a hash or goulash, a melange, a medley, an omnium-gatherum, a mulligan and a gallimaufry?

--

Mike in Brisbane on Verbs and Verbing:
My boss is having a small war with the library on campus. The library likes to use the word "loaned" as the past tense of "lend" as in lending books. He insists that this is ungrammatical, and the word is "lent". Comments, please?

--

Paul in Sydney, NS:
The following quote from The Random House Unabridged may be of interest to Mike's boss: Usage Sometimes mistakenly identified as an Americanism, LOAN as a verb meaning "to lend" has been used in English for nearly 800 years: Nearby villages loaned clothing and other supplies to the flood-ravaged town. The occasional objections to LOAN as a verb referring to things other than money, are comparatively recent. LOAN is standard in all contexts but is perhaps most common in financial ones: The government has loaned money to farmers to purchase seed.

So, if one lends it, it's lent, but if one loans it, it's loaned?

--

Rich in Rindge, NH:
Aside from the obvious terms "canine" and "feline", can anyone fill in the equivalent terms for:
    1. birds

THE POWER OF WORDS ~ 49

    2. Goats
    3. Frogs
    4. Fish
    5. Bulls
    6. Bees
    7. Pigs
    8. Wolves
    9. Deer
    10. crows

How about it, any others?

Sara in Boston: Animal words - a thread to play with!

    Equine – horses
    Bovine – cows
    Ovine – sheep
    Feline – cats
    Canine – dogs
    Caprine – goats
    Porcine – pigs
    Corvine – crows

Any other -ine's?

Phil in Salt Lake City:
I can add:

    Lapine – rabbits
    Lupine - wolves (as well as a flower in the pea family)

Kat in Rochester:
How about:

    Piscine – fish
    Murine – mouse
    Avian - bird (sorry, not -ine, but as close as I could get)
    Taurine – bull
    Leonine - lion

And Steven in San Antonio:
1. birds - avine
2. goats - caprine
3. frogs - anurine?
4. fish - piscine
5. bulls - bolline?
6. bees - apine?
7. pigs - porcine
8. wolves - lupine
9. deer - cervine
10. crows - corvine
11. bats - chiroptine
12. chicken - galline
13. snake - serpentine
14. bear - ursine

Patrick in Collegeville, MN:
Three more -ine animal words:
> vulpine, from vulpes/fox
> passerine, from passer/sparrow
> vulturine, obvious

Another non-ine one:
> simian, form simia/ape (from simus/snub-nosed)

Many of these adjectives are applied metaphorically to humans, with considerable injustice to the animals they denote; we unload our human vices onto them, whether we use the Latinate or Anglo-Saxon words--e.g., porcine/piggish/hoggish, lupine/wolfish, vulpine/foxy (the word has acquired other meanings, of course; but sly, devious. . .) Makes it easier, I suppose, for us to treat them as we do.

--

Mick enquired:
I recently read that the antonym for EUPHEMISM is DYSPHEMISM. I must confess that I have never seen that word in print

nor heard it in speech. Does anyone know another, more common antonym?

--

David in Ritner, KY offered:
Names of those special symbols:
>! bang, yipe
>@ snail
># hash, pound
>$ string, bux
>% percent
>^ carrot
>& et, and, ampersand
>* splat, star, asterisk

--

Bob in Chicago shared:
There was an item in the news recently whereby President Bill Clinton was castigated for his use of the word "welsh" as in "America does not 'welsh' on her debts". Apparently, some people of "Welsh" (or Welch) descent took umbrage of his remark and labeled it "a racial slur". Why they didn't label it an ethnic slur is not known. Maybe the Welsh consider themselves a breed apart. I think that the president's choice of the word is accepted usage and some folks are just wrapped a little too tight.

John in Keele added:
The letter page of today's London TIMES concludes with a contribution which expresses pleasure that the offensive use of "to welsh" has now been, er, scotched...

Jesse in Sunnyvale, CA observed:
Interesting. I've used the term "welch" before, but never knew the origin. The same thing holds true for "gyp" and I never had the slightest reservation about using the term, until someone pointes out the likely heritage from "gypsy." Normally, I would agree that those folks might be "wound to tight," but on the other hand, it grates on my ear to hear

someone "jew" someone else down in a negotiation of price. I've met folks who didn't know the origin of that term and didn't mean offense by it, but I can certainly see how it could cause offense.

And then Allan from Sydney, NS added:
The origin of 'welch' (or welsh) in the sense of failing to pay a debt or go back on one's word is unknown. In all likelihood, it has nothing whatever to do with the Welsh people. The word is considered absolutely standard English. It is not offensive usage, and no one except maybe ignorant hypersensitive types would think it has anything to do with the Welsh, any more than describing something as a turkey has anything to do with the Turks or their country.

In sharp contrast, the word 'jew' in the sense of hard bargaining is listed as offensive usage in every dictionary and reference book of English; it should never be used in this sense.

--

Mike in Brisbane responded to Caleb who asked: "Why are they URBAN legends? Didn't rural folk also make up stuff?"

Caleb, I have it on good authority (which means I dreamed it up) that they might be called urban legends as opposed to 'tribal legends', 'ancient legends', 'classical legends' and so on; i.e. they are part of modern (or post-modern) culture. Certainly, rural people made them up too, but they remain 'urban legends'.

And Allan in Sydney, NS followed up:
The term 'urban legend' was popularised (though not invented) by Jan H. Brunvand, a professor of English at the University of Utah. In addition to scholarly works, he published a number of popular books which listed many legends of contemporary folklore. The first, published in 1981, was 'The Vanishing Hitchhiker: American Urban Legends and Their Meanings'. This was followed by several sequels.

In his introduction to 'The Vanishing Hitchhiker' Brunvand notes that the juxtaposition of the terms 'modern', 'contemporary', and 'urban' may seem contradictory to those who think of folklore as charming, obsolete, unsophisticated traditions passed along by gaffers and crones in backwoods villages. The term 'urban legend' is used because they are told and believed by some of the most sophisticated 'folk' of modern society – young people, urbanites, the well-educated. The storytellers - assume that the cases are true.

Most - but not all - urban legends take place in urban settings. Almost all involve the modern urban world, most invoking modern technology of one sort or another - microwave ovens, automobiles, sewage systems and the like, usually in an urban setting. They are promulgated by the mass media, adding to their urban outlook and feel.

You could call them modern fairy tales - which, of course, they are - but the folklorist term 'urban legend' seems to have caught on.

Bill in Columbia, CT added:
"Urban" refers to the city and "urbane" refers to one's state of sophistication (which is acquired from city living of course).

--

Caleb in Albany, NY responded to a query which asks:
"I recall my grandmother using some of her mother's cookbooks which had measurements like - a pinch of this, 2 dashes of that..."

According to my Dad,
    2 pinches = 1 dash
    4 dashes = 1 dollop
    2 dollops = 1 amount

--

Katherine in Oakland commented in regards to "^ carrot":
Meant to comment before: AFAIK that's "caret", not "carrot" (nor, for that matter, "carat"--anybody wanna play with those three? I'm too tired!)

David in Ritney, KY weighed in too:
A carat is a unit of mass equal to 200 milligrams in all of the civilized world, or one bean equal to four old grains (3.168 Troy grains) in the United States of America and in Myanmar. (Source: The American Society for the Historical Preservation of Weights and Measures)

A caret is what Ms. Ninnywicz calls that funny little pointedly hat thingy in her Sophomore English class.

--

Pat in Collegeville, MN expressed:
My Merriam-Webster, BTW, conjectures that gam comes from gammon, obsolete for talk--gam also means a gathering of seamen, especially whalers, for friendly conversation.

Mike in Brisbane reposted:
And don't forget, that as well as bacon, there's 'gammon' as a verb, meaning to trick or deceive, and as an adjective, meaning 'false'.

Mike in Aurora, IL opined:
I believe the term veteran means retired, only when it refers to soldiers. However, in all other professions it usually refers to someone who is still in the profession and has a lot of experience. i.e. in 10 years, I might consider myself a veteran tax accountant (if I'm still practicing) however, when I retire, I won't consider myself a veteran accountant just a retired one. After I'm retired, I may be considered a former veteran of the tax profession (God help us all, and save the Queen)! :}>

--

Jack in London responded to Janet in Calgary, re kerfuffle:
This is in common use in the UK, probably more in the north than the south. Collins defines it as follows:
kerfuffle (carfuffle, or kurfuffle) n. 1. Informal, chiefly Brit. commotion; disorder; agitation. vb. 2. (tr.) Scot. to put into disorder or disarray; ruffle or disarrange. [from Scottish curfuffle, carfuffle, from Scottish Gaelic car twist, turn + fuffle to disarrange]

Lee in Sacramento remarked:
There you go, Jack. The difference between Brits & Mericans. You get kerfuffled while I get in a swivet! Guess we're equally disturbed, however. (And you can take that to be either meaning.)

--

Janet in Calgary enquired:
I completely confused a group of people the other day by describing someone as "having been thrown into a complete swivet" by a turn of events. Does anybody else use this phrase, or will it turn out to be my family thing?

--

Allan in Sydney, NS brought up enquire vs inquire:
I vaguely recall this being discussed at some length in the earlier days of this group. The two words are completely synonymous and interchangeable, though inquiry seems to be far more common in North America, Canada included. The Economist Style Guide lists inquire as preferred American usage. However, Oxford claims that (recent) UK usage tends to distinguish between enquire (ask) and inquire (make investigation) e.g. convene a Court of Inquiry, but enquire about a patient. The distinction is not made in North America, and I suspect it is not made anywhere else.

--

Lori wrote:
The more languages I learn, the more I appreciate the word sibling (gender unspecific, encompasses one generation). Does anyone know any other languages with similar meaning words?

Steven in Austin, TX answered:
In German, there is "Geschwistern", (no, not the same as Schwester). Although, grammatically, the word is feminine, it translates to "siblings" in English.

--

Dave in Glendale, CA shared:
Sometimes I get enthralled, besotted and enchanted by words which have come to be interchangeable (as in describing a person who is deeply in love with another), but whose past reveals subtle differences in meaning now ignored... case in point being, er..um.., "enthralled", "besotted" and "enchanted".

"Enthralled" carries the notion of being enslaved, "besotted" of being intoxicated, and "enchanted" of being under a spell (probably one that was uttered in a sing-song pattern).

[Insert name of preferred deity here], but I do love this language!!!

--

Bill in Mobile made a distinction:
Meanwhile, "historic" refers to some unusual happening (i.e. "This is one small step for man and one giant step for *mankind.") that is in another class that warrants an infinite life. "Historical" refers to the mundane information that leaves a personal informative trail for our ancestors.

--

Kat in Rochester had a suggestion:
There is a thread running on another list about the proper term for a female curmudgeon. So far (after several days) the only possibilities we have come up with are:
curmudgeoness
curmudgeonette

Otherwise, folks are falling back on nasty pejorative words like -bitch- and -copyeditor-, which lack the semi-affectionate tone of -curmudgeon-. Any suggestions?

Hep followed up on the same theme:
Aren't we past trying to turn words into a diminutive form for women? The ette/ess is rapidly disappearing. The other day Maya Angelou was referred to as a poet, not a poetess. When was the last time Emily Bronte was referred to as an authoress. Even the term actor is being used to refer to both genders of that profession. The female term for curmudgeon is curmudgeon.

Richard in Tempe, AZ wondered:
But will we use traditional terms, such as "waiter," or create awkward, "gender-neutral" terms like "waitperson?" I vote for "waiter." If the gender of the individual is "unusual" for the trade, we can always say "male midwife." (Hmmm, perhaps that's a bad example, but surely, we

wouldn't change that one to "midhusband," would we?) On the other hand, I think I might object to "chairman" and "spokesman" if I happened to be non-male. <g>

I don't mind "chair" (or even "committee director," "leader," "supervisor" or "manager") for "chairman." (I expect some opposition to "chair.") Neither am I bothered by "company representative" for spokesman. I wish we had something shorter, though...any suggestions? (Please don't ask me to endorse "spokesperson." Or to use "author" as verb!)

And, I would add, the *term* for a *female* curmudgeon is curmudgeon.

--

HAR enquired:
What about ensure and insure? According to my Webster's, they're synonyms except in the sense of "indemnification," which only applies to "insure."

Steven in Seattle responded:
The American Heritage suggests the same. It's definition for ensure is "To make sure or certain; insure." It also contains in a usage note: "Although ensure and insure are generally interchangeable, only insure is now widely used in American English in the commercial sense of 'to guarantee persons or property against risk.'"

And Lisa in Charlotte, NC shared:
I'm having a friendly row with my manager, who's a great guy but can't spell his way out of a wet paper bag. We've got a beer bet riding on this one, and I like good beer! He is continually sending out email & various postings using the term "insure" where I assert he should be using "ensure". His assertion is that the 2 terms are interchangeable. My assertion is that the 2 terms are *somewhat* interchangeable but that in the context he intends, the term ENSURE is more accurate. The context of his notes is always something along the lines of "Let's insure that our processes are documented", i.e. to "make certain of" or guarantee.

He sent me an excerpt from the dictionary which he feels proves the 2 are interchangeable. I assert that they are synonymous but that since ENSURE has "to guarantee or make sure" as its PRIMARY definition, and INSURE has "to obtain insurance" as its PRIMARY definition and "to make certain" as its SECONDARY definition, that ENSURE is most appropriate for his context.

BTW I have an English degree, and better taste in beer...

And Linda weighed in:

I think one of your best examples is the different connotations of either ensure or insure, and assure. OK, they are KIND OF interchangeable, but "ensure" implies forward-thinking, while "assure" clearly gives an image of reassurance - more of a reaction than an action. If it "doesn't really matter," (when folks say that to me, I often suggest taking the word out - seems to open their eyes a bit) how important can the word be to your message?

Bill in Mobile aded:

A dictionary reflects usage and simply because something is used a lot ("insure" as the same as "ensure" doesn't make it correct. Snuck (according to the dictionary) is also used frequently but the grammarian says "sneaked." The dictionary is not the place to determine the best English.

--

Phil in Salt Lake City asked:

Can anyone tell me what "hugger=mugger" farming is? It's rather hard to look up.

Mike in Brisbane answered:

Phil, the Concise Oxford says Hugger-mugger means 1. secrecy, confusion, and 4. proceed in secret or muddled fashion. probably from O.E. hoder = huddle and mokere = conceal

So my guess is that it was "highly disorganised farming", or "muddled farming". Interesting that Kipling uses the word "mugger" to describe a crocodile who lies in wait for people at an Indian watering place – lying concealed, of course.

Jim in Philadelphia enquired about "mangle" and David in Glendale said:

if memory serves, is a professional ironing device especially good for flatwork (although a skilled operator can iron practically anything with it. Not to be confused with a steam ironing device, the mangle consists of a cylindrical, cloth-covered surface, about four feet long and about 10 inches in diameter, which rotates slowly (the machine holds it horizontal) when the thing is engaged by a foot pedal. The foot pedal also brings down (or forward on some models) a hot "shoe", which is heated metal, the exact fit to the cylinder; it covers a third of the "roundth" cylinder and usually all of its length. The hot metal irons anything between it and the cylinder (including, occasionally, the operator's hands or other anatomical protrusions). Workers do not wear ties while operating the device...at least not for long.

Suad asked:

I would really be thankful if someone can help me with this word "flabbergast"? what does it mean? and examples of its use would be great :)

And Mike in Brisbane had an answer:

"Flabbergast" - a condition of extreme surprise - caused by an event which "took your breath away". My dictionary says 18th century, possibly derived from "aghast".

Marjorie in Boston suggested:

Raul asked for the meaning of the word "rudesby." I can't find it in a dictionary either, but from the context of the sentences in which it appeared, I'd say that it means a boor. Reminds me of another word I've run across more than once: moonling (also not in the dictionary), meaning a callow, silly youth. Both of these words appeared in novels (written in recent times) that took place in Georgian/Regency England. Has anyone else come across either of these words? They're too good not to be real!

Anders in Stokholm also had a take on it:
According to "Webster's" it means 'turbulent person', without further remarks (apart from 'archaic'). In Scandinavia there are quite a few places beginning with Rud- or By- or ending with -rud or -by. The 'rud' means clear or remove and is particularly associated with forest. The 'by' means settlement. So Rudesby may originally have been a place somewhere on the British Isles. Perhaps it is still extant but under a different name. If one accepts a geographical origin of the word one may suspect that this was considered low-standard origin. One can perhaps replace the rudesbies above with (equally?) pejorative Londoner, New Yorker, Texan, Cockney, etc. Any comments?

And John in Keele, UK added this:
Or as the Germans call it, "Volksetymologie", is probably behind the "rudesby" question, and I suspect it's Shakespeare who's doing it rather than the WordPlayers. In other words: the derivation from Scandinavian terms for clearing forests is probably the right one [cognate with German "roden", no doubt], but misuse of the term to mean "a rude person" is a natural thing to do once you've heard the term, whether it's an unconscious mistake or a conscious piece of WordPlay.

--

Frank in Ottawa offered:
Somebody asked about "Twee". According to Eric Partridge it means dainty; chic; pleasing: colloquial 1905. Obsolete.

Bill in Columbia, CT noted:
On a side note, obsolete means it has fallen into disuse and obsolescent means it is becoming obsolete.

--

On the topic of the various forms of kissing, Mike in Brisbane added:
And then of course, there's vanity kissing, which is when the gentleman bends over the lady's hand, but actually kisses his own.

Kent was puzzled:

I have never heard of such. Was it a social standard, or a personal eccentricity?

Ken in Victoria, BC queried:

I have never heard the term "twilight" used for the morning. Is there another term?

Sara in Boston answered:

Twilight at sunrise - I've heard this referred to as "dawnlight," when the sky is bright but the sun's not yet up. I don't know if this is correct, but it sounds nice!

Kent had his own take:

For the start of the day, I know of both false dawn and daybreak. I don't believe either one, though, is actually the term being requested. The search continues.

Personally, I don't believe there is a term. People only create words for what they experience; how many people are ever up that early? Of those who are, how many are awake enough to create a neologism? :)

Mike in Brisbane had his own version:

Yep, in Australia it's "pikkininni daylight", from an Aboriginal word "pikkininni" meaning baby or small child. There's also "at sparrowf*rt" or "first sparrowf*rt" which denotes a very early hour.

Bob in Chicago had a literary reference:

How about the word "brillig" as used by author Lewis Carrol (aka Charles Dodgson) in his poem "The Jabberwock". If my memory serves me correctly the poem begins " 'Twas brillig and all the burogroves did gyre and gimbal on the wabe..." The word "brillig was used here to denote a kind of false daylight or dawn/dusk. I am sure that there is some English major out there in WP-Land who will correct me if I am wrong.

And Har observed:

"Aurora" is a beautiful word for the light at the beginning of the day. "Crepuscule" is an even lovelier word for twilight.

Bill in Columbia, CT added:
Several people have written comments on "Twilight." Twilight is the time either between full night and sunrise or sunset and full night. Twilight occurs in the evening or early morning. "Crepuscule" is another name for it. In its essence it refers to an intermediate state.

--

Frank in Ottawa said:
[Tuque] is Quebecois French, a slight variant of toque, which in France meant a cap that knocked (toquer) against the back of the neck or shoulders because it had a long, droopy end.

Karen in Manchester, UK retorted:
And of course now it's the word for a chef's hat.

--

Matt in Minneapolis, MN took us back to the subject of toponymical names:
In the same _Crazy English_ with the marvellous discourse recently cited, the word describing where someone is from, or from where someone is, is listed as "domunym".

And Mike in Brisbane followed up with the names thread, in Australia:

>From Queensland = Banana Benders
>From NSW = Cornstalks
>From Victoria = Mudgrubbers
>From South Australia = Crow eaters
>From Western Australia = Sand Gropers
>From Tasmania = Taswegians
>From Northern Territory = Territorians

And there's Novocastrians, Sydneysiders, Brisbanites, Adelaideians, and a whole lot more ites".

--

Gerald in Ottawa wrote about road traffic rules:
... Jug handles are very big in Spain. For sheer horror, however, I'd like to nominate the system in Melbourne, Australia where - it must be

borne in mind - people drive on the left. In the 1970's at least, those wanting to turn right at certain designated intersections in the middle of the city had to get into the extreme left-hand lane, move well out into the middle of the intersection, sit there until the light turned red, and then pull a fast 90-degree turn to avoid being broadsided by the three lanes of impatient traffic that had been sitting there all this time, vrooming their engines and waiting for their own light to change. They did mark these particular intersections in advance, I'll give them that, but it wasn't always apparent to the uninitiated what they were talking about...

Jane in Hobart, Tasmania followed up:
A beautiful description of Melbourne's "hook turns" Gerald! They certainly are horrific. They serve a useful purpose though. Without them, cars waiting to turn right (in the right-hand lane) run the risk of having an impatient tram driver run into their rear-end. So, they head over to the left to run the gauntlet of the waiting cars instead. Do they have similar rules for left-hand turns in downtown San Fransisco? "Jug handles" is a term I have never heard before. "Traffic circles" is also a new one for me. In Australia they are called "roundabouts" which I think is particularly apt. It sort of sums up peoples' attitude towards them, "Oh, I reckon I can enter this intersection 'roundabout now..."

--

Lorianne from Saskatoon was reminded:
Remember the name and related profession thread? Well, I recently found out that such names are referred to as aptonyms.

--

Dave in Glendale, CA said on jibe vs jive:
Back in The Old Days, when I was tech consultant on inventing the wheel, we used "jibe" as the verb meaning "to fit with, to agree with," as in "The conclusion that the concoction was jam did not jibe with its evident tendency to deform and reform in a manner more consistent with its categorization as a form of jelly."

"Jive" came later, originally as an alternative to one of the seven words that got George Carlin a couple of contracts. Only then did it become the adjective/noun of choice for what was thought (in Those Days) to be a form of music that represented energetic foreplay.

--

Kent asked a while back:
I hope you have jaffles? In the Midwest, just about where the Mason/Dixon line blurs between family members, it is a novel word. Is it related to waffles as jandals related to sandals on a recent post?

Mike in Brisbane responded:
Well, sorta. To make a jaffle, you take two slices of bread, put some savoury stuff in between them, and put the assembly into a jaffle iron, which crimps the bread slices together, and toasts them. You finish up with a little pie with a toast casing. Nice on rainy days. You can get electric jaffle irons now, but in the olden days, they were a long-handled appliance which you used over the glowing coals of a campfire.

Ken in St Paul, MN budded in:
Mike, yeah, we got'em, too! Pudgy pies is what we call 'em. Along with the long-handled implements for cooking them over a campfire.

Andy in Chichester, UK observed:
Continuing the food thread, it would seem that Mike's Jaffle is Jesse's Toastie is Kenneth's Pudgy Pie is Lorainne's Bush Pie is my Breville (TM). Are we all talking about the same thing?

--

Ken in St Paul offered:
Bob brought up "dum aisel". My dear old departed father used to call us children "dummerissel" which I later discovered during my German lessons was probably "dummer esel" - means dumb jackass :-)

--

George in Revelstoke, BC suugested:
To Kat: A suggestion for a word expressing extreme emotion - phreatic ("Her response to the crisis was to assume a most phreatic disposition.")

THE POWER OF WORDS - 65

Andy in Chichester enquired:
I was amazed to find that the word yokel is used outside England. My dictionary (shorter Oxford) also tentatively suggests it is from a dialect word for Green Woodpecker. First, does anyone have any idea which dialect? Secondly, has anyone come across the words emmet (sp?) and grackle (sp?)? These are both antonyms of yokel in a way, being used by (I think) Cornish and Devonian locals to describe tourists.

Monika asked:
Now, I have a question that has been bothering me for some time. English is not my native language, and three terms I have always had a lot of trouble with are nerd, geek, and dork. Now, I understand the basic concept of a nerd is someone who is very intelligent, into science, and is socially totally inept. And I guess a geek is someone who would be a nerd, except he's not smart enough. But what exactly is a dork?

Also, I've been unable to come up with a female version for these things - are there no female nerds, geeks, and dorcs, or just no word for them, or would they be nerdettes, geekesses and dorcas ?

And David answered:
I think you have nerd right. The term geek had its origin in the world of carnivals and travelling shows. It was the term for a performer whose act revolved around grossing out the audience. The canonical example is biting the heads off live chickens. Thus, the term now has distinct overtones of a creepy or disgusting individual without any connotation of intelligence.

Dorc (or dork) has the connotation of not-so-much stupidity as lack of awareness of what is going on around him - someone who just doesn't get it. It seemed to fit a lot of my fellow undergraduates at MIT, who weren't stupid, after all, but who seemed to operate on a different plane from the real world.

I've never heard these terms applied to women.

Jesse in Sunnyvale, CA commented:

I've usually seen it spelled as "dork" and it is one of the many euphemisms for penis. Where "nerd" and "geek" have some association with intelligence, "dork" has no such shade of meaning. It usually just means stupid, which is odd, since most nerds and geeks will also be accused of being dorks. "Geek" as I understand it, was originally the term for the person who would bite the heads off of chickens in a side show at a carnival.

I believe all three are gender-neutral terms, although I have heard "nerdette" used, but only jokingly. A female "dork" however, is probably a contradiction in terms.

And Bruce in Sydney, AU added:

For what it is worth I have always spelt it with a K. It has always had two connotations, the first of which tends to preclude the application of any feminisation as it is yet another synonym for that repository in the male of all things cerebral, the "old fella", the "deep protein injector", the "love muscle" (I see a thread here), or at times just "my penis".

Now let me quickly address the second connotation lest you good people all think me obsessed. "Dork" is one of those words which can have a 'relational nuance', much like the way an Australian uses the word "bastard". "Dork" directed at a friend is almost affectionate if invariably critical. Directed at a stranger it is pure insult. Synonyms might be... 'clod', 'fool', or 'Oh thee of embarrassing social ineptitude' stuff like that. An Americanisation might be 'goofball'.

Katherine in Oakland, CA had an explanation:

My two cents' worth on use of dork/geek/nerd--this is how I use the terms, or how they seem to be used by people I know:

I've only heard "dork" used for men, and have sometimes been given what might be called a biological explanation for that (i.e., that the word started out as a specific reference...quite embarrassing, when I'd been calling idiotic guys that for a while because I liked the sound of the word as an insult!). AFAIK, it always connotes stupidity.

"Nerd", on the other hand, frequently implies intelligence—though in a not very socially acceptable way: it's the grown-up version of "brain" or all those other names we were called in grade school that meant, "eewww! she'd rather spend her time _reading_ than playing jump rope/chasing boys/engaging in normal behaviour". Seems to be mostly unisex, though I've seen "nerdette" used on occasion (and probably facetiously).

"Geeks" are like nerds, but both socially weirder and more knowledgeable. People who think nerds are too egg-headed (!) will use "geek" as an insult. The computer geeks I hang out with use it proudly, as a term connoting expertise or at least fanaticism sufficient to earn a good living.

Jack in London added:
Re geek and nerd -- in my experience geek is used by computer hackers whereas nerd is used as a term of abuse by outsiders. Both mean someone has all the personality of a cheese-grater (see The New Hacker's Dictionary ... or the Jargon file) but being a geek implies computing skills a nerd may not have. A dork, of course, is a different kind of socially-clueless individual. Nerds study science/technology subjects and wear pocket-protectors but dorks drink lager and play team sports.

Lorianne in Saskatoon observed:
I found something on slang at UCLA. There they have the word 'gork' meaning nerd. It was formed from geek+dork.

--

George in Revelstoke, BC asked:
Anyone know what a "feed dog" is? Clue: neither Alpo nor canine are involved.

Steve in Austin, TX replied:
Well, they're not involved unless you are some warped kind of a sadistic seamstress (or seamster ??) Feed dogs are what help draw fabric through a sewing machine. They are on the opposite side of the fabric from the foot.

In reply to Andy who observed "I was amazed to find that the word yokel is used outside England", Susi said:
I've heard it all over the US, as in "local Yokel", for a very countrified native.

--

Lorianne in Saskatoon asked:
Anybody know why flammable and inflammable mean the same thing?

Bob in Chicago had the answer:
It has been my observation that the government regulatory agencies tend to use the words "flammable" and "combustible" when describing materials or processes that can ignite. It seems to me that the word "inflammable' is used more often for things intangible like a situation that escalates in intensity or is growing out of control.

And Flagg explained:
When I worked in a screen-printing shop, I had our local fire inspector explain it to me, since I had been working with safety hazard warning labels long enough to be curious.

According to some regulatory agency (presumably OSHA), "combustible" and "flammable" refer to substances which will ignite (combust) when exposed to a flame or spark. "inflammable" refers to substances which, under certain circumstances, can generate enough heat to ignite THEMSELVES. The example given was lacquer thinner-soaked paint rags in a pile. If left alone, they "CAN" spontaneously combust, and burst into flames. Hence, lacquer thinner is labelled as inflammable. Mineral spirits (the common name for a chemical, not eternal soul of a rock) will not combust unless heat/flame/spark is applied from an external source; thus, it is flammable.

--

Kat in Rochester weighed in on "beaverboard":
This was originally a trademark for sheets of compressed wood pulp. As for the origin of the term: have you ever seen the ground around

a tree stump after a beaver has harvested the trunk? That's right...WOOD PULP. Very descriptive.

--

John in Keele, UK cautioned:
The Guilds list, I note, includes "potters". Have to be careful around here [next to the Potteries Towns] when someone introduces him- or her-self as "a potter". The expression may mean "born locally" rather than "employed in the ceramics industry".

--

Mike in Brisbane shed some light on an Aussie favourite:
Vegemite is a concentrated yeast extract, used as a spread for sandwiches, toast or biscuits (crackers). Believed to be a byproduct from breweries, it is very salty, and dark brown in colour, almost black. Australians consume vast quantities of Vegemite and its two major competitors, Marmite and Promite. They are all basically the same, although on a scale of salt to sweet, the run is Vegemite, Marmite, Promite, with Promite being the sweetest of the three. Each has its fanatical adherents. the product is rumoured to contain vast amounts of Vitamin B and Niacin, and it is advertised as an essential part of the diet for growing children. Also used in soups, stews, sauces. A large teaspoon of the substance dissolved in a cup of hot water is often used as a comforting drink. Much used in school lunches, and at breakfast on toast. Combines well on crackers when served under sliced tomato. Not nice on ice cream. Seems to be a peculiarly Australian phenomenon, although I believe developed by an American. Somewhat similar to Bovril and Oxo, although these are beef extracts. The television jingle which advertises Vegemite has passed into the Australian vernacular, and children are sometimes described as "happy little vegemites" or "not a very happy little vegemite". There you go - le dernier cri on Vegemite!

--

George in Revelstoke, BC was inspired:
Along the Yokel/Hick/Rube thread, I would like to explore the syn-

onym "bumpkin." According to my American Heritage Dictionary, a bumpkin is an awkward, unsophisticated rustic, as in yokel. Origin unknown. I was wondering whether this word occurs much in England, Canada, or Australia.

One might speculate a derivation from "pumpkin," or "bumption" (the state of being "bumptious"). A country pumpkin bumpkin may have no bumption, but a bumptious city bumpkin probably has no pumpkin. For further reflection we might add "hayseed," "clodhopper," "boor," and "provincial."

--

Martin in Los Angeles wrote:
A question - what word or words rhyme with "filth"?
And Phil in Salt Lake City answered:
The word "tilth" comes to mind. In case anyone is not familiar with it, it is an agronomic term relating to the looseness of the soil. A soil with good tilth will soak up rain, rather than let it run off. Tilling increases tilth.
Lorianne was puzzled:
I think we use tillage around here. Does anyone still use tilth?

--

Karen did a quick delurk to clarify the meaning between "dressing" and "stuffing".
Stuffing is cooked within the bird. Dressing is prepared and cooked separately from the bird, but is served with the bird. It isn't loose like stuffing, but has the appearance of a savory bread pudding.

--

Karen had another puzzler:
I discovered in Webster's Unabridged Dictionary (only one available) that "recipe" used to refer to formulas used in medical prescriptions. I am interested in knowing at what point did "receipt" cross over to "recipe" and did it have anything to do with earlier recipes listing only ingredients and not instructions? Was it borrowed from the pharmaceutical meaning?

Also how geographically wide spread was the word "receipt" used back then (or even now)?

Alex in Adelaide had a plausible explanation:
Karen wonders about the connection between "receipt" and recipe. I say it comes from French "recette" meaning recipe.

--

Bill in Columbia, CT clarified:
The dialogue on the spectrum of black is quite intriguing. The word "niggard" is often used as an ethnic slur by the ignorant. It has nothing to do with prejudice that is typified by the "N-word."

Catie in Arlington, VA answered:
Had to look this one up. According to my American Heritage dictionary (new college addition), Quadroon: (n). A person having one quarter Negro ancestry. [From Spanish _cuarteron_, from _cuarto_, quarter, from Latin _Quartus_.]

Also: Octoroon: n. the offspring of a white person and a quadroon; one who is one-eighth Negro. [OCTO- + (QUAD)ROON.]

--

Leo shifted gears:
The terms "tone poem" and "symphonic poem" are synonymous. My electronic AH dictionary states it is explained as "A piece of music, most popular in the late 19th century, that is based on an extramusical theme, such as a story or nationalistic ideal, and consists of a single extended movement for a symphony orchestra. Also called tone poem."

Examples that come to mind are Rimsky-Korsakov's "Scheherazade," Debussy's "La Mer," and Grieg's "Peer Gynt Suite." There are hundreds more out there.

--

Frank in Ottawa needed a clarification:
Correct me, prithee, if I'm wrong (and I'm sure you will), but I was taught that the good people of Afghanistan are Afghans. An Afghani is a unit of currency.

Katherine in Oakland added:
Also the dogs and crocheted bed-coverings are Afghans.

--

Jim in Philadelphia enquired:
I'm not sure exactly why that reminded me, but according to the Official Scrabble Players' Dictionary (before they eliminated obscenities last year, anyway) listed the following word: OFAY. I had never heard this word before my sophomore year roommate pointed it out to me, but apparently it means "a white person, in derogatory context." Is there a connection here?

Dean answered:
The OED guardedly poo-pooed this theory without being sure what the real deal is. One theory is that it comes from the Ibibio 'Afia', meaning white. The other is that it comes from the French 'Au Fait', meaning with authority outside the deed of law.

--

Catie followed up on an earlier thread:
Dave, after posting my last note, I just had to go downstairs and check out the origin of the two presents in my dictionary. You were absolutely right! Those two (present - here now, and present - gift/introduce) are from two different origins. Of course, the PREsent - gift, and preSENT - to give, or introduce are from the same origin, the derivations are as follows (from my American Heritage Dictionary, New College Edition - which I've had since college, 15 years ago).

present (1) a moment or period in time perceptible as intermediate between past and future; now. [Middle English, from Old French, from Latin past and futurel; now. [Middle English, from Old French, from Latin _praesens_, present participle of _praesse_, to be before one, be present: _prae_, in front of + _esse_, to be.]

present (2) tr.v., 1. to introduce. 2. To bring before the public. 3. To make a gift or award. n. Something presented; a gift. [Middle English _presenten_, from Old French _presenter_, from Latin _praesentare_, from _praesens_, present (adjective).]

Alex in Adelaide reminded us:
On the topic of heteronyms, there was one discussed here previously: unionized unIONIZED--for atoms, UNIONized for industries.

Bill in Columbia, CT was grateful:
Dave Moody, nice word ("cavil"). "Cavil" is a pleasant defensive intransitive verb that is appropriate in detoxifying verbal unrest. It can be used in the progressive with one or two l's.
Thanks for keeping me verbally alert.

David in Glendale, CA reminded us:
Someone suggested (in jest) that one should have reservations about a culture (like the Spanish) for which the word for being pregnant is a cognate of our word meaning to be ashamed ("embarazada", I believe).
   Actually, it is our culture that has added the concept of shame to a word which used to mean merely "hampered," or -- at worst -- "perplexed," or so my Oxford Dict. of Etymology says.

Bill commented on the saga of mop/mope/moped/moppet:
mop (v) - to clean and *mopped* (v) - past tense of mop;
mope (v) - to brood and *moped* - past tense of mope;
moped (n) - a motorized bicycle.
   Another word that is often confused with this group is *moppet* (n) - a young Child.

Phil in Salt Lake City learnt something new:
When I asked about "New Year's Revolutions", I didn't anticipate getting taught a new (old) word: ...widdershins. I had to look it up under "withershins". It means (in case I'm not the only one needing help): in a direction contrary to the usual --in the wrong direction. Thanks, Sara.

The most misspelled (or misunderstood) words in family history:

Geneology – not a word : Genealogy – family history
Interment – burial : Internment – confinement in prison
Emigrant – relocated from : immigrant – relocated to
Calvary – a hill near Jerusalem : Cavalry – a horse soldier
Decent – socially acceptable : Descent – downward on a family tree
Cemetary – not a word : Cemetery – a burial ground
Grantor – property transferer : Grantee – the recipient of property
Copywrite – create business text: Copyright – legal rights to intellec. property

From GopherRecords.com – Records Retrieval from the National Archives.

--

Little known words:

Aglet: the tiny plastic or metallic sleeve at the end of the shoe laces
Agraffe: the wire cage that holds the cork in a bottle sparkling wine
Armscye: armhole in clothes, where the sleeves are sewn
Bannock device: the metallic contraption used to measure one's foot at the shoe shop
Box tent: tiny plastic table place in the middle of a pizza box
Columella nasi: the space between the nostrils
Crapulence: the sick feeling one gets after eating or drinking too much
Dysania: difficulty in getting out of bed in the morning
Glabella: the space between one's eyebrows
Griffonage: illegible hand-writing
Interrobang; a combination of a question mark and an exclamation mark (?!)
Minimus: small finger or toe
Overmorrow: the day after tomorrow
Petrichor: the smell after a rain fall
Phosphenes: the sheen that you see when you press your hands on your closed eyes
Tines: the prongs on a fork

Tittle: the dot over an 'i' or an 'a'
Vagitus: the cry of a new-born baby
Vocables: the "na na na" and "la la la" in the lyrics of a song
Wamble: stomach rumbling

3

Etymology

Jim in Philadelphia posed a question on Raspberries:
Anyone know why the sound that usually comes with the following emoticon :-P is called "Raspberry?

Brian in London answered:
Easy: it's raspberry tart, and it's (Cockney) rhyming slang. There are a lot of expressions that are now common but people sometimes don't realise started as rhyming slang, e.g. " to take a butcher's at", "to use one's loaf", but perhaps I'm stealing your thunder?

Zeno in Minneapolis, MN added:
"Stealing my thunder", at least, is not, I think, derived from rhyming slang. It is reputed to be virtually the only thing we remember about John Dennis, the playwright who accused William Shakespeare of stealing the idea of using sheets of tin wobbled back and forth between one's hands to simulate thunder in, I believe, "Lear". Dennis claimed he invented the idea and used it in his play ... golly, the name of it slips my mind... odd, that. Dennis also had several other derogatory things to say about Mr Shakespeare.

Jim in Tacoma, WA followed up:
Yes, John Dennis invented the tin-sheet thunder for his play _Appius and Virginia_. The thunder was a hit, but his play was not. Soon after Dennis' own play died at the box office, Dennis attended a produc-

tion of _MacBeth_, where he heard his thunder issuing from backstage. Apoplectic, Dennis rose and howled, "See how the rascals use me! They will not let my play run, and yet they steal my thunder!" However, because Shakespeare (1564-1616) had been taking the long dirt-nap many years before Dennis (1657-1734) was born, Dennis did not accuse Shakespeare of the theft.

Mike in Brisbane on Raspberry:
From Cockney rhyming slang =raspberry tart. I often wondered about the British pejorative "stupid berk", and was interested to learn that it also was rhyming slang "Berkshire Hunt". Work that one out, Exon!

Bill in Columbia, CT regarding "Cop":
The verb "cop" (slang) means "to nab" - a major function of the police has always been to "nab" malefactors. A policeman was called a copper ("er" - person) and "copper" was eventually shortened to "cop."

Gennari in Stanford, CA on phrase origins:
My first post... My officemates and I were just discussing funny phrases and suddenly had to know the origin of "Bob's your uncle." Can anyone enlighten me?

Gerald in Ottawa re: Bob's your uncle:
It means roughly "and everything will be OK" but there's no agreement at all on its origins. It's usually listed as "of mysterious origin." Some say it was based on the flagrant nepotism shown by one or another British politician, presumably named Bob. Others trace it back to an earlier slang term "all is bob" meaning "all is safe" but no one can prove that either. About the only thing that's certain is that it suddenly turned up in England around 1890 and became popular. Sorry.

Sandi asked:
Here's my question for the group - I've been bugged by the phrase "pushing the envelope". I know what it means, but it makes no sense. What's the origin?

Bob in Chicago answered:
I first heard the phrase used as an engineering term during the quest for the breaking of the sound barrier during the Air Force "X" series test program in the late 1950's that made Chuck Yeager of "The Right Stuff" famous. I believe the origin has to do with mathematics and something about curves and tangents, etc.

Someone else weighed in:
Sandi recently asked about the phrase "pushing the envelope". Aircraft have both physical and performance limitations which together create an "envelope". Thus, the phrase. I heard this expression many times while in Vietnam from the flyboys.

Haney in Rock Hill, SC:
From the "Do we all speak English" desk... While traveling in Europe in the 60s, I was visiting ("crashing" was the word in vogue back then) at a student hostel at the University in Lund, Sweden. I needed to catch a ferry back to Denmark but didn't have a clock. A lovely British woman said that she would make certain I got up on time, and that she would "come around and knock me up in the morning". For a boy from the south of the U.S., this was an exciting prospect! Down here, "knock up" means to impregnate. Now, where did that phrase come from!!

Dean answered a query:
John asked about the origins of 'call a spade a spade'. The OED attributes it to a misinterpretation of a Greek phrase by some guy named Erasmus. Mistaking the (almost identical) words for bowl and spade, he wrote "...Macedonians wer feloes of no fyne witte in their termes but altogether grosse, clubbyshe, and rusticall, as they whiche had not the witte to calle a spade by any other name then a spade."
The original phrase '...tin skapsin the skapsin onomason' could have meant much the same thing ('call a bowl a bowl'.) It seemed to me that

it more likely meant something along the lines of 'a bowl doesn't contain it's name'. Any other ideas?

Jeff in London weighed in on "I have learned to call wickedness by its own terms: a fig a fig and a spade a spade" John Knox.
I think old JK was some kind of religious guy... This caused me to look up "figs". What did they ever do wrong? Answers:

1. The tree of knowledge wasn't an apple tree but a fig tree according to scholars (would you Adam and eve it?)
2. Judas hanged himself on a fig tree.
3. DH Lawrence mentioned its resemblance to the female genitals in "Women in Love"
4. The Greek word for fig was used as a euphemism for the female genitals
5. The French word for fig, "figue" is still used this way.
6. Similar with the Italian "figa"
7. In English, the word "fig" is given to an insulting gesture, with the fist closed and the thumb pushed through the index and middle fingers, and is supposed to represent...yes, you've guessed it.
8. The fig was once thought to have supernatural powers
9. Shakespeare used it as a synonym for "fuck"
10. The word "sychophant" comes from the Greek and means "fig displayer".

Just found a reference for Holy Mackerel. It has one of two origins:
1. Jesus fed the 5,000 with mackerel. Indentations either side of its head are said to show where it was held by him.
2. Mackerel were once exempt from Sunday trading laws because their flesh goes off quickly.

Anders in Sweden on Holy Mackerel:
It was a long time since I read the Bible but if I remember things cor-

rectly Mr. Josephson fed the 5,000 on the beach of Lake Kinneret (sp?). Mackerels are marine fish which do not occur in that lake. Therefore, any suspicious fingerprints on mackerels may perhaps better be checked with the FBI archives. Besides, Holy Mackerel sounds like a (we're back) euphemism for Holy Moly/Holy Moses which in turn may be euphemisms for Holy Jesus, or?

Roger in Fayetteville, AR wrote:
I heard that Gadzooks came from God Zeus, but that was 25 years ago from an indeterminable source.
Mike in Brisbane answered:
I think it's one of those moderated religious swearing, deriving from "god's hooks", i.e. the nails which pinned Jesus to the cross.

Heath in San Antonio, TX:
I just read (in a communication evaluation survey) the line: "I 'gunny-sack' when I argue with people." Any ideas of what that means?
Katherine in Oakland, CA answered:
As I've encountered it, this refers to saving things up for the fights. For example, I have a friend who often irritates me; since I don't like getting angry at her, I tend to "stuff" the little irritations—the metaphor is of shoving them all into a large bag always hanging at my side. Now, if she does something that makes me too mad, or if all the little things suddenly outweigh everything else--whoosh! Out comes the gunny sack, and everything comes up: I yell at her, not just about the one thing that has aroused my ire at the moment, but about everything that I've been saving up.

Someone asked: "Question for relevance: Is the word "degree" re temperature from the same root as degree re "BSc, PhD, etc."?
Jack in London answered:
Yes. It came to us from the Latin gradus (step or grade) via the Old French degré. When you graduate you get a degree. However, I think

my favourite use of the word is in Keats' The Eve of St Agnus, where the hidden Porphyro is watching Madeline undress. She:

>Unclasps her warmed jewels one by one;
>Loosens her fragrant boddice; by degrees
>Her rich attire creeps rustling to her knees...

Hot stuff, or what? :-)

Bob in Tokyo had a query:
A Japanese student of mine has asked me for the origin of "flea market." My little paperback dictionary only has the definition. Does it have something to do with the flea-bitten items you may find at one? Or am I taking the term too literally? (BTW, they have flea markets here in Japan. My student calls them "free markets." :) Which is close, considering the prices of new items here in Tokyo!) Any help you can give is appreciated.

Leonard in Garden City, NY answered:
Bob asked about the origin of "flea market." According to Merriam-Webster's Collegiate Dictionary, Tenth Edition, the phrase dates to 1922 and is a translation of the French *Marche aux Puces*, a market in Paris.

Steve in Tempe, AZ on sports and word origins:
What is a "sticky wicket" and how do you get out of it? THANKS IN ADVANCE.

Heath in San Antonio, TX:
I think begging the question remained unexplained, though several people made fun of it in the meanwhile. Begging the question involves implicitly using your conclusion as a premise (i.e. a step in constructing your argument). For example:
How do you know God exists?
God exists, because the Bible says he does.
Why do you believe the Bible?

Well, because it is the word of God.
[1. The Bible is true because God wrote it.]
[2. The Bible says God exists.]
[3. Therefore, God exists.]

Terrence in Bermuda answered a query from Dean who asked: "...had me in stiches." (I suddenly wonder, did that phrase originate?): One definition of stitch is "a sudden sharp pain, especially in the intercostal [between the ribs] muscles". So, the phrase means "I laughed so hard my sides hurt".

--

Phil in Salt Lake City:
I was recently watching the Disney movie "Mary Poppins" when you lovely people sprang suddenly to mind. No, not because of your sugary sweet dispositions, nor because of your quick wit, which is frequently "extremely diverting". It was rather because of an "incomparable expression" (if I may insert a little Oscar Wilde) which made me exclaim: "I must ask the WordPlay list about this!" The expression was, "Enough is as good as a piece" which Mary Poppins herself uttered, in response to Michael's wanting to continue cleaning up the nursery (with Mary's magic) after it was already done instead on going on the planned outing. From the context, I infer that the meaning is: "Be satisfied with what you have", but how the actual words are supposed to convey that meaning is beyond me. Help, anyone?
One more expression from that movie that could stand a little exploration is Mary's version of "Hurry up!", to wit: "Spit-spot!" I, of course have added the hyphen, to facilitate pronunciation, Mary having been lamentably lax in her loquatial punctuation.
I would also like to know if these are particularly British expressions?
Mike in Brisbane responded:
Phil, I think you just got a movie mondegreen. The saying would be "Enough is as good as a feast." A piece, by the way, is what you have in

THE POWER OF WORDS - 83

Scotland and the North of England when you come home from school, a slab of bread and jam.

Terrence recounted an anecdote:
This reminded me of a Portuguese nun who taught me French in high school. She was very easily flustered, and if the class was getting out of control, she would scream: "Enough is too much!"

--

Jim in Schenectady, NY enquired:
Can anyone tell me the history of the term "bus-boy"? Or to "bus" a table? A bus-boy being, of course, a teenager who cleans tables in a restaurant.

Pat in Collegeville, MN answered:
He's a boy for everything (he's ordered to do), an omnibus-boy—same source as the bus you ride on. The transformation to verb is common in English.

--

Caleb in Albany, NY wrote:
BTW, does anyone here know what SPAM stands for? These are all acronyms. I'm sure.

Mike in Brisbane:
Yes, it's an acronym - Spiced Ham. The actual use of the verb "to spam" comes from the Monty Python sketch "Spam, spam, spam etc..." i.e. really spreading it around and repeating it often, if you see the connection...

Mike in Brisbane wondered:
My colleague heard these words in a song this morning = anyone know what a buffalo soldier is, and why?

Dean responded:
During the US Civil War there were two cavalry divisions (the 5th and 9th if memory serves) composed of African Americans. They were referred to as the Buffalo Soldiers.

Gerry in NY had a definition:
1. Buffalo soldiers, name given to the African-American U.S. Army regiments commissioned by Congress to patrol the American West after the Civil War. Consisting of two infantry and two cavalry regiments, they were the first such units chartered in peacetime. The regiments continued in Army service until the U.S. armed forces were integrated in 1952.
2. I believe that the term derived from the fact that the curly hair of the black troopers resembled the curly hair of the buffalo.

Guy in Cupertino, CA had a take of his own:
According to a recent article in the Occidental College alumni magazine, the Buffalo Soldiers were the 9th and 10th cavalry, stationed at Leavenworth KS. Indeed, they were organized after the Civil War to fight "Indians" (indigenous populace -- hey, that's IT -- we can call them Indigens!)
They were essentially the police force of west Texas and Arizona Territory. They helped the railroads get established by "controlling and interdicting" the opposing natives. They rode with Teddy Roosevelt among the Rough Riders at the Battle of San Juan Hill.
They continued as a distinct unit until President Harry S Truman integrated the military services at the time of the Korean War.
A commemorative postage stamp was issued in 1994.
--

Jim had a query about a familiar term:
I've been thinking about what's been going on at work lately. I've been working overnight, as in, from 10 pm to 7 am this past week and will continue to do so this week. :P Why is this shi(f)t called the graveyard shift?
--

Gerry in NY had a query:
What is the derivation of the term "at the top of his lungs" as in the statement: " He shouted at the top of his lungs."
--

Mike in Brisbane had a query:
Did anyone cover the explanation that the word barbequeue comes from the French "beard and tail", referring to the practice of cooking whole goats in this fashion. There's some memory of reading something about this that suggested that this was originated by pirates/bandits/mariners/castaways/settlers? in Florida or the Caribbean. How's that for vague?

Terrence in Bermuda had a sort-of answer:
Isn't barbecue an American word? All right taken from Spanish? ...taken from the Taino (carib Indian?) barbacoa = a frame of sticks.

--

Caleb in Albany, NY gave us a word etymology:
And, yes, I meant "perquisites" from which the term "perks" came.

--

Mike in Brisbane responded to Sara who wanted to know about the origins of "sleep tight":
In the olden days, (puts on storyteller's hat and voice) when beds were sprung with rope, the rope would stretch after a while, and you'd sink into the middle of the bed. A more comfortable sleep was to be had on a bed where the ropes had been tautened, which you had to do every so often. Hence "sleep tight".

--

Patrick in Collegeville, MN followed up on Anders who speculates that guard, garden, yard, hortus and cognate words in a couple of other Indo-European languages are from the same source:
You might have added ward and its relatives, too, Anders.
Guard and ward(en) come from French and Old English respectively. Explains why guarantee and warranty are synonyms. Both are cognate with Old High German warten (to watch) and Old Norse vartha (to guard).
Garden and yard are cognate with Old High German gart, as are the French jardin, the Italian giardino, etc. OE weard means watch or guard, gard means an enclosure. The relation between the meanings is

clear enough to justify hypothesizing a common Indo-European root--and if I could find my old book listing those roots, I'd bet it would support Anders's guess.

--

Maryanne in Tallahassee, FL wondered:
My friend Nell from the Netherlands was puzzled by the phrase, "speak to you like a Dutch uncle." What does it mean?

Mike had an answer:
To take you aside and explain things to you in a friendly caring way – but I'm Hagued if I know why.

And Jan:
A DUTCH UNCLE--is "a person who sternly or bluntly criticizes/scolds/admonishes another" -- but a DUTCH WIFE is "an open frame of rattan or cane to support the limbs while in bed"!

--

Varda in Portland, ME comments:
Of course, there's also the great "soda vs. pop" controversy. I know "soda" is used on the east coast, and "pop" is what they drink in the Midwest. What about elsewhere? What about other foods and beverages?

Mike in Brisbane:
Just to confuse the issue further, I remember English children's comics and stories from the 1950's and before where the term "soda pop" was used. In eastern Australia, they used to be called "fizz" or "fizzy drinks", "aerated water" or just "soft drinks", however in Western Australia, the term was "cooldrinks" (one word, I think).
In Queensland, there's a popular soft drink called Sarsaparilla, aka "Sars". It's probably about as disgusting as Moxie sounds, tastes like the early chlorophyll toothpaste. Some Queensland drinkers add it to their beer, which is then known as "beer with a dash". Most peculiar.

And Ruth, thanks for the story about the Plymouth Fury - Yonks ago, this kind of story was known as a "Shaggy Dog" story. Apparently, there was a story with a punchline that included the words shaggy dog, does anyone know what it was, the original story?

Zeno in Minneapolis, MN:
My father told me that the original "shaggy dog" story, much abbreviated, went something like this:
A drunk sleeping on newspaper on a bench happens to read an ad: "LOST: One Shaggy Dog. Reward. 1 Grosvenor Square, London SW1" [insert discussion of differences between English, Canadian and American postal codes here -- go on at some length, until just before your audience has lost interest]. Just then a shaggy dog walks by. The drunk takes the leash and the dog, and proceeds to London [insert various adventures and misadventures of the journey along the way -- an accomplished raconteur can make this part take up to 30 minutes; think of it as a credenza]. When he finally gets to 1 Grosvenor Square, London SW1 and knocks on the door the butler opens it, takes one look, and says "Good Heavens! Not THAT shaggy!" and slams the door.
A shaggy dog story, thus, has come to be a story in which the punchline is not worth the buildup.

--

Lomond in Sacramento, CA:
The English Disease - This question could start a thread similar to the fortunately now defunct "Hoosier" thread. Here's one answer to MDU's question about the origin of the phrase:
In my days as a health information officer (especially in the personage of my alter ego, "Captain VD") research showed that many years ago, people in Europe (especially the French) referred to syphilis as the "English disease". The English were quick to pick on another country to blame (especially the Spanish) and so the battle raged. From this battle of survival, came the phrase, "A pox on you!"

Gerry in Ottawa had a different interpretation:
The "English disease" definitely refers to homosexuality. I was reminded of it during a recent trip to Egypt when a tout suddenly ac-

costed me with, "You are English, yes? You wish small boy?" "No," I said. "I'm Canadian and I wish you to bugger off." "Oh, that is very amusing, sah," he replied cheerily. "How about nice post card?"

Gerry also explained the origin of Scot:
"Scot" is a Middle English term for a local tax, a contribution, a payment - especially for entertainment - or for one's share of such payment. The meaning of "scot free" accordingly seems self-evident.

Anders in Stockholm picked up on the English reference:
When I studied German some (two-digit) years ago we learned that 'to shop-lift' was called 'zu Englisch kaufen'. Why and how was never explained, however. Does anyone know? Besides, I am not quite sure why our tutors chose to incorporate such a phrase in our vocabulary to be; such expressions tend to be outdated rather quickly. (Is it still called 'shop-lifting'?)

--

Caleb asked: "Mike D.U.: Is " kambucha tea" from Cambodia? (Kampuchea)."

Mike in Brisbane answered:
No, it's originally from Mongolia, or certainly the eastern side of Asia. It's a health drink, made by floating a "mushroom" on a bowl of strong black sugary tea. A fermentation takes place, producing a drink that is about 0.5% alcohol. You have a small glass each morning, and it helps to detox the system. The "mushroom" grows to fill the bowl, whatever the size, and grows a new mushroom on top of itself. This you give away to a friend. It's actually a plot so that these mushrooms can take over the world. – They might actually do a better job than some I wot of. - The drink is believed to have amazing properties - I'm sure you'd be able to find details at your local health food store.

--

Barbara in Stephenville, TX asked:
Anyone able to verify the phrase "sold down the river" originated in the deep south from slave owners who threatened to sell off members of families of their slaves if they misbehaved?

Jim in Philadelphia answered an old query that came from Anders in Sweden, which asks:

"The expression 'never throw the axe in the sea' was in my ears a very Swedish expression, until I heard it used by an Englishman on TV. I thought it had Viking origin and reflected a duel on a small island between two chiefs - the one who throws the axe in the sea surrenders. The expression may also have been the precursor to towels and boxing. Does anyone know how the 'axe' became English?"

Sorry it took me so long to answer... My guess is that it's through a Russian fairy tale, often retold. I'm not certain, but I believe it was Leo Tolstoy who told the following tale about a serf and the Vodianoy (the spirit of the water in Russian mythology... It is pronounced vuh-dyuh-NOY) The story goes as follows:

A serf was in the forest chopping down trees, and he was getting tired, so he sat down on a log. As he reached for something to wipe the sweat off his brow, he accidentally kicked his axe into the lake (let's take a little bit of license and move from the lake to the sea...) The serf started to become concerned, for he didn't have the money to buy a new axe, and he couldn't go in and get it, for it was too deep. Suddenly, the Vodianoy appeared, holding a gold axe. He asked the serf if that axe was his. The serf, the good, honest man that he was, said, "No, I'm sorry. That's not it." And the Vodianoy disappeared. The Vodianoy reappeared, this time with a silver axe. "Is this yours?" Once again, the serf replied in the negative. And the Vodianoy disappeared again. Then the Vodianoy appeared a third time, holding a rusty old metal axe. "Is this one yours?" The serf said, "Yes, it is! Thank you very much." The Vodianoy was impressed with his honesty and gave the serf all three axes. The serf went home and some of his friends saw the shiny new gold and silver axes, and he explained that he had gotten them from the Vodianoy. Another serf went out to that lake, and threw his axe into it. Soon after that, the Vodianoy appears, holding a gold axe. Vodianoy asks, "Is this yours?" The serf excitedly exclaims, "Yes! Yes it is!" The Vodianoy looks angry and says, "Liar! This is not yours! For that, I will keep the axe that is REALLY yours."

Mike in Brisbane followed up:
Anders, the custom of the two chiefs fighting it out on the small island was called "holmgang", wasn't it? And it might be that the expression passed into English as a result of the large numbers of Vikings who settled in the British Isles - that's drawing a pretty long bow - but there's lots of other expressions which have made it down through the centuries.

Mike also followed up on Jim's tale:
On the Axe and Towel thread, Jim, thanks for the Russian folk tale - I think that's a great explanation - I'm not sure that it isn't in "Old Peter's Russian Tales" by Arthur Ransome - any Ransome (Swallows and Amazons) fans out there? But I digress - axes in the sea, yes, fine, but wasn't "throwing in the towel" derived from boxing? If the fighter couldn't get up to start the next round, his second threw in the towel?

There's another expression - "He couldn't tell a hawk from a handsaw" which I thought was ok, and then I remembered that there is a plasterer's tool called a "hawk" or "hauk" - it's that little flat tray with the handle underneath, which is used to hold the plaster when you're plastering - and I wondered if that's the hawk referred to in the saying? Any thoughts?

John in Keele, UK answered:
"I can tell a hauk from a handsaw, when the wind...". This [from memory] is Hamlet, protesting his sanity while pretending to be mad, if you see what I mean. Yes, I suspect it _is_ a plasterer's hauk [haven't seen one in the D.I.Y. shop recently, but I think they spelled it "hawk" last time I did].

Probably every annotated edition of Shakespeare you can lay your hands on will give you a different explanation, but one which preserves the general reference to workman's tools seems most plausible to me!

--

Mike in Brisbane had another etymological query:
Gerald, thanks also for the bit on "excelsior" - now here's another one. when I was a kid at school, we used, in craft lessons, a brown sticky paper in rolls (long before sticky tape) called "passe par tout". Why was it so called? Any takers?

--

Penelope in Michigan enquired:
In Dutch a rabbit is called a 'konijn'. Is coney or cony a well-known word?

Caleb in Albany, NY answered:
Here's what the inimitable Webster has to say: co. ney \'ko--ne-\ n [ME conies, pl., fr. OF conis, pl. of conil, fr. L cuniculus] 1a1: RABBIT; esp: the European rabbit

--

Matt in Minneapolis answered to Susan:
I have 'boon' coming from Latin 'bonus' when used in its lesser-known sense of 'jolly'. Used as you meant it, as a benefit or blessing, it is from Old Norse 'bon', meaning prayer.

--

Terrence explained "the board":
In the 1600's, table and chairs were luxury items; the common man would set up a wide board on a few trestles to act as a table - these were in fact called boards and not tables. Similarly, common folks would seat themselves not on chairs but stools, chests, upturned buckets, etc... If one owned a chair, it would be reserved for someone of importance to sit in, who would, of course then be the _chairman of the board_! Although not further mentioned, I suspect that _boardroom_ shares this derivation.

Lomond had a related question:
On your subject of "boards", is this where we also get "room and board"?

--

Heath in San Antonio, TX asked:
Does whiskey originate from water of life? I mean, I agree with the notion, at some level, but definitionally...?

Katherine in Oakland, CA answered:
Notionally, I believe, is the point. "Whiskey" is an Anglicization of the Gaelic, spelled "uisquebaugh" (or something like that--it's a language I haven't learned, and its spelling is always a problem) (well, do _you_ trust a language in which "dh" can be silent, and "mh" can be pronounced as "v", and...). This Gaelic word is, I'm told, a direct translation of "aqua vitae"... or do I mean a cognate?
Recommended listening for Wordplayers: the song "The Humours of Whiskey". The version I know is on a Tim Lyons album, "Easter Snow".

--

Gerry in Ottawa gave us the skinny on the origins of "Wendy":
The name was first used by J.M. Barrie in his play "Peter Pan" which came out in 1904. It started as a pet name given him by little Margaret Henley, the daughter of William Ernest Henley, a well-known English poet, editor and close friend of Barrie's. It began as "Friendy," then became "Friendy-Wendy" and ended up as just plain "Wendy." Margaret died in 1894 at the age of six but Barrie never forgot her.

--

Mark in Winnipeg, MB:
Regarding the origin of the name "Pamela", I don't think Fielding invented it: Sidney named one of his heroines "Pamela" in his 1586 _Arcadia_.
It derives from the Greek "pan", meaning "all" (as in "Pan-American"), and "meli", meaning "honey", as in "mellifluous" and even as in "mildew" (literally "honey dew", although the sense shifted in the fourteenth century).

Pat in Collegeville, MN added:
It would be Richardson, Mark. Fielding wrote _Shamela_, the delightful burlesque of _Pamela_. In any case, your intelligence about

Sidney's use of the name in _The Arcadia_ moved me to get that romance out for the first time in many many years (I never did get it out much), and there was Pamela, daughter of silly Duke Basilius and Duchess Gynecia, sister to Philoclea. Since the names are Greek, I whipped out my trusty Liddell and Scott to see what Pamela might mean, but could find nothing convincing. Mela suggests dark complexioned; but the Pa- suggests nothing (pan(m)/all would keep the m and result in Pammela). So maybe Sir Philip made the name up.
In any case, a posthumous demerit for my still admired 18th-century prof.
Memory bump: didn't Charles I quote Pamela in prison, a kind of prayer? Which Pamela?

--

Bob in Chicago:
I was surprised to learn recently that the Mexican town named Guadalajara received the name from one of Cortez's men who deserted to that location to found his own renegade empire. Apparently, he named the place after his own hometown in Spain which in turn was named by the invading Arabs who named it after a dry stream bed in their old neighborhood in the desert called Wadi Alahara. It seems like once a name catches hold you just can't shake it.

--

Pat in Collegeville, MN:
Cat is in old English as catt, probably, says my hand dictionary, from late Latin cattus, -a. But whence puss? Both my easily available dictionaries say source unknown. But I had a book (Muriel Beadle's _The Cat_?), lent and thus lost, that had a list of cognates for cat and for puss in Indo-european and some other languages; and puss went back pretty far. Are its cognates common in Slavic languages?
Terrence in Bermuda rebutted:
I have always thought that puss/pussy must be a back formation from the psss-psss-psss percussive-sibilant cat calling noise which seems to

be so effective at catching a cat's attention, but perhaps this is the other way around and I'm putting the cat before the hoarse.

--

From Michael in Mesa, AZ:
So, last night, I read Turn Of The Screw (speaking of sentences in dire need of diagramming), and I came across the phrase "hang fire," which I had previously heard only from Mick Jaggar. What does it mean and where does it come from? In James' context, it appears to denote a dramatic pause in a tale or a sincere hesitation in speech. I was initially thrown by the fact that the first character to "hang fire" was also, quite coincidentally, rearranging the logs in the fireplace at the time. Anyone?

Steve in Austin, TX chimed in:
I know the term "hang fire" as used by Army mortarmen. It refers to a mortar round that has become stuck in the barrel of the mortar tube before it reached the bottom of the tube and, therefore, didn't fire. I can see where this phrase might have come to refer to a dramatic pause, since, in the case of a mortar hang fire, a squad of soldiers would be hunkered down with their fingers in their ears waiting for the damned thing to go "BOOM!"

--

Mary wondered:
... All of this made me wonder, from where does the word "hello" originate??**

I'm aware that I'm probably far behind the curve here, responding a whole two days after the original posting (and geez, you guys are flight enough of finger, I presume that by now the debate has been addressed, joined, hotly debated, laid to rest, revived and finally decided). But this might be useful.

Ed in River Forest, IL answered by quoting "Made in America", c1994 Bill Bryson:
" At first people weren't sure what to say in response to a ringing phone. Thomas Edison is sometimes credited with inventing the word

'hello' specifically for use on the telephone. In fact, 'hello' (a variant of 'hallo,' 'halloo,' and much older salutations) was current in English for at least twenty years before the telephone came along. What Edison actually favored was a jaunty 'Ahoy!' and that was the word habitually used by the first telephone operator, one George Coy of New Haven. (Only male operators were employed at first. As so often happens with new technologies, women weren't allowed anywhere near it until the novelty had worn off.) Others said, 'Yes!' or 'What?' and many merely picked up the receiver and listened hopefully."

Gerry in New York:
Finally, someone asked about "gerrymander". Herewith, the answer:
A gerrymander sounds like a strange political beast, which in fact it is, considered from a historical perspective. This beast was named by combining the word salamander, "a small lizard-like amphibian," with the last name of Elbridge Gerry, a former governor of Massachusetts-a state noted for its varied, often colorful political fauna. Gerry (whose name, incidentally, was pronounced with a hard g, though gerrymander is now commonly pronounced with a soft g) was immortalized in this way because an election district created by members of his party in 1812 looked like a salamander. According to one version of how gerrymander was coined, the shape of the district attracted the eye of the painter Gilbert Stuart, who noticed it on a map hanging in a newspaper editor's office. Stuart decorated the map with a head, wings, and claws and then said to the editor, "That will do for a salamander!" "Gerrymander!" came the reply. A new political beast was created then and there. The word is first recorded in April 1812 with respect to the creature or its caricature, but it soon came to mean not only "the action of shaping a district to gain political advantage" but also "any representative elected from such a district by that method." Within the same year gerrymander was also recorded as a verb.
The American Heritage Dictionary of the English Language, Third

Edition copyright 1992 by Houghton Mifflin Company. Electronic version licensed from InfoSoft International, Inc. All rights reserved.

Gerry in Ottawa had a take on this too:

Gerrymander comes from Elbridge Gerry who was Governor of Massachusetts between 1810 and 1812. A violent anti-Federalist, he was largely responsible for redrawing the boundaries of the senatorial voting districts in that state to ensure a Jeffersonian majority. Someone, looking at the new, twisted and almost reptilian outline of the electoral district for Essex County, is said to have remarked, "It looks like a salamander," to which a friend replied, "No, it's a gerrymander." Gerry later served as Vice-President under Madison.

--

Hans in Holland gave us an update on Dutch berms and asked: Wonder where the name "Bermuda" came from...

Terrence in Bermuda obliged:

Bermuda is named after Juan de Bermudez, a 16th century Portuguese mariner who first put us on a map and we were known as "the Bermudas". After Sir George Somers was shipwrecked here and claimed us for England, we were for centuries called "the Somers Isles". I'm not sure when or why we reverted to Bermuda and became singular (though we are a singular tourist destination).

--

Gerry in Ottawa on Scaring the Living Daylights:

Since no one else seems to have dealt with this yet, let me try one on. In my youth, every story about pirates seemed to have some surly character with a cutlass who'd say things like, "You'd better talk, lad, or I'll cut out yer liver and lights," lights being an archaic term for lungs. By the same token, I assume that you could also "scare the liver and lights" out of someone. Is it remotely possible that, in time, this could have been corrupted into the more familiar "scare the living daylights?" A bit far-fetched, you say? True, but I've seen worse. In the immortal words of Pogo, I await your scornful laughter.

--

THE POWER OF WORDS - 97

Dave in Glendale, CA enquired:

I know what a "hat trick" is (hockey: three goals by one player, and, by extension, a "three-Pete" by anyone not named Pete). Where did it come from? Is it related to de-coneying a chapeau ("at sixty bucks a t'row!")? (bows to Welles, Blackstone, and Kaye)

Zeno in Minneapolis, MN:

When the Maple Leaves were winning all the trophies there was a world-famous hatter who gave a free hat to any player who scored three goals in one game; in exchange the hockey players would hang around his shop for a day waiting for him to block their new hat, and he got all kinds of business from people stopping by to congratulate the player, see the new hat, and perhaps buy one themselves. The world was smaller and more innocent then, and the sportswriters, instead of righteously exposing this naked bribery as the felonious assault on civilized values which is how it would be viewed today, simply started referring to the three-goal phenomenon as "the hat-trick"; as with so many inside jokes, it quickly caught on.

Gerry in Ottawa weighed in:

"Hat Trick" may well be used in hockey but its original application was to cricket where it meant taking three wickets with successive balls. A collection was either taken up for the player concerned or he was given a new hat by his club. It seems to have been first used in 1882. On the other hand, I like the story about the publicity-conscious hat seller better.

--

Matt in Minneapolis, MN answered a previous query:

I believe that "brownie points" have to do with the Junior Girl Scouts earning merit.

Pat in Collegeville, MN:

Brownie points: military slang for the increase of rating points on fitness reports, earned by brown-nosing one's superiors.

--

Gerry in Ottawa continued:
There's one thing I'm curious about, however, and that's the origin of the Australian phrase "open slather" in the sense of no holds barred, open house, free access or "Liberty Hall' as they say in the States. No, it's not in Wilkes or Morris and Baker does no more than define the meaning. I'd really like to know. I guess it's just that I admire the word "slather" which I know otherwise only in the sense of heavily buttering a piece of bread.

It's certainly a relief from most of the other words beginning with "sl" which, to say the least, are a pretty negative lot. Just look at slam, slander, slap, slash, slattern, slaughter, slavish, sleazy, slime, slink, slippery, slipshod, slither, slobber, slog, slop, slosh, sloth, slouch, sloven, slow, sludge, slug, slum, slurp, slush, slut and sly. Really depressing. Yeah, I know there are a few positive ones but why ruin a good argument?

Incidentally, does anyone know the origin of "Liberty Hall?"

--

Susan in Spokane, WA:
While watching "Beauty and the Beast" Gaston (I think that's his name) is trying to incite the townspeople to hunt and kill the beast and he sings for them to "screw your courage to the sticking point" or spot or something. I have heard that before; I don't think it's a Disney original. My daughter asked where that came from and I said with a smirk "I'll find out." Help, pleeeze!

Zeno came to the rescue:
Macbeth: If we should fail --
Lady Macbeth: "We fail! But screw your courage to the sticking-place. And we'll not fail." Shakespeare's Macbeth. First act.

Katherine in Oakland CA:
Not a Disney original, indeed! It's Shakespeare--Lady Macbeth says it to her husband, inciting him to regicide.

--

THE POWER OF WORDS - 99

Rich in Rindge, NH:
During my vacation I pondered the following: The terms "blarney" and "baloney" have similar meanings. Are they also etymologically linked? My dictionary does not enlighten me. Any thoughts?

Patrick in San Jose. CA:
Blarney, from the 16th/17th Century Earl of Blarney (a spot a few miles outside Cork in Ireland). Said Earl was apparently a noted windbag and was less noted for successful execution of his promises. Elizabeth I is said to have remarked on hearing about one such incident: "This is all Blarney: what he says, he never means." Nowadays tourists dressed in green polyester pants kiss the 'Blarney stone' (an unremarkable and dried-tourist-saliva-stained stone atop Blarney Castle) in order to attain "the gift of the gab." We Irish, on the other hand, are said to be born with same; hence no need for stone-kissing. :-)
Baloney... no etymological linkage that I know of. Is the origin not from "Bologna"?

--

Barbara in Stephenville, TX said:
I Believe I missed this question in a trivia battle once. The answer, as I recall...'mad as a hatter' refers to an old practice of hatters who treated their wares with a form of mercury to make the hats retain their shape and thus the hatter frequently suffered the consequences of mercury poisoning. Anybody else have a version for the origin of this phrase?

--

Stephanie in the Colorado Rockies had a query of her own:
Thanks for your kind words of welcome. When I was a child, my father (of Davy Crockett fame) occasionally referred to me as a "scallywag" or a "rapscallion". Has anyone else ever been called those names? Does anybody have an idea of where they might have come from?

--

John in Keele, UK highlighted the rift between American and British English:
According to my bilingual Chinese cookbook [English and American]

what us Brits call a Spring Onion is in the US called a "scallion".
But I'd guess that "rapscallion" is more likely to be connected to "scullion", with the vowel slipped a bit. Stranger things have been known: there are still parts of the British Isles where "bad" and "bed" are indistinguishable in pronunciation... [Well, it's a class thing really.]

--

Gerry in Ottawa on "Drop of a Hat":
Surely "at the drop of a hat" was a sports metaphor, rather like the referee dropping the puck between the two sides, at which point everyone whizzes into action. I'm not sure which particular sport involved dropping a hat although I mean to find out. It may have been bear-baiting for all I know.

--

Steve in Austin, TX:
Where did the phrase "coming out of the woodwork" come from? My guess is that it referred to the sudden realization that a house was infested with termites. Any help?
How about other phrases that mean an abundance or excess of something? Such as:
    Through the nose
    Coming out of my ears
    Up the "wazoo" (note euphemism)
    More _____ than Carter's has liver pills
    More _____ than you can shake a stick at ___ for days
Let's see some more!

--

Sara in Boston had another colloquialism:
To "barge in" - I assume that refers to nautical barges; is it just because barges are so big?
To "canvas" (or fundraise) - where did this one come from?
BTW - the canvas(s) question - I was wondering if it had any folklore sort of background. Did people carry canvas bags when asking others for money? Any ideas?

Terrence in Bermuda:
The original meaning of the verb canvass was to toss a person using a canvas sheet. I'm sure you would agree that this would be a sure way to elicit an opinion from the tossee! How this led to the modern meaning, I cannot discern from my sources.

--

Steven in Atlanta, GA:
The first reference in my Webster's Third describes the practice of placing the victim in a canvas sheet held by a gang and throwing him around. Sailor fun, no doubt, coined in Elizabethan times or earlier as it appears in Shakespeare (I'll canvass thee between two sheets!) with this meaning. Also, I didn't realize before that "canvas" derives from "cannabis." It seems that the fiber of choice for sailmaking was hemp. Puts a whole new spin on "three sheets to the wind," eh?

--

Jody asked:
Why is a second full moon during a single month referred to as a "blue moon?"

And Terrence in Bermuda:
Charles Funk, in "A Hog on Ice", devotes 28 lines to this phrase, which can be summed up as "no idea".

Bill in Columbia, CT:
I understand that a "Blue Moon" was thought to be impossible; however, it has been observed not only through the debris-strewn air resulting from volcanic eruptions but also in a smoke-filled fog-laden atmosphere. Therefore, it has come to mean "rarely ever."

Gerry in Ottawa:
For what it's worth, there was a long debate last year in one of our local papers on this "blue moon" business. A full moon occurs every 28 days. Since most months have more days than that, it will occasionally come along twice in the same month. This second one is called the blue moon which, because of its rarity, gives rise to the expression "once in a blue moon." As to why its blue, several readers suggested

pollution but one tied it down specifically to the Krakatoa eruption of 1883 which tossed huge amounts of volcanic dust into the stratosphere, causing the moon to appear blue all over the world for several months. Since such a thing had never been recorded before, it too came to typify a rare event.

Then, of course, some smarty-pants came up with a 16th century author who had written "They say the moon is belewe" in the sense of "some people will believe anything." So take your pick. There was also a 1953 movie called "The Moon is Blue" but I doubt if that has much to do with the case.

--

Di in Melbourne responded to a query on "baulderdash":
According to _A Dictionary of Slang and Unconventional English_, balderdash is "a nonsensical farrago of words from ca. 1660".

Andy in Chichester followed up:
The Concise Oxford says that an earlier (16th c.) sense of balderdash was a frothy liquid. It says the word is of unknown origin.

--

Alex in Adelaide, AU asked:
Can someone enlighten me on the origin of these two expressions:
It's raining cats and dogs
There is more than one way to skin a cat
Now then, why on earth is a sausage called a hotdog? (Only in USA!)
What is the origin of the phrase: A ballpark figure?

Sara in Boston answered:
"ballpark figure" - From what I understand, this refers to an American baseball park. To keep the ball "in the ballpark" was not terribly difficult since the parks are *quite* large... ergo, a ballpark figure is an estimate that's anywhere near the actual figure. If it's out of the ballpark it's completely off.

"Hot dogs" - Time for another episode of Sara's Urban Myths! Maybe! I had heard that there was a vendor selling frankfurters who painted a picture of a dachshund standing in a roll on his awning, with the caption "Get your hot dogs here." Supposedly the name caught on.

Bill in Columbia, CT answered:
"Raining Cats and Dogs" comes from Norse mythology. The cat symbolizes heavy rain and the dog (an attendant of Odin) is the storm god, which represents heavy gusts of wind. The animosity between cat and dog was used to represent the conflicting elements within a storm.

--

Frank in Ottawa also quoth: "It has just struck me that the expression "Gone to the Dogs" may not be used in the USA and other parts. It means Gone into decline, finished, six feet under."

And Mike in Brisbane responded:
In Australia, this expression means that someone has fallen from grace, gone into a moral decline, degenerated, gone on the grog, - also "gone to the pack".
Which brings me to another question - why do we say "gone for good", when the passing of the item may not have been a good thing at all?

--

Andy in Chichester, UK responded to an earlier query:
Mike... The Three Estates of the Realm (in England) are the Lords Spiritual (i.e. bishops and archbishops in House of Lords), Lords Temporal (i.e. peers of the realm in House of Lords) and the Commons (i.e. MPs).
I don't know who coined the phrase Fourth Estate for the press, but I'd guess s/he was a journalist! To what three estates are Americans alluding when they use the phrase? Not the above, surely?

Katherine in Oakland, CA added:
I think the press is the fourth estate. First was nobility, second clergy, and I forget what third was--common folk maybe?

Pi@cup chimed in:
In my dictionary under "estate," it says: formerly, especially in feudal times, any of the three social classes having specific political powers: the first estate was Lords Spiritual (clergy), the second estate the

Lords Temporal (nobility), and the third estate the Commons (bourgeoisie). The fourth estate: journalism or journalists.

And Patrick in Collegeville, MN added:
On the Fourth Estate thread, didn't the first Three Estates get designated as such when the French parliament, les états généraux was founded in the late Middle Ages? If memory of a too-long-ago gradschool class serves me, Macaulay writes in the early 19th cent. that Burke in the latter half of the 18th cent. referred to the journalists who hung out in the gallery of the House of Commons as the Fourth Estate (Commons was, of course, the Third Estate). M. implies, as I remember, that Burke coined the term. During the early 19th cent., Hazlitt refers to Cobbett's reform theories and agitation as related to the Fourth Estate, meaning the laboring poor.

--

Frank in Ottawa was stumped:
"Curry favour"? Now where did that come from?

--

Marilyn in San Francisco enquired:
Anyone know the origins of this phrase? I used to think that maybe it had something to do with American Football, but wouldn't it then be "the whole ten yards"?

Zeno in Minneapolis, MN answerd:
Nine cubic yards is the amount of cement in a cement truck. When you order cement, you have to calculate how many cubic yards of cement you'll need to make your driveway or foundation or flotchy-doo (yeah, try to pick THAT flotchy-doo up and hold it over your head, Dani!). So if you need a truck-full of cement you need "the whole nine yards". That is to say, all of it, the whole thing, etc.

David in Cary, NC weighed in:
Two other possible origins I've heard are: In the days of sailing ships, it supposedly took nine yards of cloth to make a set of uniforms for an officer. An officer wanted to make sure he got the whole nine yards of cloth, i.e. wasn't short-changed.

The other explanation was that a three masted sailing vessel had three main yardarms (or yards) on each mast. If you had all sail set, you had sail on the whole nine yards. BTW, there are cement trucks with six, ten and twelve yards of concrete ;-)

Bill in Lexington, KY added:
I've seen that debate in another forum several times. I think the phrase preceded concrete trucks, although I have no proof of that handy. The conclusion each time of the debate was "we don't know its origin".

--

Marjorie in Boston asserted:
The phrase "seventh heaven" derives from the concept, in Jewish mysticism, that there are seven levels, or spheres, of heaven the first level being the closest to us on Earth and the seventh being the closest to the Divine essence. So the saying "I'm in seventh heaven" means that you are, figuratively, in that highest, and most delightful, sphere of heaven.
I learned this recently from a most brilliant friend with a rabbinic degree and a PhD in Medieval Jewish Philosophy and Mysticism. (He's also a plumbing contractor, professional actor, and sometime poet. Talk about your Renaissance men!)

Patrick in Collegeville, MN added:
Marjorie gives the source for seventh heaven, which accords with what I have read more than once. And the theory of the seven heavens goes back a long way. They appear in the apocryphal 2nd Apocalypse of Enoch (got its final form in the 5th cent. c.e., but parts go back to 1st cent. c.e.) and the Ascension of Isaiah (got its final form in the 3rd cent. c.e., but parts go back to the 1st cent. b.c.e.). In his second letter to the Corinthians, Paul the Apostle tells of being caught up into the third heaven, and this while he was still alive; presumably there were more to go--probably four more.

Bill in Columbia, CT said:
The Mohammedans believe there are seven heavens - one piled on

top of the other with God and the angels at the top (in the seventh heaven).

MIKECINDYJ also added:

Marjorie, Interesting comments about the Jewish tradition of 7th heaven. I believe the idea behind the tradition goes back to Aristotle, Greek Philosophy. The Greek idea was that the heavens are in seven crystal spheres; the earth at the center, the sun, moon, stars respectively in the spheres. This idea continued into Christianity through the days of Keppler and Copernicus. Amazing how these things get passed on from society to society.

Marjorie in Boston rebutted:

Nice try, but the Jewish concept predates Aristotle by a very long time. However, it is widely known that Aristotle and other Greek philosophers learned from and discussed ideas with Rabbinic sages of their day. This is the case with the concept of seventh heaven; in fact, the brilliant man who held a series of lectures on this topic cited that Aristotle learned it from Rabbinic scholars (it's been documented).

--

About Caleb's query on "OZ", Sara in Boston enlightened us:

The name, I believe, comes from L. Frank Baum's "Oz" books (the series which also spawned the movie "The Wizard of Oz." He coined the name in his office, when, while trying to think of a name for his new land, he looked over at his filing cabinet and saw one of the drawers labeled "O-Z."

How this came to refer to Australia I've no idea.

Mike in Brisbane:

The Oz Thread: Caleb - it's just a spelling of the abbreviation "Aus" for Australia. There're quite a few uses of it here, "Circus Oz", a performance group, is one that comes to mind. In the earlier days of the internet, .oz was used instead of .au as the country part of the address. The University of Queensland still preserves this in their address, which now ends with .oz.au

Janet in Calgary, added:
The whole question of Australia as Oz makes more sense when you realize that Aussie is usually pronounced with a z sound as if it was "Ozzie", not with the s sound that the Americans use.

And Anders in Stockholm:
Australia comes from the Latin word 'australis' which means 'southern'. The English name of Oesterreich is 'Austria' which might have the same etymology as 'Australia' whereas 'Oesterreich' means 'eastern kingdom'! How?! How can a present day 'eastern kingdom' be called 'southern' when the district originally was situated along the NORTHERN border of the Latin-speaking Roman Empire?! Should it better have been Borea? :)

Sara in Boston:
When one is on the phone and tells the other party to "hang on," is there any background to the phrase other than the obvious mental image? Any ideas, all?

Steven in Atlanta had a hunch:
Here's a guess: In the early days the telephone earpiece was a Bakelite disc without a handle. Instead, there was a metal loop on it to attach it to the wall-mounted body of the phone. There were two hooks on the box, one on the front attached to the line switch (from which we still have "on-hook" and "off-hook") and one at the side to *hang* the earpiece *on* while you go call your sister in from the barn.

--

Dean in Manhattan:
I haven't been around for a while due to a move to the 'Big Apple' (I've been making informal inquiries about the origin of this inappropriate nickname, so far the best one I've heard is that jazz musicians used it to refer to this most lucrative of venues.)
I've been wondering (arguably in part due to my new environs) about the etymology of the pop-culture term 'dissed', referring to acts of psychological violence, as in: 'Dude, I had a date with that girl last night and she totally dissed me.' [stood up]. Any theories?

Steven in Austin responded:
That's an easy one. It's short for "disrespect".

--

Bob in Chicago:
So, my mother told me that her TV set was "on the fritz". I have heard this term before in regard to radio receivers, washing machines and other electrical appliances. I take it to mean "not acting properly" or "somewhat broken" or "acting strangely for some unknown reason". Does anyone know where this term comes from, and whether it has a recognized definition?

--

Lyn asked:
Does anyone out there know where the phrase "wet behind the ears" came from?! We're having a lively debate, but, alas, are reduced to mere speculation.

--

Someone saw this in an informal job posting discussion: <<"Smart-aleks need not apply." "Smart-aleks" looks wrong somehow. Anyone know the origin of the phrase?>>

Terrence in Bermuda had an answer:
This should be "smart aleck" (from Aleck, short for Alexander) with no hyphen. To which Alexander aleck refers I do not know. He was obviously a smart Aleck - Alexander Graham Bell? - but also a haughty one, and it's my impression that Bell was a nice guy. Perhaps Aleck is a polite substitute for Ass?

Heath in San Antonio, TX:
The American Heritage suggests smart aleck may come from Aleck Hoag, 19th-century American confidence man and thief. It then defines a smart-ass and a smarty-pants as a smart aleck.

--

Dave in Glendale, CA:
Canadians, especially Maritime Provincers: Does the word "loonie" have a special meaning up Nawth, or does it double for a victim of lu-

nacy there, as it does here below the longest undefended border in the world...

--

Gary had a query:
A recent digest talked about someone "getting off scott free". Anyone know where this phrase comes from? Is it anything to do with Scotland? Should it be scott free or scot free?

Barbara in Stephenville, TX has a hunch:
Doesn't the expression 'scott free' have origin in the Dred Scott decision of the Civil War....even though Dred wasn't set free in that decision which helped start the U.S. Civil War.

And Hep confirms:
The term Scott free derives from the Dred Scott supreme court decision concerning runaway slaves. Dred Scott was a runaway slave who made it to the North and, he thought, to freedom. The Supreme Court decided the case against him. One of the worst decisions in U.S. jurisprudence.

And Bill in Columbia, CT has a different take:
The "scot" comes from the Anglo-Saxon meaning "putting money into a general fund" - therefore a tax. The "scot" was the original income tax" -since it was levied on people according to what they could pay. "Scot-free" first meant "tax-free."

And Gary:
Thanks for that Bill. Your explanation certainly seems to pre-date the tale about Drew Scott escaping. Expect to have some people disagreeing with you though. I've had dozens of replies, through this list and direct to me, who like the Drew Scott version.

Bob in Chicago:
You mean the DRED Scott version, right? I'm afraid I have to side with the crowd that favors the "tax" version since my dictionary shows scot-free as having a lower case "s" and only one "t" and defined as "completely free from obligation, harm, or penalty" and "scot" by itself is defined as "money assessed or paid".

Bill in Columbia, CT:
Yankee comes from "Jan Kaas" (a nickname for the Dutch), meaning cheese because of their expertise with that item (many of our attacks on particular groups of people come from food). In the days of pirates, the English referred to the Dutch (free boaters) as "John Cheese" to insult them, a little problem with pronouncing "John Kaas." When the Dutch colonized on our soil they referred to a melded form of the word "John Cheese" and "Jan Kaas" which came out "Yankee." They made it worse by saying; "Damn Yankee!" in particular reference to those who lived farther north. The Dutch, angered by the criticism, used it like kung-fu and hurled the epithet back at others to demonstrate superiority.

Dean said:
Ha Ha! I enjoyed reading the difference between a "Yankee" and a "Damn Yankee". (Recall, a "Yankee" is someone from the North who visits the South while a "Damn Yankee" is someone from the North who never leaves the South.

And Elle followed up:
And, in my best scarlett accent, may I remind you of: "damn carpetbaggin' yankees"? (recall in history, travellers using bags made from old carpets, salesmen from tha' north: damn carpetbaggin' yankees)

And Leslie:
Yankees are found north of the Mason-Dixon line. That's the definition always used in my family (good Texans all!)

Susi in Louisville KY responded to a query, which asked where did "stomping grounds" come from???
Buffalo, deer, and horses have salt cravings almost as bad as mine. In an area where there are salt deposits on the surface, herds crowd in and stamp the vegetation flat. They return frequently, especially in the summer, when they lose a lot of trace elements to perspiration-

evolution's Gatorade. Thus the phrase "to return to one's old stamping grounds". Stomping is a regionalism, but not from around these parts- I've been to Stamping Grounds, KY. Now if someone could only explain Monkey's Eyebrow and Big Bone Lick, KY.

And Sara in Boston:
Stomping grounds - this brought to mind, for me, the Native Americans who lived on the grass plains. When they were having a celebration or a gathering, they would send a group of people to the site early to stomp down the grass and create a clearing. Maybe not the derivation, but it makes a nice mental image...

--

John in Keele, UK:
I suppose I should ask an expert first, but the word "dictator" is of course Latin, and they certainly used it rather differently in Ancient Rome than us twentieth-century folk do. Further depth-diving in recollections of school Latin suggest to me that the term belongs to the days of the Roman Republic, when they appointed a dictator or two to run the show in times of great emergency. Later on they had Emperors who rode roughshod over everybody all the time anyway. Will that do?

--

Bill in Columbia, CT asked:
I was curious about the origin of "dudes"; so in my investigation, I discovered that "duds" is middle English for clothes. An Easterner who went west would often dress in a flashy manner to impress the Westerners, however the Westerner thought the Easterner had an "attitude" and added an "e" to "dud" to create "Dude." Dud + Attitude = Dude.

Bill also answered to Cat who asked: "Where does hell bent for leather come from?"
"All for lather" originally was used to describe a fast, reckless horseback ride where people were describing the race in terms of sweat. Lather didn't seem to add the vitality necessary to express "the real vibrance of the race" so it was changed to "Hell Bent for Leather."

Susi in Louisville, KY proposed:
"Off the cuff"- I have no reference for this except the lore passed by word-of-mouth through generations of costumers, but the starched collars and cuffs of the Victorians were detachable-starching included boiling and ironing by heating heavy hunks of metal, and the vests were cut so high at the neck that only the collar and cravat showed anyway, so one could-and did-wear a plaid shirt without anyone knowing. Anyway, the heavy starching produced a paper-smooth surface with the consistency of Kevlar, so it was a convenient place to jot a note when paper wasn't available-or to conceal a crib sheet (don't know anything about that phrase). So, remarks made with few notes were "off the cuff". NOTE: please don't ask me about Napoleon and sleeve buttons- I have several cans of Spam that someone left me that can be opened and mailed by snail-mail -much more effective than email "spamming".

Bill in Columbia, CT:
It's my understanding that "off the cuff," came from "on the cuff," when waiters in public houses used to keep a record of what was ordered on the cuffs of their shirts.

Peter in Melbourne enquired:
I've heard two phrases used by Americans, and I'm keen to find the origin before I use them in polite company. They have one word in common, but I can't see the connection.
1. The phrase: "Home and Hosed". Used in the sense of "Completed", "Goal Achieved" etc.
2. Calling Canadians "Hosers".

Linda in Delaware answered:
Here's a guess on "home and hosed." After you get "home" from a horseback ride, the horse needs to be cooled-down and cleaned-up before being put in a stall or released into a pasture. Often they are "hosed"-off and scraped with a special implement to get the grunge

and sweat off. Rather the alternative to being "rode hard and put up wet," which is comfortable for neither human nor beast. We often use the expression "rode hard and put up wet" to describe someone who looks pretty beat-up, as in, "she looks like she's been.... Not polite, but pretty descriptive.

--

Jo-Ellen in Minneapolis wrote:
In another vein... (and that expression came from?). Count Dracula, perhaps?
Martin in Los Angeles suggested:
My guess is that it comes from mining – when one vein of ore was played out, they tried another vein.

--

Susi in Louisville, KY asked:
I await with baited breadth an explanation for "more than one way to skin a cat" -I always assumed it was a euphemism.
Mike in Brisbane corrected:
Well, "baited breath" is what a cat has when it eats cheese and then breathes down a mousehole.
If you're waiting in anticipation, you're waiting with "bated breath" - hence the expression "don't hold your breath".

--

Jane in Hobart, AU asked:
As an aside, does anyone know the derivation of the word 'alphabet'? Did someone start with alpha, move on to beta and then get bored with the whole exercise? :) My on-the-spot hypothesis. Seriously though, does it have Greek origins?
HAR: About "alphabet": Greek, maybe. Or Hebrew: aleph, bet.

--

Someone asked:
Three feet make a yard I know. The UK has recently given up on such words in favour of metric measurements. Has the yard already died everywhere else or do other countries still use it?

Steve in Seattle:
We still use good English measurements in the Colonies -- and I'm glad of it. The English measurement system is based on human scale rather than some rigid mathematical concept.
A foot is exactly what it sounds like, the length of some king's foot. (An inch is a bit more obscure, from the Latin uncia, twelfth.) A mile (milia, cf. mille) is a thousand paces (at two steps per pace). Of course, I wish we still had cubits <g>.
Temperature is an even better match of measurement to humankind. The range 0-100 is either the range at which we can comfortably survive or the range at which water is liquid -- which scale is more meaningful and intuitive to most of us? (Of course, the most important temperature of all to those in the Great North is the same on both scales; -40C/F is reputedly the temperature at which spit freezes before it hits the ground. Isn't that special?)

Anders in Stockholm had another take:
The thousand paces appear somewhat mathematical! So does the twelfth! Besides, the Swedish name of inch is 'tum' and means 'thumb' and represents the good old arbitrariness: just a thought, who would buy rubber bands by the inch? Besides, metric was originally determined as 1/10,000,000 of the distance from the equator to either of the poles. If that does not render it human it must at least be _global_!
The C in 'centigrade' stands for Celsius. (His first name was - Anders!) His original use of the scale was with the zero at the boiling point and 100 at the freezing point (of water, of course). Later, that was switched to the reverse by Carl von Linne (Linnaeus) to the present usage. So much for 'scientific' consistency!

--

Rich in Rindge, NH:
I was explaining the meaning of "brownnosing" to my 10-year-old son when it occurred to me that the origin of this common figure of speech might be a lot less than polite. Could the "brown" on the nose be the residue from butt-bussing (THAT thread again!) or is my mind

just in the gutter (as usual)? [Someone DID comment that Wordplayers tend to be more scatological]. Any thoughts?

Katherine in Oakland:

Rich, I've always understood "brown-nosing" (yes, I want that hyphen!) to mean precisely that. Of course, my mind may be in the gutter too...

Lee in Atlanta:

For Rich -- My, my, but you did have a protected childhood yourself. You bet that brown nosing is scatological. The corollary to the term is "He/she follows so close behind, that if (the person being followed) stops short, (the follower's) nose will be brown."

--

Barbara in Stephenville, TX responded to a query:

'Feeding a dog on its own tail' is from a 1900 speech by Mark Twain relating to cutting funding for education in order to build jails... what you gain at one end, you lose at the other... it don't fatten the dog.

--

Mike in Brisbane had a question:

Um, what did the "C" in C-rations stand for? Similarly, "D" and "K" rations? Anybody know?

Bob in Chicago answered:

I asked my 76-year-old "Dubya Dubya Two" army veteran father and even though it has been fifty years since he ate any of that stuff he remembers how it tastes just as if it were eaten yesterday. I wonder why? Anyway, he said that the "C-Ration" was a canned food serving for one soldier consisting of things like corned beef hash or kidney stew. The "K-Ration" was a waxed cardboard box containing a small can of food like "corned pork and apple flakes" along with a few items like cigarettes and toilet paper and perhaps some crackers or a fruit bar. The "D-Ration" was a big candy bar. There was also something they called a "ten-in-one" which was a box holding enough rations for about ten men. Am I making you hungry yet, Mike?

Steve in Austin, TX:

The C in C-rations stands for "combat". (It was printed on the side of the case). I'm not sure, but I believe K-rations came with an amenity "kit". (So did C-rations later). I've never heard of D-rations. They must have been before my enlistment. Now, when we're in combat or in the field, we eat MRE's, Meals Rejected by Ethiopians.

Gerry in Ottawa gave us the skinny:

I can confirm that the "C" in C-Rations stood for "Combat" but can't shed any light on K-Rations apart from the story that they were originally intended for paratroopers who presumably didn't want to leap into space festooned with tin cans. I always liked K-Rations. They kept you, so to speak, in a constant state of flux. The fruit bar in the breakfast package had an almost lethal effect on the bowels, which was offset in the luncheon package by a wad of toilet paper and a large piece of cheese which had the effect of binding you up again until dinner when you were offered a fairly bland menu to get you through the night. The most popular item, of course, was the little box of cigarettes that came with them. It's hard to imagine now that any government would actually hand out free butts. Or do they?

--

Peter in Melbourne commented:

On "A Dog's Breakfast": Excuse any offence caused but I believe the origin of this is reaction of a stray (hungry) dog to finding vomit on the pavement in the morning - left there by late night revelers. Hence, a "Dog's Breakfast" is a mess, something to be avoided, a poor result, a shambles (and there's an interesting history to *this* word - refer the King James Bible).

Incidentally, discovered yesterday that "resent" used to carry the meaning of "appreciate" and even "to smell strongly". Comes from old French (should this be capital "f"?) meaning "to feel strongly".

--

Gerry in Ottawa:

Just back from a month in England and have a couple of language questions. First, does anyone know the origin of the word "yonks" in the sense of "a long time" as in "I haven't seen him for yonks." The only place that I've even seen it listed is in "Street Talk: The Language of Coronation Street." which seems to suggest that it's fairly recent. So why does no one in England seem to know where it comes from? People don't suddenly start going around saying "yonks" without questions being asked.

Jane in Hobart had a guess:
My theory is that the word is a form of rhyming slang. The term "donkey's ears" (ie. years) is rhyming slang which is used here in Australia (originally from England no doubt). I guess it wouldn't be too much of a stretch to imagine that this was shortened to "donks" which eventually became intermingled with "years" to form "yonks". "Yonks" is also quite common here.
Just on the topic of rhyming slang, my favourite is "dead horse" in place of "tomato sauce" (ketchup/catsup for those Northern Hemispherians). The look of confusion on the faces of guests when politely asked to pass the dead horse is rather amusing.

And on rhyming slang, Mike in Brisbane recalled:
One that had me puzzled for years was "Bristols", meaning breasts. I finally discovered it comes from "Bristol Cities" which rhymes with "titties". Then of course there's the obvious "Kick up the Khyber" (Khyber Pass)

Someone asked a while back what the British policeman meant when he said "Sorry, I'm rubberducked". No-one seems to have replied - it was rhyming slang - he meant that he was excessively tired or exhausted. (rhymes with f***ed).

--

Bill in Columbia, CT explained:
"Throwing the axe in?" "Throwing the sponge in" has its roots in the early days. The boxing contestant's seconds would wipe the defeated boxer's face and throw the sponge into the middle of the ring as a sign of a lost cause. Today the word "towel" has been substituted for

"sponge." I suppose throwing the axe in is similar to giving up one's weapon. [Humor: It could be victory if the warrior hit his opponent in the process of acknowledging defeat.]

--

Jesse in Sunnyvale, CA:
Wordplay question for all you experts: What is the origin of the phrase "flipping [or giving] someone the bird"? This particular obscene gesture seems well understood across most language barriers, although I've heard the British version uses two fingers instead of one. What I can't figure out is where the "bird" came from. Any help?

Mike in Brisbane had an answer:
On the "Giving someone the bird" thread, from long ago, I did some research at the weekend, and discovered that the expression comes from the hissing sound made by the audience - i.e. the sound of the bird - the goose. Probably why we refer to someone who's a bit of a dork as "a bit of a goose". (In Oz, anyway).

--

George in Virgina:
Leigh-Anne: My idiot dictionary has this to say about "out of sorts": slightly unwell, not in good spirits or temper. Origin: possibly from the use of the phrase as a printing term - literally, "with some of the letters of the alphabet used up and unavailable." For example, I may be out of sorts if I lose my sorts at the cleaners.

Rich in Rindge, NH was aptly positioned to answer:
As a student of the printing trade I've happened upon a number of common phrases which stem from that profession:

OUT OF SORTS: Ottmar Merganthaler's great invention of the late 19th century, the Linotype, uses brass molds to create type with molten lead. These molds (or "mats") were also called "sorts" and were stored in large metal trays called "magazines." The machine returns the mats to their proper slot in the magazine after casting, but every now and then one might fall out. The Linotype operator needed to be careful to replace fallen mats or he (they were almost always "he" back then) would run out of a particular letter. When this happened, jobs would be delayed, and the printer would not be happy if he were "out of sorts."

GET THE LEAD OUT: Another common problem with a Linotype would occur if it was not adjusted properly and then, when it attempted to inject molten type metal against the letter mats, caused instead what was known as a "squirt," with molten lead spraying every which way and immediately hardening. This resulted in the poor apprentice having to clean the entire machine which could take an hour. The printer would nag him to "get the lead out."

MIND YOUR P's AND Q's: Foundry type is the old-style individual metal letters which would be set by hand. After use, the apprentice would clean it and replace it into the proper compartments in the wooden drawers where it was stored. Since the type characters were mirror-image and since lower-case "p" and "q" look similar, the apprentice would be reminded to be careful to watch out for which went where, therefore to "mind one's p's and q's."

--

Toni in Minnesota remarked:
I've already fixed one bug today, so can I go home now? [Why do we call them "bugs", anyway?]

Katherine in Oakland answered:
Because a moth flew into ENIAC one day and gummed up the works, Toni.

Also, Bev chimed in:
The term bug as applied to errors in software is attributed to Grace Hopper, who, after experiencing problems on her mainframe computer, opened it up to find a *moth* inside! (This is true, folks.)

Also, Flagg had a take:
Actually, the term "computer bugs" originated circa 1859, when Blaise Pascal created one of his many "computing machines". It was a mechanical beast, full of gears and cranks. It seems he was demonstrating his device to a colleague, when they noticed several computations

coming back with the same answer. Upon closer inspection, they discovered a moth had been squished inside the machine, jamming up one of the clockwork-sensitive gears. Hence the term, "bug" as it refers to computers and programs.

And from Gary in New castle, AU:
Actually Blaise Pascal, the mathematician and computing pioneer, died in Paris in 1662.
The on-line Dictionary of Computing at Imperial College London includes this: (which might or might not explain how the word bug was coined in this context).

Admiral Grace Hopper (an early computing pioneer better known for inventing COBOL) liked to tell a story in which a technician solved a glitch in the Harvard Mark II machine by pulling an actual insect out from between the contacts of one of its relays, and she subsequently promulgated bug in its hackish sense as a joke about the incident (though, as she was careful to admit, she was not there when it happened). For many years the logbook associated with the incident and the actual bug in question (a moth) sat in a display case at the Naval Surface Warfare Center (NSWC). The entire story, with a picture of the logbook and the moth taped into it, is recorded in the "Annals of the History of Computing", Vol. 3, No. 3 (July 1981), pp. 285—286.

Richard in Berkeley, CA interjected:
Whoever told the bug story about Pascal probably meant Babbage. The link is that Pascal and Ada are programming languages, and Ada was Babbage's programmer.

Gerry in Ottawa vented off:
Heavy serendipity traffic today, beginning with "booze" which derives from the Middle Dutch word "buisen,' a verb meaning "to carouse" and which passed over into English sometime in the 13th century. This naturally made me think of the view of the St. Lawrence River from the ramparts of Quebec City, a view which used to be rather spoiled,

to say the least, by a tavern on the far side with a large sign advertising "Beer, Wine and Hooch." This, of course, was before the "French Only" language law kicked in. Now it probably says "Biere, Vin et Hooch." In any case, I found that the last dates back to Klondike gold rush days when the miners stumbled across an Indian tribe in Alaska called the Hootchinoos who brewed up a particularly lethal brand of liquor. This came into heavy demand later during Prohibition when the name was shortened to "hooch." Now, can anyone tell me what the meaning of "good" in the expression "She left me for good" is? I know it's short for "good and all' and dates back to 1520 but then I can't imagine where "good and all" comes from either.

And George in Virginia:
Seems that, during the 19th century, there was a Kentuckian named Colonel Booze who made and marketed his own whiskey. Years ago, I heard another account which said that embossed on the bottles were the words "B.E. Booze Bottling Co." It is likely that Booze boozed booze as part of his quality check...

--

Lorianne in Saskatoon cited:
Etymological Dictionary of the English Language- Skeat, 1884:
Myriad: fr. Greek: ten thousand
Naphtha: fr. Latin, fr. Greek, and ultimately fr. Arabic: an inflammable Liquid

--

Catie in Arlington, VA: noted:
Interesting fact about Dungarees coming from Dungri in India. Also, Denim - from serge de Nimes - a heavy strong twilled cotton, used in making uniforms and work clothes - manufactured in that French town.
And then of course, we have "Jeans" or blue jeans, a heavy strong twilled cotton, used in making uniforms and work clothes - manufactured in Genoa (iene fustian - geane fustian - from Middle English Jene, Gene, Genoa, where it was first made) (Am. Heritage Dict/)

Dave in Glendale, CA made a correction to a common error:
On another thread, isn't it shoo-in (as opposed to shoe-in), based on the "shoo" that comes from many origins as the sound one makes when cat-scatting and fly-fleeing (LG: schu; It: scio; Fr: shou)?

--

Peter in Gelong, AU asked:
Is a *thread* unravelling on the names of textiles? How about "corduroy"? Is it true that this cloth - that has become common attire for manual work - was once so expensive that it came to be called "the cloth of kings" or, in French, "cord du roi" (spelling?)? Can anyone confirm?

--

George in Virginia asked:
Still looking for the origin of the word "booze;" suggestions welcome. Also, would like to explore the words scutage, weasel, and dungarees. Thanks.

Mike in Brisbane answered with:
And there were some very erudite answers. I don't know that anyone defined "weasel", though. Usually similar meaning to "welch", i.e. to wriggle out of an obligation. I imagine from a weasel's ability to wriggle through confined spaces and narrow gaps, also from the perceived unpleasant character of the weasel. Most of the ones I've known have been ok though...

In Australia, Booze = Grog = Beer and any other alcoholic drink, although wine can be known as "plonk" or "steam" and spirits as "the hard stuff".

--

Gerry in Ottawa wondered:
There's another definition of "weasel" in the old nursery rhyme: "Up and down the City Road, in and out the Eagle. That's the way the money goes, pop goes the weasel." The weasel here is some sort of pressing iron or small tool that could easily be "popped" or pawned

after drinking up all one's pay at the Eagle Tavern. Any precise definition of this tool would be more than welcome.

I've forgotten the original question but wasn't Osric the foppish courier in Hamlet? Finally, "trouser trout" rather than "trouser snake?" Well, I know we all have our physical differences but still....

Mike in Brisbane followed up:

The weasel in question was a tool used by hatters - as you said - a kind of iron, probably either a blocking or a felting iron. The OED doesn't give it a mention, but it does say that "weasel" is US Colloq. for "a native of South Carolina". So there.

Gary in New Castle, AU shed some light on "pop":

I heard that the pop in Pop goes the Weasel meant pawn, i.e. take to the pawnbroker, and that the weasel was a corruption of whistle, i.e. whistle and flute (suit). So, our songs hero, having drunk his money away in the Eagle pub, got his hands on some more by pawning his suit. This might all be rubbish of course but it sounds plausible. Mind you, I have a feeling that popping is the opposite of pawning, i.e. redeeming something from a pawnbroker, which would rather throw a spanner in.

Karen "Delurker" offered:

While on a tour of a historical house in Little Rock, Arkansas I was told a "weasel" was a colloquial name for a spindle (or some mechanical device on a, maybe specific, spinning wheel - I don't remember all the details) that would "pop up (or out)" when full. I was told this was the origin of the song. I don't claim this is fact, but I thought "you guys" might enjoy exploring the possibility.

Rich in Rindge, NH offered:

My wife is a weaver/spinner/knitter who has worked in museums, and I believe she once told me that this is true (partially.) She has an old yarn winding device she calls a clock reel (because of a dial arrangement which counts the number of turns.) A standard skein of yarn consisted of 40 turns of the reel which is about 2 yards around, therefore 80 yards per skein. Many of these reels (which were called weasels in some places -- I don't know why) had a cam which loudly clicked once every 40 revolutions, hence the "pop." What I can't figure is where the "cobbler's bench" fits in.

--

Jim in Philadelphia on black boxes:
... the same kind of "black box" that they use on airplanes? And, never having been in the cockpit of a plane (why do they call it that anyway?) I wonder, is the black box originally black, or is that the color of it after the plane has burnt up and is lying in pieces on the ground?

Brian in London:
I assumed for a long time that it was "black box" in the sense of something enclosed that achieves a purpose without one's knowledge of how it is accomplished. I was very surprised to discover that it is not "black box", but "Black box" having been named after its inventor/developer/designer (or whatever), called Black. It is never black, of course, but rather fluorescent orange, the better to be found amongst the wreckage.

--

David postulated:
The phrase "politically correct" has a long history. It was used in the Communist Party as the term for the correct (Party) stance on a political issue. It became a kind of in joke among the New Left and feminists (probably mostly among the children of the Old Left, who knew where the term came from) as the term for a leftist stance on a political or social issue. It came to mean the term for a more doctrinaire stance where it probably conflicted with your gut reaction. Now the term has been co-opted by the Right as a pejorative term, just like they co-opted "liberal" as a pejorative term that once upon a time referred to a political strain that believed in using public money to stimulate trade and economic development, and now tends to mean (pejoratively) government intervention into everything.

Jim in Philadelphia:
For some reason, this made me wonder about the houseplant "Wan-

dering Jew." (It's not much of a stretch to see where this came from...) Any ideas as to why it's so named. Before anyone comments, I understand the "wandering" part of it. But the Jew?

Mike in Brisbane had a theory:
There's a legend that a man mocked Jesus Christ as he was carrying his cross on the way to Calvary. Jesus is supposed to have stopped, looked at him, and said "I go, but thou shalt tarry until I return." And so this Jewish man is supposed to be still wandering the earth - "The Wandering Jew". There's been quite a few novels and things written on the theme. As with the man of the legend, you can't kill the houseplant of the same name, - and it wanders.

--

Youngblood posited:
Watching a BBC television production the other night brings a question to mind. Where did the term "getting the sack", meaning having one's job terminate unexpectedly, originate? "I'll be sacked for that." "Are you giving me the sack?" etc.

Court in Wayne, IN answered:
The phrase was current in 17th century France (On luy a donne son sac); and the probable explanation of the term is that workmen carried their implements in a bag or sack, and when discharged took up their bag of tools and departed to seek employment elsewhere.

--

Bill in Columbia, CT observed:
Your verbiage bubbled through and again titillated my grey matter to contemplate Greek and Roman mythology. Pandora's box is a common misconception. It was really a bottle or jar. Incidentally, mythology has given rise to many words that inhabit our "verbal dome."
Also, the labyrinth was on the island of Crete and was designed by Daedalus, which you so eruditely explained in a brilliant cadence of polysyllabic expression. The Minotaur, King Minos II and Taurus combine to create "Minotaur," (half man and half bull). The upper half

was a pulchritudinous man, which proves that we are evolving, not devolving.

Interestingly enough, Queen Pasiphae (King Minos's wife) was placed in a trance by Poseidon, and Pasiphae passionately copulated with a bull and gave birth to the "Minotaur." Poseidon was angry because King Minos II had cheated him out of a prize bull so he had the bull engage in an ejaculatory romance with Minos' wife.

--

Someone enquired:
Does anyone know the traditional or accepted meaning of the word Boxing in the name of the holiday which falls on Dec. 26th? I know that it is an English holiday (also celebrated in the "Colonies" including Canada and Australia).

Giles in New Castle, AU:
Boxing Day is the day that people used to go around giving Christmas presents or Christmas "boxes" to family and friends.
BTW, is anyone else annoyed at the current trend to regard the "Twelve days of Christmas" as the 12 days *before* Christmas, i.e. 14th-25th December. In fact, they are the 12 days after Christmas, finishing on "Twelfth Night", or 6th January. The days before Christmas are "Advent" (which means "coming" in Latin).

Alex in Adelaide added a side note:
There is no such thing as Boxing Day in the USA, but rather what is called National Whiner's Day where people take back to the stores those unsuitable presents they've received for exchange or refund. For that reason only it's been declared as a national holiday.

--

Bill in Columbia, CT answered a query:
The query several postings back was about "No skin off my nose." Well, while browsing through several aisles in search of a good book, I bumped into a succinct explanation of this idiom. Other related idioms are as follows: "No skin off my elbow (or back, or shoulder, etc.) Of course, the most popular expression is "No skin off my nose." It

comes from a miscreant's being thrown (literally) out of an establishment for inappropriate behaviour. The individual being thrown (the throwee) generally sustains some abrasions on the nose, shoulder, back, elbow, etc. So, if you say, "No skin off my nose." It means that you are clear of this kind of trauma.

Toni in Minnesota added:
Which reminds me of a similar expression that makes somewhat less sense: what about "by the skin of [one's] teeth"?

Robert in Pompano, FL:
"The skin of [one's] teeth" comes, if I remember aright, from the Old Testament book of Job, referring to a near escape from disaster.

Bill in Columbia, CT also said:
"by the skin of *his* teeth is a literal translation from the Hebrew text of the Book of Job. Since teeth have no skin, for a person to get by the "skin of [one's] teeth" is to get by with no margin at all.
Incidentally, mnemonic comes from Mnemosyne (Goddess of Memory), mother of the Muses.

--

Bob in eastern Washington:
Gerry in Ottawa explained the meaning of the numbers in the song "Green Grow the Rushes." I heard that the term Gringo was coined during a war with Mexico. Our soldiers sang the song, and the Mexican soldiers started calling us "green-grows." I don't say it's a true story, but it is true that I heard it.

--

Gerry in Ottawa, in turn answered to Bill:
Bill Skoog asked about straw polls. That was a tough one. Books all over the floor there for a while but I finally ran it down in William Safire's "Political Dictionary." Before sophistication set in, it was simply an informal survey of a small group to determine opinion and derives more or less from the advice of John Selden (1584-1654): "Take a straw and throw it up into the air. You may see by that which way the wind is." The expression was used in 1866 by the Cleveland Leader in

a way that suggested it was already familiar. "A straw vote taken on a Toledo train yesterday resulted as follows:
Andrew Johnson 12, Congress 47." Apparently, earlier surveys of this sort had been carried out on river steamboats and were known as "steamboat votes."

--

From Facebook (author unknown): Isn't it funny how certain phrases go in and out of fashion?

'A SHOT OF WHISKEY' - In the old west a .45 cartridge for a six-gun cost 12 cents, so did a glass of whiskey. If a cowhand was low on cash, he would often give the bartender a cartridge in exchange for a drink. This became known as a "shot" of whiskey.

BUYING THE FARM - This is synonymous with dying. During WW1 soldiers were given life insurance policies worth $5,000. This was about the price of an average farm so if you died you "bought the farm" for your survivors.

IRON CLAD CONTRACT - This came about from the ironclad ships of the Civil War. It meant something so strong it could not be broken.

RIFF RAFF - The Mississippi River was the main way of travelling from north to south. Riverboats carried passengers and freight but they were expensive so most people used rafts. Everything had the right of way over rafts which were considered cheap. The steering oar on the rafts was called a "riff" and this transposed into riff-raff, meaning low class.

COBWEB - The Old English word for "spider" was "cob".
SHIP STATE ROOMS - Travelling by steamboat was considered the height of comfort. Passenger cabins on the boats were not numbered. Instead, they were named after states. To this day cabins on ships are called staterooms.

SLEEP TIGHT- Early beds were made with a wooden frame. Ropes were tied across the frame in a crisscross pattern. A straw mattress was then put on top of the ropes. Over time the ropes stretched, causing the bed to sag. The owner would then tighten the ropes to get a better night's sleep.

SHOWBOAT - These were floating theatres built on a barge that was pushed by a steamboat. These played small towns along the Mississippi River. Unlike the boat shown in the movie "Showboat", these did not have an engine. They were gaudy and attention grabbing which is why we say someone who is being the life of the party is "showboating".

OVER A BARREL - In the days before CPR, a drowning victim would be placed face down over a barrel and the barrel would be rolled back and forth in an effort to empty the lungs of water. It was rarely effective. If you are over a barrel, you are in deep trouble.

BARGE IN - Heavy freight was moved along the Mississippi in large barges pushed by steamboats. These were hard to control and would sometimes swing into piers or other boats. People would say they "barged in".

HOGWASH - Steamboats carried both people and animals. Since pigs smelled so bad, they would be washed before being put on board. The mud and other filth that was washed off were considered useless "hog wash".

CURFEW - The word "curfew" comes from the French phrase "couvre-feu", which means "cover the fire". It was used to describe the time of blowing out all lamps and candles. It was later adopted into Middle English as "curfeu" which later became the modern "curfew". In the early American colonies, homes had no real fireplaces so a fire was built in the centre of the room. In order to make sure a fire did not get out of control during the night it was required that, by an agreed upon time, all fires would be covered with a clay pot called-a "curfew".

BARRELS OF OIL - When the first oil wells were drilled, there was no provision for storing the liquid so they used water barrels. That is why, to this day, we speak of barrels of oil rather than gallons.

HOT OFF THE PRESS - As the paper goes through the rotary printing press friction causes it to heat up Therefore, if you grab the paper right off the press, it's hot. The expression means to get immediate information.

SHIP STATEROOMS– Traveling by steamship was considered the height of comfort. Passenger cabins on the boats were not numbered. Instead, they were named after states. To this day cabins and ships are called staterooms.

4

Grammar

Jane in Hobart, AU asked:
Can anyone shed light on the reason why people in the USA would write "Please write me as soon as you get the chance.", while in Australia it is correct to use "Please write <u>to</u> me as soon as you get the chance"?

Jim in Philadelphia responded:
Actually, Jane, both seem correct to me. It's the indirect object syndrome (Dativitis?????) Just as both "He gave the book to me" and "He gave me the book" seem correct...

Kristofer in College Station, TX:
People also say "fax me" and "page me." Is it a result of our technological advancement that we automatically allow those items which can do something to have their names verbed?

--

Someone noted: Freres Volokh Productions, in its manifesto, gave us: "We ONLY accept electronic submissions."

Terrence in Bermuda corrected:
You mean you don't publish them? Or should this be "...submissions ONLY." or "...ONLY electronic...

Punctuation

Jeff in Edinburgh on commas: ... escalator, kerosene, and zipper? Is it correct to insert a comma before "and", as after "kerosene" above? I was once told it was optional.

Brian in London answered:
I have a theory that some false ideas are promulgated in a society by being recycled by schoolteachers whose only experience of them has been their own time in school. I don't make this comment cynically: I was a schoolteacher myself for twenty years and I know that it occurs in my own then subject.

"What has all this got to do with commas?" I hear you ask. Well, I feel that in the school teaching of English, punctuation suffers from this problem. Most teachers of English have been taught and are interested in literature, and their experience of the nuts and bolts of language is often just their own school learning. They teach children how to lay out a business letter, for example, based on what _they_ were taught in school, and not on, say, a modern business style guide. Most of them will teach you _not_ to put in the last comma in Jeff's example, but - certainly in Britain - you will be hard put to find a usage or style or language guide that agrees: they all say put it in.

If you like your punctuation to be logical, the reason for including the comma is simple: it clarifies compound lists. If I say that I have been unable to buy something, despite looking in "Boots, Marks and Spencers and Woolworths", you do not (from the sentence itself and without cultural knowledge) know whether the three shops I tried were (1) Boots, (2) Marks, and (3) Spencers and Woolworths, or (1) Boots, (2) Marks and Spencers, and (3) Woolworths. Jeff's final comma (after "Marks" or "Spencers" as the case may be) would make it all clear. And - the theory goes - if you need it sometimes, you should use it always, for consistency.

--

Pat in Collegeville, MN said:
Jeff gives an admirably clear description for the layperson of the difference between bacteria and viruses. I missed the preceding discussion, so I'm grateful for something I can understand--and enjoy.

Interesting to me, by the way, that we use the Latin plural for bacterium, but the English for virus. I suspect that we get viruses because those who applied the word to the pernicious little buggers weren't sure whether virus is second or fourth declension (it's second, and the Latin plural is viri). Or they might have had reservations about viri because it also is the plural for vir, a male homo sapiens.

Alex in Adelaide observed:
Thanks to Lee (*the woman*) who noted that scissors are used only as plural. This would immediately suggest that _a pair of scissors_ is redundant.
Yet on second thought I realized that _a pair of_ is needed to distinguish a single set of scissors from many (a singular within a plural if so to speak).
Other words that are used exclusively in plural are: pants/trousers/slacks/jeans/...,news, etc...
Words that are always singular are: information, air, heat, etc...
Any other such words fellow wordplayers?

John in Keele, UK commented:
With the exception of underwear, "pants" in the meaning quoted is American usage; I don't think you'd come across the singular in English, even in the context given.
Minor exception: we seem to have acquired "hot pants" somewhere along the road...

Allan in Brandon, Ca picked up on Jeff's "can I have one bottle of each of your whiskies":
Jeff would appear to be very nicely and politely challenging the

spelling that I used for the plural form of 'whiskey' in my posting. But the Random House Dictionary specifically lists 'whiskeys' as the correct plural form for 'whiskey'.

It is true that the general rule for forming plurals for words ending in 'y' is to change the 'y' to 'i' and to add 'es' (eg mysteries, parties). However, the rule usually applies only if there is a consonant before the 'y'. This would suggest that the plural form for the Scotch and Canadian distilled product (whisky) is 'whiskies', and sure enough, this is what the Random House Dictionary lists for them (as does Oxford).

This now allows for the subtle demonstration of correct English at a bar. Patrons of the American and Irish varieties of aqua vitae who wish to demonstrate their grammatical knowledge of hard liquors at a bar should specify (and insist on) 'whiskeys' when ordering. Those of us with preferences for British Commonwealth spirits will order and drink only 'whiskies'. However, given that some American whiskey producers label their product incorrectly (as noted in my earlier posting) it might be wise to first inquire of the bartender what spellings are stocked when going for the American variety.

--

Patrick in Collegeville, MN:
Katherine asked what the plural of census is. In Latin it's census (4th declension, like status and cursus). I suspect most Americans would do censuses, although we don't seem to have a problem with some other Latin plurals that are the same as the singulars (species, series, congeries).

--

Guy in Cupertino, CA asked:
Is anyone else noticing an increased occurrence of the misuse exemplified here:
"Between 50 to 75 persons attended." Namely the use of "to" rather than "and" with "between"?

Janet in Calgary jumped in:
You beat me to this post by about one day - we have a sign a the office that says "Please alert the guard if you plan to enter this area during the restricted hours between 10:00 p.m. to 6:00 a.m.", and it's been bugging me too.

--

Charlie in Memphis, TN:
Anyone out there remember the old Winston cigarette commercial (or even the fact that we had cigarette commercials in the USA) where their slogan "Winston tastes good like a cigarette should" was corrected by a horn-rimmed professor-type to "Winston tastes good as a cigarette should"?
Some of the old commercials and slogans were clever - remember any??

--

Spelling
Wes said:
I thoroughly enjoyed Michael's latest, but I must correct one commonly misspelled word. "...to computer, computer to internet. That *miniscule* electro-chemical seed ". It's 'minuscule'

--

Pat in Collegeville, MN:
Michael then asks tolerance for the orthographic jamming together of a and lot. As subsequent digests show, Mike, you won't get much sympathy from linguistic conservatives. But in time you'll be vindicated. "A lot" is clearly on the way to becoming alot as "a while" has become awhile in most contexts. All right / alright is a little further along, but not so far as already and altogether.

Anyway, as you practice tolerance, you'll also have to practice patience. I tell my students, if you spell it that way, you're readers will understand you clearly, but many will peg you, unfairly, as semi-literate, so you got choices.

Penelope in Michigan:
Alot vs. a lot: I work for 12 composition instructors. Even though most of us would like to throw in the towel and let our students use "alot" we all carry on the battle and insist on "a lot".

Katherine in Oakland, CA:
Somebody's comment about professors trying to hold the line on "alot" reminded me of the time I took a proofreading test for an employment agency--a story I don't think I've told on this list: The test consisted of about a dozen sentences, which were to be corrected if they had errors, and marked "correct" otherwise. One of these sentences was, "While we're gone, mow the lawn everyday." I changed it to "...every day", of course. _My_ doing so was graded "incorrect"; when I said, "Huh??", I was told that since "everyday" was now accepted usage in this context, my correction was itself erroneous. *Sigh*

Steven in Atlanta, GA:
Arrgh! Take it to the tester's boss and steal the job. "Everyday" is only an adjective, at least in American (cf. Webster's Tenth Collegiate '94, that most liberal of descriptive dictionaries).

--

John in Keele, UK:
Jeff comments [from Australia] on the, to me, American usage "write me when you get there".

Obvious inference: "me" is in the Dative, normally expressed in English by preposition "to". Further guess: like much characteristic American speech, this is derived from German [possibly via Yiddish, which is a dialect of Medieval German]. "Schreib mir!" [where the form "mir" is clearly Dative] probably lies behind it. Another example: "What gives?" = "Was gibt's?". But I've no idea where the extraordinary "Visit with" comes from...

--

Steven in Austin, TX:
Toni wrote: "BTW, I have yet to figure out how to use 'fail' as a noun." That always puzzles me, without fail!

Terrence in Bermuda:
"Fail" (along with "Pass") is frequently used as a noun by students and teachers, as in: "If you had submitted your essay on time I would have given you a 'Pass', but despite the quality of your work, I'm afraid I am going to be forced to give you a 'Fail'".

Less informally, is the common expression "without fail" in which fail is clearly a noun.

Cindi in Southern Illinois:
Confusing the possessive and plurals *really* (ha ha) irks me. I know that most of the time, as with most grammar mistakes, it happens only because people aren't sure or just plain don't know how to use or distinguish the two. It doesn't help when one walks into a store and sees:
"VCR'S ON SALE!!"
"GET TWO FREE CD-ROM'S WITH PURCHASE!"
"TOTALLY 80'S"
Adding to the issue is that we are increasingly becoming a visually-oriented (someone explain oriented and orientated please!) rather than a print-oriented society. The less one has to use grammar rules that only apply to written language, the easier it is to forget them.

Steven in Austin, TX:
All of these are correct. When pluralizing an abbreviation or numbers, an apostrophe is used to separate the 's' from the number or abbreviation. i.e. Johnny can say his ABC's., I'll take the size 13's., Several AK-47's were discovered.
But you don't have to take my word for it. I learned it in the New York Times Manual of Style for Journalists.

Andy in Chichester, UK:
If only it were that simple. You may, if you wish, take the word of the New York Times as law, but ask any other publisher and they are likely to give you a different answer (sounds vaguely familiar, can't think what group that reminds me of). Neither of the academic publishers I have worked for allow this use of apostrophes, the Chicago Style Manual does exceptionally (I's for example) and Hart's Rules says they should be omitted. You pays yer money and you takes yer choice. My preference? I can't see what function they serve so I take them out.

Cindi in Southern Illinois:
[to which I respond:] Being a librarian, I had to run to the reference stacks. (oh, and I felt a need to look this up.) :)
From the Chicago Manual of Style, 14th edition, p. 197
Letters, Noun Coinages, Numbers, and Abbreviations
6.16 So far as it can be done without confusion, single or multiple letters, hyphenated coinages, and numbers used as nouns (whether spelled out or in numerals) form the plural by adding s alone:

xs and ys	all SOSs
the three Rs	several YMCAs and AYHs
thank-you-ma'ams	CODs and IOUs
in twos and threes	the early 1920s

6.17 Abbreviations having more than one period, such as M.D. and Ph.D., often form their plurals by the addition of an apostrophe and an s. Noun abbreviations with only one (terminal) period usually form their plurals by the addition of s before the period.
M.A.'s and Ph.D.'s   ed., eds.   vol., vols.   yr., yrs.
However, on p. 215:
LETTERS AS LETTERS
6.82 In some proverbial expressions the distinction [that letters of the alphabet be italicized] is ignored, and in that case, the plural is formed by adding an apostrophe and an s:
Mind your p's and q's. Dot your i's and cross your t's.

John in Keele, UK:
The transitive version of the verb "protest" appears usually in phrases such as "to protest one's innocence"

[Since it happened to be to hand, my source is A.S. Hornby, _Advanced Learner's Dictionary of Current English_; I'd be interested to know if the "protest something meaning protest against" sense appears in American reference works. It doesn't feature in Hornby.]

Katherine in Oakland, CA:
About W as a vowel: The explanation I've been given, if we're talking about English (yes, I know W is a vowel in Welsh) (and for that matter that R is a vowel in Serbo-Croatian), is that W is a vowel when it forms diphthongs: e.g., in "hollow" or "pew". Or, I suppose, "vowel"...

And David in Glendale, CA:
Laurie, maybe your non-believing friend might be helped (to the true faith, of course) by contemplating the word "ewe," where the w serves its true and original purpose of "uu", a looooong looong u. It changes the sound from long-e to long-uu, so forms a diphthong -- and a diphthong is by definition two vowel sounds jammed together so closely (ligated) that it is practically impossible to determine where one ends and the other begins. Lately, of course, we efficient modern types solve the problem by dropping the first vowel entirely, but not in words like "ewe".

As to the final e in the word, it is (in these modern times) silent, but serves the usual purpose of underlining the preceding vowel's being long (in the Anglican sense, whereby we parochial English speakers consider a vowel to be long if it has the pronunciation we give it in our alphabet).

P.S. Thanks for spelling words like "diphthong" and "diphtheria" with a "ph" instead of just a "p"; spelling those two words traditionally means that you probably pronounce them equally traditionally with a dif (instead of a dip) at the start.

--

Phil in Salt Lake City: Avoid the "hopefully"'s misuse:
I also want to apologize to our non-U.S. friends on the list] for the (hopefully) brief digression into "local" politics] On usage: I am aware that some will find fault with my use of] "hopefully" in the above paragraph. I searched for several minutes for] an alternative, but found none. Any help?

Guy in Cupertino, CA:
Howzabout: "I also want to apologize to our non-U.S. friends on the list for what I hope has been a brief digression into "local" politics."

--

John in Keele, UK:
A quick survey of my American e-mail correspondents some while ago suggested that it is a matter of ["official"] indifference whether to use the 'c' or the 's' form of verb/noun pairs that English people are taught to distinguish [thus: I did a lot of piano practice yesterday/I was practising all day]. The one you "remember it by" as a rule of thumb is of course the case where you can hear the difference: "He advised me to desist"/"She gave me good advice".
This ring any bells among you teaching folk, or is it obsolete? Or just very British?

Mike in Brisbane responds:
Very much so John. May be very British, but Australian as well. If you get them wrong, you can really stuff up the meaning. "Licence" and "License" for example.

--

Monika asked:
Lately I keep seeing the word 'advise' used as a noun - as in ' I can't give any advise on that issue'. Is this becoming accepted usage in English,

or is it just a typo people make often?
Any input?

Leo responded:
From Leo's skool of first-rate cool writing, it's a typo, nothing more. Certainly it's not acceptable. Some people my have a hard time distinguishing which to use.

--

Bill in Columbia, CT:
There is one grammatical blunder that boggles my mind: "Kids graduate elementary school." All I can see is the elementary school going on for further education, while the kids stay behind as receptacles for incoming schools.

Katherine enquired:
Do you mean as opposed to "graduate _from_"? Interesting...I'd always head that "graduate from" was the blunder, with the other being the older (and therefore of course the more formally correct form).

HAR added:
Graduate means to confer a degree upon. Therefore, students are graduated from schools, schools graduate students.

--

HAR also asserted:
I don't think mistakes like "alot" for "a lot", "there" for "their" or -- especially -- "it's" for "its" are typos at all. I believe these errors reveal either ignorance of or indifference to the correct spellings.

Bill in Lexington, KY:
Agreed, HAR. An author may have an important message presented with impeccable (and I had to check that spelling) logic, but if it is presented with poor spelling and grammar, it is less likely to be accepted by its readers ... at least the readers who know the difference.

--

Toni in Minnesota:
Just curious ... when did "pairs" become the plural of "pair"? I've heard it used several times recently, and each time it grated on my ears like fingernails on a blackboard.

--

Rogers said in the same vein:
The word "thanks" is a true plural that has no singular. We say "a million thanks" and "his thanks were sincere" but we never say "a thank" or "his thank was sincere."
Can you think of any similar words? ("Physics" doesn't count. It's not a True plural)

--

Leo wrote on the subject of new tech terms to English:
My preference is "e-mail," but not for any particular reason. It's simply what I've gotten used to writing.

Richard in Tempe, AZ in response suggested:
Seems to me the logical progression starts with "electronic mail," evolves to "e-mail" and then to "email." I've already completed my evolution...at least with respect to "email."
Just like "on line" to "on-line" to "online."
"Real time" to "real-time" to "realtime."
And like so many less tekkie (techie?) words and non-technical words that started out as two, became hyphenated and finally became compound words. The more we use these terms and words, the more *real* they become.

--

Bill in Washington, DC said:
It has been suggested that "realtime" and "online" and "email" are solid, non-hyphenated words, having evolved from compounds right before our eyes.
Point 1: This is English, not German.

Point 2: Yes, it's true that compounds tend to evolve from two words to hyphenated to solid, but let's not forget that this change takes place over dozens, if not hundreds, of years (and it has NEVER taken place with a word like e-mail). I deal with striking examples of this every day: As a newspaper editor who, like most U.S. newspaper editors, is bound by the AP Stylebook and Webster's New World Dictionary, I still must use "hot line" instead of "hotline," "town house" instead of "townhouse," and "teen-ager" instead of "teenager," among other anachronisms.

While I would change those style rulings in a second, I humbly submit that the truth lies somewhere between typing "cross fire" forever and jumping to solidify "realtime" because some kid somewhere coined the term yesterday.
I think questions such as "Should 'online' be one word?" are perfectly proper matters of debate for, say, a mailing list of dictionary editors -- and perhaps there are dictionary editors among us on this list. But for other editors, those of us who are slaves to Official Usage, this kind of linguistic vigilante plotting is pointless, fun as it may be.
BTW, the day I see "realtime" in a real dictionary, I'll be listed in Guinness as the oldest living human.

Allan in Brandon, Manitoba commented:
Surely the debate on whether or not certain computer-related terms should be hyphenated or not is yet another example of the major differences in style that exist between American English and English as used by the rest of the world. On this topic The Economist Style Guide notes that 'American English is far readier than British English to accept compound words. In particular, many nouns made of two separate nouns are spelt as one word in American English, while in British English they would either remain separate or be joined by a hyphen'.

--

Bill in Lexington, KY responded to a query from Ruth, who asked: "I used to know but I forget, my English comp teacher used to accuse me of splicing commas – I didn't even own an editing machine, let alone a splicer. En/Inquiring minds (well, mine anyway) need to know - just what *is* a comma splice???"

A comma splice occurs when two main clauses are joined by a comma rather than a semicolon.

--

John in Keele, UK:

Alyssa, I think your spelling of "straightjacket" probably disguises the true etymology, which is 'strait' = narrow, confined. And the Collins Cobuild English Dictionary _only_ gives the spelling "straitjacket". Now that the oldfashioned [old-fashioned?] sense of the word 'strait' is disappearing from usage, I increasingly see the spelling with a 'gh' as writer interprets the word in terms of his or her modern limited vocabulary

---

HAR:

Ending a sentence with a preposition => I think it was Winston Churchill who said, "Ending a sentence with a preposition is something up with which I will not put."

Reg interjected:

Oh No! It was Winnie, all right, but the context was a young man correcting him for ending a sentence with a preposition. What he said was, "Impertinence, young man, is something up with which..." etc.

--

Bill in Lexington, KY on stacking of prepositions:

The young boy was sick and in his upstairs bedroom. He asked his mother to read to him. She selected a book about Australia and took it up to his room. When he saw it, he said "Aw, Ma, what did you bring that book that I didn't want to be read to out of about Down Under up for?"

Bev on language inconsistencies:
Night and day are opposites, right? So why can we say "at night" but not "at day"? Most other references I can think of apply to both: during the night/during the day, in the nighttime/in the daytime, at nightfall/at daybreak
Maybe "at night" simply isn't correct English and we should properly be saying "during the night." (?)

--

Gary responded to Richard who asked "If you enjoyed that, then here's another poser for you. Why can animals leave teethmarks but not clawsmarks? Why can a house be mice-infested but not rats-infested?":
Good question Richard, I hope to see the answer here shortly. While you are at it could you explain why people 'put their best foot forward'. Doesn't this imply (at least) three feet?

Rich in Rindge, NH also weighed in:
This one seems simple. None of the plural constructions ends with an "s." Therefore, if the plural is normally made by adding "s" then we use the singular; if the plural is irregular or has no ending "s" we use it.

--

Phil in Salt Lake City was puzzled:
I received an ad today that said: "Sometimes a few centimeters make a big difference."
This is an example of what seems to me to be a problem that a lot of people have with plurals. Unless I'm mistaken, the above should be "Sometimes a few centimeters _makes_ a big difference" since it is one distance, comprised of a few centimeters. Nez pas?

Bill in Lexington KY answered:
Phil, my ear seems to be happy with either a singular or plural verb, which scares me. Grammatically, the verb has to be plural unless you

take into account the possibly implied phrase ("Some- times [a distance of] a few centimeters makes a big difference").

Phil rebutted:
The fact that we were talking about _one distance_ was basically the point. If you have a stick, you can say that it's 10 centimeters or 4 inches, but it is still one stick. The units are really arbitrary. The ubiquitous "someone" recently posted a statement like:
"Twenty minutes is not a lot of time." The twenty minutes is singular because the sentence is talking about one span of time, _consisting_ of 20 connected, uninterrupted minutes. The minutes are also being equated with the singular "time".
Another example: "Fifty dollars was paid for the coat." It is understood that we are talking about one payment (or one amount) of $50. No one expects that someone made 50 payments of $1 each.

--

Virginia on jarring phrases:
My favorite example of a dangling participle: Having eaten our lunch, the steamboat departed.
In sentences like this, the first participle phrase ("Having eaten our lunch," in this case) is always understood by readers and hearers as modifying the next noun or noun phrase (here, "the steamboat").

--

Jane in Hobart asked:
G'day all, is it possible to have two apostrophes in the one word I wonder?

Jack in London answered:
Indeed, it's possible to have two apostrophes in a three letter word, as in Rock'n'Roll :-)

--

Lorianne in Saskatoon:
Canadian spelling: We mostly refer to it as British spelling, but we do

not use it consistently, as sometimes we use American spelling. Canadian spelling is, therefore, easy to screw up. I know of an example where a Canadian stylist manual (writing style that is) switched back and forth from British to American spelling of the same word, even though it informed students not too! My dad would write GAOL (instead of jail) and the secretaries would type it up as GOAL. He's the only person I know who uses the British spelling of this word over the American spelling, and I don't understand why he would. I guess it's some kind of elitist thing and he didn't care if nobody understood him.

--

Bob in Eastern Washington had a problem parsing the sentence:
One person replied, "Very succinct. Would that such brevity and clarity were also ubiquitous."
How about that second sentence? The author pointed out that it was a common sentence structure in England, where she went to school. I'll take "were" as the verb in the subjunctive. But what function does "would" fill? Is it the only thing left after losing an assumed subject and predicate, "(We) would (wish) that such...."

Bill in Lexington, KY responded:
have seen such constructions before, but I have to admit that I don't know how to parse it or if it can be parsed. And, yes, the mood should be subjunctive, but even if it were not, "were" would be correct because of the plural subject, "brevity and clarity".

Matin Los Angeles, added:
It seems to me that "Would that such ..." is a shortening of "I would wish that such ...". If this is so (or as Picard said to the tailor, "Make it sew!") then the sentence is grammatically correct.

--

Ken in Victoria, BC wondered:
O.K. I'll buy that but why is it "I'm going to the bedroom"?, but "I'm

going to bed"?
I think the answer lies somewhere in the difference between "I'm going to the jail" and 'I'm going to jail". But I can't put my finger on it.

   Bev came to the rescue:
Sure you can, Ken. (Why did I just think of a chorus line?) It has to do with the simple matter of going to a place vs. going to and taking part in a thing or experience. *The bedroom* and *the jail* are mere places. But bed and jail in the indefinite examples describe more an experience. Trust me, it's clear. I'm just having a helluva time describing it.

   Lorianne in Saskatoon, SK followed up:
Which brings us back to the original phrase, "George is in hospital" (I hope that's what it was). I don't think people really say "going to hospital", so we just don't have this problem. Good analysis though, Bev. Short and precise.
--
   Martin in Los Angeles on opposites:
Possible new thread - words that look like opposites but aren't. Example - "within" and "without".

   Brian in London obliged:
"Without" does normally mean "not possessing" these days, but certainly once could mean the opposite of "within". Most of us will be familiar with the words of that wonderful hymnographer Mrs Cecil Frances ("Fanny") Alexander, later wife of the Archbishop of Armagh, who wrote (in the last century):
> There is a green hill far away
> Without a city wall, ...

At the age at which we probably first came across these words, we may well have wondered why anyone should expect a hill to have a wall or be surprised that it didn't. But here, of course, "without"

does mean the opposite of "within": the hill is Golgotha, outside the city walls of Jerusalem. (Some recent hymn books have rewritten this "... Outside a city wall".)
A slightly different word, "outwith", is still in common use in Scottish English to mean "outside", though not heard at all in English English.

Frank in Ottawa ventured into old English realm:
Now I see it probably did. I bow my head and beseech thees (Old English for You-all) to show forbearance.
Katherine was quick to correct him:
Nope, OE for You-all is "Ye".

Frank again:
And I thought, listening to this typical North of England usage, why do I and most of us say "Give it to him"? Him is the Dative case isn't it, so why do we need the "to"?

Bill in Lexington, KY answers:
Because "Give it him" means "give him to it". The indirect object normally precedes the direct object. When the direct object comes first, we insert the "to" to indicate that.

David in Glendale, CA:
Alyssa asked, So, IS "w" ever a vowel? Yep, not to get one's vowels in an uproar, vowel *sounds* are represented in English by the *letters* a, e, I, o, u, y and w (and in other languages by other letters, like j, for example). One word where W is a real UU (double-U is its name, and UU is its game....) is "ewe," in which there are two vowel sounds (diphthongish, that) represented by e and w; the final e serves the usual purpose, of indicating that in English the "long" version of the central vowel (in this case, the uu) is to be used. It also appears in Wye (the uu sound starts the word) and ends a *few* others.

Steven in Seattle added:
How now, brown cow? 'Tis a vowel in all four of those words.

Laurie also weighed in:
The explanations I got, both online and off, seem to center around "W" as a vowel when used in a diphthong. Therefore, a word like cow would have "W" as a vowel. A more specific reason given me by an English teacher was that "W" is used as a vowel in a diphthong where "U" would be used, except that "U" is not commonly used to end words. Therefore, cow, law, etc. would have "W" as a vowel.

Steven explained:
The W was originally a U (V glyph -- think Roman writing). Sometimes it was a single letter, sometimes it was doubled (originally written "vv," as it commonly appears in Shakespeare's quarto and early folio editions, but occasionally "uu"). As an example, Cow was written Cou in Middle English.
We treat it as a consonant when it's partly voiced at the beginning of a word, such as "we," but remember that the French spell the same syllable, more or less, "oui" -- all vowels. One could perhaps make an argument that it's always an open and free sound and thus should always be a vowel – but (a) even I'm not that perverse, (b) that's beyond my knowledge, and (c) I sure wouldn't want any part in confusing schoolkids even further.
--

Alyssa in San Francisco complained:
It wasn't me who asked about w as a vowel, but thanks.

Bill quickly corrected:
It should, of course, be "it wasn't I who asked ...", but I have to admit that that doesn't sound right to my ear. I would say "it wasn't me", too. However, I would say "it was not I who ...", and "it was not me ..." doesn't sound right. Any suggestions why?

John in Keele, UK elaborated:
It is indubitable that lots of English speakers, including well-educated ones, habitually say "It wasn't me!" and similar. The problem is not _whether_ it's correct, just how to describe it. Where can we look for an indication of the difference between verb-to-be, followed-by-complement [rather than "object"] and exclamations such as the example given? Answer: the French language, where there is an extra pronoun for just this purpose.
Il te voit [he sees you; 'te' is "accusative object"]. [Perhaps I should translate "he sees thee"?]
Ah! C'est toi! [oh, it's you!; 'toi' is emphatic pronoun]
The nominative is of course 'tu' [tu vois = you see].
Similar provision in the first person singular as well: je; me; moi. It wasn't me in French is "Ce n'etait pas moi!" [Imagine an acute accent on the 'e' of etait]
And of course 'il, le, lui' in the third pers. singular.
[There is an overlap with the dative, BTW: 'Donnez-le moi!' = give it to me.]
So the mechanism at work is an instinctive use of an "emphatic" pronoun, which happens in English to be identical with the accusative case of the pronoun. Feel better now?

Abbreviations and acronyms
Allan in Brandon, Manitoba noted:
the virus first known as LAV (by Dr Luc Montagnier in Paris), then HTLV-III (by Dr Gallo of the NIH in Washington) was renamed HIV in 1985 by an international committee. That transmission of HIV-1 in Central Africa preceded transmission elsewhere was recognized by this time, but it is news to me that geographic factors had anything to do with the name chosen. The change to HIV was primarily because of an increasingly acrimonious dispute between Montagnier and Gallo as to who had first discovered the virus. The committee decided

that Gallo did not have the right to give it the name he had chosen, and settled on HIV. Gallo, of course, has been thoroughly discredited since then, and need not worry any longer about winning a Nobel Prize.

As for the acronym AIDS, the disease entity was first called GRID (Gay Related Immune Deficiency) in January 1982. Other names at the time were ACIDS (Acquired Community Immune Deficiency Syndrome) and CAIDS (Community Acquired Immune Deficiency Syndrome). 'Community' was of course a synonym for homosexual. The Centre for Disease Control in Atlanta, Georgia detested the GRID acronym. In August 1982 someone there came up with AIDS, which stuck.

--

Dean followed up with:
Of course, there is also K.I.S.S. It stands for Keep It Simple Stupid and is an editorial comment often made on engineering text.

--

On **pedantry**, Brian Bilston once wrote a poem about "pedants":

> Foot soldiers in the War on Error,
> they're here to save us from ourselves,
> with *Fowler's Modern English Usage*
> (first edition, nineteen twelve).
>
> They scrutinize each word we write
> for typos, gaffes, et cetera,
> correcting all our dumb mistakes
> to make our grammar betterer.
>
> They sigh and tut and tell us off
> for the rules we have forsaken
> and chart this nation's steep decline
> by the care we should of taken.

Custodians of the King's English,
they merely serve to keep it pure
and restrict, they hope, the ignorant
to three mistakes or less.

In doing so, they hold no fear
they will deprive a thing of life:
for it's not important what is *said*,
what matters is that its *right*.

5

Style and Syntax

Maryanne in Tallahassee, FL asked:
What does it mean when someone says (e.g.), "Farmer McGregor has what is arguably the best garden in town"?
When someone makes a statement like that, I infer that to the writer or speaker Farmer McGregor's garden *is* the best, period. But, "arguably"? It seems to me they're saying "it could be argued by someone else that another garden is better, but I can argue back." Help me out here, Wordsters.

    Jeff in San Diego, CA answered:
I've always inferred it to take on the second meaning you offered, that someone may have a better garden, and we can argue about it. Further, I only envision this use of "argue" as more of a debate. If someone has the wherewithal to prequalify their boast ("the best garden in town") with the word "arguably," then I gather they are recognizing, practically conceding, that there are probably other very good gardens around that could qualify as "best." By prequalifying their boast, they've prevented any argument from ensuing. I'm arguably in over my head, so I'm going to be moving on now.... ;)

--

Jesse in Sunnyvale, CA:
For those of you who deal with Marketing departments, how about this bit of nonsense:
"I'd like to proactively dialogue with you offline about our market-driven, quality strategy, and assign some relevant action items to the issues."
Does anyone else quake with fear to hear such utterances?

--

Verbing

Patrick in San Jose, CA:
PS a colleague recently told me that in order to get something done, we would have to "incentivize" the relevant person. Now *that's* an emetic word if ever there was one...

--

George in Virginia:
Computers will never be able to distinguish between the syntax of -
Time flies like an arrow
and
Fruit flies like an apple.
(I hope)

John of Keele, UK interjected:
No no no! The time/fruit flies saying is authentic Groucho Marx [again] [From the _Flywheel_ scripts? No time to check!]
And it goes: "Time flies like an arrow; fruit flies like a banana"
The apple was Isaac Newton, and that's Physics!

--

Sara in Boston responded to Mike on quotation marks: "double or single?":
The way I learned it, " is used for a direct quotation. ' is used for a quotation *within* a quotation, i.e. "So, I was talking to Myrna, and I says 'Hey, Myrna! Is that your face or did your neck throw up this morning?' and she says 'Hey, Norma! Sit on a flagpole and spin!' and

then we both did laundry."
Another interesting note; when something is written in narrative, I've noticed the closing quotation mark is dropped if the narrative continues after a paragraph break, but the opening quotation mark is repeated:
"So there we were, holding six baskets full of cherry tomatoes, and not knowing what to do with them.
"Later on, someone suggested eating them, and..."
Is this an American trait? Any thoughts?

Patrick in San Jose, CA remarked:
I'd always thought of this not as a closing quote being dropped, but as an opening quote being repeated.
(Is the glass half full or half empty? :-))
After all, normally you shouldn't have to close the quote and reopen it immediately afterwards. I assumed it was a device to remind the reader that the new paragraph she's reading is still quoted speech rather than a return to narrative.

Allan in Brandon, Manitoba quoted:
From The Economist Style Guide (1991)

In American publications (and those of major Commonwealth countries) the convention is to use double quotation marks, reserving single quotation marks for quotes within quotes. In British publications, the convention is the reverse (except in The Economist): single quotation marks are used first, then double. However, the American style is becoming more popular.

The relative position of quotation marks and other punctuation is far more contentious. The British convention is to place such punctuation according to sense. The American convention is simpler but less logical: all commas and full stops precede the final quotation mark (or, if there is a quote within a quote, the first final quotation mark).

Other punctuation - colons, semi-colons, question and exclamation marks - is placed according to sense.

--

Phil in Salt Lake City, UT was intrigued:
Hospital question: Why do people of British leaning say "George is in hospital" while Americans (from the US, at least) say "George is in _the_ hospital"? What do the Canadians say, Ken?

Elliot in Van Nuys, CA:
The discussion of Going to hospital vs. going to _the_ hospital, etc. reminds me I, and everybody I knew, always said graduated _from_ high school, so I always start when someone says they graduated high school.

--

Gerry in Ottawa answered a similar query:
Peter, you hear both "on holiday" and "on holidays" in Canada. I tend to use them indiscriminately myself, rather like "toward" and "towards." There may be a slight suggestion that the plural refers to something more extensive like a summer at the cottage but I can't say that I make a deliberate distinction. Sometimes one just sounds better than the other.

--

On a similar vein, Sara in Boston:
I heard "come with" used all the time in Illinois, which is definitely not southern US. I remember the first time I heard it, too; I had no idea what the person was saying. (Do I want to come with? HUH?)

Poems, quotations etc.

Leo shared:
Mike Ceccarelli, now of professor of something-or-other somewhere in Michigan, was formerly an interlocking operator at Metro-North's New Haven, Conn., run-through terminal. But it's so funny I thought

I would share it with you... at least, it's funny to me. Now *I* work there, only on the other side of the "aisle" on the Amtrak side.

The Day After Thursday
    'Twas the day after Thursday
    and all through the plant,
    employees were heard
    to grumble and rant.
    The trains were all inbound
    the switching began,
    while I did the routing
    and Curt lent a hand.
    The stationmaster was tucked
    in his trailer with care,
    while orders for switching
    came sharp through the air,
    From the east end of six,
    to the west end of three,
    then back to the east
    he broadcast with glee.
    Then cut three pair
    from the belly of four,
    and bring them up close
    to the shop's middle door.
    When down on track nine
    there arose such a clatter,
    that we sprang to the window
    to see what was the matter.
    And what to our wondering
    eyes should appear,
    but an itinerant drunk
    with a six pack of beer.
    While down on track four

some suits grew irate,
while the CDOT they were taking
departed from eight.
The locals were stoning
the trains with great glee
and piling each track
with mounds of debris.
While off in the station
a woman forlorn,
had learned that her Amtrak
and children were gone.
And who left his briefcase,
and who left her hat,
their coat or computer,
their this or their that.
Some folks in the tunnel
were harassed by a goon,
while information demanded
a flag from the moon.
The drunkard on ten
began a new show,
as the Amtrak protect crew
refused the signal to go.
And off on the branch
they ran half a crew,
and the trainmaster in training
wondered what he should do.
There's a wrench cut on four
and a cold car on three,
The outbound on six
has a door light, you see.
When the engines aren't ready
and the wire's gone dead.

it's really no wonder
that my voice fills with dread.
And I shook my head
cause you never can tell,
if the night is sublime
or straight out of hell.
But I heard form a deadhead
as he pulled out of sight
"At least keep it cheerful,
it's stupid people night."
--Mike Ceccarelli

--

Dean asserted:
"The older I get the better I was"
Corollary: "I'm not as good as I used to be, nor never was."

--

And Chris said:
... and hope is a letter that never arrives delivered by the postman of my fears . . .

To which Phil in Salta Lake City replied:
That is more positive than the expression it made me think of:
"We promise according to our hopes and perform according to our fears."

--

The origin of the term spam:
Stanton McCandlish shared a ditty with us:
I have firsthand experience of a likely alternate philology for the Internet-ly use of "spam".
Hearken back to the prime days of Monty Python (if you have good cable stations, you don't even have to hearken much, MP is still being syndicated.) One skit had a horde of Vikings invading a local greasy-spoon restaurant, whose menu consisted entirely of spam. The clerk/

cook/waitress begins a litany of the available menu items which runs something like (I don't >have a transcript so forgive the paraphrase), "We've got spam, spam and eggs, eggs and spam, spam eggs and spam, spam and spam, spam spam and eggs, spam spam eggs and spam, spam spam eggs and spam spam, spam spam spam and spam..." at which point the (thoroughly anachronistic and absurd – but this is Monty Python, so it is to be expected) vikings begin chanting, "SPAM SPAM SPAM SPAM, SPAM SPAM SPAM SPAM, SPAMMETTY SPAM SPAMDY SPAM SPAM SPAM SPAM..." over and over again. The effect of course is a complete drowning out of all dialog (especially that of the hapless and confused client) with "spam".

At least as early as early-to-mid 1993, and probably at least a year earlier, on MOOs, MUDs, MUSHes, MUCKs and other "text-based virtual realities" (collectively, M*s), the term was used to refer to the blather and gibberish that appears on one's screen when one's M* persona is "in" a "room" trying to read something or carry on a textual conversation (M*'s are real-time, like IRC) and another person "in" the "room" begins reiterating the same thing over and over again, in rapid succession (usually just to be obnoxious), so one cannot carry on the conversation except with extreme difficulty.

Without specialized client software (i.e., via plain telnet connection), each character's comments and emotes and actions scroll up the screen one line at a time. If many people are "talking" and doing things at once it is all but impossible to keep track of a thread of conversation, because it is drowned out by others' gibberish. If someone is deliberately abusing this fact of telnet life by throwing up garbage at a fast pace (usually with macro keys), your conversation is completely drowned out by the garbage, much like choruses and litanies of "spam": Incredibly annoying.

As far as I can tell this is the origin of the term. I tend to suspect it next spread to IRC and only after that to Usenet, but I could be wrong.

I've no idea if the term was first used in Usenet to apply to someone posting obnoxious messages to a single newsgroup, or maybe a few cross-posted groups, but tend to suspect this was the case. In fact I'll posit (but cannot at this point prove) that the Sirdar Argic "bot" was the catalyst. The Argic posts, I believe, appeared at first on only one or a limited number of semi-relevant soc.culture newsgroups, stayed there a while, then rapidly spread to other newsgroups when the perpetrators clued to the fact that as long as his/her identity was shielded, what we now call spamming was feasible. If this is the case, and if the term spam was first applied in Usenet to the early Argic posts, the term would have carried over, probably in follow-up (and cross-posted) flames against the Argic posts, which by the time of their heyday appeared to be auto-posted by software (a "bot"). NB: Argic was several month before Canter & Siegel. I'm not sure how it compares, age-wise, to "MAKE MONEY FAST". I'd guess MMF is older, but wasn't called spam until later. This is just a guess though.

That's a lot of ifs, but I think the clear analog of "SPAM SPAM SPAM SPAM" is at least fairly strong circumstantial evidence, even if the "migration point" to Usenet from M*s can't be pinpointed.

I'd be grateful if anyone can shed light on the missing pieces (or correct me if I'm astray here.) I don't say that just for the heck of it; I'm genuinely interested in tracking this bit of lost net history down, and archiving the results if we can ever put together anything serious on this. Blame the linguist in me, I guess.

      Stanton McCandlish -- Relayed by Mike of Brisbane

--

Jesse of Sunnyvale, CA mused:
Jim, what is a "meta" for any way if you can't mix it up?

And Alex in Adelaide noted:
Was it Will Rogers who's credited with the saying: "I never metaphor I didn't like"?

--

Mike in Brisbane:
You've reminded me that the phrase originated when an enormous animal was washed into the Thames estuary. No one knew what it was, and so it was handed over to the Worshipful Company of Sausage-makers, who proceeded to deal with it in a workmanlike fashion - or perhaps a workpersonlike fashion. The results fed the city of London for weeks. Great sausage sizzles were held in Hyde Park, and the air was fragrant with the smell of frying sausage. It was this event which prompted C. Dickens to write - "It was the Beast of Thames, It was the Wurst of Thames".

--

Phil in Salt Lake City shared:
For example, we have (at work) in one of our male/female (multipurpose?) restrooms, the following sign:
"Oh, kind gentlemen, please believe me
There is something that doth grieve me
When you find yourself hiding
behind the bathroom door.
"It appears, dear sirs, you must be dreaming
Because when it comes astreaming
You are leaving your deposit on
the seat and on the floor.
"Therefore I do humbly beseech you
That when the urge doth greet you
that you focus your attention to
the commode and no place more."

--

Lauren in Raleigh, NC followed up with:
"If you sprinkle when you tinkle,
Please be neat and wipe the seat."

--

Katherne in Oakland, CA:
I remember seeing a book (circa 1970), "Jail Keys Made Here". All photographs of signs of that sort, I think, and lots of fun.

--

Bill in Columbia, CT shared few funnies:
I just finished reading some words of wisdom in Funny Times from our political elite. I thought it would be most circumspect to bring some of this politicalese into the realm of cyberspace.

Bill Clinton, "I believe that this country's policies should be heavily biased in the favour of non-discrimination."
Bill Clinton, "If we don't make some changes, the status quo will remain the same."
Dan Quayle, "I support efforts to limit the terms of Congress, especially members of the House and members of the Senate."
Janet Reno, "I always wait until a jury has spoken before I anticipate what they will do."
George Romney, "I didn't say that I didn't say it. I said that I didn't say that I said it. I want to make that very clear."
Martin Fitzwater, "The highly fortified chemical weapons are dangerous and becoming more s
Marion Barry, "Outside of the killings, we have one of the lowest crime rates in the nation."
Barbara Boxer, "Those who survived said, Thank God I'm still alive' But, of course, those who died, their lives will never be the same."

--

Alan passed on this short poem:
The Naughty Preposition
> I lately lost a preposition;
> It hid, I thought, beneath my chair.
> And angrily I cried: "Perdition!
> Up from out of in under there!"
> Correctness is my vade mecum,

And straggling phrases I abhor;
And yet I wondered: "What should he come
Up from out of in under for?"
 -- Morris Bishop

--

Bill in Lexington, KY responded to John on "Beecham's Pills:
Hark, the herald angels sing,
Beecham's pills are just the thing.
Two for adult and one for child,
They are really very mild.
They will make you feel all right,
Keep you running through the night,
Hark, the herald angels sing,
Beecham's pills are just the thing.
Learned from my mother, long ago.

--

Jeff in San Diego, quoted the following poem:
How he clothes his family
They tell me you work for a dollar a day;
How is it you clothe your six boys on such pay?
I know you will think it conceited and queer,
But I do it because I'm a good financier.
There's Pete, John, Jim, and Joe, and William and Ned.
A half dozen boys to be clothed up and fed.
And I buy for them all good plain victuals to eat;
But clothing - I only buy clothing for Pete.
When Pete's clothes are too small for him to get on,
My wife makes 'em over and gives 'em to John.
When for John, who is ten, they have grown out of date,
She makes 'em over for Jim, who is eight.
When for Jim they've become too ragged to fix,
She just makes 'em over for Joe, who is six.
And when little Joseph can wear 'em no more,

She just makes 'em over for Bill, who is four.
And when for young Bill they no longer will do,
She just make 'em over for Ned, who is two.
So you see if I get enough clothing for Pete,
The family is furnished with clothing complete.
But when Ned has got through with the clothing, and when
He has thrown it aside - what do you do with it then?
Why, once more we go round the circle complete,
And begin to use it for patches for Pete!
   (Sam W. Foss, circa 1902)
--

Richard in Berkeley said <<When I was a lot younger -- about 45 years ago -- I had a book of jokes that contained, among other things, a set of "Little Willy" rhymes.>>

And Bob in Chicago responded:
I dunno, Rich, I think I liked the "Little Dicky" rhymes better :)
   "Fall frost is on our pumpkin,
   Ain't no time for Dicky dunkin'...
   When the weather's hot and sticky,
   Thaaat's the time for dunkin' Dicky".
--

Barb in Stephenville, TX:
I saw this on a sig line from someone from Australia:
   I come from the land down under
   Where women glow and men chunder.
   What the heck do men do when they *chunder*???

Jane in Hobart answered:
The word "chunder" is an Australian euphemism for the action of vomiting. The sig that you read didn't have the lines of the Men at Work song quite right. It should read;
   I come from a land down under
   Where beer does flow and men chunder

THE POWER OF WORDS ~ 167

I would prefer to think that it is beer which causes men to chunder than the sight of women glowing.....:)

Bruce in Sydney picked up on the exchange:
Hopefully they go straight off and clean their teeth!
Actually Barbara, they do exactly what women do in the same circumstances. Although in the 'Horses sweat, men perspire, women merely glow;' vein, one might say that 'Men chunder, women merely suffer transient reverse peristalsis'.
You know, like that Reagan kid in "The Exorcist".

The derivation of the term is contentious but I buy the explanation that as an act of decency when about to unload from the upper decking of a ship or higher floors of a building, it was the call one made to warn those below. "WatCH UNDER"

Gerry in Ottawa also had a take on the subject:
To expand a bit on "chunder," it's said to derive from the expression "watch under," meaning "look out below." Rather like "gardyloo" in Scotland. I believe it had some early currency among schoolboys but it didn't really take hold until it was popularized by the comedian Barry Humphries (aka Dame Edna Everage, Sir Les Patterson and others). Humphries has a lot to answer for in that he's almost single-handedly managed to add an entire artificial vocabulary to Australian slang, including terms like "technicolour yawn: for "vomit" and "pointing Percy at the porcelain" for "urinate." Not to mention "trouser snake" for "penis." I guess they're all clever enough in their way but I can't help but feel that the old traditional ng was picturesque enough as it stood. I know, language should be free to develop, but surely not on the basis of one man's comic turns. So there.

--

Phil in Salt Lake City relayed this nugget:
"Never attribute to malice that which can adequately be explained by ignorance."—Hanlon's razor

Katherine in Oakland, CA followed up:
Lazarus Long, via Robert Heinlein: "Never attribute to malice what can be adequately explained by stupidity." I knew people who used that for their yearbook quote in high school. (No, I used a different LL-ism: "Yield to temptation; it may not pass your way again.")

--

Laurie remembered a joke:
A mohel (ritual Jewish circumcisor for those of you who missed this thread) met a friend and was showing off his new wallet. The friend commented on the fine quality and unusual texture, asking what it was made of. The mohel indicated it was manufactured of years' worth of scraps from his trade. The friend noted that this was an awfully small result, so the mohel remarked that if you rubbed the wallet, it would become luggage.

--

Janet in Calgary reminisced:
One of the highlights of my high school career was correcting my English teacher when he used the phrase "gilding the lily". I idly corrected him, which stopped him dead in his tracks, and he finally sent me off to the school library to borrow a copy of Bartlett's Quotations to prove it. He was tickled pink - he was that kind of teacher. BTW, the quote is : "To gild refined gold, to paint the lily,/ To throw a perfume on the violet,/ To smooth the ice, or add another hue/ Unto the rainbow, or with taper-light/ To seek the beauteous eye of heaven to garnish/Is wasteful and ridiculous excess.

--

Gerry in Ottawa responded to a query on the Songs of the Civil War:
"All Quiet Along the Potomac;" "Aura Lee;" "Battle Cry of Freedom;" "Battle Hymn of the Republic;" "Bonnie Blue Flag;" "Goober Peas;" "Grafted Into the Army;" "I'm a Good Old Rebel;" "The Invalid Corps;" "Just Before the Battle, Mother;" "Kingdom Coming;" "Life on the

Vicksburg Bluff;" "Marching Along;" "Marching Through Georgia;" "Maryland, My Maryland;" "Mister, Here's Your Mule;" "Sherman Will March To the Sea;" "Stonewall Jackson's Way;" "Take Your Gun and Go, John;" "Tenting Tonight on the Old Camp Ground;" "The Vacant Chair;" "We Are Coming, Father Abraham;" "Weeping Sad and Lonely;" "When Johnny Comes Marching Home" and "Who Will Care for Mother Now?"

"Aura Lee," of course, which probably came second only to "Lorena" in the hearts of homesick soldiers on both sides, was later changed by Elvis Presley into "Love Me Tender," a piece of cultural savagery which us purists still find hard to forgive.

--

A question for the ages: What happens to the doughnut hole after the doughnut is consumed?

Tyson said:
As you ramble on through life,
Whatever be your goal,
Keep your eye upon the doughnut,
and not upon the hole.

Mark said: Obviously, it becomes holier than thou ...

James said: The hole turns into guilt which makes you take the stairs instead of the elevator next time.

Jim said: When one eats the donut, one frees the hole to become more than just a hole!

Maurizio said: The hole of the doughnut can't be swallowed. When you open your mouth, it will fly away.

Bruce said: Doughnut holes are collected in the upper atmosphere and are dumped over various parts of the world in the form of hail. (Smaller hail is usually the result of eating bagels or cheerios.)

Henry said: When you eat the doughnut, "not-you" eats the hole.

John said: It stays floating right in front of the mouth for several hours which explains why people who have too many doughnuts during meeting can be hard to understand.

It goes to the hall of lost socks and communes with laps of standing folk.

The hole contains all of the calories of a doughnut. As long as you only eat the doughnut, the hole (along with the calories) disappears into THIN air!!

Most doughnuts are consumed on Monday mornings as a means of overcoming the stressful transition from Weekend to Weekday. As they are eaten, the holes fall to the floor and pile up. (The holes are why doughnuts are not normally allowed in computer rooms, not the sugar on the doughnuts.)

Doughnut holes clinging to the legs of workers are the cause of the "dragging" appearance commonly referred to as "Monday Morning Blues" (MMB).

Owen said:
As the day wears on, air conditioning units (or the wind if eaten outdoors) carry the holes away. (On most days, AC units can handle the volume of holes so that the level does not create MMB.) Movement through the air cause them to inflate and float away to be caught in the OZONE layer of the atmosphere. THAT is the real cause of the

OZONE depletion, and for that reason, I try to sacrifice and ALWAYS EAT JELLY-FILLED.

Lezanne said: The hole liquifies and becomes the sticky stuff that's left on your hands after you've eaten the doughnut.

Chet said: The hole goes to my wallet!

Steve said: They are recycled of course! Ever notice that your company usually seems to have a shortage of doughnuts on Monday mornings? By the time you get there, the doughnuts are almost all gone? Thats because your company, like all companies, is on allocation for doughnut holes. There are only so many in the world. When they are all in use, then doughnut makers have to resort to making jelly filled doughnuts.

Malcolm said: The answer is simple - it becomes wind.

The hole remains and returns to haunt genteel people in the form of a burp.

Fred said: It goes to 'sock heaven'. You know, that's the place where the mate to your one sock that comes from the washer has gone. The donut holes go there, also, so that if any one, unmated, sock ever happens to find its way back it arrives in your sock drawer with a hole in it!

Rob said: It disappears faster than our fleeting youth.

Philippe said: Thanks to its calories, the hole hides your voidness.

Teddi said: The hole is there, we know it is, but you can't see it, you can't feel it. You cannot prove its existence, and yet by its very existence it defines and shapes the doughnut. Therefore, I believe the hole is the soul of a doughnut. When you eat a doughnut, you have fulfilled its reason for existing, and you set free its immortal soul -- the hole. Woe to those half-eaten doughnuts whose souls are doomed to purgatory, and those stale, unbitten doughnuts whose immortal lives will continue in doughnut hell!

Angela said: Why, I flavor my coffee with mine -- and you? Tastes great, less filling --

It all depends on how you eat the donut. If eaten from front to back then the hole is eaten as well and turns to "bad" gas in the intestine and is ultimately "passed on." If you eat the donut around the hole, then you can throw away the hole and eliminate the possibility of discomfort later (this also makes the donut taste better).

Tim said: I always eat it, too--for dessert.

Mahaney said: As you take the last bite of doughnut, the hole falls onto your desk, table, whatever . . . . and that's where all the pencils, pens, notes, paper clips and other miscellanea drop through and disappear forever. (If you've ever eaten doughnuts in the laundry room, now you know where the missing socks are!) .

My boss uses them to hold his ears apart.

Shari said: A sly elf once told me the secret to donut holes. Since then I always make sure I eat them along with the donut. When consumed, the airy, tasteless portion of a delicious, fat-filled donut collects all the nasty, unhealthy ingredients and makes sure they make a hasty exit. The hole does not allow anything bad to stay around long enough to leave any permanent damage.

Ragnar said: The hole becomes exclusively a part of your imagination, which is good because it rids the poor hole of its doubtful real existence and defines it more properly as an imaginary product.

Stan said: Not being attached to anything anymore the hole is now free, and floats upwards to eventually reach the "hole-zone" layer ... this is where all doughnut holes congregate and is the reason why eating too many doughnuts is not healthy for us.

Doughnut holes contain all the calories - so, never eat the hole!

Connie said: Doughnut hole calories, however, being invisible, float about secretly mixed with air molecules - and attach themselves to hips and bellies while you sleep. Hint: don't eat doughnuts in bed!

Janetze said: Think back to where you last saw it and there it is! Open up and there is a hole right between your lips.

Lori said: The hole is an absence of doughnut and a presence of Space. When you take a bite, you increase doughnut-absence and Space-presence. When you're finished, the hole has taken over -- the doughnut, in its original form, is completely absent, and Space is completely present (save for a few pesky air molecules and some random crumbs). The hole and Space are one. What you have done is increase entropy, or disorder -- the Second Law of Thermodynamics wins again. That's why I don't bother trying to keep my desk in order.

Rhonda said: The donut hole didn't go anywhere because it was never really there. ...

Langdon said: When you eat a donut, the hole transcends into the pastry energy realm and, assuming it learned enough about life when it was in the donut, is reincarnated into a new donut (or maybe a bagel).

Mark said: They are gathered-up and recycled by doughnut shops for use in new doughnuts.

Gene said: I thought everyone knew what happens to doughnut holes. They are lighter than air, thus float away after the doughnut is gone. In fact, due to their negative polarity they tend to gather over the South Pole. And in fact, what is seen by scientific instruments as a hole in the ozone layer is nothing more than massive amounts of doughnut holes displacing the ozone. It makes sense! We never heard squat about the ozone layer until the late '60's, when we were inundated with doughnut shops. Mr. Doughnut, Doughnuts-R-Us, Doughnut Delight, Krispy Kream, Dunkin' Doughnuts....and on and on. They're all at fault! Un-holey doughnuts are o.k., but the ones with holes are a real problem.   I say we begin a national orginization to fight this hideous problem.
Sorry to carry on so, but it's time everyone knew the truth about
    doughnut holes. ...

James said: And I wonder where the numbers go when you turn off your calculator.

But then that's a whole 'nuther question.
    --
Court in Wayn, IN shared this ditty:
From a 1951 - South Dakota Peace Officers - magazine. **The Morning After**
< Wife Speaking >:

> Good morning, my bright international mate,
> My outstanding genius in problems of state,

I trust all is clear in the wonderful mind,
Which last night remodeled the whole of mankind.
Your handling of Russia, The Ruhr, Palestine,
And China and Greece; it was masterly fine!
You're sure to be named as "The man of the year."
Here's four or five aspirins -- swallow them dear.
Awake my fine songster! It's well on toward noon,
All morning I've waited, just hoping you'd croon.
A measure from "Chloe" or "Deep Rolling Sea"
Which last night you sang till half past three.
You awakened the neighbors, you tripped on the mat,
And one of your props was your hostess's hat.
I'm sure she will want you again for tonight --
The life of the party whenever you're tight.
Arise, sweet Prince, but be careful, don't skid
Arise and consider the things that you did.
The uprooted garden, the splintered garage;
It sounded just like an old-fashioned barrage.
Go see your hostess -- and carry a check,
I think if you sign just "Pain in the Neck"
The bank will o.k. it -- it would have to be you --
The clown that went beserk "twix dawn and the dew."
So drink up the seltzer, you chattering drone,
It's said to be good for the splitting dome.
I wish I were Sandow; how far would I through you,
For the next thirty days, please pretend I don't know you.
My Juvenile Jackass, my dim-witted duffer,
You say you feel awful? Well, damnit, then suffer.

--

Bruce in Sydner NSW had ditty to share:
From the New South Wales State parliament comes this wee gem. The speaker was an opposition member who rose with this point of order when the Premier strayed from his subject.

"Mr Speaker, the Premier's answer is based on the premise that if you don't know the answer to the question, answer another one. Not only is the answer full of blether but it is well punctuated with calumny of a type totally unbecoming of this House. It is not even a good example of the casuistry of which the minister is sometimes capable. It is achromatic drivel lacking acuity and clearly indicates the minister's present cataonic state. It is also both contumacious and prolix and I ask you to rule accordingly and, with respect, to excoriate the minister forthwith".
Surprise surprise the Speaker declined.

--

Jeff in Sandiego quoted from Knight-Ridder Newspapers By Emily Hancock:
...The strange thing about "Auld Lang Syne" is that hardly anyone -from the most musically educated to the most musically illiterate - knows what the song means or why singing it has become practically mandatory for New Year's Eve celebrants...
...Like most of those interviewed, [Dick] Clark, who prides himself on being a master of music trivia, said he did not know what the ballad meant or why people sing it annually.
...For the official word on the song's meaning and origin, inquiries were made at Hal Leonard Corp., the Milwaukee-based company that publishes "Auld Lang Syne" sheet music. Hal Leonard's president provided some answers. "I don't think people stop to think about what it actually means," said Keith Mardek.
...Mardek offered some insights that explain the song's origins and rise to popularity:
In 1798, Scottish poet Robert Burns adapted the "Auld Lang Syne" lyrics to a Scottish melody that was first published in 1711. But music experts are still at odds over the melody's age, where it came from, and who really wrote the lyrics.

It was band leader Guy Lombardo, however, not burns, whom we have to thank for making the song a traditional New Year's Eve ballad, Mardek said.

The tradition of singing "Auld Lang Syne" on New Year's Eve started in 1929 when Lombardo and His Royal Canadians played their first gig at the Grill Room in New York's Roosevelt Hotel. The show was broadcast over the radio. From that point, the tune not only became Lombardo's theme song, but also the traditional song for heralding the arrival of the New Year, according to Mardek.

So what do the words "auld lang syne" mean in English?

According to the Oxford English Dictionary and Hal Leonard Corp., "auld" means "old," "lang" means "long," and "syne" means "since."

That means Americans sing "Old Long Since" every year. Doesn't make sense literally, but the phrase "auld lang syne" is generally taken to mean "days gone by," Mardek said.

Put that phrase in the context of the song and you've got a ballad that resonates with the emotions of New Year's Eve celebrants, even if they don't know exactly what they're singing..."

--

Ten rules for aspiring poets (courtesy of Brian Bilston - Facebook)

1. Poetry does not have to rhyme. Well, at least not always.
2. Metaphors can lend a poem power (although mixing them isn't good). Should they start to fly in all directions, nip them in the bud.
3. Focus and concentration are important skills to hone. Close the door. Turn off the Wi-Fi. Don't get distracted by your phone.
4. Avoid clichés like the plague.
5. Don't write stuff that's a bit vague.
6. The use of unnecessarily long words may result in reader alienation. Curb your sesquipedalianism. Obviate all obfuscation.

7. Always proof-read you're work. Accuracy can be it's own reward! And remember that the penis mightier than the sword.
8. Check haiku closely for lines which have too few or too many syllables.
9. Never ever follow rules.

David in Ritner, KY quoted:
Some of um is black on the outside,
and some of um is white on the outside,
and some of um is yaller on the outside,
and some of um is brown on the outside;
but they is all red on the inside.
    -Shitting Bull, Rainbow Tribe

--

Jim in Philadelphia experimented with AI:
I asked ChatGPT to rewrite "Green Eggs and Ham" in the style of Shakespeare. I think it turned out pretty good.

> Oh, dearest friend, I must protest,
> For I have found myself quite distressed,
> By these curious eggs of green,
> Which in my sight have oft been seen.
> I dare not try them, I must say,
> For fear that they will cause dismay,
> And leave me in a state most foul,
> With illness and a fevered scowl.
> But nay, my friend, he will not rest,
> He implores me to put them to the test,
> To try them here and there and then,
> To eat them in a box or den.
> Oh, what to do, my troubled mind,

This friend of mine, he can be quite unkind,
Yet still he pleads with all his might,
For me to take a little bite.
And so I think, perhaps I might,
Try these green eggs, despite my fright,
And see what pleasure they might bring,
When eaten with a joyful ring.
And lo and behold, to my surprise,
These eggs of green, they do not despise,
For they are truly quite delicious,
And leave my palate feeling most auspicious.
So let us raise a cup of cheer,
To these green eggs, so full of cheer,
For they have proven themselves divine,
And brought me joy in every line.

6

Pronunciation

Sara in Boston was curious:
Is there a word for botching pronunciation of words you've only seen written? I have a friend who's extremely well read, but he does this all the time, because he's never heard most of the words used in conversation. For example:
"Veh-mince" for vehemence
"Bed-raggled" for bedraggled
"Ahw-ree" for awry

Jeff in Edinburgh related:
I remember one of my swatty (swotty?) classmates at school, coming across "chaos" while reading out load, pronounced it as "chowce" we all ROFL... etc

Katherine in Oakland was reminded:
oh, about mispronounced words--"col-o-nel", of course! (First grade, reading "Johnny Tremain", I'm pretty sure.)

Andy in Chichester, UK:
On words mispronounced, one of the classics has to be hyperbole. It is not the venue for an American football final (credit to Andrew Moncur and the *Guardian*)

--

Haney in Howell, NC recounted:
My mother taught English and Latin in mountain schools for 40 years. She gave her children a real appreciation for the language and carefully pointed out the differences between what we heard and what was "acceptable". When I was a young radio announcer in high school, mother would post all the words I'd blown on the air on the refrigerator door for me to see when I returned home.

However, my high school English and Latin teacher (yes, we had four years of Latin at my school of 200+ children) treasured the mountain language. She searched for the Anglo-Saxon roots, and explained how many of the expressions came about.

In the North Georgia/East Tennessee/North Carolina mountain region, people will still ask you to "carry them to the store". "There" and "chair" rhyme with "spar". A translation tip. Few local folks bother to pronounce the "ed's" and "ing's" on the end of words. Too much work!

The folks came to this country, made it into the mountains, and preserved their unique usages and pronunciations. Television and radio have neutralized some of this, but you can still find folks who speak this way.
Want a big dose? Go to a NASCAR Stock Car race.

--

Pat in Collegeville, MN:
Thanks to Jeff in San Diego for the pellucid explanation of what Golytely is and does. Having gone through the ordeal once, it's fascinating to know just why what was happening did. Your classmate's pronouncing it go- lee-telly, Jeff, reminds me of a student's talking about the Hittites in one of my classes (can't remember why in God's name they would have come up), and calling them several times the High-titties.

Pat continued:
Terrence in Bermuda notes that the switching of letters within a word is metathesis, giving aks for ask as an example. I've noticed that the

transposition of s and p is not uncommon--graps for grasp, raps, crips, lips for lisp.

My sister, when but a tot, regularly transposed m and n in alunimum, crinimal, pernament.

--

Patrick in San Jose, CA:
Allow me to disagree politely with the implication that native-born Americans somehow automatically don't have English pronunciation problems!

And finally, may I humbly point out that there are *some* people who are not native-born Americans but who, nonetheless, miraculously manage to speak English as a mother tongue? Incredible, I know, but true...

--

Michael in Mesa, AZ on mispronunciation:
I've heard "breffix" for "breakfast" from a friend as a kid, and from my niece: "yesternight" and "last day."

--

Someone enquired: <<Where does the whole "boyd" for "bird," "goyl" for "girl" thing come from? I've noticed it also works in reverse: "terlet" for "toilet," "pernt" for > "point.">>:

And Katherine answered: That's a Brooklyn accent!

Zeno added: And the even more famous "Did you pahk yah cah in Hahvahd Yahd?"

--

Lee in Sacramento, CA:
Mispronouncing words you've only read brings back anew my embarrassment when, in high school, I read something aloud in class which included the word -clandestine-. I knew what it meant, but had never heard it, and pronounced it -clan-des-tine, rather than clan-DES'-tine. Needless to say, no one being crueller than kids, I got royally laughed at. My face still burns when I think of it.

--

Bill in Lexington, KY:
Our son is hearing impaired, but is quite bright and an avid reader. He has a large vocabulary, but many of the words he has never heard. He's now 27 years old and we still have to correct his pronunciations often. Even after correction he still pronounces "legislature" with the wrong "g" sound (leg is lay chur).

--

Sara in Boston on pronunciation:
Has anyone heard the bit called "Thirty Dirty Birds?" Unfortunately, I can't remember the name of the band that does it, but it goes like this:
   Thoity doity boids, sittin' on the coib
   Choipin' an' boipin' an' eatin' doity oithwoims
   Along comes Hoib, sees the thoity doity boids, sittin' on the coib
   Choipin' an' boipin' an' eatin' doity oithwoims
Man, was he distoibed!
Say it with a thick New York accent and it makes sense...
I'm off like a prom dress (oh, my apologies, Mr. Exon!!)

--

Toni in Minnesota:
Am I wrong to cringe every time I hear someone say pre-FER-able or com-PARE-able?

--

Jim in Philadelphia observed:
Matt was ROFL over VISUALISE WHIRLED PEAS. Say it out loud. Visualise World Peace. Too much sax and violins for my taste...

--

Patrick in Collegeville, MN responded to Patrick in Sacramento who asked about pronouncing harem:
ha-REEM. I remember the pronunciation from technicolour Baghdadi epics of the '40s and '50s about the likes of Haroun al Rashid and Ali Baba. Such as evil viziers and scruffy low-grade villains would say, with hideous leers, "Thou shalt never see her more; she languishes in

the hah-REEM!" In real-life American English, I've never heard anything but HAIR'm.

--

Marilyn in San Francisco asked:
My husband wants me to ask the group "When did harASSment become HARassment?" Newsreaders are constantly using the latter. Are they afraid to say "ass"?

Katherine in Oakland answered:
My tenth-grade English teacher claimed that "HARassment" was in fact the older and more correct pronunciation. (I'm not sure we believed her.)

Bill in Columbia, CT weighed in:
I'm a tenth-grade English teacher, and I teach HARassment as opposed to harASSment because the reverberation of "ASS" tends to adulterate the discussion to those with a sensitive ear. Some people are sloppy in their pronunciation and bring in images of male chauvinism when one can only hear "Her Ass." It's no big deal, but my tenth-graders tend to think this word is fun to use because they hide behind the multiple meanings inherent in the pronunciation. Immaturity? Hypersensitivity? *Sophomore (*the wise moron) - *this is no put down of my students because they are great. I thought I would simply interject the meaning of "sopho" and "more" since wordplay is the name of the game.

--

John in Keele, UK answered a query from Guy who asked about the phonetics of English 'wh' sounds:
Since I am not by profession a phoneticist, nor an historical phonologist, and haven't studied English Language since I left school, I am uniquely unqualified to reply; but somewhere at the back of my brain is the recollection that this sound was actually _spelled_ 'hw' in Anglo-Saxon times, and it seems to me that it is still pronounced that way in modern English "who" though with virtual disappearance of the 'w'. The 'w' sound is at least potentially a semi-vowel, which may account

for the effect Guy describes, though I don't get all the "ia" stuff. "Aspiration" is the right term for an 'h' in most contexts; some languages indicate an _initial_ aspirate [which is what we're on, right?] without an actual LETTER 'h': in Greek it's called a "rough breathing" and is indicated by a back apostrophe: `

I detect no difference in pronunciation between "which" and "witch" or between "what" and "Watt". Collins German Dictionary [don't ask!] boldly states that "whimper" and "whip" are just pronounced with initial 'w'; what looks like an aspirate sign in the pronunciation guide for those words just indicates that the STRESS is on the first part of the word. But *I* think that you can hear the 'h', at least when "whip" or "whimper" is spoken emphatically [no, not _now_, Lisa...]

Oh, and for the record, Collins shows the sound of "who" as starting with an 'h', and having no 'w' at all, which is approximately what I said above. I also think that when native speakers of English are trying to emphasise which word they are saying of the homophones what/Watt or which/witch, they PUT IN an aspirate sound for clarification. And they do it in the Anglo-Saxon manner: "Hwitch?"

Alot of this is just to do with how individual speakers of English in various parts of the world hear each other talk, so the problem is [with all respect to Guy] not so much a question of how to transcribe the sounds, but what folks actually say.

Katherine in Oakland rebutted:
Most people don't pronounce them differently, I think. I've tried to do so ever since listening to a friend who does--it sounds good! (English isn't her first language, and that may have something to do with it—the aspiration is _always_ clear in her speech.) I'm also reminded of the passage in "The Story of the Trapp Family Singers" (yes, that, not "The Sound of Music", is the title of the book) where Maria is practicing English on the boat to America, and a nice lady takes her aside

and tells her that she should say "Hoo-wat", "Hoo-ware", etc. instead of Vat and Vere...

And David in Glendale, CA weighed in:
My early training (note, not "education") _did_ make a distinct difference in pronunciation to follow the difference in spelling between words like "which" and "witch", "whale" and "wail", "where" and "were[wolf]."
I've noticed that people understand what one is saying better when they don't have to step back and consider the context to decide which of these pairs is being used.
Certainly, a whole bunch of spellcheck- proof mis-spellings would be avoided if the traditional "hw" were used, at least mentally.

About the "w" not being used as a vowel because it's only a lip-shaper... aren't all vowels determined not only by the amount the jaws are separated and the posture of the tongue but _also_ the position of the lips? If you don't believe (more True Faith!), look in a mirror and see the difference between "oo" and "ee" (as in "boo" and "be").
Also check the difference in tongue posture between the w and the e of "we"...

John in Keele, UK observed:
Dave commented on mouth shape in pronunciation: I certainly agree that you can detect some speech mechanisms that way [with a mirror or introspection] which escape dictionary-makers trying to explain English to Germans [somewhere I have a copy of Daniel Jones, but it hasn't surfaced yet...].
I've a feeling that the 'w' in my pronunciation of the word "who" is entirely a matter of lip-curl, and probably makes no difference to the sound I produce.
What's more, you can go a long time trying to pronounce sounds in certain foreign languages _without_ conspicuous success unless you know the secret; for instance: the retroflex 'r' in Chinese [sometimes also transcribed as a 'j' sound!] is impossible to even get close to unless

you know to curl your tongue back.
As I nearly said on the glottal stop thread: it's unlikely that any Cockney actually makes a clicking sound [!] as his/her glottal stop, and certainly not in the glottis, always excepting badly slipped teeth... So I used [|]. The idea is to transcribe the actual sound produced.

Pat in Collegeville, MN had a take as well:
On the hwich /witch thread: in my dialect (Hoosier? Puke? Gopher?) which is definitely pronounced hwich, whale /hwale, what /hwat. But who is hoo, whole is hole. Don't know why. TV and visits to England tell me that the the Queen's English (a whomped /hwomped -up dialect that changes faster and unsystemicaller than the "natural" speech of the natives) doesn't pronounce the h in wh- beginning words. So the Prince of Wales and the Prince of Whales are the same, whatever the Welsh may think--although it fits, because, if memory serves, the whale is a kinges fishe, as the swan is the kinges brid, and maybe Liz has delegated dominion over Leviathan to Chuckers.

--

Lee in Sacramento, CA:
John--I'm sure that glottal stop stopped in NYC, Brooklyn & Bronx particularly, & then hied itself over the Hudson River into NJ. Bottle is pronounced bo'le, butter is bu'er, the name Martin becomes Mar'in. Very unattractive sounding.

--

Brian in London responded to Pat who asked if Celts is pronounced Selt or Kelt?:
Always kelt, I thought, except that (Glasgow) Celtic (Football Club) is pronounced seltic.
FYI - "Celtic" should be pronounced Keltic as opposed to Seltic. A large part of the reason for this common mispronunciation is the basketball team here in Boston, which is pronounced Seltics. Oh well.

And Allan in Sydney, NS objected:
Why? Regardless of the origin of the word, the Random House and Oxford Dictionaries list both pronunciation forms as correct. The

Oxford Companion to the English Language notes that the word was formerly pronounced mainly with a soft 'c', and now currently mainly with a hard one. However, in these (Western Canadian) parts of the world, on the relatively rare occasions that the word is used, in my experience it is almost always with a soft 'c'.

Pronounce it whatever way you prefer, and accept the fact that it is a word with two different correct pronunciations just like 'shedule' and 'skedule' for 'schedule'.

Sara in Boston has a different take:

Three cheers for the Celtic religion finally gaining some ground – it took people (in general) an awfully long time to realize that it's a true nature-based religion; the holidays are related to the turning of the seasons, and quite a bit of it was adopted by other cultures and changed around a bit. The Celtic New Year, Samhain, is November 1. The ending of the old year falls on October 31 - this should sound familiar to those of you who celebrate Halloween (All Hallow's Eve), a night of ghosts and dead and witches.

--

Bob in Chicago:

If anyone goes to Minnesota to visit Pat, they will notice that Minnesota has a lot of places named for the saints similar to those in California. There is St. Paul, of course, but there is also a St. Peter, St. Anthony, St. Charles, and St. Clair, etcetera, all the way down through the litany and including some saints that you may not even have heard of like St. Bonifacius, St. Hilaire or St. Rosa.

The one that made me take a closer look was St. Cloud. I couldn't figure out who St. Cloud was until it dawned on me that "Cloud" is the American English pronunciation of the French name "Claude" or in English "Claud".

--

Mike in Brisbane:

Listening to a radio quiz last night – my wife is just back from having a colonoscopy (all OK) - and the radio announcer asked "what is episcopacy" she pronounced it accented in the same way as endoscopy, colonoscopy etc. - and, my mind being on such things, I tried to find a medical answer. The contestants were floored. Imagine my surprise when the answer was "government by the prelates of the church". Yeah, right.... Her pronunciation threw me completely. Anyone think of any other examples like this?

And Pat in Collegeville reacted:
Mike dumps epiSCOpacy on me. A monster, Mike. The -scop- is the same as in proctoscopy and colonoscopy (I chose those two as particularly appropriate to the subject), from skopein, to look (epi- means over, so the literal translation of episcopos / bishop is overseer). But they are 20th-cent. medical jargon, whereas episcopacy was Latined and then Englished a long time ago (I'm too lazy to consult the NED). It's ePIscopacy.

I suspect the perpetrator of the bizarre pronunciation was impelled by the tendency of the English accent to move rearward at least to the antepenult (e.g., LAMentable becomes laMENtable, irREParable become irrePARable). The final result of this shift will probably be the accent of all more-than-one-syllable words on the penult (e.g., INfluence becomes inFLUence, AFfluent becomes afFLUent, DeTROIT becomes DEtroit, poLICE becomes POlice).

--

Bob in Chicago:
I'll never forget the first time I read the word Chihuahua out loud. I was about 12 years old and I was reading an item from the newspaper to my father. I came to the word Chihuahua and pronounced it "Chi-who-ah-who-ah". My father couldn't help laughing and I was very embarrassed. The same thing happened with my first pronunciation of the word "psuedo" which I pronounced "swaydo". I'm not embarrassed to talk about it at all now and have much empathy for people who are trying to learn a language, any language...including their own :)

--

Jane in Hobart responded to Richard who asked 'So how do you pronounce "emu"?':

This reminded me of when I was living in the United States and a friend of mine asked me about 'that bird called the 'eee-moo'. This struck a particularly funny chord with me having never heard the word pronounced other than by the Australian way of 'eeem-ew'. My friend was rather put out by my tears of laughter. But I guess it made up for all of those guffaws I was subjected to in the U.S. when I mentioned 'chewna' rather than 'toona-fish'...

BTW, I don't think emus bury their heads (do ostriches _really_ do that?). I do know that they will chase humans if they so much as think that you are being rude to them (I still have nightmares from a childhood visit to a wildlife park!)

And Bob in Chicago:

So, do you also say "chewn", as in "You Can Tune a Piano But You Can't Tuna Fish"?

To which Jane in Hobart said:

Yep, that dolphin-friendly stuff that comes in a can we call 'ch-yew-na'. (To add to the confusion, it's also what we would call the person sitting at the piano, fiddling with it's hammers and strings. "Who's the bloke on the piano?" "Oh, he's the ch-yew-na (tuner).") The piles of sand in the desert or at the beach are 'd-yew-nes' (dunes) and the moisture on the grass in the morning is 'd-yew' (dew). There's no 'u' in dew but I thought I'd throw that one in anyway because, if I remember correctly, North Americans would say 'd-oo'.

Ann in Davis, CA weighed in:

Jane said they in Oz pronounce dune "dyune" and "emu" "eem-yew" (I may not be spelling these pronunciations as they did) and I thought you (-all) might be interested in the fact that when I was a kid, in Arkansas in the '40s, we pronounced our name (Stewart) "Styoo-urt". (I pronounce it "Stoo-urt" now (been in California for 30 years)). My grandmother, a refined upper-middle-class sort, used to answer the phone saying "This miz Styoo-urt". We also said "nyews". Is there a

term for this yewing?
Also, I pronounce "emu" "ee-myew", not "eem-yew". Do you really put the m on the first syllable?

--

From Susi contended:
Rumor has it that in a few hundred years, those that speak and understand U.S. English will not be able to understand British English. I heard on Nova last year that in 60 yrs., people in Baltimore won't be able to understand people in NYC, and anyone's guess about Alabama. I know, having worked on a national toll-free number, switching between talking to people from Boston to Texas to S. Carolina could be pretty taxing!

To which Lorianne in Saskatoon replied:
I'm of the opinion that English dialects are dying out, in North America at least. Differences will smooth out with increased ease of communication between dialect areas: either other dialects will borrow irregularities, spreading them to even more dialects, or else the irregularities will disappear. Standard dialects will take over. This will probably take several hundred years (depending on the individual dialect), so we won't notice it happening. Radio and television have probably already set the changes in motion.

--

Aren in Manchester, UK:
On another thread, the one about common mispronunciation, how about people who say "paremfeses" for "parentheses," "supposably" for "supposedly," and "all the sudden" for "all of a sudden." Re "heighth" instead of "height," Webster's says it's "a variant that occurs in educated speech but that is considered by some [ME!] to be unacceptable." [I just learned that that's what the division symbol next to a variant pronunciation means!]

--

Lorianne in Saskatoon said:
Today in my historical linguistics class the words (and name) MARRY,

MARY and MERRY came up. In some dialects these words are all pronounced differently, while in others they are all pronounced the same. I would like to find out how they are pronounced in YOUR dialects, where your dialect is, most likely, the one you learned when you a kid. (Wow I just created a garden-path sentence!) Send me a response stating which words you pronounce the same, or whether they're all the same or all different.

Please state your dialect. I will post any results I come up with. Feel free to ask questions, too.

Richard in Oakland:

I pronounce them all differently, but the last two are closer together than either is to the first.

Matt in Minneapolis, MN:

Continuing on Lorianne's thread, as a Midwesterner, I've always pronounced Mary, marry, and merry NEARLY alike, as well as Barry, berry, and bury. There's perhaps a slight vowel and mouth position difference between the first syllable of hairy and heron, but not something noticeable during normally enunciated conversation. Of course, I also pronounce which and witch; whether and weather; wheel, weal, and we'll alike. As I said above, I'm a tech-type, not an English major.

Bill in Lexington KY:

Someone in another discussion on English said "Anyone who doesn't hear the differences between those words isn't trying." My response was "if you hear any differences between those words when I say them, you're hearing something that isn't there." I make no difference and don't hear differences around here except once in a while. However, since I don't make any distinction, I'm probably less likely to notice if someone else does. I'm from and in urban central Kentucky.

And Karen in Manchester:

The flip side of that coin is when I know my usage is correct but I can see people squirming and thinking, "I can't believe she thinks that's right!" For example, Henry David Thoreau pronounced his own last name just like "thorough," not with the accent on the last syllable as most people think. I like to honor his preference, but it's clear that not everyone agrees with me!

--

Lorianne in Saskatoon:
How kids pronounce food words- NEW THREAD: I had a friend who said psghetti (spaghetti), I said hangaber (hamburger), and my nephew called popsicles pockidles. Any others out there?

Katherine in Oakland:
I think "psghetti" is fairly common. I said "brekfix" for breakfast, I'm told. My little brother said "mamalade" for "marmalade"; my parents often set out a choice of marmalade or a darker jelly (yes, I know that sounds funny, but now I'm not sure whether it was grape or crabapple), and one day Danny suggested that if one was "mamalade", the other ought to be "papalade"...yes, so wordplay runs in the family; what can I say?

Matt in Minneapolis, MN:
On to mispronunciation and kidspeak: I also believe 'pasketti' and 'hangaber' to fairly common among the wee folk. My son called brussels sprouts (is that what they're called in Belgium?) 'eat balls'. He loves them, BTW.
My problem is with announcers and other 'professionals' who say "athaletes" or "relators". Neither the 'thl' nor the 'alt' combinations seem very difficult to say.

Kat in Rochester added:
My juvenile contributions were ... hopsital (hospital) ...

And Toni in Minnesota:
After having listened to Justin Wilson, I can't say it any way except "horse-pistol".

Jacquie in Arlington, VA:
When I was little I used to call those funny webbed-footed birds "gucks." And stepping into the opening I made—a friend's daughter referred to her dad's briefcase as a "griefcase!"

Phil in Salt Lake City:
My wife's little brother used to say "plidow" for pillow. My 18-year-old said "prolly" for probably

Bev remarked:
Someone I work with consistently pronounces "similar" as "sim-u-ler." That's with a long u sound.

Bob in eastern Washington:
On the kiddyspeak thread, a pronounciation that makes me want to ralph all over the rug is "sammwich." This barfolus sounding word is, sad to say, also used by many adults. I wretchedly retch.

--

Peter in Gelong, AU was inquisitive:
What is the 8th letter of the alphabet called? I'd always thought "aitch", until I came to Australia. Here, many people call it "Haitch".
Is this uniquely Australian? Or do any Wordplayers know of its pronunciation like this elsewhere? Interesting...

Matt in Minneapolis, MN answered:
Peter asks about 'H'. I was unaware that there was any letter besides 'Z' = zee/zed, that had differing pronunciations.
The American Heritage says 'aitch' is from French 'hache', but I still don't know why the rough breathing mark = 'h', or 'y' and 'w' have such strange names. All the others have one of the sounds the letter makes in the name. Shouldn't 'w' be called 'wie' and 'y' be called 'ye'? 'H' could be 'hey'.
Then, of course, there's the fact that we have 26 letters to represent 40+ sounds and 3 of those letters - C, Q, & X - make no sounds not already covered by other letters.

--

Kimberly in Fort Lauderdale:
I'd like to ask about the pronunciation of "oil". Everyone that I know, except my mother, pronounces it "oy-ull."

Bob in Chicago answered:
I am always "tickled" by the accents I hear when down around the

Texas, Oklahoma, Arkansas, & Louisiana border convergent areas. The residents there sometimes pronounce the word "oil" as "all". They also say "bob war" for "barbed wire". I went into a self-serve gasoline (petrol) station in Arkansas one time (North Little Rock) and there was a crude, hand written sign attached to one of the pumps that said, "hep ur sef".

George in Virginia also contributed to the discussion:
To Kimberley, on pronunciation of "oil:" I am from Northern Virginia and my wife is from Bogalusa, Louisiana. She used to ride me about my Yankee accent and, of course, I bugged her about hers. She pronounces it "ohl." Interestingly, she also observed that Brooklynites (and New Orleans...ites?) come out with the sound "earl." Aside: I am willing to try everything southern except two things: assume a southern accent, and... eat hominy.

--

Bob in Eastern WA:
Many years ago I read a piece on strange pronunciation guides. I think the title was "Ghoti spells fish." The pronunciation guide was:
- GH as in cough
- O as in women
- TI as in nation

Another long word included guides such as "P as in pneumonia," and was a totally silent word.

--

Sara in Boston responded to Dani:
Your spelling of "karaoke" is correct, in fact. And the word in Japanese is pronounced just as it is spelled, "kara-okay." Somewhere along the line the Americans transmogrified it into "karry-okee."

And Steve to Dani on karaoke:
Nope, you got it right, all right. The big question is how you pronounce it. Most folks in the States seem to render it as "carry-OH-kee," which sounds plainly bizarre to this old Japan hand. (To be fair, there plenty of English words that sound pretty strange when bor-

rowed by the Japanese.) I'd like to see any regional variations on this and other non-English words in the mouths of English-speakers. Lessee:

kimono = kuh-MAON-uh
sake = SA-kee   ("sa" as in "sad")
sumo = SOO-mow

--

Karniotis on old characters:
I think I read that Katherine had corrected someone who said that Thee is Old English for You-all. She correctly said that the actual word is 'Ye'. I remember hearing that the actual Old English character in question here is the 'thorn,' which looks sort of like a Y with a horizontal line going through it about half-way down. The thorn is pronounced 'th,' and therefore the Old English word 'Ye' should be pronounced 'Thee'. I could be way off on this, though. Does anyone know anything about this?

--

Giles in New Castle, NSW:
There are two archaic English words written "ye", which are often confused. The first "ye" is a plural form of "you", pronounced as "yee", in which the "y" was originally the letter yogh. The second "ye" is a variant form of "the", which should be pronounced as "the" (but often isn't), and which is based on misreading the letter thorn as a "y".

An example of the first "ye" is "Ye banks and braes ...". An example of the second "ye" is the fake archaic "Ye olde Englishe tea shoppe".

The word "thee" is different again -- it is the accusative form of the singular of "you". Just as you have "I", "me", "my" and "mine", you have "thou", "thee", "thy" and "thine".

Incidentally, I once saw a question about which English word had no letters in common with the singular and plural forms. The question gave one answer, but I think that "thee/you", and "thine/yours" are better answers. So, what was the original answer?

And Rogers enquired:
On to another subject: I had a linguistics prof who said that the voiced th (as in these) and the unvoiced th (as in thesis) are the only phonemes in English that are never exchanged for one another but never are the difference between two words. Is he correct? Can you think of two words whose only difference is whether the th is voiced or unvoiced?

--

From Virginia at UVA:
There's another interesting pair of phonemes, too: the medial sound in "mission" (voiceless, known as s-wedge) and the medial sound in measure (voiced, known, naturally, as z-wedge). Can you come up with one or more minimal pairs that will prove that these are phonemes--i.e., find one or more pairs of words in which the difference between s-wedge and z-wedge is the only difference in sound?

Katherine in Oakland, CA:
Only one occurred to me immediately: tressure/treasure.
Tressure is a heraldic term, which I find I'm having trouble defining--something like a border, but placed slightly within the frame instead of at the edge so that there's a small border of the original background color. If you can either imagine or find a picture of the coat of arms of Scotland, that includes a "double tressure flory counter-flory": two tressures, one within the other (again with a slight separation), with fleurs-de-lis at intervals and pointing alternately left and right (or up and down, on the top and bottom edges).

--

Bill & Sue wrote, concerning voiced and unvoiced th's and whether they are the sole distinction between any word:
Wouldn't thou care to bet a few thou on that?

And Roger remarked:
Wonderful! I had thought of eth (voiced) and eth (unvoiced), the names of two letters we no longer use in English; didn't know if they counted since they're no longer in common use.

Alex in Adelaide had something to relate:
My grandmother who lived in Paris in the 40's amused us few times with the following anecdote. On a Paris street there was this elderly man who was sweeping his store front. He has lost most of his front teeth and when he talks the 's' comes out as 'sh' sound. An old woman passes by and in her good manners utters "Shalom". The man slowly turns toward her with anger in his face and shouts back "'Sh'ale femme!!"

Matt in Minneapolis, MN:
Phil of alt Lake City challenged me (and the rest of this motley crew) this weekend with words where the same letter makes two different sounds. He cites the letters which "normally" make two sounds: c (in circus, accept, conceit, success, and so forth) and g (in gorge, garbage, gauge, gorgeous, etc.) and added x (in Xerxes and Xerox - can't think of any improper words). He offered two points for other consonant examples "if there are any".

Well, I can't account for EVERY consonant in the alpha-beta, but I'll start with c, g, and x making two different sounds other than k/s, g/j, and z/ks. There's *cacciatore* [c/ch], *garage* [g/zh], and *executrix* [gz/ks]. Moving on, d gives *deciduous* [d/j], n gives *junction* [ng/n], and t gives *torture* [t/ch] and *traction* [t/sh]. S is even more versatile, as seen in *says* [s/z], *sugars* [sh/z], *lesions* [zh/z], and even a THREE-WAY, not to be confused with a menage a' trois, in words like *sessions* [s/sh/z].

If the second sound may be a vowel sound rather than a consonantal sound, our two sometimes vowels may be added: *yearly* [y/ee] and *wallow* [w/silent].

Since, the use of 'w' above sidesteps the debate about its vowelity by using a silence as a second sound, I will extend to other letters with a second "sound of silence". b in *bomb*, k in *knock*, m in *mnemonic*, p in *psychotherapy* (an apropos word for someone expending brainpower on this, nicht wahr?)

Furthermore, if a letter makes another sound when coupled with a second letter, further examples may be added. c in *coach* or triple play in *conscience*, h in *withhold* or *hash*, p in *periphery*, s in *shores* or *shorts*, t in *that* or *thirteen* or *tilth* or *thistle*, and w in *whipporwill* (if you count 'wh' as pronounced 'hw'. The dictionary is the only one I know doing so.)

Ursine cum me a while longer. The list above leaves out f, l, j, q, r, and z. The only word I can find with 'f' pronounced as anything other than 'f' is British *halfpenny*. If they had *halffarthing*, we'd be somewhere. 'L' also is nearly always 'l' with the exceptions of silence in *half* or *salmon* or [y] pronunciations for the ewe-eye-double-l in words like *guillotine* or *bouillon*. Likewise, 'j' in words from our southern neighbo(u)r, like *jalapeno* or *jojoba* does not say [j], but no mix'n'match. V only says [v] except in Germanic or Dutch words when followed by 'r', when it is unvoiced. 'R' works if you pronounce *Worcester* as Elmer Fudd might say *rooster*. For 'q', might a follower of American statesman or TV doctor Quincy be *Quincyesque*? A particularly harsh interrogation is maybe *Inquisitionesque*? A regal lady or 70's rock group *queenesque*? Are there any real words with qu as both [kw] and [k]?
Any help on 'z'?
"All right, already", all altruists (also alumni) altercate. Stop wasting bandwidth! Aren't you on a corporate server? Don't you have work to do?
Right you are! I am not blessed with a sinecure - a marvellous word; look it up!

Ere I go, might I trouble those who found rhymes for filth to attempt the same for other words ending in <consonant>-th? How about month, breadth, width, twelfth, sixth, or eighth? No lithping allowed!

--

Dani in Atlanta asked:
What about colonel? How in the world we got the pronunciation "kernel" out of *this* spelling escapes me.

--

David in Glendale, CA was waxing philosophical:
Is there a relationship between getting sacked (Brit: fired) and what the DEfense keeps trying to do to the quarterback in USA football? (BTW, the peculiar pronunciation of DEfense is an emphasis gone wild -- differentiating between that and OFfense; two questions: has anyone heard as much about the OFfense as we hear about the DEfense? and is there a term for a pronunciation that has proliferated from a very specialized jargon pronunciation?)

John in Keele, UK weighed in:
The English proverb is "Attack is the best form of defence".
Likewise, any other context [sporting or military]: the American "offense" (which Brits don't spell like that anyway) is replaced by "attack". "Offence", for me, is what offensive language gives to those who are sensitive to it.

--

Phil in Salt Lake City:
I have a question about two or three words that have different meanings when pronounced differently. I don't think I said that very well. They are pronounced differently in their different uses. Well, keep listening and you'll see what I mean.
Used: can mean "previously in use", which I pronounce "UZED". It can also mean "formerly", which I pronounce "USST". For example: "That UZED car USST to belong to Fred.
Next example:
Supposed: meaning "assumed", I pronounce "SUPPOZED". If it means "was intended to", then I pronounce it "SUPPOSST". "I SUPPOZED that it was SUPPOSST to look like that.
Third and final example:
Has, indicating possession, I pronounce "HAZ".

Has, indicating obligation, I pronounce "HASS".
"He HASS to leave now. He HAZ a busy schedule" (We won't get into the pronunciation of *schedule*.)

First question: Are these pronunciations, combined with these particular meanings universal? How about in Canada, the UK and Down Under? I am fairly sure that these hold as far away as California, since a soft drink (which I also call "pop") company which takes its name from Mt. Shasta in northern California had the slogan:
"It hassta be Shasta"
"Haz to be" just doesn't rhyme.

Second question: Can anyone think of any other words which have different meanings when pronounced differently? (I have a feeling that Matt is going to inundate us again.)

Third question: Is there a name for this phenomenon? Any of you "English Types" have anything here?

Later Phil added:
Note: The third example has a parallel in the first person:
I HAV a book from the library that I HAFF to return today.
First of all, I have only had one confirmation of my way of pronouncing these, and no refutations. I will therefore assume that my pronunciations are universal. But I don't really think that these are heteronyms, because they seem to be subtle variants of the same word. In this last example, for example, HAFF can be read as "have the obligation to", in which case the pronunciation reverts to HAV.
I HAV a book ... that I HAV (the obligation) to return today.
The same with the third person example:
He HAZ the obligation to leave now. He HAZ a busy schedule.
So, the two forms seem to be really the same word. Also, the change in pronunciation involves only a single consonant, and the degree to which it is vocalized. It's not the same as emphasizing the first or the second syllable (converse, incense), or changing the vowel sound (bow, bass). Anyone care to think a little deeper on this?

Court in Wayne, IN suggested:
The only other word that quickly comes to mind, is close.
Close 1. to shut something, 2. to be near something.
Cloze the door. He is close to the window.

--

Bill in Columbia, CT:
Hey, Phil, they're called heteronyms.
> minute (seconds) & minute (small),
> bow (pretty) & bow (no way),
> buffet (food) & buffet (ouch),
> sewer (sewing) & sewer (stinks),
> sow (pig) & sow (sewing),
> row (boat) & row (fight),
> resume (personal history) & resume (go),
> refuse (PU) & refuse (no),
> resigned (accept) & resigned (signature),
> entrance (mesmerize) & entrance (entry),
> content (course) & content (happy),
> moped (sad) & moped (cleaned),
> incense (scent) & incense (make angry),
> putting (on) & putting (golf),
> lead (in front) & lead (metal),
> liver (organ) & liver (life),
> number (count) & number (comatose),
> wind (blows) & Wind (tightly),
> pussy (cat) & pussy (infected),
> dove (bird) & dove (splash),
> secretive (dribble) & secretive (sealing one's lips), etc.

Phil, a tip:
Heteronym - sow (as in female adult swine) and sow (as in scattering seed): *different name (heter & nym)
Homonym - box (as in verb) and box (as in noun): *same name

THE POWER OF WORDS ~ 203

(homo & nym)
Homophone - to, too, two: *same sound (homo & phone)

Catie in Arlington, VA adds few more:
    Wound: (WOOND) an injury
    Wound: (WOWND) Past tense of wind (like wind a watch),
which leads us to:
    Wind: (WYNDE) (like wind a watch)
    Wind: (WINND) The air that blows
    Refuse: (REFYOOSS) Trash
    Refuse: (REFYUZE) (I refuse to do that)

    Matt in Minneapolis, MN remarked:
Catie, the grammatical conjugation case your grandmother referred to is "ablative" [ab' luh tiv] as opposed to reference to surgical excision which would be [uh blay' tiv].
As Catie mentioned, there is a distinction between *real* heteronyms, unrelated words with different etymologies (e.g. does - 3d pers. sing. Of do [duz], plural of doe [dohz]) and "pseudoheteronyms", related words pronounced differently (e.g. convict - the noun and the verb; or read - present and past tenses). The *real* heteronyms, aka homographs (no relation to Mapplethorpe), of which I am aware number (#, not 'more numb') about 100. The variant pronunciations are left as an exercise for the reader.
Inundation mode on:
ablative, agape, appropriate, are, as, ate, axes, bases, bass, bow, brat, buffet, coax, commune, compact, console, content, converse, desert, dingy, divers, do, does, douse, dove, entrance, fiasco, fillet, flower, formal, genial, gill, glower, hinder, incense, intimate, invalid, is, jargon, lather, lead, lineage, liver, lower, lupine, mare, minute, moped, mow, number, os, overage, pace, palatine, pan, pasty, (pate), peaked, peer, poll, primer, project, pussy, re, recreate, redress, repent, represent, resent, reserve, resign, resolve, resort, (resume), river, (rose), row, salve,

severer, sewer, shower, singer, skied, slaver, slough, sow, stingy, stipulate, supply, tarry, tear, thou, thymic, tier, tower, unionized, us, violist, wind, wound.

The parenthetical ones have foreign diacritical marks, but are so commonly spelled without them that they count.

Dave in Glendale, CA observed:

Then, there are "ghost" heteronyms, words that should exist, but which turn out to be mispronunciations. Case in point: the classic librarians' cautionary tale about the little boy who marched up to the librarian and complained about truth in advertising, at least, as far as a book's title having anything to do with its contents:

"I looked all through this book, and doesn't say a word about how to capture moths for my collection!" The book: *Advice for Young Mothers* ...Then there was our earlier thread on being annoyed by a deliberately duplicated message: "I resent the post you resent even more the second time than I did when you sent it the first time..."

--

Matt in Minneapolis, MN:

Dave and Jim already answered coax. The pro-Duce version is good, but methinks that would fall under the heading of capitonyms, wherein capitalizing a letter changes the pronunciation, e.g. job/Job, herb/Herb, said/Said, begin/Begin, polish/Polish, tangier/Tangier, et cetera ad nauseum.

--

Steve in San Francisco contributed:

With regard to the often-asked questions about phonetic spelling: I am reading a great book called "The Language Instinct" by the psycholinguist Steven Pinker. In this book he describes the benefits and necessity of using a non-phonetic system. Just a couple of examples: 1) Without context, how would we know the difference between "meat" and "meet" (or "mete" for that matter)? 2) Due to a phenomenon called "co-articulation", every letter's sound changes when adjacent to other letters. We also have diphthongs and all kinds of bizarre idiosyncratic dialectical variations that would be impossible to reflect in written text (is "written text" redundant or what? That's kind of like saying "visual image").

7

Language Oddities

On unfortunate names, Gerald in Ottawa suggested: Places: Fauquier County, Maryland?

Elizabeth in Madison, WI:
Steven, are you from the upper peninsula of Michigan? In Michigan and Wisconsin (and other places, I'm sure) the upper peninsula of Michigan is called "The U.P." Persons from there are called "yoopers." (I don't know if they are bitter about it.) There is a polka band from the U.P. called "The Yoopers" or "Da Yoopers." Do you know anything about this, Steven, or is your email address just a coincidence?

On limericks, Bill in Lexington, KY:
Scientific American once presented a small study of limerick endings. From memory:

> There was a young poet from Japan,
> Whose limericks never would scan,
> When someone asked "Why?"
> She said with a sigh,
> It's because I always try to get as many words in the last line as I possibly can.

THE POWER OF WORDS - 207

Another young poet from China,
Had a feeling for rhythm much fine-a,
But his limericks tend,
To come to an end,
Suddenly.

There was a young person from Crewe,
Whose limericks end at line two

There was a young man from Verdun

--

Jim in Philadelphia gave us a reference for palindromes:
From the New York Times review, two books of palindromes are "Go Hang a Salami! I'm a Lasagna Hog" and "So Many Dynamos" by Jon Agee (Farrar, Straus & Gilroux)
From the first book:
A drawing shows two groups of men in sombreros throwing fruit at each other across a street. An old man steps out of a doorway into the fray and one of the combatants shouts, "No Sir! Away! A papaya war is on." Another drawing shows two nuns at a bar where a bartender pours a drink for one of them. The other, who is holding a golf club, looks ruefully at the nun awaiting her drink and says: "Flo, gin is a sin! I golf."
Soda, bra, bottle, belt to Barbados.
Ned, go gag Ogden.

--

Maria in Austin on slogans:
Heard they had a contest for a new motto for the state of Wisconsin to replace the current motto, "The Dairy State". Someone submitted the slogan "Wisconsin. Come and smell our dairy air "
When I was somewhat younger, we used to say "You don't have to be a brain surgeon..." to indicate that something would not overly tax the

little grey cells. Nowadays, and universally, the surgeon is replaced by the rocket scientist. Why is this? Has brain surgery become easier?

David in Glendale:
Add to the homonyms for which your word processor isn't worth a tinker's dam (damn/curse, dam/coin or dam/Grendel's Mama?):
sight (something you see, or the faculty of seeing)
site (a place, like, for example, a battle site, and by verbing to emplace)
cite (to list, or quote, and by nouning, a listing or quotation, as in one of the lists on the internet -- but I still would rather see it as Contemporary Citations, not Current Cites...)
I think the 10 9 8 7 6 5 4 3 2 1 on page op title may have to do with current editions. It would seem to me that it would be child's play to remove numbers from the right as output mounts.

Mary Beth answered a query:
Someone asked about the line on the "frontispiece" of a book (I know I mispelled that...) that reads 10 9 8 7 6 5 4 3 2 1.
Those numbers represent the printing number of a book (by the way, we in the publishing biz call that page the copyright page). If the number one is included in this line, it means you have a copy of a first printing book. When a book reprints, the printer will then delete the lowest number in that line, thus indicating the 2nd, or 3rd printing.
Hope that answers your question. If you have any other "book/publishing" questions, just ask, I have been a print buyer for about five years now...

On superfluous expressions, Mike in Brisbane offered:
Thought of you all during one of the conference presentations, when the presenter said "Of course, you all know..." and went on to tell us what we all knew for the next five minutes. I guess it went without saying...

Gerald in Ottawa:
Actually, Khyber Pass IS rhyming slang, as in the expression "You can stick it up your Khyber." Always wondered why though since the Brits

say "arse" rather than "ass." On the other hand, may be they say "parse" rather than "pass."

Gerry also weighed in on the temperature scale conversions:
I've always found the easiest way to go from Celsius to Fahrenheit is to double the figure, subtract 10 percent and add 32. 20 degrees Celsius would thus be (20 x 2) -4 +32 = 68.

Frank in Ottawa elaborated:
 I say ass for a donkey
 bass for a singer or a fish or an instrument
 lass for a girl
 mass for a horde, crowd or service
 sass for cheekiness
 tass for a former Soviet news agency
 vass if I'm trying to say 'Was' in German.
 I say arse for bum (not hobo by the way)
 clarse for the many definitions of class
 glarse and glarses for windowpanes and spectacles
 parse for what I'm too old to make at an attractive girl in a Pub.
And I must be right 'cos I was born wivvin the sahnd of Bow Bells, wasn't I.

--

On pronunciation, Alyssa in San Francisco wrote:
Rollo gave us the pronunciation key with the following line in it: "Wauchope (ugh) WAR-hope"
How the heck do you get an r sound out of "wauchope"??

Jack in London responded:
Waugh is a common surname, pronounced War. It's well known in many places these days because of the brilliant Australian cricketing brothers of that name. There's also Evelyn (Arthur St. John) Waugh, the author of Brideshead revisited, amongst other things.
I've actually met someone by the (sur)name of Wauchope and he pronounces it Walk-up.

Puns

"How can you tell a dogwood tree from the rest? – From its bark!"

Gary in Manchester said:
Here in England many shopkeepers use puns when they choose a name for their shop. Hairdressers seem fond of this e.g.
- A Cut Above
- Headlines
- Shear Magic

Fish and chip shops go for the plaice/place similarity
- The Plaice to Eat
- Our Plaice
- The Filleted Plaice

These are all real shop names I've seen here, 'The Filleted Plaice' seems bizarre but someone must of thought it was a good name for a shop. Likewise, a local greengrocers called 'The Potato Centre'. There's a pet shop called 'Sophistocats' in my home town.

Any others? I live in hope that there is a 'Making Great Strides' tailor's shop in Oz.

Jesse in Sunnyvale, CA:
How about "Curl up and Dye" Saw that one in a movie somewhere.

John in Keele, UK:
In Hanley, Stoke-on-Trent, there is or used to be a shop called "Shampoodle and Setter" [dog grooming, of course]. And on a slightly different but related theme, a van passed me the other day with the slogan on its rear doors: "We strip for you!" [painters and decorators...]

Sara in Boston:
 Hair It Is
 Shear Excellence
 Hair Today (<-- groan tomorrow?)

About Hair

Katherine in Oakland, CA:
Hair salons etc.: My favorite for a long time was in Philadelphia: Julius Scissor, Existential Hair Sculpture.
That favorite has been superseded by the local one: Alexander Pope Haircutters...

Rich in Rindge, NH said:
One of my favorite cartoons from our regional magazine called _Yankee_ (published down the road from me - I've worked for them from time to time) was one of a dentist and his patient. The patient was labelled "Yankee" and the dentist "Yanker."

Dani in Atlanta:
I thought I'd pass along a name of a fabric store in the area "Sew-it-Seams"

Susan Marie in Atlanta:
My favorite name is Plant Parenthood, a California florist.
There's a self-service LaundraMutt in Manhattan for the pooches (they're so cute with their little noses pressed to that round glass door).. Not to be confused with Groomingdale's in Louisville KY. There's also a pet store that specializes in "marine fish", to distinguish them from the popular Walking Catfish franchises, I assume. Or try Doggy Do's or Groom n Zoom.

Hairstylists must take a class in bad puns somewhere between Lethal Plastic Nails and Pink Hair for Old Ladies. Locally, there's Hairport, Clip Art, Shear Delite, Hair it Is, Hairum (and Hair-em), Parting Company, Still Cutting Up, Wave Reviews- and who really thought that "Medusa" or "The Chop Shop" would draw customers? And we have "Larry's Haircutters"," Curley's", and "Mo Hair"- Wu!wu!wu!

Maeve in Champaign, IL said:
Hi, I'm new to the group and have been enjoying the bar names. My favorite located here in Champaign, Illinois is Tumble Inn

Karen in Manchester, UK:
I heard of a bar called The Office, as in, "Honey, I won't be home for dinner; I have to stay late at The Office."

Rich in Rindge, NH said:
The other day I noticed that the faculty member who teaches stained glass in our art department received a catalog from a supplier named "PANE IN THE GLASS"

Marjorie in Boston, MA:
I saw the following sign on the door of a shop this morning: PLEASE GO AWAY OFTEN!
This shop is a travel agency! (I've seen this sign more than once, yet it gets me every time!!)

Anders in Stockholm:
In Gothenburg there used to be a pub called 'Dirty Dick' and in Stockholm there is one pub called 'Halfway Inn'. Even if written in English, the latter may be a pun to Swedes only?

Nancy, Columbus, OH:
When I was in Dublin (Ireland) years ago, I took a picture of a pub sign that struck me. It said, "If you're bored, come here and be fed up."

Bob in Chicago, IL:
I worked at a gas station/garage (aka filling station, aka petrol station) in my youth where they had a sign that said: "Let us shock you, brake you, tune you up, and tire you out".

Jim in Philadelphia:
I suppose that's kind of like the sign in a local drug store that reads "Try our cough syrup. You will never get any better."

Mike in Brisbane had a whole bunch of fun puns:
I once dated a guy who broke up with me because I only have 9 toes. Yes, he was lack toes intolerant.

Did you know ants never get sick? It's because they have anty bodies.

I've started investing in stocks: beef, vegetable, chicken. One day I hope to be a bouillianaire.

If you boil a funny bone, it becomes a laughing stock. Now that's humerus.

I accidentally rubbed ketchup in my eyes. Now I have Heinzsight.

Did you know muffins spelled backwards is what you do when you take them out of the oven?

I tried to come up with a carpentry pun that woodwork. I thought I nailed it but nobody saw it.

Singing in the shower is fine until you get soap in your mouth. Then it's a soap opera.

The Black-Eyed Peas can sing us a song but the chick peas can only hummus one.

How much does a chimney cost? Nothing, it's on the house.

Once upon a time there was a King who was only 12 inches tall. He was a terrible King but he made a great ruler.

My friend Jack says he can communicate with vegetables. That's right...Jack and the beans talk.

I want to tell you about a girl who only eats plants. You probably haven't heard of herbivore.

I was struggling to understand how lightning works and then it struck me.

Six cows were smoking joints and playing poker. That's right. The steaks were pretty high.

I went to the paint store to get thinner. It didn't work.

--

On puns, someone shared with us quite a selection that was unattributed:
1. Dad, are we pyromaniacs? Yes, we arson.
2. What do you call a pig with laryngitis? Disgruntled.
3. Writing my name in cursive is my signature move.
4. Why do bees stay in their hives during winter? Swarm
5. If you're bad at haggling, you'll end up paying the price.
6. Just so everyone's clear, I'm going to put my glasses on.
7. A commander walks into a bar and orders everyone around.
8. I lost my job as a stage designer. I left without making a scene.
9. Never buy flowers from a monk. Only you can prevent florist friars.
10. How much did the pirate pay to get his ears pierced? A buccaneer.
11. I once worked at a cheap pizza shop to get by. I kneaded the dough.
12. My friends and I have named our band 'Duvet'. It's a cover band
13. I lost my girlfriend's audiobook, and now I'll never hear the end of it.
14. Why is 'dark' spelled with a k and not c? Because you can't see in the dark.
15. Why is it unwise to share your secrets with a clock? Well, time will tell.
16. When I told my contractor I didn't want carpeted steps, they gave me a blank stare.
17. Bono and The Edge walk into a Dublin bar and the bartender says, "Oh no, not U2 again."
18. Prison is just one word to you, but for some people, it's a whole sentence.
19. Scientists got together to study the effects of alcohol on a person's walk, and the result was staggering.

20. I'm trying to organize a hide-and-seek tournament, but good players are really hard to find.
21. I got over my addiction to chocolate, marshmallows, and nuts. I won't lie, it was a rocky road.
22. What do you say to comfort a friend who's struggling with grammar? There, their, they're.
23. I went to the toy store and asked the assistant where the Schwarzenegger dolls are and he replied, "Aisle B, back."
24. What did the surgeon say to the patient who insisted on closing up their own incision? Suture self.
25. I've started telling everyone about the benefits of eating dried grapes. It's all about raisin awareness.

--

Kutzd had more puns:
Feline fine: I enjoyed reading Terrence's oh-puss on hurricane Felix-the-cat-egory 2 storm that tried to pun-ish Bermuda. His lynx between the hurricane and the cat thread were purr-fect. It was good to hear that onions don't take storms like this lion down.

--

Katherine in Berkeley, CA shared a pun:
Does anyone remember this exchange in a Marx Brothers film (possibly "A day at the races")? Groucho and Harpo are discussing a contract and turning over copious pages reading out pseudo-legalese like "the party of the first part" and so on.
Harpo: What's that bit?
Groucho: That's the sanity clause.
Harpo: Don't be silly: there ain't no sanity clause.
She added:
Nitpick alert: It's Chico and Groucho, of course, rather than Harpo and Groucho. And, if I recall correctly, what Chico says is, "You can't fool me! There ain't no Sanity Clause!" (And I think it's in "The Cocoanuts", but it could be "A Day at the Races".)

John in Keele added a correction:
No, I think it was _A Night at the Opera_ before they get on the boat [on stage/backstage at the opera house, with a _very_ large pair of scissors to cut the contract?]. And Margaret Dumont somewhere in attendance. What's more, it's an insurance contract, and the gag "You lose a leg, we help you look for it" is also in there somewhere. Or perhaps I haven't properly woken up yet this morning.

--

Gerald in Ottawa on puns:
Being in a curmudgeon mood, I'd also like to complain about the growing efforts of headline writers to be witty. It's not so much the obvious ones like "Relationship Cut Short" in the Bobbett case but those that keep appearing every day in the business section of our local paper. "Submarine Contract Torpedoed," "New Head for Molson's Beer," "Company claims Leak in Dam Bid," I suppose it's something of a release for the poor devils but still...

Terrence in Bermuda responded to a suggestive pun:
"Relationship Cut Short in the Bobbett case..."
Did you hear about the new movie about this case? "Free Willy"

More on puns, Terrence shared this:
Driving through town with an old friend, she remarked that the Bishop was selling his house, "that one there - the one that looks like a castle". To which I was forced to rejoinder:
"You mean, a Manse home is his castle?"

Anders in Sweeden had a self-referential pun of his own:
I keep forgetting what the word 'mnemonic' means. Can anyone, please, help me with a memory aid?

Terrence in Bermuda came to the rescue:
* Memory's Not Everything; Manage Obscure Notions: Initial Characters
* Memorize NE(any)thing: Make Odd Naughty Idiotic Catchphrases

--

Turn of phrases:

John in Washington, DC:
I see more and more people misusing the phrase "begging the question." It has become very popular with newspaper writers: "He was in New Orleans on July 4th, so that begs the question how could he have committed the crime in Memphis?"
No! That does not beg the question, it raises the question.
I'm appealing to WordPlayers, because while I recognize the incorrect usage, I'm unable to give an example of proper usage. It's something about using the conclusion of a syllogism as one of the premises -- a violation of the rules of Logic. Are there any logicians in the group who can give a couple of textbook examples of a logical proof which begs the question?

--

On metaphors, Bill in Lexington, KY wrote:
Anybody remember when "hot pants" was a lifestyle rather than an article of clothing?

--

Dave in Glendale, CA discussed:
D'J suggests one has been pulled by the nose, a Hollandaise equivalent of having one's leg pulled. Even more persuasive is being strong-armed. Are there other persuadable anatomical areas (apart, children, from that which seems to take over all thinking at puberty)?

Jim in Philadelphia responded:
I don't know. It seems as though having someone's ears is a good sign that you can persuade them to do something. And those persuadable anatomical areas that seem to take over all thinking at puberty seem awfully persuasive at times to me... :o

And Katherine interjected:
I forgot about answering this first time around. Arms (having been twisted) are pretty persuadable--does that count?

Matt in Minneapolis, MN added:
Persuasive body parts suitable for this forum, as opposed to Penthouse's, include twisting your arm, getting on your back, bending your

ear (if you will lend it), and breathing down your neck; along with catching your eye and turning your head, inasmuch as getting your attention can persuade you.

--

On homographs, Dani in Atlanta shared:
A note that landed on my desk says: "Dani, I resent your fax. Al"
It took me a minute to figure out that Al was NOT mad at me; he only put the fax through the machine because the transmittal did not go through the first time.
Martin in Los Angeles:
raise / raze. Antithetical homonyms

--

Rollo in Adelaide wrote:
Delving into a grammar textbook to answer questions like this usually yields fascinating exceptions. The word "news" is plural, yet we say "The news is good".
Mike in Brisbane chimed in:
There was once a famous American journalist who insisted that "news" was plural. When his editor cabled him with the message "Any News?", he would reply with a cable saying "Not a new." Might have been Thurber, I can't remember.

--

Maya asked:
When I was a kid, we used to change the first letters around of some words--we'd say "Beeping Sleauty" and "beet selt". I was wondering if anyone else did this kind of thing--and if it was only with "b" and "s" phrases.
Jim in Philadelphia responded:
That would be a spoonerism, named after the legendary Reverand Archibald Spooner. "It's kisstomary to cuss the bride." and "Excuse me. You are occupewing my pie." Happens all the time, and I find myself guilty of it at times. I'm going to go shake a tower, I find myself announcing to no one in particular... (Beats baking a tath, anyway...)

Anyone have any favourite spoonerisms?
I hate going into my attic. There are too many crooks and nannies there....

Pat in Collegeville, MN said:
Considerably advanced age wise beyond Bill, I am still fond of fog as thick as sea poup.

And Sara in Boston:
One of my Favorites was one an old friend used to use: "Oh, you get that, huh? Wow, you're a real fart smeller."

Ben in Trent, NJ answered Maya:
What you quote are almost (but not quite) 'Spoonerisms'. Almost, because they involve the transposition of initial sounds of words (a sort of metathesis). Not quite, because a true Spoonerism has a real meaning in its transposed form. The term comes from the Revd W A Spooner, Warden of New College, Oxford early this century. He is reputed to have dealt with an offending undergraduate by telling him, 'Sir, you have been caught fighting a liar (lighting a fire) in the quad. You will leave by the next town drain (down train).'

Bill asked:
Is swapping letters or syllables with[in?] a word a Spoonerism?

Terrence in Bermuda said:
No. This is metathesis. A common metathesis is aks for ask.

Gerry chimed in:
"heffalump" for elephant is, of course, from Winnie the Pooh.

Dave in Glendale, CA had a few:
Several folks have written about pisgetti, flutterby, etc.
My son (almost 9 yrs old) says 'vegebatle' (maybe vegebadle), even though he's been able to spell it correctly for several years.
A couple of other cute phrases are 'quite a couple' for 'quite a few', and "I amn't" for "I'm not"
Actually "I amn't" makes a bit of sense; after all, the other contractions are "he isn't" and "they aren't", why not "I amn't" ;-)

Caleb in Albany, NY:

My guess is that that WAS said, until it corrupted into the word "ain't". "Amn't" is a bit hard to say and so probably got corrupted in that way.

Marjorie in Boston, MA:

I never called spaghetti "pasghetti," although quite a few of my friends did. However, I did pronounce ravioli "raveloli"as my mother fondly reminds me from time to time.

Continuing on with spoonerisms, Mike in Brisbane:

I think my favourite one of all time was by an ABC Radio announcer, in a news bulletin some years back: "In Sydney today, a lady working in her garden was bitten on the funnel by a fingerweb spider....."

Richard in Boulder, CO:

One Spoonerism that I think is better than the original word is "flutterbye" (butterfly).

Mickelbear had one:

My favourite spoonerism is definitely keys and parrots - for peas and carrots.

Mike added:

Caleb, a sly drool is the same as a slipstick - sounds like it would be handy for working it out?

Jan had a couple:

Usher to wedding guest: "May I sew you to your sheet?"
He was riding a "well-boiled icicle".
After the avalanche, the town was buried under "sons of toil."

Matt in Minneapolis answered the metathesis query:

Someone (Caleb perhaps?) recently asked for a word for the punning, letter-switching sort of WordPlay. Peter Bowler's "The Superior Person's Book of Words" (published in Australia, BTW) offers paronomasia and those who engage or delight in such things paronomasiacs.

Patrick in San Jose, CA:

Finally, I read recently about a speech delivered in the House of Commons in London. The speaker had referred to something or someone as being "about as useful as a flat cap in a submarine" and the commentators were trying to figure out what he had meant. The best theory I heard (reaching, I know) was that if for some reason you *had* to wear headgear on a submarine with its restricted headroom, a flat cap might not be a bad idea (as opposed to a tall helmet, or a sombrero, or whatever), and perhaps that was what the speaker had had in mind...but then it turned out to have been a delightful spoonerism: it seems he had meant to say "about as useful as a cat flap in a submarine" which is pretty unequivocal... :-)

   Jim in Philadelphia on switching letters around:
For more Weird Al Yankovic, how about his parody of Greg Kihn's (Our Love's in) Jeopardy: (I Lost On) Jeopardy. (For those of you not in the U.S. Jeopardy is a tv game show with varying shades of difficulty in their trivia questions, where they give the "answers" and you have to supply the "questions.")
Tom Petty and Stevie Nicks's Stop Draggin' My Heart Around became Stop Draggin' My Car Around
Madonna's Like a Virgin became Like a Surgeon (now THAT one's a classic!)
Nirvana's Smells Like Teen Spirit became Smells Like Nirvana (the one line in there "Boy this ought to bug your parents!" really hits it...)
And the oft-covered (forgive me if I don't remember who did the original... Tommy James, by chance?) I Think We're Alone Now became I Think I'm a Clone Now
   Matt added:
Having been a big fan of Dr. Demento (host of a radio show which plays obscure, humorous, and/or parody songs) in my high school days, I've heard many of Weird Al Yankovic's songs. Some of his parodies (in the order I think of them, not necessarily chronologically):
"My Bologna" (to the tune of The Knack's "My Sharona")
"Like A Surgeon" (to the tune of Madonna's "Like A Virgin")

"I Want A New Duck" (Huey Lewis & the News' "I Want A New Drug")
"Eat It" (Michael Jackson's "Beat It")
"Ricky" (an I Love Lucy version of Toni Basil's "Mickey")
"Smells Like Nirvana" ("Smells Like Teen Spirit")
"I Lost On Jeopardy" (from "Our Love's In Jeopardy". I can't think of the artist at the moment.)
"King Of Suede" (from The Police's "King of Pain")

On parsing, Jeff in Edinburgh, UK asked:
Is there a name for the following type of wordplay?:
man's laughter = manslaughter or psychotherapist = psycho the rapist

Zeno contributed:
Attributed to Dorothy Parker:
Horticulture: You can lead a whore to culture but can you make her think?

Caleb wrote "there must be another term for taking the words and collapsing them?"

Matt in Minneapolis, MN suggested:
I believe the word you want is portmanteau (French-derived word for suitcase). The undisputed master of these was Lewis Carroll [Fairly easy trivia question: What was his real name? Bonus: How about his questionable hobby?] The Alice-Humpty Dumpty conversation is full of portmanteaux. (what a wonderful plural form!)

Words that ought to be words but aren't
DYSTYPIA: I love the word dystypia for when your fingers miss on the keyboard. I always find myself typing fo (of) and teh (the), and for some odd reason, reserach (research).

Jim in Philadelphia returned to mondegreens:
It's interesting that we should be bringing up the topics of ear-

worms... I recently purchased the CD "Jagged Little Pill," by Alanis Morissette. (One of the best albums released so far this year, IMNSHO)) There's one song on it that's played fairly often on the radio right now called You Oughta Know. It's a sexy, perverted break up song, kind of like Like the Way I Do, by Melissa Etheridge. When I read the lyrics to You Oughta Know, I laughed at myself because here's the chorus:

> And I'm here to remind you
> Of the mess you left when you went away
> It's not fair to deny me
> Of the cross I bear that you gave me
> You you you you oughta know.

This makes a lot more sense than what I thought she was singing, or "It's not fair to deny me / Of the cross-eyed bear that you gave me")

--

Jan brought up the topic of odd names – Places:
These are actual names of towns in Texas:
Bee House, Bigfoot, Big Lake, Big Sandy, Big Spring, Big Thicket, Big Wells, Box Church, Chihuahua Farm, Coffee City, Cuthand, Dime Box, Fair Play, Friday, Gay Hill, Goodnight, Gun Barrel City, Halfway, Heckville, Jolly, Lovelady, Magnet, Needmore, New Deal, New Home, New Hope, Old Glory, Pluck, Ponder, Quicksand, Rainbow, Raisin, Seven Sisters, Sour Lake, Sugar Land, Sweetwater, Telephone, Three Rivers, Twin Sisters, Utopia, Wink, Wizard Wells.
[How about this for a newsbrief: "Jolly Man Drowns in Three Rivers -- Relatives in Fair Play Suspect Foul Play. Memorial Service to be held Saturday in Friday, Followed by Interment in Quicksand."(!?!)]

--

Susan in Cheney, WA answered a query:
About the similarities between Michoacan and Michigan: I have not read that book mentioned but being Hispanic and having lots of Latin American studies under my belt I know that those two terms are Indian words meaning something like "land of many lakes" in both

languages. Michoacan, by the way, is a beautiful and not-too-touristy state to visit and enjoy the real Mexico.

--

On the naming of gadgets, Jack in London observed:
About a year ago I wrote an article about the topic, where I noted that the most popular names on the Internet were the names of the planets (Mercury, Venus etc). What I was too thick to notice, until a reader told me, was that this was probably because most Internet servers are Suns. (groan)

--

Lomond in Sacramento said:
Funny sayings: Heard during the TV coverage of a basketball game during the US Olympic Festival - "They have had an innumerable number of chances to score."

Penelope in Michigan answered a query on odd names – people:
Louis Carroll: real name was Charles Lutwidge Dodgson; his questionable hobby was taking picture of naked little girls.

--

Frank in Ottawa wrote:
For them wot don't know, "Taffy" is a generic name for Welshmen, as "Jock" for Scots and "Paddy" for Irish.

Mike in Brisbane commented:
Yep, and "Taffy" is a diminutive(?) of "David"

--

Matt in Minneapolis, MN recalled the alternate US national anthem: America the Beautiful:
> God mend thy ev'ry flaw. (the first verse). Read the others.
> O beautiful for spacious skies,
> For amber waves of grain,
> For purple mountain majesties
> Above the fruited plain!
> America! America! God shed His grace on thee,

And crown thy good with brotherhood
From sea to shining sea!
O beautiful for pilgrim feet,
Whose stern impassion'd stress
A thoroughfare for freedom beat
Across the wilderness!
America! America! God mend thine ev'ry flaw,
Confirm thy soul in self-control,
Thy liberty in law!
O beautiful for heroes proved In liberating strife,
Who more than self their country loved,
And mercy more than life!
America! America! May God thy gold refine
Till all success be nobleness,
And ev'ry gain divine!
O Beautiful for patriot dream
That sees beyond the years
Thine alabaster cities gleam,
Undimmed by human tears!
America! America! God shed His grace on thee,
And crown thy good with brotherhood
From sea to shining sea!

--

In a discussion about snakes, John in Keele said:
"The good news about poisonous snakes is that they aren't well adapted to killing humans, so even if you have the bite marks you may not have been injected."

Bob in Chicago responded:
This brought to mind a little poem that I memorized in the Boy Scouts many years ago to aid in differentiating between the deadly coral snake and the similar looking but harmless king snake by noting the order of their colorful red, yellow, and black marking bands...
"Red to yellow, kill-a-fellow. Red to black, venom-lack".

Phil in Salt Lake City countered:
Wouldn't this depend on whether one is reckoning from the head toward the tail or vice versa? If there are only three colors, any two are going to be adjacent in one direction or the other.

Rich in Rindge, NH recalled the mnemonic:
I learned the rhyme as:
> Red on black, venom lack.
> Red on yellow, kill a fellow.

--

Dana said:
"Westinghoused is what one became when the then-new AC current entered homes".
To which Wes objects the terminology: Is this the same as alternating current current? Many people use this term, but I think it is redundant.

--

Bill in Lexington, KY had a pet peeve:
While we're on the subject, I've seen the abomination "alot" appear in the digest twice lately. Does the writer mean "a lot", "allot", or the absence of "lot"?

--

Jane in Hobart, AU wanted to discuss speech fillers:
I'm interested to hear if anyone has special words that they use in conversation when they can't recall the name of the object they are describing. My family has at least three of these (I guess we are somewhat absentminded). For example, "Could you please pass me that...ah..thingamajig." and "I saw a blue...um..whatchamacallit..yesterday." and "Where did I put that little..um..doobilacky?" No, they're not Aboriginal words, just conversation-fillers. Any others?

Katherine in Berkeley answered:
Thingamajig and watchamacallit, definitely. "Doohickey" is another one, though not used in my family. And some of my friends use

"whatshisface" for the equivalent when it's a person's name (rather than an object's) they're trying to recall.

And Kat in Rochester, NY:
Regarding the thread on alternate names for 'that thing over there', another list I'm on discussed this several months ago. The variety of synonyms was impressive. Can't find my archive disk at the moment, but off the top of my head:
froomis, framiss, thingamahoozie, whatsit, dinglezapper, itsyzit, youknowwhat

And Pat in Collegeville, MN:
Whatchamacallits: The U-speaking English I have conversed with refer to them as doodahs, which I can't remember anyone's noting so far. I wonder what they must think of the Camptown ladies in the song of the same name.

Dani in Atlanta, GA:
Re 'whatchamacallit,' 'thingmabob,' and I have some to add. These are courtesy of Mz. Feezuhkyl Thayruppeee: 'whoozywhatzy,' 'mombodoozie,' and, my favorite, 'flotchee doo' as in "Daaaneeeeh, hon, see if you can pick up that flotchee doo over there [two syllables: Thayr-RR] and raise it over your head."

Sara in Boston:
My favorite word for something you can't remember the name of is "whozeewhatsis."

Frank in Ottawa said about fillers: Umm, err, etc.
When Brits are briefly searching for the next word in conversation, they tend to say "Um", as in, "I'll have a pint of ... um ... Best Bitter please"
Canadians tend to say, "What about them ... er ... Blue Jays, Eh!"
Russians use "Nu" or "Znachit"
What expressions, usually monosyllabic, are used in other parts of the world to fill in these brief gaps. Is there a word for them?

Mike in Brisbane, AU:
On that Numbers thread - did any one mention:
The fourth estate? Which I think means the press - what were the other three?
And The Third world
> Alex in Adelaide added:
>> First and ten,
>> On all fours
>> $64000 question
>> Mach 1
> And Marilyn in San Francisco
On the number phrases thread, how about "the whole nine yards"?
> And Paul in Sydney, NS:
Number phrases: anyone mention "fifth column" yet?
> And Nite Owl:
>> Cloud Nine
>> Three's a crowd
>> Two cents worth.

--

Mike in Brisbane invoked the Pet Peeve Department:
Many of our Australian politicians use the phrase "The reality is" frequently and often. Of course, it never is.
And the number of people who pepper their speechifying with "I mean", is beyond belief. I mean, it's really terrible.
> And Kent proposed:
A pet peeve is "What it is, is..." Now that I have noticed it, I catch myself saying the dreaded words. I can't stop myself; I have no substitute phrase. Help!

--

Someone submitted a list of oxymorons, unattributed: Some favourite oxymorons:
> Assistant supervisor
> New tradition

Original copy
Plastic glass
Uninvited guest
Highly depressed
Live recording
Authentic reproduction
Partial cease-fire
Limited lifetime guarantee
Elevated subway
Dry lake
True replica
Forward lateral
Standard options

--

Marjorie in Boston: Oxymorons:
The erudite Mike Down Under muses: "Original meanings department: I was looking at a novel recently which was printed in the 1700s, which made it intrinsically interesting, but was struck by a passage which made it clear that the original meaning of "terrible" was "to inspire terror". Makes the phrase "terribly good" a bit of an oxymoron, doesn't it?"
Yes! Another good example is "awfully good." There must be other oxymorons that we use daily without thinking about it. Can anybody think of others?

--

Cindy in Montpellier, VT on redundancies:
I was thinking once about redundant terms. Soon the phrase "equal justice for all" came to mind, and I began to consider how repetitious it is. If something is equal and for all, naturally it is just. Something for all and just has to be equal. If Something is not given equally, it is not just, and if only a few people can use it, it is neither equal nor just. Therefore, since equality involves using all, and justice cannot be served without equality or everyone being included, the phrase "equal

justice for all" is doubly redundant. So much for a wonderful saying. I challenge someone to find more redundancies.

Richard in Tempe, AZ rose to the challenge:
I find your challenge *very* unique...

Caleb in Albany, NY disagreed:
This is not redundant. It is incorrect. "Very" does not repeat "unique"; it modifies it in a syntactically incorrect manner. But I get the gist of where you're going, Richard. How about "3 a.m. in the morning"? That would be a redundancy.

David in Glendale, CA picked up on the "equal justice for all":
IMO, the phrase is well-carpentered, and any sins are those of omission of a specific detail, not commission of redundancy.
Justice has more overtones of being what one deserves, and may or may not be equal, indeed, is more likely than not unequal. (I deserve better than you deserve, because you have been evil and I have been pure and good...)
Ergo, "equal" qualifies "Justice," so is not redundant.
"Equal justice" need not be for all -- it could be equal for only two people, thee and me.
Ergo, "for All" pins down the meaning of "Equal Justice" somewhat, so it is not a redundancy.
Actually, "equal" justice is impossible...which is probably why the original phrase is "with liberty and justice for all."
IMO, its major flaw is that it does not explain who "All" are. Some folks do not regard this ambiguity as a flaw, since it has enhanced its lasting power (though it has not lasted as long as some people think, since the Pledge of Allegiance is a Johnny-come-lately among USA revered rites -- and I do mean "rites"). Because it does _not_ specify who-all Equal Justice is for, it adapts easily to our changing beliefs as they become more inclusive than landowning, non-indentured or enslaved males.
As for being a Johnny-come-lately, more and more people in the USA do not realize that the Pledge of Allegiance was not created at the

same time as the Declaration of Independence, or even the Constitution, or that the phrase "under God" is a relatively recent addition.

Zeno in Minneapolis, MN continued the argument:
Why is it just if something is both equal and for all? Let us say that everyone were equally hungry, would you call that, ipso facto, just? Suppose everyone were equally in pain, would you call that just? Suppose everyone were in the midst of great pleasure, would that be just? Imagine that we took away your computer because there are people in India who don't have one, and since we can't afford to give everyone a computer we decided to take eveyone's away -- would that be just?

And responding to the assertion from Cindy that "Something for all and just has to be equal":
So death for all Jews is just, because it is for all of them? Cheap gasoline for all Americans is just because it is for all of them? Expensive gasoline for Europeans is just because it is for all of them? No gasoline for anyone is just because we can't afford gasoline for everyone on earth?

Tommy in Minneapolis, MN also commented:
Actually, the phrase "equal justice for all" is redundant only if you ASSUME that equality is just. You're reading this phrase with a cultural/political/historical prejudice. I would venture to guess that if we were to root out the origin of this phrase the redundancy might not be so obvious.

And Johanna in New York:
The Pledge of Allegiance was written by Francis Bellamy, a socialist Baptist minister, who is buried in Rome, New York. The words "under God" were added shortly before I began kindergarten in 1954. Bellamy's original words were previously modified slightly, though I can't quote the original.

Brad quoted the _Encyclopedia Britannica_:
The pledge of allegiance to the flag of the United States of America was first published in the juvenile periodical _The Youth's Companion_ on September 8, 1892, in the following form: "I pledge allegiance

to my Flag and the Republic for which it stands; one nation indivisible, with liberty and Justice for all." The words "the flag of the United States of America" were substituted for "my Flag" in 1924, and the pledge was officially recognized by the U.S. government in 1942. In 1954, at Pres. Dwight D. Eisenhower's urging, the Congress legislated "under God" be added, making the pledge read: I pledge allegiance to the flag of the United States of America and to the Republic for which it stands, one nation under God, indivisible, with liberty and justice for all.

According to the legislation of 1954, one is supposed to stand upright, remove any headdress, and place the right hand over the heart while reciting the pledge.

--

Ann-Elizabeth, Boulder, CO asked:
Speaking of which, why do we use the phrase "Upstate NY" when the state is nearly as wide as it is tall. And, why don't we use "Upstate California" which at least generally runs north and south?

--

Barb in Stephenville, TX brought up Idioms/metaphors:
Any other sport out there infiltrated our grammar to describe someone's opinions on any topic like baseball terms have done:.....examples:
> Way off base
> Way out in left field
> Off the wall

However, "off the wall" in baseball usually means something almost as good as a home run. While in conversation it is usually a put down. Any ideas?

Hep countered with:
I always thought off the wall was not a sports reference but, rather, referred to padded cells in asylums. For example, an idea is off the wall, the idea is crazy.

--

Martin in Los Angeles referred to one of the messages in a recent word-play (about a phrase - "And so to bed" by, I believe, Pepys (spelling?)):
It made me think of two from two novels that, for whatever reason, have stuck in my mind. They are:
"Always merry and bright" from a Henry Miller novel (possibly one of the Tropics)
"And so it goes" from Kurt Vonnegut's "Slaughterhouse Five"
Are there others that fellow W-Pers recall fondly?
The phrase (since I started this, I can set the rules and you can disregard them (though that would be dissn' me)) must occur a number of times in the novel and be used in such a way as to emphasize and add emotional overtones to the situations where it is used.

--

On mixed metaphors, HAR offered:
It can be amusing when someone mixes metaphors. I once heard a sports commentator describe a player as being "green behind the ears".

--

Alan asked about the origin of a phrase:
What is the meaning and provenance of the phrase "to eat a peach." I am wondering as it is the title of one of my favorite records (Allman Bros.) and I have also seen it used once in print but was unable to fathom its meaning from the context.

Janet in Calgary answered:
The only reference I know to eating a peach is in Eliot's "The Love Song of J. Alfred Prufrock". The interpretation put on the line "Shall I part my hair behind? Do I dare to eat a peach?" given to us by my high school English teacher was that Prufrock was a middle-aged man constantly second guessing his impulses, worrying that he would appear eccentric or odd.
Daring to eat a peach was, in my teacher's theory, all related to the

possible indignities of having peach juice dribbling down your chin, or a piece of skin caught in your teeth.

Hep added:
Actually, the meaning of eat a peach changed in the mid-70's after one of the Allman Brothers was killed when his motorcycle rammed into a truck carrying a load of peaches. After that the meaning changed to die, to buy the farm. The last album with all the Allman Brothers on it was titled Eat a Peach.

--

Euphemisms
Anybody have any idea why so many of the euphemisms for sex and sexual organs are related to carpentry? (Hammer, Screw, Nail, Drill, Bang, Ream, Joint, Nuts, Tool) Was sex invented by carpenters? Is that also why they call it a "woody"? Just some mental meanderings on a Saturday morning before I bolt

Barbara in Stephenville, TX asked:
Anyone have any idea how the word 'moonshine' came to define illegal brew? Does the word predate US prohibition?

Jeff in Edinburgh, UK:
Re "Moonshine": This term was originally used in Britain to denote brandy illegally smuggled by moonlight.

Phil in Salt Lake City:
My guess is that the production of said "illegal brew" was mainly done when the *moon shines*, at night in the back woods. It may be appropriate to note that the use of the word "was" in not really correct. Apparently some still carry out such brewing activities, presumably to avoid taxes.
I lived in Georgia for several years, and we heard cautions about driving around in unfamiliar country well off the main roads—especially at night. People carrying out such nocturnal brewing activities seem

to be a bit touchy about intruders. Not really safe to trespass. Also, we had the amusing experience of buying a larger-than-usual quantity of sugar for home canning and storage purposes--and receiving some veeeery strange looks from the grocery store clerk. I'm sure she thought we were stocking up for the night's brewing activities.

Penelope in Michigan:
Moon shine is corn liquor, I know because my grandfather was a Moonshiner and I was about 10 years old when I and an assorted group of cousins found his still and got introduced to Moonshine. Glen Fiddich is much better.

Katherine in Oakland:
In American English (and maybe elsewhere, but I don't know) we speak of "moonlighting" by anyone who has an additional job for extra money.
Don't know of any connection with (our) "moonshine"...anybody else?
--
Jeff in Edinburgh:
On the subject of latrines (I call it the "bog" or "loo") The synonyms I hate most are the "restroom" and the "bathroom", since if there's only a tiolet in it, you do neither of the above. An American (for it, I presume, is they that use these phrases oft.) visited the labs I work in a couple of months ago and asked where the restroom was. It took me a few seonds to work that one out.
My fav'e euphemisms are: "gingerbread office", "temple of cloacina", "cackatorium" and "thunder box" (all from McDonald, DOTAE).
Oh, yes, a newspaper clipping quoted in "Private eye" last week mentioned that "the Japanese language has more than 650 expressions to describe the task of visiting the toilet" -- Shee-it!

Mike in Brisbane:
"Loo" comes from the custom of calling out "gardy loo" (a corruption

of French - gardez l'eau) before the contents of the chamber pot was precipitated into the street below.

Alex in Adelaide:
On the toilet names I remember a phrase from my childhood used at times by my grandmother who refers to it as "Là où vont en ruines les delices de la cuisine" which can be roughly translated as " There where fall in decay the delicacies of the day"

Katherine in Oakland, CA:
That one's good!
A new (to me) one for the related activities: I spent some time this weekend with an old acquaintance who refers to "euphemizing"--"OK, I have to euphemize, and then we can go to the bookstores."
--
Michael in Mesa AZ responded to a remark:
"You must remember that it's X in the states and E across the pond." Ecstasy or XTC. "E's are good" according to Ebeneezer Goode. Personally, I've never been "on X," although I have read Alice in Wonderland about a godzillion times.
Cool wordplay from my childhood was on Mr. Roger's Neighborhood: in the Land of Makebelieve there was a donkey named Donkey Hoty.
--
Penelope in Michigan:
Question: When a person dies it seems that no one is able to say the word dead. You hear the terms passes, passed over, passed on, gone, gone away, at rest, or at peace. Ok so what is my question. Is the US the only place that it is damn near impossible for a person to say "I am sorry that your loved one died"? What other terms have any of you heard?

Pat in Collegeville, MN had suggestions:
Some expressions, given in context, not to use when referring to the

dear departed:
I'm so sorry your grandmother kicked off / bought the farm / kicked the bucket / went west.
My deepest sympathy. And where's the stiff?

Jim in Philadelphia weighed in:
Hang on a second. I've got the dead parrot routine on a CD. Let me transcribe that list:
He's bleeding demised! He's passed on. This parrot is no more. He has ceased to be. It's a stiff, bereft of life. He rests in peace. He snuffed it. He's up the creek and kicked the bucket. He shuffled off this mortal coil, run down the curtain, and joined the choir invisible! He's extinct. THIS IS AN EX-PARROT!

--

Bill in Lexington, KY responded to a remark:
"Who said: I'm not fat, I'm just short for my weight?":
My version is "I'm not overweight, I'm just underheight."

--

Bob in Chicago:
Judge Ito used an interesting euphemism yesterday during the "OJ" trial. He had sent the jurors on an excursion to Catalina Island by boat and some of them got seasick. He said that they returned from Catalina "barking at the seals" which he explained was an old fisherman's term for throwing up.

--

From Facebook (author unknown):
These insults are from an era before the English language got boiled down to 4-letter words. (As a Blogswallop follower you will know we don't like swearing!)
1. "He had delusions of adequacy" Walter Kerr
2. "He has all the virtues I dislike and none of the vices I admire."- Winston Churchill

3. "I have never killed a man, but I have read many obituaries with great pleasure. - Clarence Darrow
4. "He has never been known to use a word that might send a reader to the dictionary."-William Faulkner (about Ernest Hemingway)
5. "Poor Faulkner. Does he really think big emotions come from big words?"- Ernest Hemingway (about William Faulkner)
6. "Thank you for sending me a copy of your book; I'll waste no time reading it." - Moses Hadas
7. "I didn't attend the funeral, but I sent a nice letter saying I approved of it." - Mark Twain
8. "He has no enemies, but is intensely disliked by his friends." - Oscar Wilde
9. "I am enclosing two tickets to the first night of my new play; bring a friend, if you have one." -George Bernard Shaw to Winston Churchill
10. "Cannot possibly attend first night, will attend second... if there is one." - Winston Churchill, in response
11. "I feel so miserable without you; it's almost like having you here" - Stephen Bishop
12. "He is a self-made man and worships his creator." - John Bright
13. "I've just learned about his illness. Let's hope it's nothing trivial." - Irvin S. Cobb
14. "He is not only dull himself; he is the cause of dullness in others." - Samuel Johnson
15. "He is simply a shiver looking for a spine to run up. - Paul Keating
16. "He loves nature in spite of what it did to him." - Forrest Tucker
17. "Why do you sit there looking like an envelope without any address on it?" - Mark Twain
18. "His mother should have thrown him away and kept the stork." - Mae West
19. "Some cause happiness wherever they go; others, whenever they go." - Oscar Wilde

20. "He uses statistics as a drunken man uses lamp-posts... for support rather than illumination." - Andrew Lang (1844-1912)
21. "He has Van Gogh's ear for music." - Billy Wilder
22. "I've had a perfectly wonderful evening. But I'm afraid this wasn't it." - Groucho Marx
23. The exchange between Winston Churchill & Lady Astor: She said, "If you were my husband I'd give you poison." He said, "If you were my wife, I'd drink it."
24. "He can compress the most words into the smallest idea of any man I know." - Abraham Lincoln
25. "There's nothing wrong with you that reincarnation won't cure." -- Jack E. Leonard
26. "They never open their mouths without subtracting from the sum of human knowledge." --Thomas Brackett Reed
27. "He inherited some good instincts from his Quaker forebears, but by diligent hard work, he overcame them." -- James Reston (about Richard Nixon) —Robert L Truesdell

--

On euphemism, Mike in Brisbane queried:
Knowing your own language: I was browsing the Macquarie Dictionary of Australian Colloquialisms at the weekend, and came across a phrase I'd never heard used - 'to shoot a fairy' - meaning audible flatulence. I mentioned it a dinner party the other night, and no, no-one had ever heard it either, but each person came up with a variation which none of the others had heard, including 'to shoot a bunny' and 'to shoot a possum'. Any others?

Sandi said:
Mike asked for phrases that mean audible flatulence. In these parts it's known as "cutting the cheese".

And Barbara in Stephenville, TX:
Barking spiders - another definition for cutting the cheese.

And Steven in Atlanta:
Incidentally, I always thought "cutting the cheese" denoted *non*-au-

dible flatulence, i.e. the silent killer. Must be a few more colorful euphemisms out there ....

And Dave in Cary, NC:
Last year Spinal Tap came out with a new album called 'Break Like the Wind'

Susi in Louisville KY:
On flatulence, ladies "poot" in these parts. Back home, Mother had squeaky shoes in public, but stepped on a frog at home.

And Ken in Victoria, BC:
On the "What do you call it thread" my grandmother's group always referred to the posterior expulsion of flammable gases as a "pardon me. e.g. "Oh dear. I just made a pardon me."
According the medical reference text I have on hand, men average 14 expulsions per day. There is no figure listed to women.

David in Phoenix, AZ:
"I thought I heard a buck snort!" is a phrase that I have heard in the midwestern US. My sister-in-law has taught my two nieces that they make "fluffs." "Squeeze a duck" is one I heard from a friend who is originally from the northeastern US.

Richard in Tempe, AZ:
Years ago a friend's child used the word "rumble." Ours picked it up – we giggled over it -- and started saying, " 'Scuse me! I rumbled!"

Jeff in Melbourne:
Ooh, and BTW, while we are talking about grandmothers and anal eructation, my Nana refers to the seepings as Windibobs. Now, there's a goody.

Dave in Glendale:
And finally, in respect to my neighbor's flatulence ("You might very well do so; I, of course, could never comment"), is there any better word for a seeper than ... seeper?

Bob in Chicago:
Several times when visiting the southwestern United States I have heard the expression "drier than a popcorn fart" :)

Steve adds to Alyssa's growing list for "pregnant":
There are also gravid, enceinte, anticipating a blessed event, brooding, wearing her apron high, in a delicate condition, carrying young, and I can't believe no one's mentioned expecting, but the one that fits is: great with child. "

Mike in Brisbane added:
And a variant - from the old "Careless Love" - "Now my apron strings don't pin, and you pass my door, but you don't come in".

Giles in New Castle, AU said "Not a pot to piss in," meaning broke.

Lee in Sacramento countered:
I've always heard (and used) the phrase "not a pot nor a window to throw it out of."

Euphemistic names for kissing came from Sara in Boston:
Kissing, buss, peck, smooch, suck face, tongue tango.

Bob in Chicago had some more:
Smack, lip nibble, pucker suck, labium lick, labellum latch, labial embrocate, amorous embouchure, lippy sip.

Bill in Columbia, CT:
This discourse on kissing is rather fascinating. Now at last I know why I have bad breath. All I can think of is the movie On Golden Pond when the kid told Henry Fonda that he enjoyed "Sucking Face."

Sara in Boston posed a challenge:
Another word question: how many euphemisms for "money" can we come up with? Examples:
Cash, Moolah, Clams, Samolians, Bananas, Poundage, Bucks, etc.
Running short on cashish,

Katherine in Berkeley added:
Dough, Bread, Greenbacks, smackers.
I'll think of more. Never heard "bananas" before in this context! And

I've always seen "samolians" spelled as "simoleons"...but I wish I knew the derivation thereof! And is it related to "simony"?

Susi had few of her own:

In the US: dough, dead presidents, pocket change (not to be confused with pocket pool), long green, greenbacks, and the mad (cabfare if you fought with your date), pin, and egg varieties (the money a woman socked away for a rainy day).

Wayne in Indiana: Names for money....

    A lot of money = A bundle
    A fin = A five dollar bill
    An Xer = A ten dollar bill
    A C note = A hundred dollar bill
    American currency = Greenback, lettuce and cabbage

Mike in Brisbane:

And on the money word thread - an expression for being broke that I like is "Haven't got a brass razoo." Does anyone know where brass razoos were current?

In the interests of preserving the remnants of Australia's pre-decimal culture, the old names for Australian currency were:

    threepence = a tray, threepenny bit
    Sixpence = a zack
    shilling = a deener, a bob
    two shillings = two bob
    ten shilling note = ten bob
    one pound note = a quid
    Five pound note = a spin
    Ten pound note = a brick

With the advent of dismal currency, all we seem to talk about now is dollars and bucks. Inflation has caused the smaller coins to disappear, and the note denominations get larger and larger.

Gerry in Ottawa chimed in:

Serendipity strikes again. While looking unsuccessfully for synonyms for money, I ran across "monkey wrench" which came up recently.

According to Paul Dickson's Word Treasury, it was invented in 1856 by a man named Monk who worked for the Springfield, Massachusetts firm of Bemis and Call. First called Monk's wrench, it later became monkey wrench. By the way, my Dictionary of Americanisms tells me that "simoleon" as another word for dollar, was formed on the analogy of "napoleon," an earlier French coin. It doesn't explain the "sim" part except to say that it may be derived from the name "Simon." But why Simon?

And on the topic of trouser snake, Gerry said:
Moving on to another thread, a trouser "trout?" Well, I knew we all had our physical differences but still...

--

Matt in Minneapolis, MN on contextual usage:
[The following was written by someone else. Possibly Richard Lederer - I know I saw something similar in one of his books.]
There is a two-letter word that perhaps has more meaning than any other two-letter word, and that is "UP."
It's easy to understand UP, meaning toward the sky or at the top of the list, but when we waken in the morning, why do we wake UP? At a meeting, why does a topic come UP? Why do we speak UP and why are the officers UP for election and why is it UP to the secretary to write UP a report?
We call UP our friends and we use it to brighten UP a room, polish UP the silver, we warm UP the leftovers and clean UP the kitchen. We lock UP the house and some guys fix UP the old car.
At other times the little word has real special meaning. People stir UP trouble, line UP for tickets, work UP an appetite, and think UP excuses.
To be dressed is one thing but to be dressed UP is special.
And this UP is confusing:
A drain must be opened UP because it is stopped UP.
We open UP a store in the morning but we close it UP at night.
We seem to be pretty mixed UP about UP!

To be knowledgeable of the proper uses of UP, look UP the word in the dictionary. In a desk size dictionary, takes UP almost 1/4th the page and definitions add UP to about thirty.

If you are UP to it, you might try building UP a list of the many ways UP is used. It will take UP a lot of your time, but if you don't give UP, you may wind UP with a hundred or more.

When it threatens to rain, we say it is clouding UP. When the sun comes out we say it is clearing UP. When it rains, it wets UP the earth. When it doesn't rain for a while, things dry UP.

One could go on and on, but I'll wrap it UP, for now my time is UP, so... I'll shut UP...!

Richard added:

I tried to look up "up," but I was so upset that I was unable to come up with the original source (I don't believe it was Lederer), that I decided to give up before I threw up.

--

HAR took us back to the subject of fillers:

I've heard them called, uh, hesitation phonemes. A very common one in Spanish is este...

Terrence in Bermuda noted:

The Brits I know, especially Public School Brits, generally don't say "Um" but rather a very long and very annoying "Aaaaaaaaaaaahhhhhhhhhh" in a pained tone like a death rattle, which, after four or five of them are used in a single sentence, is just what one longs to really hear.

Patrick in San Jose:

The one I normally come across in French is "euhhhhhhh".

Steven in Atlanta, GA:

On language bits that are essentially meaningless except perhaps as verbal punctuation: In Japanese sentences "ano" is frequently used as a think-filler and attention-getter, and most any declarative sentence ends with the semi-interrogative "ne" (that's nay not neh, you knights who say knee).

Sara in Boston:
Um, well, er... the other space-filler-when-trying-to start-one's-brain I've often heard in Japanese is "eto" (pronounced "ay-toe," and dragged out).

--

On couplets, Richard in Boulder, CO asked:
Hugger-mugger, not well done! Patched together.
For extra points, words like the above follow a certain pattern: razzle/dazzle, hankie/pankie, hocus/pocus, etc. Can you find the rule they operate under? Hint - try to reverse the words.

John in Kansas City, MO answered:
I don't have the answer at hand, but enthusiastically direct word lovers to linguist Steven Pinker's new book "The Language Instinct." Within the first few chapters he deals in precise terms with this very question. It has to do with the formation of certain sounds by the tongue and the ease with which it moves from one formation to other. I only wish I could summarize his thoughts more accurately. I can't, so read the book. It's a delight of common sense, clinical research, world history, and intelligent supposition.

And Richard in Boulder, CO:
The rule according to Pinker is that the less obstructive consonant leads the dynamic duo. I went over his list of these words (there must be a name for them) and could not argue with him. However, the obtrusiveness of consonants is not the most obvious thing.
But remember vowels? They are all unobstructed! If he is correct then a vowel will never follow a consonant is such a construction.
I checked and could not find any. Your itsy bitsy and also abbra/cadabra, antsy/pantsy, eeny/minee etc. Find one and you can prove him wrong (although I would say he is still right most of the time).

--

David in Glendale on political correctness:
If you've had it with waiter/waitress (the word, not the long-suffering person), try the simple: "server." Much more descriptive (waiters don't

wait, except when I can't make up my mind about what to choose) and gender-neutral.

HAR again:
On the "he/she" and "gender-neutral" thread: What's wrong with "he and she", "him and her"? For my money inventions like "s/he" and "s/him" are semi-literate abominations. And why not "chairman" and "chairwoman", etc? Ever notice that a "spokesperson" is almost always a woman?

Someone noted:
I don't mind "chair" (or even "committee director," "leader," "supervisor" or "manager") for "chairman." (I expect some opposition to "chair.")

Steven in Seattle, WA:
Chair is a perfectly good use of synecdoche, in the same vein as using "crown" to represent the British royal personage. No contest from me.

Lorianne in Saskatoon, Ca:
Gender-neutral third person Pronoun, I like to use they/them. Its usage in this way goes back a few hundred years, so I feel justified. However, professors tend not to like this too much. It's more acceptable in spoken, rather than written English, at least in my dialect.

--

Johanna in NY introduced us to a peculiar usage:
Over much of upstate New York, among children and the uneducated, it is common to indicate agreement in the negative. Examples:

> Child 1: My brother still wets the bed.
> Child 2: So doesn't Jimmy. (Meaning he wets the bed also.)
> Adult 1: My kids are driving me crazy!
> Adult 2: So aren't mine!

My husband, who comes from New York City, and my mother, who came from the Middle West, are and were completely mystified by this. My mother trained it out of her children through much teasing, though she failed on other native speech habits.

--

On similes, someone enquired:
>> Carrying coal to Newcastle"?...or
>> "Selling refrigerators to the Eskimos"?...or
>> "Preaching to the choir"?...or

??? (help me out somebody)

And Susi in Louisville KY answered:
Somebody made a fortune sending coal to Newcastle during a coal strike. Eskimos still buy refrigerators-to keep food from freezing (those 50s-vintage ones with the Dodge bodies and 4" of insulation would be preferred, I guess). As for preaching to the choir, anything to keep them awake! My hubby is an operatic bass-bari with a snore like a foghorn in heat.

--

Mike in Brisbane changed gear:
Here's a try for a new thread, too...
What expressions do people have for persons who talk a great deal? Some of my favourites are:
>> "He'd talk the leg off an iron pot." (Why?)
>> "She'd talk under six feet of wet concrete."
>> "He'd talk till the cows come home."
>> "He'd talk the hind leg off a donkey." - There's those poor donkeys again!

Whaddaya reckon?

Linda commented on the favorite simile: COLD AS A....
The whole phrase is, "Cold as a witch's tit in a brass bra." Sounds darn nippy to me! Why a witch, in particular, would wear a brass bra I don't know.

Then, Court in Wayne, IN:
Penny your "How cold is it?" was timely and I enjoyed it very much. I put it on both BBSs that I run. Hope you don't mind. Some time back there was some references to the cold and the anatomy of a witch's breast. Most often heard in this area for very cold weather is the loosing of parts from a brass monkey. The most used expression involving

parts of the breast is when you are in serious trouble, parts of it get "caught in the wringer."

--

Gerry in Ottawa, picked up on British vs. American:
Secondly, and this almost gets us back to the earlier biscuit thread, there's the problem of "cake" and "gateau." It all started when we saw Black Forest Gateau on a menu and, assuming that this was just your usual bit of restaurant pretension, told the waitress that we'd both have the Black Forest Cake. "You mean the Gateau," she replied. "Why do you call it that?" I asked peevishly. "'Cos that's its name, innit?" she said. Well, that was a hard argument to beat so I let it go. Someone later suggested that "cake" in England was normally reserved for good old straightforward stuff like pound cake and sponge cake but that, once it was gussied up with icing, whipped cream, cherries and other foreign foofaraw, it became a "gateau." Since that someone was our daughter Janet's mother-in-law, perish forbid - as they used to say on Duffy's Tavern - that I should question this but I still wouldn't mind hearing from others. Incidentally, shouldn't there be some easier way of saying "our daughter's mother-in-law?" Seems a bit roundabout.

Maeve in Urbana, IL, followed up:
Gerald wrote about his recent trip to England and why they call cakes gateaux. I don't know why but I've always been intrigued by the Franco-isms of British English, especially in food (my favorite thing to think about). They also call eggplant aubergines (which makes more sense than eggplant re: a recent posting), and zucchini are courgettes. Considering that both of these items are not indigenous to England or, I would assume, France, I find it surprising that, in the case of zucchini, the French term is used and not the term which I would suppose to come from other origins (Spain? Italy? South America?). Can anyone shed any light on this?

Gerry continued on the same theme:
Jeff asked the other day whether the English had apartments, as op-

posed to flats. Well, they do but I'm a bit puzzled myself by the distinction. The Shorter Oxford gives two definitions. The first, which it says is archaic, is: "a suite of rooms in a house or building allotted to the use of an individual." It's in this sense, I suppose, that you often see references to "the Queen's apartments" in Buckingham Palace. The second and more recent is: "a single room in a house" but with the same meaning as before if used in the plural. What confuses me is that my wife and I rented what was called a "junior apartment" in London last month which was always referred to in the singular by the management but consisted of two rooms plus a miniscule bathroom and kitchen. Since the whole thing measured no more than 15 by 20 feet, you could hardly call it a suite but, on the other hand, it was more than a single room.

I'm beginning to suspect that "apartment" simply may have more snob appeal. I've just finished an English murder mystery, for example, where the hero sees an advertisement which says, "Rare opportunity to acquire remaining three years of seven-year lease in Luton's most prestigious apartment building." Checking it out, he asks "You got a flat in Samgarth House?" "That's right, sir," the receptionist tells him. "An apartment." Go figure.

    Dean responds to Gerry:

Gerald pointed out that 'apartment' has snob appeal in the UK. Of course, here 'flat' is très chic. Anglophilia being de rigueur for the American snob.

    Johanna in NY protested:

Dean - Where do you live? Around here "flat" and "apartment" refer to two different types of living spaces. A flat is one floor of a house - good old-fashioned two and three-flat houses, where a family lives on each floor. They may rent or own. Frequently a house is owned by two or three families, each of which has its own flat. An apartment is a portion of a floor which is rented out. A duplex is a more modern architectural arrangement, in which two families share a house, but live side by side, instead of layered.

My husband and I happen to live in a second-floor flat. That's enough flattery for now.

--

Mike said:
"Can someone please explain to me the bit about people looking at their hand when asked where they're from?"

Phil in Salt Lake City answered:
I recently heard the comment that you can always tell when someone is from _Michigan_ because when they explain where they are from, they always hold out their left hand and point to the back of it (shaped like the state) to show where in the state they live.

--

HAR answered a query:
Residents of Buenos Aires are Porteños.

--

Jesse in Sunnyvale, CA asked:
This reminds me of a bit of wordplay from a different list. How do you parse the following sentence?
"We need protection from the government.
"Without context, is there any kind of rule to determine if the speaker wants to be protected from the government or receive protection from (provided by) the government?

--

Phil in Salt Lake City brought up a sexist expression:
The phrase, as I am acquainted with it, refers to a man marrying a woman, perhaps after a period of cohabitation. I think of it in connection with the "Old West" for some reason. In marrying her, the man "makes an honest woman" of her. My comment referred to the one-sidedness of the phrase, as I have heard it, relating, I suppose, to the "double standard" in play, suggesting that in cohabiting, she was more "dishonest" that he. Anyone else familiar with that expression, or its application by gender?

Linda commented:
HONEST WOMEN / MEN: "Making an honest woman of her," as I am familiar with the phrase, means marrying her because you've had sex with her or even worse, (gasp!) gotten her pregnant (thereby making her "dishonest," one assumes).

Susi in Louisville, KY added:
In a like vein, one definition for honest is chaste or virtuous- remember when Hamlet asks Ophelia if she's honest and she's aghast? Presumably when you make an honest woman of her you restore her virtue, since anything else would require surgery.

Susi also answers a query from Andy in Chichester who asked "who, apropos the recent professions thread, is wondering why Smith is a more common name than, say, Farmer?":
Probably because there were so many farmers, but usually just one smith per area. The idea of English surnames was to be able to differentiate between the 20 "John the farmers" in the area, so you got one John Farmer, and the rest took something else – John whose farm was on the hill took Hill, etc. with Dale, Downs, River, Bank, on to town name, road name, etc. So, you start out with a pretty even distribution of surnames; maybe the Farmer extinction comes from farming being still a much higher mortality job than smithing, or maybe they just had more girl children. on a trivial note, it is now for persons in Korea surnamed Kim to marry each other-it was forbidden for years to marry someone with the same surname to avoid inbreeding (but then why are there so many Kims?).

--

Hank returned to the topic of collective nouns:
And now my contribution/puzzle: I noticed a month or so back a thread on the topic of collective nouns. For example, the collective noun for geese is gaggle. I was too busy at the time to actively participate here, but I think I will now be able to do so.
Some time ago, my sure-to-be-sainted mother asked me why a group of crows was called "a murder". (Is it only me, or do all mothers bother

their favorite son late on a Friday with questions like this??) After some reflection I was able to draw at least two conclusions. The first was that the term was rather odd and might be worth investigating. The second was that we should increase mom's medication.

I thought the best place to begin was to figure out the proper name for collective nouns. I have variously seen them called nouns of assemblage, nouns of multitude, etc. The earliest printed reference I've located which lists collectives, The Edgerton Manuscript; appr 1450, uses the phrase 'terms of venery'. It seems to come from the Sanskrit 'vanoti': he conquers or he hunts. This eventually became the Latin 'venari': to hunt game ... Eventually leading to venison. Unfortunately, crows were not mentioned here.

The Book of Saint Albans published in 1486 uses the term 'a murder of crows' but does not give a pedigree for the term. My two questions are:

    1) Is there a word which means 'collective noun'?

    2) Why is a murder of crows called a murder of crows?

Hank continued:

The term used was 'a murder of crows'. Most collective nouns are in some way descriptive of the animals themselves (sound, look) or of the group itself. My favorite oddball one was 'a school of fish'. I find that turned out to be a transcription error ... some medieval monk or another blew it... It was originally 'a shoal of fish'. The closest thing I've been able to find for crows was a phrase from a Middle English book dating from 1470 stating "... the rooks were crying bloody murder ...".

Sara in Boston suggested:

"Murder of crows:" has anyone considered that crows and ravens were historically the carrion birds who would gorge on the remains of a battlefield? In that sense, "murder" is probably quite appropriate. Does anyone know what the collective for ravens is?

Kat in Rochester answered to Sara:

I learned it as an 'unkindness' of ravens. Don't know where it came from. I suspect some poet is responsible.

THE POWER OF WORDS - 253

--

Gerry in Ottawa:
To enrich your lives even further, if that's possible, here's as comprehensive a list of so-called "nouns of assemblage" as I could put together from stuff around the house:

A shrewdness of apes; a pace or herd of asses; a cete of badgers; a sloth of bears; a swarm or grist of bees; a raft of birds(sitting on the water); a brace or leash of bucks; a drove of cattle; a clowder of cats; a chattering of choughs; a pod or covert of coots; a murder of crows; a herd of curlews; a gang of elk; a fesnyng of ferrets; a skulk of foxes; a gaggle of geese (on the ground); a skein of geese (in flight); a herd or tribe of goats; a charm of goldfinches; a down or husk of hares; a cast of hawks; a sedge or siege of herons; a haras of horses; a pack or mute of hounds; a kindle of kittens; an exaltation of larks; a leap of leopards; a pride of lions; a sord of mallards; a stud of mares; a labour of moles; a watch of nightingales; a muster of peacocks; a nye or nide of pheasants; a wing or congregation of plovers; a pack of ptarmigan; an unkindness of ravens; a building or clamour of rooks; a herd or pod of seals; a walk of snipe; a dray of squirrels; a murmuration of starlings; a herd or bevy of swans; a sounder or drift of wild swine; a flock of swifts; a spring of teals; a dool of turtledoves; a school, gam or pod of whales; a pack, rout or herd of wolves; and a fall of woodcock.

--

Giles in New Castle, NSW answered the query
"Can you think of a word containing all the vowels in order, once each, including y?":
I could answer this abstemiously, with just one word, but I choose to answer facetiously, with two!

--

A gentleman interjected and said:
I shall not name names, but, Janet, when you find a way for us men to figure out when a woman is *NOT* extremely hormonal... Hmmmmm...

Susi in Louisville, KY rebutted:
As a member of the Fighting Feminists (our mascot is the Blind Mohel), I'll carry the ball on this one. May I observe that women have a change in hormonal balance monthly. Men, however, have a constant flood of sex hormones to their brains. That is why their judgement is not to be trusted, why their mood is dependent on their recent sexual activity, why they cannot say the words "hey, buddy, how do you get to 1st and Main", why they cannot distinguish red from white and therefore wash them together, why they never want a Screaming Yellow Zonker at 3am, and why they cannot appreciate women's usual superiority. Here endeth the text from St. Lorena of Bobbit, cut 3. Be thou glad she didn't have pinking shears.

--

Frank in Ottawa answered to Amy who asked about a name for the transposition of initial letters of two or more consecutive words.
This is known as a Spoonerism, after the Reverend W.A. Spooner (died 1930) who was known for such inadvertent slips. A couple from the OED are:-
"He has just received a blushing crow."
"For real enjoyment, give me a well-boiled icicle."
Then there's the famous Australian ditty about the pheasant plucker. A couplet from it:-
"I'm not a pheasant plucker, I'm a pheasant plucker's wife,
And when we get together it's a pheasant plucking life."

--

Hank picked up on the topic of redundancies in naming objects:
I mentioned in response to a post from Linda how 'tautologies by translation' can occur, and asked for other examples. The one I used was "Schuylkill River". Schuylkill translated from the Dutch means "hidden stream"; thus, the current English derivation is "hidden stream river". In Lancashire, England is a place called Cheetwood; cheat being an old Celtic word for wood. I am sure there are many in

Australia (although I personally don't know of any) as well as more in the US and elsewhere. Any takers?

Elliot in Van Nuys, CA suggested:

Don't have the reference at hand, but in addition to such local favorites as The La Brea Tarpits (The the tarpits tarpits), there is a lump somewhere in England called Torpenhow Hill, which translates as Hill Hill Hill Hill.

--

Bill in Columbia, CT:

A litotes is a figure of speech consisting of an understatement in which an affirmative is expressed by negating its opposite. "Not bad" is an example of a litotes. If somebody is not unwelcome he or she is welcome. A synecdoche is a part to denote the whole. Twenty sails were seen on the horizon. (Sail is part for the whole boat.)

--

Steve in San Francisco:

This is my first contribution to this forum. My interest is in words/terms/derivations. I noticed some complaints about word abuses. I have a few pet peeves as well. For instance, the term "workaholic" or "chocoholic"... They all make no sense. If an alcohol abuser is an "alchohol"-ic, then a chocolate abuser would be a "chocolat"-ic. Likewise for "work"-ic, etc, etc,... Is this old news to everyone (to use that tired old oxymoron)?

Steve continued:

Here's one for you all to contemplate: "Blind Faith". Isn't faith by definition "blind"? If it weren't, it would be "knowledge". As for oxymorons, at the library I saw a magazine called "Current History". That's all for now.

--

On proper parsing, Toni in Minnesota said:

I started being careful to use "re-sign" precisely because folks had trouble parsing "<player> resigns with <team>" (or worse, "<player> resigns as <team-member>"). After your comments above, however, I finally went to my dictionary, which does indeed define "re-sign" as "to sign again". That same definition is NOT given as one of the possibilities for "resign". Resigned to re-sign,

---

Idioms about food from www.spellzone.com

A bad apple/egg – a bad influence or someone who brings trouble
A couch potato – an idle person
A hard nut to crack – a difficult person to understand or a difficult problem to solve
A piece of cake – easy
A smart cookie – a clever person
Big cheese – an important person
Bread and butter – the necessities
Doesn't cut the mustard – doesn't meet the required standard
Food for thought – worth considering
Gone pear-shaped – gone unexpectedly wrong
In a nutshell – simply put
In a pickle – in trouble or mess
Like chalk and cheese – opposites
Like two peas in a pod – very similar
Not my cup of tea – not the type of thing I usually enjoy
Selling like hotcakes – selling quickly and in large quantities
The apple of my eye – the person I adore
The cream of the crop – the best
The icing on the cake – something positive that happens in an already very good situation. Sometimes, something quite bad that happens in an already very bad situation
To be handed something on a (silver) platter – to acquire something easily, usually without any effort on the receiver's part
To bring home the bacon – to earn the income

Our strange language from Lord Cromer:

When the English tongue we speak,
Why is 'break" not rhymed with "freak"?
Will you tell me why it's true
We say "sew" but likewise "few";
And the maker of a verse
Cannot rhyme his "horse" with "worse"?
"Beard" sounds not the same as "heard";
"Cord" is different from "word";
Cow is "cow", but low is "low";
"Shoe" is never rhymed with "foe".
Think of "hose" and "dose" and "lose";
And think of "goose" and yet of "choose".
Think of "comb" and "tomb" and "bomb";
"Doll" and "roll" and "home" and "some",
And since "pay" is rhymed with "say",
Why not "paid" with "said", I pray?
We have "blood" and "flood" and "good";
"Mould" is not pronounced like "could".
Wherefore "done" but "gone" and "lone"?
Is there any reason known?
And, in short, it seems to me
Sounds and letters disagree.

8

Greek, Latin, and other languages

Kristopher in College Station, TX: Latin phrases interpreted: One of my previously unanswered questions (which is why it was a question [I don't know, why was it {Why was what what?}?].) was if anyone had a list of those commonly used Latin phrases...you know, the kind politicians like to spout...such as:

>pro bono
>quid pro quo

Zeno in Minneapolis, MN answered with his own interpretations: Well, since you ask:

>Pro bono -- What Cher was for years, although not so much lately.
>Quid pro quo -- A progression: from amateur to professional.
>Festina lente -- Every Lent a festival
>Post hoc ergo propter hoc -- Therefore it is right to spit at posts.
>Sic transit gloria mundi -- The subway's broken: Gloria won't be there for the weekend.
>Cui bono -- Oral sex.
>Delenda est Carthago -- It's so far to Delenda we ought to drive.
>Dulce et decorum est -- There's good interior design at est sem-

inars.

Ars longa vita brevis -- The longer your member the shorter your life.

Odi et amo -- Love stinks.

Stat magni nominis umbra -- Quick get the big umbrella!

Nil posse creari de nilo -- No vigilantes can catch me, none! More colloquially: You'll never take me alive, copper!

Spiritus mundi -- Monday-morning sermon critiquing.

Arma virumque cano -- I'm a virile dog.

Nervos belli, pecuniam infinitam -- A weak stomach is a sin forever.

Dux femina facti -- Look out when the woman boss is right.

Equo ne credite -- Don't borrow money to bet on a horse.

Bella, horrida bella -- An extremely prescient movie review.

Spiritus inter alit -- The soul is drunk.

Experto credite -- Roman Express.

Hoc genus omne -- Spit on all smart people.

Summum bonum -- The largest member.

O tempora! O mores! -- What Cicero said eating Japanese batter-fried shrimp the first time.

Mike in Brisbane followed up with:

sic transit gloria mundi = Gloria threw up in the bus on Monday --

Jan in Hobart, AU had a hefty contribution:

Kristofer asked for a list of useful Latin phrases. Here are some Latin and French ones I could think of, mostly ones I've heard or read at some time or other--and had to look them up:

ad hoc (Latin--"for this"--as a committee formed for one particular end or case at hand)

ad litem (Latin--for a particular legal case or action)

bourgeois (Fr--"middle class"--usually meaning very materialistic)

carpe diem (Latin--"seize the day")

carte blanche (French--"white paper"--used to denote full author-

ity to use one's own judgment)
    cause celebre (French--"celebrated cause"--a notorious incident or celebrated legal case--such as the O.J. SIMPSON TRIAL!)
    caveat emptor (Latin--"buyer beware"--usually means item is sold 'as is,' with no warranty)
    c'est la vie (French--"that's life")
    coup d'etat (French--"stroke of state"--sudden exercise of force in politics, as when a government is overthrown)
    coup de grace (French--"stroke of grace"--decisive finishing blow or act, especially one to put someone or something out of its misery)
    creme de la creme (French--"cream of the cream"--the very best)
    cum laude (Latin--"with honors")
    docendo discimus (Latin--"we learn by teaching")
    dolce vita (Italian--"sweet life"--hedonism)
    du jour (French--"of the day")
    ecce signum (Latin--"behold the sign"--look at the proof)
    e.g. (Latin--exempli gratia--"for example")
    e pluribus unum (Latin--"one composed of many")
    errare humanum est (Latin--"to err is human")
    esprit de corps (French--"common spirit" or regard for the common good of the group)
    et al (Latin--"and others")
    etc. (Latin--et cetera--"and so forth")
    ex animo (Latin--"from the heart"--sincerely)
    ex libris (Latin--"from books"--from the library of)
    excelsior (Latin--"still higher")
    faux pas (French--"false step"--a social blunder)
    fiat justitia (Latin--"let justice be done")
    haute couture (French--"high [standard of] sewing or fashion")
    haute cuisine (French--"high [standard of] cooking")
    hors d'oeuvre/s (French--"outside the main body of work"--used to denote foods served as appetizers)
    ibid. (Latin--"in the same place")

i.e. (Latin--id est--"that is")
ipso facto (Lat--"by that very fact"--by nature of the situation)
jeu de mots (French--"play on words"--pun intended!)
joie de vivre (French--"joy of living")
justitia omnibus (Latin--"justice for all")
laissez faire (Fr--"let the people do as they please"-- "let live")
lapsus calami (Latin--"slip of the pen")
lapsus linguae (Latin--"slip of the tongue")
locus in quo (Latin--"place in which")
magnum opus (Latin--"great work")
maitre d'[hotel] (French--"master of the house"--headwaiter)
major domo (Latin equivalent of preceding entry)
me judice (Latin--"I being judge"--in my judgment)
mea culpa (Latin--"through my fault)
modus operandi (Latin--"method of operation"--as in a criminal's M.O., or usual way of doing things)
nil desperandum (Latin--"never despair")
noblesse oblige (French--"nobility obligates"--the obligation of responsible behavior associated with high rank or position)
nosce te ipsum (Latin--"know thyself")
obscurum per obscurius (Latin--explaining the "obscure by means of the more obscure")
omnia vincit amor (Latin--"love conquers all")
onus probandi (Latin--"burden of proof")
par avion (French--"by airplane"--used on airmail)
paucis verbis (Latin--"in a few words")
pax vobiscum (Latin--"peace be with you")
per diem (Latin--"for the day"--amount of money given for daily expenses)
per se (Latin--"in or by itself")
persona non grata (Latin--"unacceptable person")
pleno jure (Latin--"with full right")
post hoc (Latin--"after this")

post partum (Latin--"after birth")
post mortem (Latin--"after death"--usually means an autopsy)
post obit (Latin--post obitum--"after death")
pro bono (Latin--"for good"--usually used to describe legal services rendered at no cost to a client, because it is for the good of others)
pro patria (Latin--"for one's country")
q.e.d (Latin--quod erat demonstrandum--"thus it is shown"—used primarily in mathematics to formally end a proof.)
quid pro quo (Latin--"something for something"--something traded for something else)
quo ad hoc (Latin--"as far as this"--to this extent)
quo vadis (Latin--"whither are you going"--as in court when the judge asks where a lawyer is going with a line of questioning)
regnat populus (Latin--"the people rule")
respice finem (Latin--"look to the end"--consider the outcome)
sans doute (French--"without doubt")
sans souci (French--"without worry")
se defendendo (Latin--"in self defense")
semper fidelis (Latin--"always faithful"--Marine Corps motto)
semper paratus (Latin--"always prepared"--Coast Guard motto)
sine qua non (Latin--"without which not"--an essential or indispensable thing)
si vis pacem, para bellum (Latin--"if you wish peace, prepare for war")
sotto voce (Italian--"under the voice"--very softly, as in a whisper)
status quo (Latin--"state in which"--existing state of affairs)
suo jure (Latin--"in one's own right")
suo loco (Latin--"in its proper place")
tempus fugit (Latin--"time flies")
totidem verbis (Latin--"in so many words")
tuebor (Latin--"I will defend")
ultima ratio (Latin--"the final argument")
uno animo (Latin--"with one mind"--unanimously)

veni, vidi, vici (Latin--"I came, I saw, I conquered")
vincit omnia veritas (Latin--"truth conquers all things")
vis-a-vis (French--"face to face"--in relation to)
voir dire (Fr--"to speak the truth"--jury select. by questioning)
vox populi (Latin--"voice of the people"--popular sentiment)

Now, can anyone adequately explain to me what a writ of "habeas corpus" is? (It translates literally into Latin as "You should have the body.")

Qui Docet Discit,*

Katherine in Oakland, CA added:

Thanks for the list, Jan! May I nitpick?

ad hoc (Latin--"for this"--as a committee formed for one particular end or case at hand): "to" rather than "for", really...as in "addressed to this case", I think.

bourgeois (French--"middle class"--usually meaning very materialistic): And originally "of the city".

obscurum per obscurius (Latin--explaining the "obscure by means of the more obscure"): Not sure I'd seen this one before, and I like it!

post hoc (Latin--"after this"): Ergo propter hoc. :)
"Post hoc ergo propter hoc": "after this, therefore because of this". The fallacy of thinking that because B follows A (temporally), A must have been the cause of B.

q.e.d (Latin--quod erat demonstrandum--"thus it is shown"—used primarily in mathematics to formally end a proof.): Are you sure? I'd learned it as meaning "that which was to be shown".

Pat in Collegeville, MN:

Welcome, Susanne of Chagrin Falls, and thanks for the list of foreign words and phrases. Interesting how they, like formulae in our mother tongue, get abbreviated--e.g., pro bono for pro bono publico, and Fiat justitia, dropping ruat caelum (let [though] the heavens fall).

Gerald in New York also chimed in:

Jan Radclyffe asks about habeas corpus.

Habeas corpus ("you should have the body") is a writ issued by a court commanding that a person held in custody be brought before a court so that it may determine whether the detention is lawful. It is meant to ensure that a prisoner is accorded due process of law, and does not determine guilt or innocence. Habeas corpus originated in medieval England, and is a right guaranteed by the U.S. Constitution.

Bo in Malmo, Sweden concurred with Katherine:
"Post hoc propter hoc" (after this, therefore because of this) is used to describe the logical fallacy that because one event precedes another the first must have caused the other.

Allan in Brandon, Manitoba gave an example for "Post hoc propter hoc":
The first truly effective anti-epileptic drugs were bromide compounds; they came into use in the last century because in those days, it was believed by some that epilepsy was caused by masturbation (the list of evils and illnesses that this practice was supposed to have caused is astonishingly long). It was also believed that bromides (in very common use as sedatives) had specific anti-aphrodiasic properties (which they do not). This led to the experimental treatment of epilepsy with bromides, and they were found to be very effective. Unfortunately, the 'post hoc ergo propter hoc' argument was applied, resulting in a fallacious origin of epilepsy being kept alive for some time. It is not clear, however, if the very common use of bromides as medicines had anything to do with another meaning of the word (a commonplace saying, a trite remark, etc). This meaning of 'bromide' seems to have its origins in American slang in use in the first years of this century.

Pat in Collegeville, MN followed up:
My Wentworth and Flexner attributes this use of it to Gelett Burgess, of purple cow fame, and his book _Are You a Bromide?_ (1906), and remarks, ". . . Burgess coined the slang meaning of this term from the medical usage = a sedative; perhaps influenced by the Spanish 'broma'

= a joke."
The latter conjecture seems far-fetched, though Bostonian Burgess lived and edited in San Francisco before publishing the cited book.

--

Mike in Brisbane responded to Ken the Strong who said "While I can find much information on "Panis Angelicus" by Franck, I can't find a simple thing like a translation of the title into English. One would be appreciated.":
Bread of Angels, or more often - Bread of Heaven

--

Kat in New York:
Brian in London reports that -Spam- is used as a nickname (origin of that phrase?) for the Tallis motet "Spem in alium nunquam habui..." which he translates as "I have never had hope in another". Interesting. in the archives of the Classical Language Translators Club we have that one listed as: "Spam in garlic? Never had it!"

--

Pat in Collegeville said:
Dave did a bravura piece with stand and many of its derivatives, and asked why to understand should mean to comprehend. Don't know, although it literally means the same as substance, which gets Frenchified as sustain. You might, Dave, want to do a job on the related stat-words (state, status, station, e.g.). Stand comes from the present participle of the Latin stare (to stand); status, -a, -um is the perfect participle.

--

Jim in Philadelphia had a peculiar version of the pledge of allegiance:
I led the pigeons to the flag of the Untied States of Uh, Merica. And to the republic, four witches stand, invisible, with libber's tea, injustice for all.

--

Mike in Brisbane about the sign on the gate:
When I was a little lid in wartime Sydney, I used to stay with my great-aunt and get spoiled rotten - but, as usual, I digress. Auntie Mollie had a brass plate on the front gate - the property name - "Mori Alto". I assume it to be Latin, but have never been able to make any sense out of it - is it a classical allusion or quote - any clues? And no, it wasn't a cemetery on the top of a hill.

Bob in Chicago answered:
Just a guess but I believe it means "Halt be to Death" or "Death do not pass", or "Stay Death".

Kat in New York had a different interpretation:
How about "Death to Female Singers with Low Voices"?

--

From Jesse in Sunnyvale, CA offered:
As a public service to readers of this group, I am providing this updated list of the correct definitions of traditional musical tempo markings.

1. LARGO: A type of key, found in Florida.

2. LENTO: A) The period immediately before Easter; B) A type of small legume, especially suitable for making soup; C) The host of a late-night talk show on NBC, usually preceded by "Jay" (but not accompanied by Branford).

3. ADAGIO: An old saying, e.g.: To err is human. [But if humans naturally err, can we conclude that ermines naturally hume?]

4. ANDANTE: Author of a mediaeval manuscript commonly called in modern English "The Andivine Ancomedy."

5. MODERATO: The person on some of these groups who decides what gets posted and what doesn't.

6. ALLEGRO: What you see when a line of chorus girls does that kicking thing.

7. PRESTO: Stop playing and do a magic trick.

    By John McCoy (uni of Chicago)

--

Jim in Philadelphia interjected:
No one ever explicitly states that "e.g." stands for Exempla Gratia," but that's irrelevant. I started wondering, what, exactly, does "i.e." stand for??? I know when it's used, but I never knew exactly what it stands for. Anyone?

John in Keele answered:
i.e. stands for Latin "id est" = that is [or, that is to say]. BECAUSE English speakers tend not to know the full version, they tend to say "eye eee", pronouncing the abbreviation; whereas in German [yes, I know!] the equivalent abbreviation is d.h. for "das heisst", so German-speakers tend to SEE the abbreviation and SAY the expanded version.

--

Bill in Lexington. KY gave the equivalences:

US	UK
Bumper	Fender
Fender	Wing
Hood	Bonnet
Trunk	Boot
Truck	Lorry
Windshield	Windscreen
Gasoline	Petrol
Left	Right

Okay, folks. What did I miss, and what did I get wrong?

--

Catie in Arlington, VA:
That brings me to another thought. Words like Warranty and Guarantee essentially mean the same thing because of that G/W shift.
Anyway, that's why we have William/Guillaume, Warranty/Guarantee, Warden/guard etc. I can't think of any more. Anyone else know any?

--

Marjorie in Boston clarified:

Dani, "schlimazel" is definitely a person, as in "A schlemiel is a person who spills the soup; a schlimazel is the person the schlemiel spilled the soup on." "Mazel" means "luck" in both Hebrew and Yiddish, so it should be easier to understand the meaning. The humor of the word lies in the fact that unfortunate things keep happening to the unlucky "dumpee" through no fault of his own; the schlemiel may be a clumsy dork who can't do anything right, but the schlimazel is the one who suffers for the schlemiel's actions. (BTW, the word is generally spelled as I've written it here; a less common spelling is "schlimazl.")

--

Richard in Boulder, CO responded to a query which asked "What other anatomy words are used as insults? (Without crossing the line into blatant vulgarity.) Bonehead, birdbrain, weak tit.":

I am surprised that no one has brought up the Yiddish word schmuck in this regard. It has a similar etymology to dork. First it was a jewel (from the same word in German). Late in the last century it became a fancy decoration on a man s watch chain. Then it followed the same path as dork. In the 70 s it was fun to see it held as a vulgar term on NYC talk shows but it was acceptable on the West Coast.

--

Bob in Eastern Washington said:

The discussion of "f***" reminded me of a story about a newspaper account of a traffic accident. The reporter wrote "A woman had her breasts lacerated..." The editor called for a rewrite because breasts might offend the readers. The article came out saying: A woman had her (.) (.) lacerated...

--

Dan on profanities:

I try to be inventive and use other words besides the standard and mundane "four letter" variety.

For example, instead of using the word sh*tt*r, try "essence of excrescence" or perhaps "disappointing bowel movement." Much more

evocative, I think.
And it usually takes the recipient of such a remark a few moments to translate the insult, realize they have been insulted, react to the insult, realize that they have been both verbally and MENTALLY abused, and realize the person who delivered the remark has epitheted and egressed (this last step is HIGHLY recommended). All of which adds to the indignity of which they have been made the subject.

--

Har responded to Anders who asked: "What does the family name Jaffe mean?"
Jaffe is the transliteration (again) of the Hebrew Yafeh which means "beautiful".

--

Steve in Seattle responded to Phil who asked "Goy: as I understand it, means gentile. Is that right? Is it gender-specific?":
It literally means nation, in the sense of "other than us" rather than "from another political-division-called-a-country." It's gender neutral, pluralized goyim (GOY ihm). It's used by some Jews to refer to non-Jews in a slightly pejorative sense, although that might be regional; when I was growing up, it was always a neutral term in my family and my shul (congregation).
Katherine in Oakland: Yes, it means gentile; no, it's not gender-specific, AFAIK.
Does anybody know--I've been wondering this for a *long* time, ever since I learned the words--whether there's any connection between "goy", "gajo" (the Romany equivalent: non-Gypsy, outsider), and "gaijin" (the Japanese equivalent, if I've been informed correctly)? They look to me as though there ought to be a common root way back when, but yes I know that the languages are from families at least not recently connected, and all...
And about "Shaigetz":
Ever hear of "shiksa"? If a nice Jewish boy marries a shiksa, his parents go into mourning (sit shiva) (and no, I'm *not* looking for connec-

tions with Hindu deities, thank you). At least according to popular folklore. "Shiksa" is a female _goy_ --maybe only one who marries a Jew, I don't know. "Shaigetz" is the male equivalent. For some reason, it's regarded as a status increase for a man to marry a shiksa, while women are supposed to marry Jewish men. (Maybe that's why nobody knows from "shaigetz".)

--

Matt in Minneapolis corrected:
Phil harangued & Lee was overwrought about Uff Da: Michael Valentiner already summed it up by equating it with Oy Vey! It isn't so much a Minnesotan saying as it is Norveegian. As in, "Uff Da! Hey dere, Sven, ya can't be havin' a Christmas dinner widout lutefisk!"

--

Catie in Arlington, VA did some research:
OK, I sifted through a box with a pile of papers, and came up with the book. So, for your enjoyment, here are some more sounds from different languages:

Upsy-daisy! (accompanied by a picture of a baby being thrown up into the air to be caught with waiting arms)
Arabic:	Hoppa!
Danish:	Upsedasse!
German:	Hopp!
Italian:	Opla!
Japanese:	Yoisho!
Portuguese	Upa!
Russian:	Noo Davai!

Chugalug (with picture of person drinking)
Arabic:	Gur-gur-gur
Chinese:	Gu-du Gu-du
Hebrew:	Gloog Gloog
Hindi:	Gat-gat
Russian:	Bool-bool

Hic
Chinese: Da Grh
Hindi: Utch
Spanish: Hip

Drip...drip...drip
Chinese: Di-da...Di-da...Di-da
French: Floc...Floc
German: Plopp!
Hebrew: Tif...Tif
Japanese: Pota...Pota
Portuguese: Pinga...Pinga
Russian: Cup...Cup...Cup
Spanish: Clop...Clop
Swahili: Tah...Tah...Tah
Swedish: Dropp...Dropp

Uh-oh
Chinese: Zao le
Greek: Am-an
Italian: Ay-may
Japanese: Aa-ah
Swahili: Wee
Swedish: OY-OY

Yum-yum
Arabic: Allah (accent on second a)
Polish: Niam-niam
Swahili: Mmmm
Swedish: Mums
French: Umm-umm -umm

--

Pedro in Peru answered a query:
Someone asked what (hmmm, how?) people from Buenos Aires are

called. the Royal Spanish Academy's (21st edition) Dictionary showed an interesting me-too sequence of definitions:

Porteño, a: adj. applied to people from various cities in Spain or America with ports. (Notice their order...) – from the Argentine city of Buenos Aires, from Valparaiso (that's in Chile), from Puerto Carreno (in Colombia).

--

Pablo in Venezuela:

Recent thread on foreign words: I have heard that Toyota had trouble introducing their MR-2 car in France because its pronunciation in French sounds like a lot of French asterisks.

9

Foreign Phrases

Marjorie in Boston, MA:
"Ben" is a Hebrew word meaning "son of." "Bar" also means "son of," but it is Aramaic. Aramaic is an ancient Semitic language similar to Hebrew.
Interestingly enough, in those ancient days, Aramaic was the popularly spoken and written language, and Hebrew was not the spoken language, but was learned mainly for studying the holy books and for prayers. Today Aramaic is not spoken (as far as I know), but it is still taught so that the biblical commentary written in Aramaic can be understood and discussed. Some of the key Jewish prayers and legal documents used today are uttered or written in Aramaic. I find that Aramaic is harder to read than Hebrew; some of the words really twist my tongue. But then, I'm not practiced in it. My husband can pronounce it fine.

Janet in Calgary:
Re: Fock-eer County. In high school, a friend had to do an oral presentation in her French class. Since it was a trendy topic at the time, she chose ro talk about the seal hunt. The word for seal in French is "phoque", (rhymes with rock). In an attempt to make it visually interesting, she brought in a stuffed toy of a baby seal. In the middle of her

talk, she put the toy down on the desk of one of her fellow students, who immediately looked up and said "Get the phoque off my desk".

My vote goes for Olly Olly Oxen Free and shouting home free.

Sort of on the topic of what kids hear: When I lived in Australia for a time in my youth, I took riding lessons. On the first day, I was sent off by the stable manager to find and saddle my horse, Paper. I spent several minutes reading all the names on all the stalls and finally came back to tell him I couldn't find Paper anywhere. he led me over and pointed to a black horse whose stall was clearly marked "Piper". I was so used to translating the accent, I was actually mishearing correctly pronounced words!

Rollo in Adelaide:

This letter to the editor in an Australian newspaper was brought to my attention by a friend's colleague in Noumea (via Hawaii!). Wordplay readers will probably enjoy it, assuming they can recognise Australian idiom when written in mock French. (Let's not start an argument about nuclear testing, though.)

An open letter to Monsieur Jacques Chirac:

Mon cher Jack,

> Je suis a bit fromaged off avec votre decision to blow up La Pacifique avec le Frog bombes nuclears. Je reckon vous must have un spot in La Belle France itself pour les explosions. Le Massive Central? Le Quay d'Orsay? Le Champs Elysees? Votre own back yard, peut etre?
>
> Frappez le crows avec stones, Sport! La guerre cold est fini!
>
> Votres forces militaire need la bombe atomique about as beacoup as poisson need les bicyclettes.
>
> Un autre point, cobber. Votre histoire militaire isn't tres flash, consisting, n'est-ce pas, of batailles the likes of Crecy, Agincourt, Poitiers, Trafalgar, Borodino, Waterloo, Sedan et Dien Bien Phu. Un bombe won't change le tradition.
>
> Je/mon pere/mon grand pere/le cousin third avec ma grand-

mere/la plume de ma tante fought avec votre soldats against Le Boche in WWI (le Big One). Have vous forgotten?

Reconsider, mon ami, otherwise in le hotels et estaminets de l'Australie le curse anciens d'Angleterre - "Damnation to the French" - will be heard un autre temps.

Votre chums don't want that.

Millo.

--

Someone had an objection:

Further clarifications on the JFK's mis-spoken line: I personally think the business about a 'Berliner' being a jelly doughnut in German is a complete fabrication which Jan and others may unwittingly be continuing, ie they are carrying on an urban legend.

Phil in Salt Lake City responded:

I must disagree. I lived in northern Germany from 1967 to 1969. I frequently bought jelly-filled donuts in local German bakeries. We always asked for "Berliners" and the term was in frequent usage. The way I first heard the JFK story was as a joke: "What is Kennedy full of?" Ans: "Jelly, because he said, 'Ich bin ein Berliner' ". The inclusion of the "ein" was definitely an error, according to North German usage. "Ich bin Berliner" or "Ich bin Amerikaner" or "Ich bin Wissenschaftler" (scientist) was the correct form. I believe that I also heard a tape or saw a film of the actual speech. JFK said something to the effect that as long as Berlin was not free, all men were imprisoned--no man was fully free. In this sense, all men were Berliners-- "and so I say, 'Ich bin ein Berliner' ". The crowd loved it, in spite of the error. They understood the sentiment, and the joke that followed was in the best of humor. JFK was, at the time, loved by most of the Germans I spoke with, and venerated by many. One man I visited in Berlin had pictures of Kennedy on his wall--a shrine, almost. He was very emotional about Kennedy. All of this was not because of the speech, but because of the American airlift of supplies into West

Berlin when the Russians blockaded the city, thinking they would surrender and the East would have all of Berlin under their control. The US saved Berlin, and the German people were very grateful to the US and to Kennedy.
This is not an "urban legend".

--

Alex in Adelaide recalled his French grammar:
The one that really gets people is "cimetière" where the sound and the e at the end suggest a feminine gender as most French nouns would attest, the masculine counterparts end in 'ier' with a mute r, but no this one is definitely _le cimetière_

--

Brian in London:
It is interesting that the word "Kindergarten" - and some of the Dutch words mentioned - include the plural "children", whereas English tends to use the singular in such combinations, even if more than one of the objects is present.
We talk about a "horse race", not a "horses race", even though a race with less than a plurality of horse would be singularly uninteresting.

--

Gerald in Ottawa:
On the question of "passe partout," the usual meaning is the material used as a mat when mounting a picture. I hadn't heard the other application before but, considering that it translates as "goes everywhere," could it not be an early version of "all-purpose?"

--

Frank in Ottawa:
To quote Jeff: "... Kukuruza. Sounds corny, doesn't it?..."
Do you really need a translation, or was this the best bilingual pun I've seen in donkey's years? Kukuruza in Russian means CORN (what Europeans call Maize or Indian Corn.

THE POWER OF WORDS - 277

Gerald in Ottawa:
The story about the power of "nicht" at the end of a German sentence reminds me of the woman who went to a conference in Dusseldorf and brought along her own translator. After the first speaker had gone on for some ten minutes, she asked impatiently, "Well, what's he saying?" One moment, madame," the translator replied, waving her to silence. "I'm waiting for the verb."

--

Hans in Amsterdam:
My country is Nederland, translated: The Netherlands (the plural comes from the past: we once had 'De Republiek der Nederlanden'). People from the Netherlands are called Dutch(men). The province where I live is South-Holland. Holland is often used instead of The Netherlands (pars pro toto). I'm a Hollander. People from other parts of the country don't like to be called Hollander.

The general rule in Dutch is that in word combinations (like the Germans, most of the time we just stick the words together, a big problem for spellchecking programs) a plural form is used if more than one object is present. The exceptions to the rule are a problem for many Dutch spellers.

That's all for now. Oops, another Wordplay Digest coming in...

--

Mike in Brisbane:
G'day again. Just got the latest digest in - and the thread about the embroidered Chinese characters reminded me of the story about the young lady in the days when tight sweaters were fashionable - are they still? oh, OK - and this particular young woman was a good knitter, and copied some characters from a menu in a Chinese restaurant and knitted them into the design of a sweater she was making. A friend who could read the characters FAOTFL when she saw them, because they said "this little dish is cheap, but very tasty". This was in the Readers' Digest, about 1950, so it's probably apocryphal.

--

Hans in Amsterdam:

Deutsch is German for German. Dutch is English for Nederlands. Duits is Dutch for German, Holländisch is German for Dutch. I can understand the confusion.

--

From Kat in New York, quoting from online:

Welcome to the Classical Language Translators Club. Your entry has been submitted to the Up-to-Date Translations Competition. Last year's winning entry was: «O vos omnes» = Yo, dudes!

--

10

Errors of Literary Logic

Bill in Lexington, KY spotted one:
Our brilliant Kentucky State Fire Marshall requires that this sign be posted in many meeting rooms (the number varies, of course):
THE CAPACITY OF THIS ROOM SHALL NOT EXCEED 150
I assume they won't let us enlarge the room.

Bill had few others:
Sign on a billboard: Most trouble-free car in America.
I don't think "trouble-free" comes in degrees. Either it is or it isn't. "Most nearly trouble-free" I can accept, but then they're admitting that it isn't trouble-free.

Caleb in Albany, NY agreed:
Right you are! also, how many times have I seen the term "most unique?"
Any other sillicisms (another neologism) can you Wordplayers come up with?
--
Patrick in San Jose, CA was reminded of a pet peeve:
This is one of my pet peeves: misuse of the word "literally". I've noticed recently that the advertising industry has been discovering the pos-

sibilities for abuse of the word. A magazine ad for a new car a few months back included the text: Looks that will literally stun you!

For several days afterward, I drove carefully past car dealers, on the lookout for unconscious victims lying in front of the display windows, but alas! none were to be seen. (Now if they'd said "a *price* that will literally stun you!"... :-))
I particularly detest this use of "literally" because it not only devalues the word, it removes *all* value from it.

--

Toni in Minnesota:
Heard on the local news whilst getting ready for work this morning: "A Minneapolis man is dead after drowning in the Mississippi River." I should think so!

--

Lee in Atlanta, GA:
As in an article in the NY TIMES (For shame!) on hepatitis c: " the most fatal" of the various types of hepatitis.   Huh?

--

Matt in Minneapolis, MN:
My pet peeve [actually, I have two, whom I've named Vex and Irk] is the advertising hyperbole: "We have more/better/greater XYZ than anyone!!" Exempli gratia: "Our store has better selection than anyone!" or "We have lower interest rates than anyone!"
Aren't these businesses anyone? Are they calling themselves nobodies, or do they live in an existential recursive loop, in which they are better than they are?

Customer: "What's the best interest rate you can give me?"
Bank Employee: "Whatever it is, we can beat it!"
Along the same line, there's the "Half the calories!" or "Better tasting!" than what? If the claim is prefaced by claiming that the product in question is "New & Improved" (a problem in and of itself, as has been mentioned before), there is some sense to it. However, the comparative claims are made by "Original & Inferior" products as well.

Mike in Brisbane:
A man being interviewed on the radio last night said "I watched the snowflakes descending down slowly..." nice tautology, I thought.

Caleb in Albany, NY made a correction:
Not a tautology. A tautology says If "a", then "a": an obvious conclusion based on the premise. To describe snowflakes as "descending down" may be unnecessary description, sort of redundant, but it's not a tautology.

Mike also gave us an example of overused expressions:
In radio and TV interviews - "you're absolutely right" - doesn't leave much elbow room for further discussion, does it?

Susan in Cheney, WA:
Which brings to mind a hilarious episode in Spokane, whereby a community college administrator declared in the media that he had done a 360 in his opinion about an issue. (Did I relate this already eons ago?) I'm fairly sure from his context that he meant a 180, not a 180 and then 180 again to come back to his original opinion.

Sara in Boston picked up on a common mistake:
Verbing: loaned vs. lent: "Lent" is indeed the past tense of "lend." "Loaned" is technically invalid, as "loan" is a noun, not a verb. I think it became verbed. My dad (the English prof.) always got annoyed by people continuously confusing "lend" and "loan," "lie" and "lay," or "bring" and "take." One that has always bugged me is "lighted;" as far as I knew the past tense of the verb "light" is "lit." When someone says "I lighted a candle" I can feel my teeth wanting to grind...
Enough anal retention for now! (And notice, no flag comments!)

Terrence in Bermuda picked up another common error in "Rhinoceroses - crash (Did you know the horn is comprised of hair..."
This should be "...is COMPOSED of..."
Composed and comprised are very commonly confused. Comprise means to include or contain, or more informally to be composed of, so that "is comprised of" means "is composed of of". If you really want to use comprise, you would have to say "the horn comprises hair".

Karen in Manchester, UK:
Here you go, Phil:
1. "comprise" means to be made up of, so the whole comprises the parts: "The Union comprises fifty states."
2. "compose" means to make up, so the parts compose the whole: "Fifty states compose the Union."
3. "is comprised of" doesn't mean anything, so don't use it! Instead use "comprises," "is made up of," "is composed of," or "consists of."

Bill in Lexington, KY added:
For purists, "comprise" is an exhaustive "include". A book comprises its pages and may include some diagrams. The U.S.A comprises fifty states and includes Kentucky. Using "is comprised of" tries to reverse the meaning of the word. However, "is comprised by" should be acceptable. Fifty states are comprised by the U.S.A. I got caught on this word several times before I finally got it figured out.

Bill in Columbia, CT:
I kept hearing my superintendent bellowing about the enormity of our task at hand. I didn't have the heart to tell him that enormity refers to something heinous and that enormousness refers to something task-oriented on a grand scale.

Guy in Cupertino, CA:
I consulted the American Heritage Dictionary, 3rd Edition, page 612

(using quotes where AHD used italics): enormity
USAGE NOTE: "Enormity" is frequently used to refer simply to the property of being enormous, but many would prefer that "enormousness" (or a synonym such as "immensity") be used for this general sense and that "enormity" be reserved for a property that evokes a negative moral judgement. This distinction between "enormity" and "enormousness" has not always existed historically, but nowadays many observe it.

--

Alex in Adelaide experienced misuse himself:
Many moons ago I used to use the word _notoriety_ improperly where I thought it simply meant remarkable or worthy of notice. I was set straight in an embarrassing situation after I introduced an imminent speaker by referring to some of his work as "...of distinctive notoriety" not realising that it meant unfavorable fame.

Patrick in San Jose, CA added:
I was recently visiting a large French company (whose name will be withheld until relatives have been informed), the English version of whose annual report proudly proclaims, "In the past year, the notoriety of the Group has grown steadily..." In French, "notoriété" simply means "renown" or "fame" without any negative connotations.

Lee in Atlanta, remarked:
Sounds like infamous vs famous--quite a difference. But unless the speaker you were introducing was just about to speak (imminent) or was well-known & esteemed (eminent), I think perhaps you meant the latter rather than the former. Of course, the case could have been both: about to speak AND esteemed.

--

Terrence in Bermuda weighed in on Healthy Debate:
There has been much debate during the last week about the health benefit of the apple vs pear-shaped physique, triggered by Bea's:

"Just so we aren't guilty of passing on inaccurate information....it is the Pear shape which is healthier...not the apple!!"
I won't contribute to the argument, but I must point out that: "the Pear shape which is healthier...not the apple!!" is a common error.
A shape can no more be healthy than it can be ill! This should be: "the Pear shape which is more healthful...not the apple!!"

--

Bill in Columbia, CT:
A parent confronted me today because I corrected her son's paper from "I feel badly" to "I feel bad." It was a rather interesting conversation. I finally convinced her that "bad" is an adjective and modifies "I," and that "badly" is an adverb modifying "feel." I asked her whether her son's sense of touch was the issue or his health. I think we parted as friends, even though she made some bizarre comment about my long curly hair that did not rhyme with any human being capable of walking upright.
A demented grammarian,

Bill in Lexington, KY illustrated:
I smell badly. Therefore, I have to depend upon others to tell me if I smell bad or good.
It was a collection of beautiful and fragile glass figurines that I felt badly. I broke many of them. Now I feel bad.
There are people who go about doing good. Some of them do good well, and others do good badly. It is better to do good badly than to do no good at all. Worst of all is to do bad well.

--

Suad in Kuwait said:
Peace be to you all. Hmm I was wondering if any of you good people can help me in winning an argument I got into .. well someone said this "I could care less" ,, so I corrected that person and said it should have been "I couldn't care less" ! explaining my point of view I said .. most people who say "I could care less" really mean the opposite, if you

want to make the point that you care NOT AT ALL, then you need to use the negative "I could NOT care less" . so what do you all think .. was I right?! thanks in advance for your help .and in God's care I leave you all :) peace.

Bob in Chicago agreed:
Yes, I think you are right. I put the phrase "I could care less" in the same category with "exedera" for "etcetera" and "for all intensive purposes" instead of "for all intents and purposes". These orthographic misfits usually result from learning a language by rote without many opportunities to view the written word. The person merely repeats what he/she thought they had heard.

And Matt of Minneapolis acquiesced:
As to our Kuwaiti correspondent, you hit the nail on the head with your response to "I could care less" (Oh, yeah? How MUCH less?) I'm glad to see that one didn't fall between the cracks. It was a near miss.

--

Reg said:
To add to the kiss list: When we were in college, we used to call it "Anatomical juxtaposition of the obicularis oris muscles in a state of contraction." We, being my girlfriend and I, mainly. Plus, those we wanted to mistify.

Phil in Salt Lake City jumped in:
That must be some slobbery kiss! About how many bystanders can the two of you "mistify", on a good day? I could never get more than my partner wet. Mystifies the heck out of me how you do it!

--

Johanna in Albany, NY observed:
Someone suggested that "I could care less" came from sarcastic humor. Does anyone know the history of "proof" and "pudding"?
In January I attended network management class. The instructor, having led us through writing a procedure, when we were preparing to

test it stated "The proof is in the pudding." I laughed and said "Don't you mean the proof of the pudding is in the eating?" Then everyone else (approximately 15 people) laughed at me and all agreed that the saying, as they knew it, was "The proof is in the pudding." They were all younger than I, though some by only a couple of years, and NONE had ever heard the "in the eating" part. When did this change take place and why?

--

Dani in Atlanta shared:
My East Tennessee born-n-bred mother-in-law (out law?) called last night, and one of the things she was telling me was, "Pacifically, Dani, I was hoping. . ." and there I am, thinking, "pacifically. . .? as if the woman has ever been to the west coast..."
Here are some of her wonderful East Tennessee-isms, or it could just be her (don't want to start any wars with our neighbor to the north):
 pacifically = specifically
 particulately = particularly (has something to do with ions in the air, I'm certain)
 flippid = flippant
 agitrative = a combo of agitated and aggravated (I guess)
 wristfully = wistfully (unless she has found a way to manipulate her wrist to grab things)
Those are just a few. She tends to be full of it --- I mean full of them, yes, that's it, full of THEM.

Andrea in Atlanta:
Speaking of word mispronunciations, I had an ex-boyfriend who insisted on pronouncing the word "especially" like this: EK-specially. AND he said it ALL the time. Of course, he ignored my corrections. He's no longer with us.

Katherine on Oakland, CA enquired:
:) In a seminar last night, a classmate presented a case discussion of a

client who spoke of somebody being "infactuated" with her. (Actually, it turned out that the client said "infatuated"--we listened to the tape of their session--but my classmate didn't notice; perhaps _she_ usually says "infactuated".) And I've heard several women in the last year refer to being "volumptuous".
Now, are these a form of portmanteau word, or malapropisms? Or something else?
--

Steve in San Francisco had the right terminology:
Dani? I think it was you who asked about the term for a verbal faux pax where an alternate, similar sounding word is used in place of the correct one. This is called a "malapropism" (emphasis on the first syllable), named for the character Mrs. Malaprop in Richard Sheradon's 1775 play "The Rivals". Mrs. Malaprop was "appropriately" named from the roots "mal", "apropos" (meaning of course, "inappropriate"). A couple of her most famous bloopers were "contagious countries" and "as headstrong as an allegory on the banks of the Nile". My friend and I collect such gems and have quite a list of them. Just a teaser from his brother (a never-ending source): "Ouch! I think I tore a filament in my leg!"

And a classic from one of my Public Speaking students this semester: "The researchers couldn't colloberate their findings"
If you're real interested, watch "Married, With Children"; Kelly (the ditzy blonde) pumps them out on a regular basis.
--

Phil in Salt Lake City brought up a classic one :
Perhaps the most common error made in this connection is with the use of fewer and less. One frequently reads newspaper items like: "Twenty less motorists were killed on county highways this year than last year." or "There were less people served on Thanksgiving than expected.". It seems to me that "fewer" is the correct word in both of these sentences. And the error always goes in that direction. One seldom hears "fewer" when it should be "less". The rule, as I recall, is that

"fewer" is used when the objects can be counted, like eggs in a recipe, but "less" if it's a measured quantity, like flour or milk. ("Two cups of milk was added" or "Five gallons of milk were drunk" if one is speaking of the gallon containers the milk was in.) Nicht wahr?

Karen in Manchester responded:
Yes, Phil, you're right! To me, the worst offender is the supermarket check-out line sign that says, "Twelve items or less."

--

HAR had another clunker:
Another one that gets me is the [mis]use of "majority" and "minority" with non-countable nouns, as in "the majority of the money".

--

Karen also wrote:
How about people who say "all the sudden" for "all of a sudden?"

Bill in Columbia, CT responded: Try suddenly.

--

Mike in Brisbane had seen few:
Pet peeve department: The people who say "B Grade Movies" instead of "B Movies" when referring to the product of Hollywood's "B" studios. They seem to think that this refers to an inferior product, when in fact, many of the B movies went on to become classics in their own right (Sweeping statement - please don't ask me to name any!) Anyhow, the B movies were the supporting features, in the old days when you got two full length movies for the price of one admission to the theatre.

--

Bill in Lexington, KY:
One barber shop I went to had a sign giving the motto of the Master Barbers of America: It pays to look well. Of course it does - especially before crossing the street. But what does it have to do with barbering?

--

Lorianne in Saskatoon:
It was -10 degrees C (-15 with the windchill) when I left this morning. When I was a kid, I thought that the weather folks were saying windshield!

--

Jim in Philadelphia said:
For instance, back when I was working at my oft-lamented retail job, I commented to someone that "Six people compromise management of this store." Of course, I should have said "comprise," but with hindsight, "compromise" is an even better choice...

Bill in Lexington KY remarked:
No, the management of the store comprises six people and compromises the entire staff.

--

Dani in Atlanta fingered:
On the knack for choosing the inappropriate word. I suppose my mother-in-law (uses "erotic" when she means "erratic" or "neurotic") is a good example of a Malaprop... anyone know if Mrs. Malaprop's first name is Wanda?

Jim observed:
Like what Red Sox pitcher Roger Clemens once commented "Sometimes I can be too erotic."

--

Phil in Salt Lake City recounted:
I once played the part of the mayor in "The Music Man". He did a lot of malapropisms. One I remember was something like: "That scoundrel should have been misapprehended hours ago." The main definition I found for misapprehend was misunderstand. The one that brought the house down, though, was when the mayor was trying to end an argument with his wife, and came up with: "Not one more poop out of you, madam!" (Whereupon the wife turns to the audience

and says: "I think he means 'peep' ".) The line came off so well that I was asked afterwards: "Did you really make a mistake?"

11

Colloquial English

In this chapter we deal with colloquialism, which by its nature is regional. However, the group focused on those expressions made popular through mass media, films, and global communications.

Radmilla in Georgia chimed in for the first time:
Hullo, all. I've been truly enjoying *wordplay*! My roommate and I have always enjoyed playing with words. Have y'all done medical words lately? I'm a nurse, and have heard such terms as "fireballs of the eucharist" for fibroids of the uterus and "smilin' mighty Jesus" for spinal meningitis. I have several others if anyone likes such things.

I love the way words evolve in people's private lexicons. In ours, we started referring to our children as "chilblains". (Anyone familiar with both children and chilblains will understand that one!) Soon "chilblains" became simply "blains". And finally, one day, I guffawed to hear girlfriend refer to our kids as "the blain of my existence". She swears it was an unintentional – Freudian slurp...

--

And on Freudian slips, Varda in Portland, ME observed:
Spotted on a list of inspirational sayings: "Life is like riding a bicycle. You don't fall off unless you stop peddling."
I guess this was supposed to have been the salesperson's credo...?

--

Mike in Brisbane commented on Happy Campers:
Someone asked a while back about the origin of the 'happy camper' expression. Didn't this come from the American institution of going to summer camp, where the counsellors insisted on everyone being happy campers?
In Australia, we use the expression 'Happy Vegemites' which derives from a radio commercial of the 1940's, which of course, promoted Vegemite, arguably Australia's national breakfast dish.

On the subject of strange town names, Aditya in Fort Lauderdale, FL contributed:
I am sure that not everyone has already read this. These are names of real towns in the US:

    Aromatic Creek, MO
    Go to Hell Gulch, SD
    Caress, WV
    Flirtation, CO
    Kiss Me Quick, SD
    Benign Peak, AK
    Bellicose Peak, AK
    Deception Creek, AR
    Delusion Lake, WY
    Another River, AK
    Peculiar, MO
    Yum Yum, TN
    Climax, OR
    Ding Dong, TX
    Do Stop, KY
    Goon Dip Mountain, AK
      --from "The Game of Words" by W.R. Espy

--

Allan in Brandon, Manitoba responded to a query:
<<What *is* the difference between a 'registered trade-mark' and a

'trade-mark'?>>

In the US, a registered trade-mark is one that has been accepted by and registered with the US Patent and Trademark Office. It is protected by copyright and trade-mark law. A trade-mark, on the other hand, is a name, logo, symbol etc which the company using it considers to be a trade-mark, and so indicates. It can mean that it is waiting for registration to be granted to the trade-mark, or that registration has been refused. Its use has virtually no protection by law. The different status of the two types of trade-marks is indicated by the different symbols used for them.

I believe that this distinction applies only in the US. Canada, I think, has and recognises only registered trade-marks. Patent and copyright laws vary greatly from country to country, though the European Union has made great progress in this area. Readers seeking incredibly dense and difficult to understand prose need look no further than texts of patent and copyright laws.

--

Kristofer of College Station, TX said:
I heard someone mention the word "dawdle" (sp?) as I was coming to the lab. The statement was "We won't get anywhere if you dawdle?" Any suggestions on its origin/history?

--

Jim's wife in Schenectady, NY contributed:
A 'Mommily' is any phrase that your mother repeated to you ad nauseum in the hope that it would stick in your brain and prevent you from going astray, or to just keep you in line. " Pretty is as pretty does" was my grandmother's personal favourite (along with "It's better to have it and not want it, than to want it and not have it." This in response to anyone's question about the wisdom of taking along a sweater, umbrella, etc...) Another: "A piece of paper will lie still and let you print anything you want to on it!" (This in response to anyone's trusting statement "I read it in the newspaper". I actually think about this one quite often during campaign season.)

My mother had one that confounded my siblings and I, though somehow it always managed to shut us up. It was her standard response when we grumbled about something. "Oh, you'd gripe if they hung ya with a new rope!"

She never could tell us what this meant or where it came from. It did manage to shut us up, mainly because we were *always* confused by it and we would stop grumbling to question the wisdom of this axiom. The scary part is I use this with my own kids now and they are just as confused as I was. So that I might break this pattern of ignorance would someone care to tell me what this means?

--

Bob in Chicago, IL said:

When I was a Boy Scout in the afterglow of WWII the term "Kybol" was commonly used to mean bathroom or more specifically outhouse. I never knew the origin and I haven't heard the term in years even though it was fairly prevalent then. Can any of you old Scouts help me out?

--

On the differences between US and UK English. Brian in London, UK observed:

I have a favourite, that points up the different usages of "Do you have ...?". In American English, this is asking about the present moment, whereas in British English it is asking about what is usually or often the case; a Briton would use "Have you got ...?" to talk about the present. So, a British English speaker, being asked "Do you have gas?" expects his dentist to be asking the question, and to him it means "Do you [normally] expect anaesthetization by gas?". To an American English speaker, the question "Do you have gas?" means [in British English] "Have you [at the moment] got any petrol?" or "Are you [at the moment] suffering from dyspepsia?".

--

Maya in Georgia responded to a query:

I don't think "home boy" or "homie" is to refer to a friendly, next-door-neighbour type – It's more along the lines of good friends that you know or grew up with in the 'hood--not necessarily a NICE person, just a good friend, someone who'd back you 'till the end.

--

Insults:

"He's so dumb; he couldn't pour piss out of a boot, even if the instructions were printed on the sole!"

Michael Verne commented:
There was one corner of Ohio called Woodsfield which was a southern as any state south of the Manson-Nixon line. I used to compare sayings with a couple guys from there:

...on it like white on rice.
...busy as a one-legged man in an ass-kicking contest.
...been doing this since God was a boy.
...so hungry my stomach's making love to my backbone.
...so hungry I could eat a baby's butt through a park bench. (credit to Dan Ackroyd on that one, from Neighbors)
...so ugly he/she could make an onion cry.
...fell out of the ugly tree and hit every branch.
...uglier'n a mud fence.

--

. . .a few sandwiches short of a full picnic
. . .as nervous as a long-tailed cat in a room full of rocking chairs
. . .feeling so low he could 've crawled under a snake's belly with his hat on
. . .so ugly that when he was born, the doctor spanked his mother

--

Connie in Des Moines, IA had few others up her sleeves:
More ways to indicate that someone's not playing with a full deck:
o   A few beers short of a six-pack
o   A few French fries short of a Happy Meal
o   A few yards short of the hole
o   A modest little person, with much to be modest about-- Churchill

- A room temperature IQ
- All booster, no payload
- An early example of the Peter Principle
- An expert on the historical significance of cottage cheese
- As sharp as a bowl of Jello
- Attic's a little dusty
- Batteries not included
- Calling him stupid would be an insult to stupid people
- Fired from McDonald's for having a short attention span
- Has no discretionary intellect
- Having a party in his head, but no one else is invited
- His memory is truly random-access
- I'd like to buy him for what he's worth and sell him for what he thinks he's worth
- If his IQ was two points higher he'd be a rock
- If what you don't know can't hurt you, he's practically invulnerable
- If you stand close enough to him, you can hear the ocean
- Mouth is in gear, brain is in neutral
- Needs another brain to make half-wit
- Needs his sleeves lengthened by a couple of feet so they can be tied in the back
- Not done evolving yet
- Not enough brain cells for the Prozac to be effective
- On the batting end of a no-hitter
- Pedalling real fast, but not getting anywhere
- Put a lens in each ear and you've got a telescope
- Puts a finger in his ear so the draft through his head isn't annoying
- Result of a first cousin marriage
- Room for rent, unfurnished
- Sort of like an inverse Einstein
- Swimming in the shallow end of the gene pool
- The twinkle in his eyes is actually the sun shining between his ears
- Took the little bus to school

- A few bricks short of a load
- The TV is on, but nobody is watching
- The elevator does not go all the way to the top
- The engine is running but the car is not moving
- The oars are not in the water
- The telephone is ringing but nobody is answering
- There is a fire in the furnace, but the room is freezing
- Paying for a Mac and finding out you bought Windows 3.0
- Riding down I 95 in a kiddy car

--

Jan of Hobart, TS added:
"I'm off like a prom dress" reminded me of other funny "exit lines", such as:

> I'm going to make like a banana...and split.
> I'm going to make like a baby...and head out.

--

John in Keel, UK observed:
The classic boot/piss saying is an Eskimo [i.e. Inuit language] proverb, evidently authentic, to the effect that the person who urinates on his/her foot does not stay warm for long...
Not applicable to current climatic conditions for most wordplayers, but those of you currently having Winter ought to understand.

John interjected in a discussion on shaggy dog stories...
Agreed: the only way of classifying shaggy dog stories [which can be made to last for hours] is by the concluding "joke", which is rarely more than a token closure [Beethoven does that sort of thing, though...]. BUT the standard model for all such stories is surely the one that begins "It was a dark and stormy night..." and works its way around, via an entire stable of large hairy canine presences, to the glorious phrase: "Oh, I couldn't send a knight out on a dog like this!"

--

Gerry in Ottawa, Ca:
Moving briskly on to "Does the chewing gum lose its flavour on the

bedpost overnight?" I'm curious to know whether there are any following words. The same goes for those grand old Sousa marches, "The Monkey Wrapped His Tail Around the Flagpole" and "How Does the Hen Know the Size of the Eggcup When She Lays the Egg?" I'd also be eternally grateful to any kind soul who can finish the ditty, "Passengers will please refrain from flushing toilets when the train..." I've been working on that one for weeks but the old mind just isn't clicking in. I often wonder just how far back some of these old chestnuts go. What for example, is the origin of "eeny, meeny, miney, mo?" Or, for that matter, the old childhood taunt "Nah, nah, nah, nah, NAH, nah" which I'm willing to bet has indo-European roots.

And Martha in Boston chimed in:

> Passengers will please refrain
> From flushing toilets while the train
> Is standing in the station, I love you.
> I believe in constipation
> While the train is in the station
> Moonlight always makes me think of you.
>
> Should you desire to pass some water
> Kindly call the pullman porter
> He'll place a vessel in the vestibule
> Use the platform at the rear
> The one in front is likely to be cool.
>
> Should these methods be in vain
> Then simply break a window pain
> This novel method is used by very few
>
> Go on strolling through the park
> Goosing statues in the dark
> If Sherman's horse can take it
> Why can't you?

THE POWER OF WORDS ~ 299

[to the tune of Humoresque]
I have somewhere a recording of Does Your Chewing Gum Lose its Flavor, but haven't memorized it, alas. Or maybe, whew!

Ken in St Paul, MN was reminded of a similar ditty:
An another old Lonnie Donnegan ditty from the past. I don't remember all the words, but the chorus is:
Does your chewing gum lose it's flavour on the bedpost overnight?
If your mother says "Don't chew it",
Do you swallow it in spite?
When you catch it on your tonsils,
Do you heave it left and right?
Does your chewing gum lose its flavour on the bedpost overnight?

Martin in LA was quick to amend: No, no, no!!!
Does the Spearmint lose its flavor on the bedpost overnight?
If you put it on the left side, will it end up on the right?
If you scratch your back in the morning,
will it itch again at night?
Does ...
The nation rose as one
and sent its favorite son
Straight to the White House
The nation's favorite light house
He said that he was sent
to ask the President
a very important question that concerned the continent
 Does ....
Here comes the bride
The groom is at her side
Straight to the altar
As steady as Gibraltar
He takes out the ring

> What a pretty thing
> And as he puts it on her hand
> The chorus starts to sing
> Does ...

(no wonder there's no room in my head for useful information!)

Yvette in Springfield, MA observed:
Concerning the recent thread about "Does Your Chewing Gum Lose Its Flavor On the Bedpost Overnight." This song was written back in the 1920's by Billy Rose ("My and My Shadow," married to Fanny Brice). It had a revival in the 1960's.

Gerry in Ottawa Ca was grateful:
Thanks to those who supplied answers to "Does your chewing gum lose its flavour" and "Passengers will please refrain." They'll still run through my mind but at least I'll have the words. It was interesting but not too surprising to see the chewing gum song attributed to the 1950's. I first heard it myself around 1932 - how time flies when you're having fun - when I thought it the height of wit and sophistication. But I guess everything gets recycled in time. "How do you know that?" my children used to cry in awe when I'd suddenly come up with the lyrics to "42nd Street." I was there at the beginning," I'd reply. "Back when the earth was formed out of chaos, when man first crawled out of the primordial slime." You want the words to "A Bachelor Gay" from "Maid of the Mountains" or "The Cobbler's Song" from Chu Chin Chow?" You got 'em. The only thing I don't got is the follow-up to "The Monkey Wrapped His Tail Around the Flagpole" and "How Does the Hen Know the Size of the Eggcup?" Oh yes, and another old "Humoresque" parody involving the words "Footprints on the dashboard upside down." Incidentally, if I may make a minor correction to Guy Haas' version of "They're Moving Father's Grave," I think the original line was "if some society twit wants a pipeline for his shit."

--

In the same vein as golf widow, Michael in North Georgia responded to the suggestion of Internet Widow:
My fiancée is the WWWW, the World Wide Web Widow, because I spend so much time on line. Also, to spin the thread of Southernisms further, are you familiar with bol' okra or mountain oysters?

--

Patrick in Collegeville, MN responded to Maryanne who asked about the poem "Taffy was a Welshman."
Mother Goose rhyme I remember from my childhood (and I still have a copy of the Vollander edition). Someone posted most of the poem, but left a little out. As I remember,

>Taffy was a Welshman,
>Taffy was a thief.
>Taffy came to my house
>And stole a joint of beef.
>
>I went to Taffy's house,
>Taffy was not home.
>Taffy went to my house
>And stole a marrow bone.
>
>I went to Taffy's house,
>Taffy was in bed.
>I took the marrow bone
>And threw it at his head.

Classic stuff for children.

--

Matt of Minneapolis responded to Michael Verne who mused:
" Am I the only one that remembers "Lolly, Lolly, Lolly, get your adverbs here...?"
Au contraire. Conjunction Junction (what's your function?) and Lolly's adverbs were two of my favourite the wonderful Grammar

Rock offerings of Schoolhouse Rock. A further trip down Saturday-morning-television Memory Lane:

"A noun is a person, place, or thing"
"VERB - that's what's happening!"
"Interjection! Shows excitement! Or emotion! Hallelujah!"

--

Mike of Brisbane asked for help with Names:
Oh, and help, please. Does anybody know for sure what the nicknames of the Hiroshima and Nagasaki bombs were? There's a discussion on another group – I go for "Tall Boy" and "Fat Boy" but others claim different.

Martha of Boston chimed in:
Oh--I think the bombs were Fat Man and Little Boy.

And Darwin followed up with:
The Hiroshima bomb was dubbed "Fat Man", and Nagasaki was clobbered by "Little Boy".
As I understand the story, the names came from the first test bomb, exploded over the Alamagordo test facility, nicknamed Fat Boy, due to its unconventional diameter. The first atom bombs had to be almost perfectly spherical, in order to focus the force of the detonator. The Hiroshima bomb was several times larger than the test bomb, hence Fat Man, and Nagasaki's nemesis was but a dwarf of Fat Man.

John in Keel, UK said: I do remember reading in Robert Jungk's _Heller als tausend Sonnen_ [or _Brighter than a Thousand Suns_, to you...] that the physicists working at Los Alamos to develop the atomic bomb were instructed to tell a standard story about what they were perfecting, so as to satisfy local gossip without being suspiciously tight-lipped about it all. They spread the story in all the local bars that they were developing windscreen-wipers for submarines...

--

Mike of Brisbane commented to Bob, on Iced Tea -
Somehow, iced tea never took off in Australia. Here, it's a case of "boiling the billy" whatever the temperature, and making a cup of hot tea.

I guess the big bush never did have ice, in the old days. Interesting to know where "billy" came from, too. The billy can is the thig you hang over the fire to boil the water to make the tea.

--

Janet in Calgary commented on felt-pens:
Somewhat on topic, but without answering the question. In Canada, and perhaps elsewhere, we call the felt-tipped pens that children use for colouring "magic markers", which must have been a throwback to the original advertising or some such thing. However, when I got to Australia, aged 9 (me, not Australia), my school friends had no idea what I was talking about until I pointed and they said "Oh! textas!" It took me another two years to figure out this was not a brand name, but a reference to textured pens, i.e., "textures"

Mike of Brisbane disagreed:
Uh, not quite, Janet. the original brand that had the big market share out here was called "Textra-Colour", which is what we all grew up with. When I went to Papua New Guinea, to Teachers' College, the leading brand was a Chinese(?) one called "Bon-Ton" our college principal used to send us in to fits of laughter talking about how "you get out your bon-tons and make up some flash cards..." I guess you had to be there...

--

Sara of Boston observed:
I love Weird Al. Some of his best have been Michael Jackson take-offs ("Eat It" for "Beat It," "Fat" for "Bad," etc.). Though, he does some very good originals too. One of my favourites is "One More Minute" which has such phrases as: "I'd rather clean out all the bathrooms in Grand Central Station with my tongue, than spend one minute with you." He'd also rather:

- pull out his intestines with a fork
- spend a lifetime eating shards of broken glass
- pull his heart out of his ribcage with his bare hands and throw it on the ground and stomp on it until he dies

Varda in Portland, ME responded to Alex in Adelaide who was wondering:

<<I have always puzzled over why the names of all radio stations east of the Mississippi start with a W and those west start with a K. My favourite news radios are BBC world service, KFWB all news all the time (give us 22 minutes and we'll give you the world), and NPR.>>

I don't know why, but I can add that the *general* rule of thumb in North America is: "W" in the eastern half of the U.S., "K" in the western half, "C" in Canada, and "M" in Mexico. (Have I got that right?) Are there similar standards elsewhere? In, say, Australia? Or Europe?

Bob of Chicago followed up with:

In Chicago, radio station WLS was at one time owned by Sears Roebuck, and Company and the call letters stand for "World's Largest Store". The call letters for station WGN stand for "World's Greatest Newspaper" since it is owned by the Chicago Tribune. We also have station WIND which refers to the Chicago nickname "The Windy City" (so named for its politicians and not from its weather or its WordPlayers).

Tom in San Diego expounded with:

Chronology. The earliest radio stations were 3-letter "W" stations, then four letters; then "K" was used as the number of stations increased. Ham radio licenses use still more beginning letters. The initial letters are assigned to countries by international agreement.

Since U.S. civilization began on the east coast (never went anywhere else, come to think of it), most of the early stations were east coast stations. WGN in Chicago is a notable exception.

Someone observed:

Concerning call letters of broadcast stations beginning with W or K: I believe that the original licences all began with W, but when it became apparent that there would not be enough combinations, they went to K. As to why most of the W's are East of the Mississippi? Where were the largest and most technologically advanced cities in the '20's and '30's?

Hep rebutted:
This is incorrect. The W/K designations (W east of Mississippi, K west of Mississippi) were formulated by international agreement (you can get a list of the international country codes from the Government Printing Office). The W and K were assigned to the US, and other countries were assigned other country codes. The W and K are also the call letters assigned to Amateur Radio operators in this country, with the addition of numbers (W1-New York, W-2 New England, W-8 Ohio, etc.). Some of the K beginnings you find in the East and some of the W beginnings you find in the West have to do with call station letters that were transferred after stations were sold, and the call letters slipped through the cracks during the move of the stations (and probably a little bribery so the person attached to a station call sign didn't have to give it up).

Elizabeth in Madison observed:
In Madison there is a television station with the call letters WKOW. Dairy state.

Lomond in Sacramento noted:
A few years ago, a new Christian station applied for a license in Japan where call letters begin with "J" (logically). Much to their dismay, they were assigned call letters which spelled out a word which pronounced phonetically was the Japanese word for prostitute.

--

Steven in San Antonio wondered:
Maybe this was already stated and I missed it, but doesn't the word 'flit' refer to a homosexual in Great Britain?

--

Bruce in Sydney queried:
I can raise a titter here in Oz by calling that which an Australian calls a "thong" and a Briton a "flip-flop", a "jandal". If you pop and soda

drinkers know of that to which I refer, what are they called in the U.S.?

Matt of Minneapolis answered:
I have heard those sandal whatchamajiggers called both thongs and flip-flops. And the regionalism of naming things is evident without traversing great expanses. I am nascent of Wisconsin (near Madison, with its newfound e-nic addiction), and have resided in Minneapolis and adjacent suburbia for the past decade. The plumbing fixture found in public places for the purpose of satiating one's thirst is known here only as a 'drinking fountain' or 'water fountain'. In my native stomping grounds, however, this was known as a 'bubbler'. Inquiries as to the location of a bubbler meet with vapid and/or nescient stares. Then there's "rubber band" vs. "rubber binder" for that thin, pliant fastener. And these differences are between locales 280 miles (450 km) apart.

Susan in Spokane, WA chimed in:
I *love* those rubbery cheapo sandals and I have heard them (and worn them) as zorries, flip-flops, thongs, depending on where along the US west coast I was residing.

Marylin in San Fransisco observed:
I've always heard the sandals under discussion referred to as "thongs" or "flip-flops". That's the view from the east coast (New York) and the west coast (San Francisco). But my Kiwi husband always calls them "jandals". The first time I heard this, I had no idea what he was talking about. He claims it was a marketing ploy for the product in New Zealand, a mix of Japanese and sandals.

--

Patrick of Collegeville interjected:
Bob in Tokyo notes that it was the USS _Indianapolis_, not the _Indiana_, that was sunk returning home from delivering the bombs to whatever place of take-off. Anyone else remember the rules for naming American warships until after WWII (don't know when they went into effect, but before the '30s)? Battleships: states. Cruisers: cities.

Aircraft carriers: battles. Submarines: marine creatures. Destroyers and lesser craft had just numbers. I think it was the nuclear-powered vessels that started breaking the rules.

--

Bruce in Sidney observed on Kiwi accent:
Gidday! You're right mite, I bet no-one will know what a "beck section" is. Unless of course they are somewhat worldly and have dropped their baggage at a "chicken counter" at an airport in one of En Zed's bugger suttees. Of course, ut uz possubull they might be thunking of "sect", as in "I've been sect from my job". Or perhaps "secks" the plural of sack, and not to be confused with the homophone "sex" as in Fifth Avenue. For the numerate amongst our literati, "sucks" is the number which when counting to, you need to change hands and should not be considered an insult. Likewise, should a Kiwi suggest a quick "fucks" he or she is being neither endearingly libidinous nor ungrammatical, offering merely a speedy solution to a problem you may have.
I shall cease shearing these un-sights unto Kiweese lest I terminally confuse you other Word Players not so familiar with the flattest vowels east of Seth Efrica.

--

Michael in Mesa, AZ observed:
When did people start replacing, "I said 'hi.' Then she said, 'hi.'" with, "I go 'hi.' Then she goes, 'hi?'" (also, was I correct to end that sentence with a question mark, for the sake of my sentence, or should I have used a period, for the sake of the quotation?) I thought "goes" was a product of the seventies, but when I looked in my Peanuts cartoon books, Schultz had the kids using this slang back in the fifties or sixties.
Anyway, it could be worse. Now, they say, "I was like, 'hi,' and she was like, 'no way.'"

--

Anders in Sweden drew some comparison in colloquial English and Swedish

English: Kiss   Swedish: Puss
English: Pussy   Swedish: Kisse
Why can't the English ever make it right?   :)

--

On the topic of city inhabitants, Lee of Sacramento remarked:
You've heard of Philadelphia? Those who are inhabitants thereof are known as Fluffyans, of course!

--

Bill in Lexington KY, observed:
Truth in advertising: And then there's "New and Improved". It seems to me that if it's new, it can't be improved because it didn't exist before. If it's improved then it existed before and can't be new.
Sign on a billboard: Most trouble-free car in America.
I don't think "trouble-free" comes in degrees. Either it is or it isn't. "Most nearly trouble-free" I can accept, but then they're admitting that it isn't trouble-free.

--

Jeff in Melbourne:
We have cackhanded politicians in Victoria....or is that cockheaded...

--

Terrence in Bermuda had a Gnawing Question:
Heard on the BBC: "The Society for the Promotion of Agricultural Research in the Developing World [an approximation] is just one of many similar groups BEAVERING AWAY at this issue."
While the meaning of beavering away was clear in context, I found it interesting that I had never heard this expression used by a North American while an English colleague at the hospital assures me that it is in common parlance in the U.K. As it is obviously of North American origin, and an evocative expression at that, why did it get lost to the New World? Any Canadians familiar with this phrase?

--

Gary in Toronto, answered:
This Canadian is familiar with it, as a British turn of phrase. ;) I

wouldn't assume that just because the beaver is indigenous to North America, the phrase must be too; after all most of the beaver hats were on British heads, no? ;) And anyway, aren't there lots of common phrases based on the qualities of exotic or mythic animals?

North Americans may shy away from the phrase because "beaver" is another vulgar term for... ummm, pussy - on this side of the Atlantic - I don't think that's the case in Britain, is it?

Bob in Tokyo:

It's not entirely lost in North America, it would just have a slightly different meaning. Beaver is slang for the female naughty bits (in the U.S.). So 'beavering away' is certainly evocative, but not for polite company. One of the funnier gags in one of the 'Naked Gun' movies starts with the line 'Nice beaver!'

And Kat in New York:

This was common while I was growing up (not quite back in the dark ages, only about 40 years ago). Usually used in the sense of 'busy as a beaver' --- lots of bustle, lots of gnawing and chomping, followed by a loud crash. The result of 'beavering' was often useful, but the collateral damage (where the tree fell) could be devastating to other critters in the area.

And Bill in Lexington, KY:

Could it come from "busy as a beaver"?

And Gerry in Ottawa wanted to set them straight:

I'm appalled by the direction that this "beaver" thread seems to be taking. Nudge-nudge, wink-wink at the entrance to the Beaver Club in Montreal? What sort of Yankee kinkiness is this? In all my days as a practicing Canadian - even as a small boy when I was on the lookout for such things - I've never ever heard of the word having any sexual connotations whatsoever. Nor has anyone else that I've asked. The beaver is a Good, Noble and Industrious Animal. It beavers grimly away day after day, building its little home, damming streams, clear-cutting forests and flooding arable land. It is truly a Paragon of Virtue. Thanks to the fur-obsessed "Governor and Company of

Adventurers of England Trading into Hudson'S Bay" or "The Bay" as we carelessly call it today, the beaver was responsible for opening up much of our West. And the Beaver Club in the Queen Elizabeth Hotel, which seems to cause such merriment, is named after an earlier social club established by the directors of a rival fur-trading firm, the North West Company. Honi soit qui mal y pense, I say. Get off the sex bit. Leave the beaver to its stolid, hard-working ways.

And Mike in Brisbane:
On the "Beaver" thread, I support Gerald. The beaver is an industrious little animal, and I have fond memories of reading about them when I was but a little boy. "Beavering away" is used quite a bit in Australia, too. Now, there was another use of the word, about a generation or two ago it used to be considered funny to race up to a gent wearing a beard, and bellow out "beaver" at him, and then run away again. Anyone know when/why this was one, or what it meant?

And Allan in Brandon, Manitoba:
What might be termed the 'gynaecologic' or 'pudendal' meaning of beaver is something that I have never actually heard used in Canada; it seems to be strictly American usage. Anyone any idea why this is so, and how this meaning came about?

And Marilyn in San Francisco:
Another observation from my Kiwi husband (Bruce, if you're still out there, he's from Wellington, Titahi Bay to be exact). He's intrigued by the nicknames of college sports teams. Once source of amusement for him was that the Beavers could play the Trojans.

And Barb in Stephenville, TX:
Have read the beaver postings with interest. Seems no one has as yet come up with the source of the connotations. First time I ever heard it used in reference to anything but the big-toothed little critters was when Citizen Band truckers used it back in the CB heydays to refer to attractive female drivers or pedestrians. Guess we should ask a trucker.

David in Glendale, CA:
Biology: A beaver is an animal well respected for its soft and shiny fur.

--

Michael in Mesa, AZ on differences:
In the south you can "cut" the lights on & off, but elsewhere, they must be >"turned." (technically, cut is much more accurate)

Mike in Brisbane responded:
Somewhere, I've got a photocopy of an old Edison Electric Co notice which was hung on the wall. It explains that you don't have to light the lamps with a match, nor blow them out, but simply turn the key on the wall beside the door. I believe it to be genuine, so "turning" would have been accurate a while back. My PNG kids used to say "out the light".

--

Mike in Brisbane related a Cream Ad:
> "Brylcreem, a little dab'll do ya,
> Brylcreem, you'll look so debonair,
> Brylcreem, the girls will pursue ya,
> Simply dab a little onya hair!"

--

Gerry in Ottawa:
On another topic altogether, I notice that Bugs Bunny is about the only character left on television who still says, "What's up?" Everyone else seems to have gone over to "What's going down?" Is there some cultural reason for this de-escalation? And what about us old-fashioned types who prefer to continue on an even keel and simply say, "What's going on?" It's not easy being a traditionalist these days.

--

Jim in Philadelphia noted:
Although it would probably be considered sexual stereotyping now, women seeking mates used to be advised that 'the way to a man's heart is through his stomach'.

To which Jack in London responded"
Women who think that are aiming their sights too high! [(c) The Museum for Old Jokes.]

--

Toni in Minnesota raised a gender issue:
Quoting another participant: "I figure that ought to hold you guys for now. The next ten will >come in a couple of days..." But what about us gals? My manager insists that is is okay for him to use "guys" in this manner and that nothing is meant by it. I consider it to be obstinance on his part, and do not much appreciate it. His attitude seems to be that there is something wrong with me if I take offense instead of something wrong with him for being unwilling to make an effort to change. I am not a flaming (or any other kind of) feminist; I just appreciate NOT being called a guy.
Maybe we could try to use "folks" if "y'all" doesn't feel proper.

Kim in Tokyo responded:
Re: the thread on the use of "guys" to refer to groups of women/girls, I was born and raised in the Philadelphia area, and "you guys" was used all the time as a gender-neutral expression in both same-gender and mixed gender groups. For example, "Wait up, you guys!" "C'mon, you guys," etc. Perhaps because of this, I don't find it offensive, and I think it's preferable to most alternatives such as you girls, you women, you gals, you ladies, etc.
I know there's quite a few Philly folks out there...whaddaya think, you guys? :)
I like "y'all," but when I use it, I always feel like I'm borrowing it, since I didn't grow up with it.

And Lucy in San Francisco:
I'm not a Philadelphian, so I can't speak from that perspective. I think, though, that "guys" may be a false generic in the same way that "men" is--that is, they are both words that, strictly speaking, refer to one gender and in some cases, very pointedly exclude the other; I think, for example, of a sign over the door of a Catholic seminary in, I think,

Cleveland, that reads, "Blessed all you men who enter here." I am sure the hierarchy would not read that use of "men" to include women. I am not comfortable being labelled a "man" as in "Peace on earth, good will to men" or a guy as in "c'mon you guys" any more than I would want to use "women" or "girls" to refer to both genders. Why not use "people" or "folks" or "humankind" or another truly gender-neutral work when we are referring to folks of both genders.

Rollo in Adelaide, began thus:
An observation, caused perhaps by watching too much TV; In England, the policeman calls the member of the public "Sir". (Reference: "The Bill"). In the US, the member of the public calls the policeman "Sir". (Reference: "Cops"). Why the reversal?
In Australia, I don't think there is a common word, either way. You might get away with "Mate". Egalitarian society, I guess.
Observations from other countries?

Katherine in Oakland, CA observed:
I've never been addressed as "sir" by a policeman :). I have been addressed as "Ma'am". (Don't believe everything you see on TV, Rollo!) And I've addressed policemen as "Officer", which I understand to be the standard form...or am I Anglicising?

--

Rich in Rindge, NH took us back to the beaver metaphor:
Had to laugh this weekend when we drove past the "Happy Beaver Campground." My wife thought I was cracking up.

On the same vein, Richard in Boulder, CO said:
I was listening to a radio program about current trends in American movies. One of the latest trends was female full-frontal nudity. The guest was describing this trend and said it was called a "beaver shot".

By sheer coincidence, Katherine in Oakland had a brush with a beaver:
When registering for classes this afternoon, I noticed that one section of the required class on "Human Sexuality" is taught by Daniel Beaver.

Lee in Sacramento, responded to Sara' query:
I think I vaguely recall that screaming meemies refers to the shells of WW I. They were called because of the sound they made while approaching and (hopefully) passing overhead.

Mike in Brisbane introduced a little known term:
"Tyke" in Australian can mean an infant of the species, as in "Poor little tyke" and also a slightly derogatory word for someone who belongs to the Roman Catholic faith. I don't know what the derivation is.

Sara in Boston took a crack at John's enquiry with regards to "hooks":
I've always heard the word "hook" used to refer to a phrase or riff within a song that tries or succeeds in "hooking" the audience's attention. It can be simply a catchy riff, like the introduction to "Jumpin' Jack Flash" by the Rolling Stones, or it can be an entire phrase, like the theme to Pink Floyd's "Run Like Hell." I think it's become jargon lately.

Steven in Atlanta gave a similar explanation:
In pop music, a hook is a usually melodic and fairly simple phrase that stands out and draws the listener in, the critical element in what makes a tune "catchy." This is most often the beginning of the chorus or a transition riff. Identifying the hook is a subjective process, of course, but here are a few fairly unambiguous examples:

The "dit-dit-dit-daah" theme in Beethoven's Fifth Symphony

The intro guitar riffs in "Johnny B. Goode" and "Memphis"

The choruses of "Don't Be Cruel" and "I Wanna Hold Your Hand"

The thematic bass/guitar lines of "Inagaddadavida," "Sunshine of Your Love," "25 or 6 to 4," and "Smoke on the Water"

... and pretty much all of "Tighten Up"

A good hook is usually necessary to selling a pop song.

Elena in Montreal asked:
Has anyone heard of the concept of "babooning"? It's a term used by a friend of mine to describe picking lint, a thread, hair and the like off the shoulder (or whatever) of a friend. (I count on my friends to keep me presentable!). I've never heard anyone else use the term and often wondered whether this was a clever coinage on the part of my friend or in use elsewhere.

--

David In Los Angeles, brought up the euphemism for old age and libido:
In contrast, there's the defensive comment among the (shall we say) "experienced" among us: "Just 'cause there's snow on the roof don't mean there ain't a furnace in the basement..."

--

Bill in Mobile, AL commented about "Indian summer":
I've always thought that "Indian" at one time meant "Bogus" or "Sham" as a result of our prejudice and that something that could not be relied on was prefaced with Indian - such as "Indian Giver." "Indian Summer," I think doesn't have the romance that people believe it has.

Heath in San Antonio thought otherwise:
I believe Indian Summer stems from the same thinking as Indian giving, that is, giving and then taking away (those sneaky Injuns). Indian Summer refers to the tricky weather at the end of the summer which makes you believe autumn has come. As in Texas presently--we have had a brief cold spell, but are sinking back into miserable heat. So, we were tricked...

John from Keel, UK added a British perspective:
I nearly contributed about Indian Summers before because I don't think the North American perspective is the correct one. The phrase has crossed the Atlantic from English English [only quote I can give off-hand is the title of Galsworthy's novel "Indian Summer of a Forsyte", where the expression is a metaphor for a late blooming in old age]. And that must mean [still without looking anything up, sorry!]

that it derives from the British in India and the climate in that part of the world.

Gerry in Ottawa took umbrage at the inference from using the term:
I'm having trouble understanding why the term "Indian summer" should be considered racist. The only even slightly derogatory explanation I can find is that it gave the Indians one more chance to attack the whites. All other sources attribute it to the fact that it was the Indians who told the first settlers about it, that it was then that the Indians broke up their villages and moved into the interior to get ready for their winter hunt, and that this sort of season was more pronounced in the lands formerly occupied by the Indians than it was in the eastern regions inhabited by the whites.
It all seems innocent enough.

He later added:
I guess I'll have to back away from my earlier statement that the term "Indian summer" shouldn't be considered pejorative. According to an expert in Nova Scotia, "British settlers in New England used it to describe a time of year which often coincided with the pleasant fall weather when the area's Indians normally left their villages to go hunting. The settlers viewed this as abandoning the real work of farming for the mere pleasure of the hunt. It fitted in with, and is one of the components of, the negative image of the lazy Indian. The Indians, of course, viewed it much differently."

--

Mike in Brisbane:
Just another thought; How many of us can remember parents' or grandparents' exclamations of agreement which are no longer in general use? I remember:

"Too right!"
"My oath!" (slightly risqe, not used in the drawing room)
"Well I never!"
"My colonial oath!" (more risque)

"My ensanguined oath!" (not used in the house)
ny others? there must be a wealth of these with our different cultural backgrounds.
Another old expression: "You don't say!" (when of course, you did.)

Ken in Victoria, BC added:
> I say!
> Blow me!
> Blow me down!
> I'm rate capped (said with broad Yorkshire accent)
> Lands O' Goshen (sp?)
> Heavens to Betsy
> Well, knock me over with a feather.

Patrick in San Jose CA raised the issue of additives:
Speaking of conversational interjections, what about the ones with which people end their sentences? I know that - at least according to Americans - Canadians are popularly supposed to end sentences with "..., eh." In Ireland (and Britain, I suspect), it's quite common to find "..., you know?" or "...like" carefully placed at the end of sentences, either singly or in combination, like, you know? In French the same function seems to be served by "..., quoi", and in southern Germany I've heard "..., ge." Any corroborations, refutations, or extensions to the list would be welcome, like. And what about words or phrases used in regional variations of English, you know?

Frank in Ottawa added some:
Then there are the shortened dialect forms of "Am I not (Aineye); "Is she not" (Inshee); "Does he not" (Dunnee); "I'm first, ayneye"; "Nice looking wench that, innshee"; "Finks he's Gawd's gift to wimmim, Dunnee."
These are statements, not questions.

--

Lomond in Sacramento asked:
My wife asks - Does the term "bimbo" apply to both males and females

or is there a separate name for men? Is there such a thing as a male blond bimbo?

Jane in Hobart, AU replied:
How about a "himbo"?

Dani in Atlanta added:
I always thought that it was odd that the word wasn't "bimba" or "bimbie" or something else with a 'feminine' ending.

--

Mike said:
<<Pete has decided that linguini with a Newman Venetian sauce is top nosh at the moment.>>

And Dani in Atlanta observed:
I've always heard "top notch" and now I'm curious. . . typo or is this really what you all in the land of Oz say? Or, 'top nosh' could be the same for the southern US term "good eatin'" It wasn't uncommon to hear somebody say "Whatchu want to nosh (could be spelled 'gnosh,' too, I s'pose) on tonight?" or "I need something to nosh" as in "I need something to snack on until it's time for dinner."

--

Catie in Washington, DC invoked some sailing lingo:
Now that I've changed the subject to sailing, the history of sailing terms is very interesting. Having spent a lot of time on a fishing boat, I got conditioned to referring to:

    Head = bathroom
    bulkhead = wall
    deck = floor
    galley = kitchen
    rack, berth, bunk = bed
    fiddle-edge = that little raised edge around the table in the galley (so plates don't slide off when the ship is rolling and pitching - of course, the FOOD still ends up in your lap!)
    roll = rocking side-to-side
    pitch = rocking from stem-to-stern

> ladder = stairs
> overhead = ceiling
> aft = behind (as in the aft deck)
> starboard = right
> > port = left (the only way I could remember these is that port had 4 letters, and so did left)

There are more, but that's all I could think of off the top of my head. Some terms also have interesting meanings:
Starboard (middle English - sterbord, OE - steorbord "rudder side" from when ships had rudders on the right side. The other side was called Larboard, but (according to a nautical friend of mine), it was eventually just called port, because that was the side that was closest to land upon arrival at the home port.

--

Phil in Salt Lake City weighed in on southernism:
I have a somewhat nostalgic fondness for "y'all" and its derivatives, having spent 6+ years in Georgia in graduate school. What I seemed to notice at the time was that y'all, as used in the Deep South, was always a plural form of "you" which we are otherwise lacking in English. " Y'all's ", therefore, was a handy way of saying: "Is that y'all's house?", meaning, "Is that the house belonging to all of you?". I have heard "y'all" used by people from the "not so Deep South", such as from Virginia, when the usage was obviously a singular "you", not a plural one. Is this the usage that others have observed? And how about usage in the panhandle of Oklahoma. And how about sweet potato pie, for that matter?

Bob ib Chicago disagreed:
I beg to differ, Phil. I grew up in Chicago where the word "youse" is part of the vernacular just about equal in frequency of use to the Southern "y'all". One of its most visible proponents was our late great mayor, "Hizzoner" Richard J. Daley.

HAR added:
Actually, English _does_ have a plural form for "you". It's "you". The

singular form, "thou" and it's possessive forms, "thy" and "thine" has become obsolete so we don't hear them except in archaic writing or speech.

Ann in Davis, CA rebutted:
Welp, I'm from Arkansas and we never used y'all for the singular. We thought it sounded geeky when we'd hear it used that way by a northerner pretending to be speaking suthun.

Ruth in College Station, TX followed up:
The y'all thread was ravelled on Copyediting-l a few months ago, and I insisted that here in central Texas it is both plural and singular. No one else agreed with me, but I later asked several natives of the area who all said it was both. (I am a proud Illinois-type Yankee. They don't have to be from New England.)
I hear "all y'all" a lot here. And I am NOT making this overheard interchange up:

> Waitress: Are y'all ready for me to take y'all's order, y'all want to wait, or y'all want me to get y'all's drinks?
>
> Obviously-Yankee customer: That's five y'alls in one sentence; I'm sorry, you'll have to be shot.
>
> Waitress: So y'all want to wait?

Toni in Minneapolis concurred:
This agrees with my remembrance that, when stopping for gas on a trip through Texas some 20 years ago, all alone and in a car with Wisconsin plates, I was invited "Y'all come back, now".

Debbie in Kalamazoo, MI observed:
Bradley Harris of the U of Memphis has written an article on "y'all" as a polite singular -- forthcoming in _American Speech_, I think. Otherwise, the prevailing opinion is - based on my collection of replies - that y'all who use y'all in the singular are not genuine, not native speakers of Southern American English.

Kathleen in Stanford, CA contributed thus:
In the Old South (i.e., below the Mason-Dixon line), we found NO instances of "y'all" used as a singular. It is ALWAYS plural. What con-

fuses naive observers is its common use to refer to people who are not physically present.

If you heard me say to Mary "You all come over this evening", you might think I was using a singular. But I would mean "Mary and some unspecified but understood other or others with whom Mary customarily visits". This could be Mary's husband, her children, her parents, her classmates, a friend, a group of acquaintances that she and I share, or almost any other group of which Mary is a part. Mary and I know who they are. Observers don't have to.

If a waitress says to a departing customer "Y'all come back, now, y'heah?", she is referring to the customer and anyone else in whatever class he includes himself--other Yankees, old codgers, teenagers, conventioneers, or whatever. The group is completely unspecified. The intent is inclusive--define your own group, but feel welcome with any of them.

"You all" is a gracious and very useful way of referring to multiple unspecified others. Perhaps it feels comfortable because it is familiar, but I much prefer it to "you guys", especially when the group is of both sexes. (Yes, yes, I know "guys" is now used for females, but it sure wasn't when I was young.)

Maryanne in Tallahassee, FL added:
"Y'all" is definitely plural. Someone using it in the singular is a phoney. It is very useful. For example, if I call up Sluggo's Gym and ask, "Do y'all give massages?," Spike, who answered, will know I mean, "Are massages given on the premisses," rather than, "Do you, Spike, give massages?". The possessive is y'all's.

--

Speaking of Southernism, Susan in San Francisco interjected:
It reminds me of a favorite southernism- don't get your tit in the wringer over it. So evocative.

--

Jim in Philadelphia picked up on the controversy of referring to days f the week:

If today is Monday, "this Wednesday" is in two days, and "next Wednesday" is in nine days. (Or we could also say, "the next Wednesday after Christmas, to mean the first occurrence of Wednesday following 25 December, non-inclusive.) If today is Wednesday, "next Wednesday" means one week from today... At least that's how I always knew it. Any of you upper-class types care to contradict me?

David in Glendale, CA added:

Out here in SO(uthern) CA(lifornia), some folks avoid the Wednesday (next or next-next?) by referring to the near one as "this coming Wednesday" and the far one as "a week from Wednesday."

Jessie in Sunnyvale, CA observed:

As for the "next Wednesday" thread, I'll have to go along with what appears to be the common opinion here. "Next Wednesday" is always 7-13 days out. This is in contrast with "this Wednesday" which is always 0-6 days away.

Ann in Davis, CA also opined:

Here's how I handle the Wednesday problem: If it's the next possible Wednesday, I say "next Wednesday". If it's some Wednesday after that, I say "Wednesday of, like, next week, y'know?" or "Wednesday, uh, October 28 or whatever the date is". I don't think I've ever been misunderstood about this.

--

Marjorie in Boston wrote:

On the subject of words that are unfamiliar (to me, at least), I ran across two more that are mystifying me: "tatie pot" and "parkin." I can't find 'em in the dictionary. Both were referred to as English foods; "parkin" was mentioned as a Yorkish dish. "Tatie pot" suggests a type of potato dish to me.

Gary in Southampton, UK replied:

From your correspondent in deepest Yorkshire. Yes, parkin is a Yorkshire dish. A consensus amongst my 'e by gum' parkin-aficionado colleagues is that it's a 'softish, stickyish, gingerish cake', much loved around here. Think soggy gingerbread. This is the time of year for parkin, with lots of outdoor parties around bonfires. Could this be anything to do with the word parky, meaning cold weather?

As for tatie pots, you might need to go over the border (to Scotland), where I think they call potatoes taties. I hail from the English Black Country myself - no, that isn't Birmingham by the way - where potatoes are taters, but we don't have Tatie (or Tater) Pots.

Frank of Ottawa added:

Tatie pot. First citation 1871, but the same dish under spelling variants much earlier.

A dish consisting of beef or mutton, cut into pieces, and put into a large dish along with potatoes, onions, pepper, salt etc., then baked in the oven ... is called in Cumberland _ taty pot_.

(Sounds like good stodge for a cold winter evening.) Other citations indicate Cumberland origin.

--

Lauren in North Carolina commented of Richard's soliloquy:

He writes, in the midst of his sparklingly witty remarks: "in the world of bidness . . . , :)"

Which got me thinking about a few other funny ways people say certain words. I once dated a "reckuhration" major 'way back when I was an undergraduate. There are a whole lot of folks out there who are concerned about "nucular" regulation. And don't get me started "axing" about "gubment" issues! My ex-husband looked through the "classifields" every Sunday, liked "Seen" Connery movies and the "buffit" at Duff's Smorgasbord in Virginia.

Anyway, I remain fascinated by the ways we express ourselves, and it's not just us Southerners who have the market on interesting pronunciations. Such variety in pronunciation keeps English both lively and, thankfully, NOT truly standard. I have a very informal collection of interesting pronunciations, particularly from folks who fancy themselves so very important.

--

Kimberly in Fort Lauderdale responded to Jim:
In Florida we also refer to stepping on the back of someone's shoe as "giving them a flat tire."

--

Radmilla in Georgia responded to Barb who said:
<<Never had a butterfly kiss...that I know of. Define. Define.>>
Gladly -- Butterfly kisses are when you put your face really close to someone you like and flutter your eyelashes most delicately against the skin. Tantalizing...... (but works best in the absence of mascara....) (Maybe it's a Southern thang?)

--

Bob in Chicago responded to Mike from Down Under who said:
<<Spot the out of towner, ay!>>
Aha, another clue. I take it that the "Ozzies" use "ay" and the "Cannuks" use "eh" when ending a sentence that would normally be declarative but ends up as a quasi question. Now I'll be sure to tell the "Up Overs" from the "Down Unders", eh!...er...uh...I mean ay! What we need now is an international "Quasi Question Mark :)

--

Lee in Sacramento weighed in on the evolution of dialect:
I don't know about none of us understanding each other dialects in 60 years, but what really bugs me now is the bent toward ending a statement with a rise in tone. It therefore sounds to me like a question? (as a for instance). I stand there (figuratively) with my mouth open waiting for the rest, but there IS no "rest." That's it. I have to admit that, initially, I thought it was those of the female persuasion who were doing it, but I now realize its both a male & female acquired trait.
Help! Am I the only one on whom this has the effect of fingernails on the blackboard?

--

Susi in Louisville, KY commented on spoken fillers:
Yes, it even has a name-Upspeaking. Isn't it, like, annoying? Doesn't it, ya know, like grate? Like if I say more than two words I have to

check to see if, ya know, you understand them both? As far as I'm concerned, it's the only legitimate reason for legal handguns. Properly done, it requires a hair-shake from the female and a Butthead head-tilt from the male. Perhaps it's a mating ritual, but they'll never. like, breed? Because they're not sure they understand?

Bob in Chicago followed up with:
I agree wholeheartedly and the only thing worse is starting each sentence with "like I said"... Know what I mean? :)

Michael in St Paul opined:
Here in Minnesota, a rising inflection at the end of a sentence is not uncommon. I always thought this was Valley Girl Speak, but didn't know why it was so pervasive (especially in rural areas).
Recently, it was explained to me that the rising inflection comes from the Scandinavian influence on the language here. The rising inflection is a natural part of Scandinavian speech and now a trait of the Minnesota accent.

Linda in Delaware also commented:
UP-TALK (or UP-SPEAK): I don't recall which term was used, but a few years ago, Connie Chung did a report for whatever show she was on at the time. She wandered around a couple of college campuses, talking to groups of students about some made-up topic. It was horrifying, to say the least. Most of the offenders were young women (though they found a few young men too). Can you imagine? Every sentence a question? Even emphatic statements? "I really think that Hitler was a bad man?" Oh really - ARE YOU SURE?

I was a graduate teaching assistant in the Communication department at the time. Try grading a persuasive speech in which the speaker never makes a statement, but only asks questions (?). One of the teaching assistants tended to up-talk when she was nervous. It was as if she was saying, "OK, did you get that? Do you understand me? Do you approve of what I am saying?" We taped the show and started using it as a teaching aide. Didn't do much good. Then again, we also tried to get the students to, like, stop, like, using LIKE as some sort of pause-filler. It was not, like disgusting - it WAS disgusting.

Gerry in Ottawa weighed in:

On the question of rising inflections at the end of sentences, I obviously can't speak for Valley girls but it's very common among older women in this part of the world. My wife, who's nothing if not emphatic in her own statements, thinks it's a hangover from pre-lib days when women tended to be so unsure of their opinions that they needed constant reassurance that what they were saying was on the right track. We have another little quirk here in Canada which is known technically as the anecdotal "eh?" and is even more maddening. "I was going downtown, eh? And I meet this old buddy of mine, eh? And I ask him how he's been, eh?" It's sort of a lower class thing now, the more educated types having moved on to "you know," but it's still more prevalent than one might think. And, I might add, very, very boring.

--

Bob in Chicago was interested in magic words:
Love the magic woids....gimme more!!
> Abracadabra
> Hocus Pocus
> Presto Change-O
> Please & Thank You (obligatory)
> Shazaam
> Alacazam
> Open Sesame
> Mumbo Jumbo
> Rumplstiltskin

And Kimberly of Fort Lauderdale contributed some:
Or the list of magic words, there's "Shimboree, shimborah, shimboree-ee, shimboraahh!" -Barney and "Bibbidi, bobbidi, boo" - Cinderella.

--

THE POWER OF WORDS - 327

John in Keele. UK interjected:

I was the one who _asked_ about rhyming slang, so don't expect me to know much about it!

More familiar to dwellers in the British Isles than they actually realize: phrases such as "to take a butcher's" at something are widely used and understood -without- awareness that it's an abbreviated "butcher's hook" [=look].

TV series set in the East End of London often feature it, leading to wider awareness; after a few episodes of "Minder", phrases such as "it's the dog, for you" become accepted without protest ["dog 'n' bone", i.e. phone]. Contrary to what was claimed by another contributor earlier this Summer [what am I saying, it's freezing outside...] the use of rhyming slang does not appear to be exclusive to the criminal classes, it's just strongly regionalized, with a certain amount of leakage that even reaches us Northerners.

--

Karen in Manchester, UK asserted:

When I was in school in London, I learned that Cockney rhyming slang began as a "secret" language for prisoners in jail to communicate. You take a word, think of something it rhymes with, and then add another similar word to that. For example, if you want to say "stairs," you rhyme that with "pears" and add "apples." So when the guard hears you say to another inmate, "I hid the knife under the apples and pears," he won't understand. Some others I remember are "frog and toad" for "road" ("Up the Frog and Toad" is the name of a book on Cockney rhyming slang, I believe), "laughs and titters" for "bitters," and "trouble and strife" for "wife."

Bruce in Sydney added on Cockney rhymes:

On another topic, my fave piece of Cockney is also one of the most convoluted.

"Shove orf or you'll get a boot up the aris'."

To translate:

aris = Aristotle

Aristotle = bottle
bottle and glass = arse
a word which I know all you well lettered wordplayers are familiar.

Gerry in Ottawa answered Kat who asked about "Beecham's."
It's rhyming slang for Beecham's Pills which rhymes with Testicles. Of course, the latter has to be pronounced as "Testi-kills" to make any sense of it.

Mike in Brisbane confirmed this:
Kat, Beecham's Pills. A popular patent medicine in the early part of this century, and perhaps before.
"Pills" of course, is British slang (not rhyming) for testicles.

--

Alyssa in San Fransisco said:
"...San Francisco! (or, as they called it at a concert i was at last night, "San Fran f*cking cisco!" ugh.) (but did you ever notice how many parts of speech that particular word can be used for??)

Karen in Manchester replied:
That particular usage is known as an "infix" (compare "prefix" and "suffix"). As I see it, "f*cking" is the most common infix around: "unbe-f*cking-lievable" and "fan-f*cking-tastic," for instance. Then there's "I guaran-damn-tee it!"

On the same topic, Ann-Elizabeth in Boulder, CO elaborated:
The 3rd edition of the American Heritage Dictionary provides typical phrases where one encounters the word f**k. After laughing my head off (always a nice visual), I decided that the meaning AmHer gave to the phrase, "f**k off" is incorrect. They say it means "to leave at once." As in, "The plane landed and we all f**cked off." This seems ridiculous and very funny and my colleagues and I are already using this meaning whenever we are in safe company. (I know, nothing better to do!) I always thought "f**k off" a variant of "go to hell".
What is your sense of the meaning of this phrase? I sense a group let-

ter to the editors to correct their meaning--finally, a potential contribution—then why this word?

--

From Angela,
I'm heading out to Boston for Christmas this year, but I've lived most of my life in the Midwest, most recently in the Northwest. Can any Boston natives enlighten me about the history and usage of the adjective(?) "wicked"? I've heard it used mostly by youngers in sentences like, "That pahty was wicked cool" or "the test was wicked hahd".

Bev responded:
I'm not from Boston. Never been there. My interpretation of "wicked" as used in your examples is as a word that adds emphasis to something. As in "That pahty was really cool" or "the test was really bahd." I once knew someone from Maine, and if memory serves, I think he used wicked in that way, too.

--

Holly inquired: What is lolliwater?

Mike in Brisbane answered:
Lolliwater is an Australian (anywhere else?) and Pidgin expression for soft drink. Sweet and sticky like lollies (candy).

--

Catie in Arlington, VA observed:
Around here (Maryland) oysters are sometimes referred to as "Ersters" by the watermen who catch them for a living.

--

Andrea in Atlanta said:
Anyway, it's really funny to both of us when people say "Come with?" as in "Are you coming with me to the store?" He points out that this only happens in the South. It also seems to work with other phrases. To say this properly, the accent always is on the "with."
What do you think? Are people just getting lazy? Is it really that difficult to finish a sentence?

--

Frank in Ottawa, wrote on nicknames:

Then there was Knobby Clark (no idea why), Chalky White (obvious), and many others that might come back to me.

Jack in London opined:

I'm sure the spelling is Nobby, since I have known at least one Nobby Clarke and he didn't have knobs on. The explanation I heard was that clerks working in (e.g.) the City of London were obliged to dress smartly even though many came from poor areas and they didn't earn much money. To their friends they dressed like nobs (members of the nobility), hence they were Nobby...

I'm not altogether sure I believe this -- it sounds suspiciously reasonable -- but I haven't heard a better explanation.... yet.

(By the way, nob is also a British slang word for head while knob is a British slang word for penis, so you have to listen out for the silent k.)

--

Jane in Indiana responded to Bruce in Sydney who inquired as to the derivation of the term "Hoosier." Well, this is the subject of endless debate here in the Hoosier state! "Hoosier" is the nickname used for a resident or native of Indiana—and the Indiana University athletic teams are called the Hoosiers. However, no one is certain of the origin of this term. There are a number of theories; the two most plausible involve an early Indiana preacher named Hoosier, and a mine or company owner over the state line in Kentucky by the name of Hoosier who employed a lot of men from Indiana--thus "Hoosier's men," and eventually Hoosier.

The funniest explanation, though, and a common one, is that the word comes from the phrase "Who's there" (pronounced "Hoo zher" in backwoods Indianaspeak), called out when someone would knock on a settler's cabin door.

Mary also noted:

The _Merriam-Webster New Book of Word Histories mentions these two origins of the word Hoosier. In addition, it states *The Indiana historian Jacob Piatt Dunn dismissed most of these explanations as

hogwash as far back as 1907. His theory was that Hoosier was of English dialectal origin. Dunn's most plausible source was a Cumberland dialect word hoozer which was applied to anything large of its kind. n support of this theory Dunn produced 1832 and 1834 citations using hoosier of a huge sturgeon and of giant pumpkins.
This does not explain how the term hoosier came to be associated with folks from Indiana.

--

Court in Wayne, IN weighed in on the subject:
I am a born and bred Hoosier. Except for about seven years that Uncle Sam needed my services, I have lived in Indiana all of my 66 years.
From everything that I have ever read, all scholars agree, that they don't know where the term Hoosier came from. They all agree however, that it was originally meant to be derogatory. Typical of the people of that time in history, it was picked up and wore as a badge of honour. Sort of like Yankee Doddle. The explanations that seems most plausible is that it came from the words "hoojee" or "hoojin" (maybe derived from "injin") for a dirty person or tramp. The southern part of Indiana was settled by mountain people from upland Virginians via Kentucky.

Jim in Phildelphia added:
Well, Dan Quayle, then a member of the house of representatives, tried to persuade Webster's Dictionary to change the definition of "hoosier" to "someone who is quick, witty, and intelligent." (Yeah, like a dictionary is actually going to change a definition to satisfy *any* politician...)

--

Gerry in Ottawa explained:
"Gardyloo" is one of the remnants of the "auld alliance" between Scotland and France. It's a Scottish corruption of the French "gardez l'eau" meaning "look out for the water" and served as a warning when the contents of a chamber pot were dumped out of an upstairs window into the street below. I suppose that, if you were dumping it on a close

friend, it might be more grammatical to say "gardloo" but somehow I doubt that such nice distinctions were made.

--

Mike in Brisbane asked:
Why did US servicemen call out "Hey Rube" when they were in trouble and needing assistance?
Gerry in Ottawa answered:
I believe that "Hey, Rube" is actually an old circus expression which was used to call for help when trouble broke out on the lot.
David in Glendale, CA likewise explained in:
Re: "Hey, Rube!" The cry for help, as I understand it, comes from carney life (circus, carnival, especially side show where the process of relieving local yokels of pelf was not always completely honest). If the bilkee began threatening the bilker, the call rallied the carney folk to the defense of their compadre. "Rube" itself was used in the sense previously noted by WordPlayers as a term for local country person, unlettered and unsophisticated, a hick from the sticks (the same as one of several similar Variety headlines, in this version pointing out the failure of pseudo-country films in the suburbs: "Stix Nix Hix Pix!")

--

Mike in Brisbane answered a query:
And the schemozzle thread (that's the Australian thread) - I'm afraid it's acquired another meaning here, that is, a great mess, or a messed up situation. In the same vein, I like "schlockmeister" as a word.

--

Peter from Gelong, AU responded to Gerry who said
<<The thing distinguishing the Australian version, it seemed, was that the Aussies have an almost pathological need to abbreviate (as in Mike's "esky"...>>:
Yes, and to abbreviate into two syllable words, ending with an -e sound.
For example:
        lippy (lipstick)

Chrissy (Christmas)
sunnies (sunglasses)
rellies (relatives).

--

Kimberly in Fort Lauderdale answered Mike about the term coon:
"Coon" is a derogatory term for an African-American, in the South (at least in Florida).

--

Phil in Salt Lake City commented on the term Kosher:
I have heard "kosher" used as a synonym for "legitimate" for as long as I can remember. When I learned what the kosher laws of the orthodox Jewish diet were, the colloquial usage of the word made perfect sense. But I never once considered it as derogatory in any way.

--

Sara in Boston opined on the colloquial term for partner:
For domestic partners/boyfriends/whatever: the common term around here is "S.O." for "significant other."

--

Karen weighed in on a familiar term:
The word "hokey" was used a lot when I was growing up. It is used as an adjective and means corny. A favorite commenting phrase back then "How hokey can you get?" (rhetorical question).

--

Catie in Arlington VA, argued about the historic use of racial terms:
Actually, people who are half white/half black were known as Mulatto. And in slave days, if you were 1/4 black, you were known as an "Quadroon". 1/8 black is an "Octaroon." Today, most people that I know of mixed race just refer to themselves as black, unless they are very light-skinned and are, as my grandfather would say, trying to "pass". This is when you were black, but looked white and could pass for white. I remember my grandmother going over the family tree with me and talking about some distant cousins of mine that I never

knew about. "Where are they now" I asked. "Oh, that line went up north, they're passin'. (we all knew what it meant). These days, no in my family cares one way or the other (which is the way I like it), but I know it is still around.

Catie continued...
Do you all know the terms applied to people of a certain race by members of their own race when they think they are acting too white?
Oreo: black on the outside, white on the inside.
Being black (and sometimes accused of being an Oreo), I knew about this from an early age. When I was grown, one of my friends (who was Hispanic/Latino) gave me a few more:
Coconut: brown on the outside, white on the inside (for Hispanic)
Apple: red on the outside, white on the inside (for Native American)
Banana: yellow on the outside, white on the inside (for Asians)
These terms are still around, I heard one pop last year in a 6th grade class. I get so annoyed when people have certain stereotypes, whether they from within or without one's own race. Sigh... Maybe one day...

--

Andy in Chichester, UK responded to Alyssa on giving birth:
You were impressed by 'to drop a sprog' then? Gross, isn't it? Sprog is a fairly uncommon slang word for child, with connotation similar to brat. I've also heard it used as a verb: so-and-so's sprogged again. I was impressed by Chambers, which suggests it may be a reverse portmanteau of frog spawn!

--

Peter in New York City responded to an enquiry:
<< Anyone else familiar with the noun "holiday" used to describe a visible lack of coverage on a painted wall?>>:
I can remember my father using this word to refer to missed spots in a painted wall... as he inspects my work...."you've got a couple of holidays in the upper left corner."
Have no idea the connotation unless it is an extrapolation of holiday being a break from work and I took a break from my painting work at

that spot. Does that make sense? This usage would be from 30-40 years ago....

--

Toni in Minesota commented on interjections, the likes of:
ISH - Several different opinions were expressed. I don't recall seeing any non-Minnesota/mid-western folks who recognized it as being somewhat equivalent to "yuk", as it seems to be used hereabouts. Took me some getting used to. (Now there's a sentence ending preposition that I have no idea how to go about "correcting".)
UFFDA - Or some spelling variation of same. Thanks to those who bailed me out on this one. I'm not Minnesotan; I just play one on this mailing list. If pressed, I would have offered an opinion that it was the Norwegian equivalent of "Oy vey", as someone else suggested. I often think of it as being accompanied by a slap to the mid-forehead with the heel of one's open hand.

--

Mike in Brisbane responded to a query on an Aussie expression:
"taking the mick" is an abbreviation of "taking the mickey" (out of someone) and means "to send someone up", i.e. to deride, satirise, etc. In Barry Humphries' case, he was taking the mickey out of us all. I have no idea where it came from. Miguel Rodente? but I think it's much earlier than "Steamboat Willie".

--

Jeff in in San Diego opined on Rich's contribution:
Rich, I enjoyed your "snippet of mohels" post! While you mentioned that "the skinny" means "the truth" (as in "Give me the skinny"). When someone asks me for "the skinny," I understand it as meaning "tell me what's going on" or "give me the information." Not necessarily "the truth." (not necessarily a lie, either). "Give me the skinny" is NOT something I'd tell a mohel!

--

Jeff also followed up on Andy's:
"A new thread suddenly dawns - names perfectly acceptable in their

own language, but which sound awful in other languages."

Andy, my wife is a physical therapist, where it's customary to ask the patients to "lift your fanny!" "Fanny," referring to the rear-end. The South African who joined the practice was shocked when she first heard this term being used with patients... because in South Africa, "fanny" refers to the vagina. Perhaps it's the same in other parts of the, er, empire? (I wonder what they think a fanny-pack is?!)

--

Famous quips on government politics and bureaucracy

"In my many years I have come to a conclusion, ... that one useless man is a shame, and three or more [useless men] is a government." ~John Adams

"If you don't read the newspaper you are uninformed, if you do read the newspaper, you are misinformed." ~Mark Twain

"I contend that for a nation to try to tax itself into prosperity is like a man standing in a bucket and trying to lift himself up by the handle." ~Winston Churchill

"A government which robs Peter to pay Paul can always depend on the support of Paul." ~George Bernard Shaw

"Foreign aid might be defined as a transfer of money from poor people in rich countries to rich people in poor countries." ~ Douglas Casey, Classmate of Bill Clinton at Georgetown University

"Giving money and power to government is like giving whiskey and car keys to teenage boys." ~P.J. O'Rourke, Civil Libertarian

"Just because you do not take an interest in politics doesn't mean politics won't take an interest in you!" ~Pericles (430 B.C.)

"No man's life, liberty, or property is safe while the legislature is in session." ~Mark Twain (1866)

"The government is like a baby's alimentary canal, with a happy appetite at one end and no responsibility at the other." ~ Ronald Reagan

"The only difference between a tax man and a taxidermist is that the taxidermist leaves the skin." ~Mark Twain

"What this country needs are more unemployed politicians." ~Edward Langley, Artist

"A government big enough to give you everything you want, is strong enough to take everything you have." ~Thomas Jefferson

"We hang the petty thieves and appoint the great ones to public office." ~Aesop

"If you think health care is expensive now, wait until you see what it costs when it's free!" ~P.J. O'Rourke

Few idioms using Food

Apple of my eye	the person I adore
All eggs in one basket	risked all on the success of one venture
Bad apple/egg	Bad influence; one who brings trouble
Beef up	give more substance to something
Big cheese	important person
Bread and butter	necessities
Bring home the bacon	earn a living
Butter up	flatter someone to earn their favour
Chew the fat	chat informally and friendly way
Couch potato	idle person
Cream of the crop	the best
Cut the cheese	fart
Didn't cut the mustard	didn't meet the required standard
Eat humble pie	make an apology and accept humiliation
Food for thought	an idea worth considering
Gone pear shaped	gone unexpectedly wrong
Handed on a platter	acquired easily and without effort
Hard nut to crack	difficult person to understand difficult problem to solve
Hot diggity dog!	expression of surprise
Icing on the cake	the extra that makes good even better
In a nutshell	simply put
In a pickle	in trouble or mess

Knows his onions	he is clever
Like chalk and cheese	opposites
Like two peas in a pod	very similar
Low-hanging fruit	person that is persuaded with little effort something that can be obtained easily
Meat in the sandwich	neutral party mediating others in conflict
Not my cup of tea	not the sort of thing I usually enjoy
Piece of cake	easy
Proof is in the pudding	quality of something must be assessed based on direct experience with it
Selling like hot cakes	selling quickly and in large quantities
Smart cookie	clever person
Spill the beans	let a secret out
Take it w/ a grain of salt	believe only part of something
Top banana	most important person in a group
Worth one's salt	good at one's job

12

Weird but Logical

Varda in Portland, ME shared a collection:
ACTUAL NEWSPAPER HEADLINES
  Grandmother of eight makes hole in one
  Deaf mute gets new hearing in killing
  House passes gas tax onto senate
  Stiff opposition expected to casketless funeral plan
  Two convicts evade noose, jury hung
  William Kelly was fed secretary
  Milk drinkers are turning to powder
  Safety experts say school bus passengers should be belted
  Quarter of a million Chinese live on water

Some become unintentionally suggestive:
  Queen Mary having bottom scraped
  Is there a ring of debris around Uranus?
  Prostitutes appeal to Pope
  Panda mating fails - veterinarian takes over
  NJ judge to rule on nude beach
  Child's stool great for use in garden
  Dr. Ruth to talk about sex with newspaper editors

Soviet virgin lands short of goal again
Organ festival ends in smashing climax

Grammar often botches other headlines:
  Eye drops off shelf
  Squad helps dog bite victim
  Dealers will hear car talk at noon
  Enraged cow injures farmer with ax
  Lawmen from Mexico barbecue guests
  Miners refuse to work after death
  Two Soviet ships collide - one dies
  Two sisters reunite after eighteen years at checkout counter

Once in a while, a botched headline takes on a meaning opposite from the one intended:
  Never withhold herpes from loved one
  Nicaragua sets goal to wipe out literacy
  Drunk drivers paid $1,000 in 1984
  Autos killing 110 a day, let's resolve to do better

Sometimes newspaper editors state the obvious:
  If strike isn't settled quickly it may last a while
  War dims hope for peace
  Smokers are productive, but death cuts efficiency
  Cold wave linked to temperatures
  Child's death ruins couple's holiday
  Blind woman gets new kidney from dad she hasn't seen in years
  Man is fatally slain
  Something went wrong in jet crash, experts say
  Death causes loneliness, feeling of isolation

Matt in Minneapolis, MN was in the mood for musings;
Made-up plurals: I don't have the same poem you had, but I could put finger to keyboard and "give it a shot". Beyond the mice and geese:

> If more than one man is a group of men,
> Then, why don't we cook food in pots and pen?
> Two shakes of a die is rolling the dice,
> so why isn't pie, when plural, called pice?
> I kick with my foot, and both are my feet.
> A tree has a root, so why not some reet?
> The plural of tooth is always spelled teeth,
> If we each take a booth, why aren't they beeth?
> I know that an ox pairs up to be oxen,
> But more than one box is never called boxen.
> I cut with a knife, and many use knives
> But no marching band has their drums and fives.
> And speaking of drum, the plural's not dra
> Then why is a list of each datum data?
> One octopus plus one more: octopi
> Yet Woodstock was never filled with microbi.
> If more than one person makes a crowd of people
> If he's called Anderson, are his family Andeople?
> If I point at that, one more would be those.
> But if that is a hat, why aren't they hose?
> I draw each graffito and make my graffiti.
> If you say 'potato' do we speak of potati?
> Each criterion meets the criteria
> For each dimension in our three dimensia.
> I know that the plural of child is children
> If I join a guild, why aren't they guildren?
> One antenna, more than one: antennae
> So if one sauna, why not two saunae?
> More than one appendix are appendices
> But I know that each annex don't make annices.

> The larynx in my throat plus on is larynges
> Still a lynx with another are not called lynges.
> The seraphim fly up with the cherubim
> No photographim of them in bathtubim?
> I've finished this matrix, or these matrices
> How many was that? Can you count them by sices?

Bill in Louisville, KY had some more to contribute:
It reminds me of one, which reminds me of some other things.
> If more than one mouse is mice
> And more than one louse is lice
> You must agree
> Quite naturally
> That more than one spouse is spice
> There are 3 kinds of marriages: polygamy, bigamy, and monotony.
> "Dad, why are there laws against bigamy?"
> "Son, that's to protect the man who's too dumb to protect himself."
> There are three kinds of people: Those who can count, and those who can't.
> There are two kinds of people: Those who divide people into groups, and those who don't.

Jack in London, related in the same theme:
> There was a young fellow of Lyme,
> Who married three wives at a time.
> When asked "Why the third?"
> He replied: "Two's absurd,
> And bigamy, Sir, is a crime!"

--

Maryanne in Tallahassee, FL:
My favourite palindrome is: Rats live on no evil star.

--

More on real newspaper headlines, Guy in Cupertino, CA:

POLICE BEGIN CAMPAIGN TO RUN DOWN JAYWALKERS
SAFETY EXPERTS SAY SCHOOL BUS PASSENGERS SHOULD BE BELTED
DRUNK GETS NINE MONTHS IN VIOLIN CASE
SURVIVOR OF SIAMESE TWINS JOINS PARENTS
FARMER BILL DIES IN HOUSE
IRAQI HEAD SEEKS ARMS
STUD TIRES OUT
PROSTITUTES APPEAL TO POPE
PANDA MATING FAILS; VETERINARIAN TAKES OVER
SOVIET VIRGIN LANDS SHORT OF GOAL AGAIN
BRITISH LEFT WAFFLES ON FALKLAND ISLANDS
LUNG CANCER IN WOMEN MUSHROOMS
EYE DROPS OFF THE SHELF
TEACHER STRIKES IDLE KIDS
REAGAN WINS ON BUDGET, BUT MORE LIES AHEAD
SQUAD HELPS DOG BITE VICTIM
SHOT OFF WOMAN'S LEG HELPS NICKLAUS TO 66
ENRAGED COW INJURES FARMER WITH AX
PLANE TOO CLOSE TO GROUND, CRASH PROBE TOLD
MINERS REFUSE TO WORK AFTER DEATH
JUVENILE COURT TO TRY SHOOTING DEFENDANT
STOLEN PAINTING FOUND BY TREE
TWO SOVIET SHIPS COLLIDE, ONE DIES
 2 SISTERS REUNITED AFTER 18 YEARS IN CHECKOUT COUNTER
 KILLER SENTENCED TO DIE FOR SECOND TIME IN 10 YEARS
 NEVER WITHHOLD HERPES INFECTION FROM LOVED ONE
DRUNKEN DRIVERS PAID $1000 IN '84
WAR DIMS HOPE FOR PEACE
IF STRIKE ISN'T SETTLED QUICKLY, IT MAY LAST A WHILE

COLD WAVE LINKED TO TEMPERATURES
MAN IS FATALLY SLAIN
ENFIELD COUPLE SLAIN; POLICE SUSPECT HOMICIDE

--

Jim in Philadelphia on odd headlines, noted from the Philadelphia Inquirer:
JOURNALIST REPORTED KILLED IN ALGERIA SAYS SHE IS ALIVE.
Is it me? Or does that not sit well with anyone else here??? I kind of expect a sub-headline to the effect of "Like we're supposed to believe HER???"

Likewise, Tony added:
Ad in the paper last night: "SEWERS WANTED". Do you think they were advertising for a main drain or a stitch switch? Sorry to needle you on this one.

--

On the topic of mnemonics, Zeno in Minneapolis, MN recalled:
Kingdom, phylum, class, order, family, genus, species.
King Phillip Came Over For Good Sex.

--

Disclaimer from a nameless person:
Any resemblance between the above views and those of my employer, my terminal, or the view out my window are purely coincidental. Any resemblance between the above and my own views is non-deterministic. The question of the existence of views in the absence of anyone to hold them is left as an exercise for the reader. The question of the existence of the reader is left as an exercise for the second God coefficient. (A discussion of non-orthogonal, non-integral polytheism is beyond the scope of this article.)

--

Martin in Los Angeles related:
I knew a mathematician who named her two cats Max and Min.

--

THE POWER OF WORDS ~ 345

John in Keele, UK shared few items from a current correspondence in the letter columns of the London _Times_, not all relating to supermarkets...

B.E. Reay, up in Perthshire [Scotland] wrote:
The Perth branch of British Home Stores has a notice on its fire exit, reading "This door is alarmed"...
How do they know?

C.A. Nelms, in Kent, submitted:
I am continually puzzled by fruit labelled "Ready to Eat".
Who is to feed it? What does it like to eat?

Mary, in nearby Shrewsbury, told us:
Morrisons supermarket in Shrewsbury sells "cod pieces" on its fish counter.

--

Still on newspapers odd headlines, Doug said:
I found this on the front page of a daily food industry newsletter this morning.
"USDA TO CUT 200 MEAT INSPECTORS"

--

Terrence in Bermuda commenting on someone's remark:
Regarding the observations that macho Yanks drink iced tea while refined Brits drink it hot: It's not the heat, it's the humility.
Also:
From an interview on U.S. Network News with a visitor to the Carolinas, "We were hoping to have a nice vacation, but this will be an unforgettable but memorable experience."
Contradictory but inconsistent, nicht

--

Michael in Mesa, AZ remembered a mondegreen:
....always thought Squeeze was singing "Pulling Muscles for Michelle." Also, I'm still trying to figure out why my car keeps telling me, "the door is a jar."

--

Jim in Schenectady, NY:
Here's another neologism for you all to ponder:
Sleptomaniac: means "the spouse who wakes up with all the covers". Another very handy neologism is philitreason: A philitreason is 'a screwed-up relationship'. It is an anagram of the word relationship, plus it contains Phili- meaning love and treason-- i.e., a treachery involving a loved one. What does everyone think?

--

Gerry in Ottawa waxed poetic:
At the request of our dog, who is still in deep mourning for our late cat, I'd like to toss the following poem into the cat thread before we're barked off the stage, so to speak. It was written by an Irish monk in the ninth century.

> I and Pangur Ban my cat
> 'Tis a like task we are at;
> Hunting mice is his delight,
> Hunting words I sit all night.
> 'Tis a merry thing to see
> At our tasks how glad are we,
> When at home we sit and find
> Entertainment to our mind.
> "Gainst the wall he sets his eye,
> Full and fierce and sharp and sly;
> 'Gainst the wall of knowledge I
> All my little wisdom try.
> So in peace our task we ply,
> Pangur Ban, my cat, and I;
> In our arts we find our bliss
> I have mine and he has his.

--

Richard in Tempe, AZ shared some trivia:
I had once read that *all* the earliest U.S. stations used the initial "W," and the initial "K" came along later for stations west of the Mississippi.

THE POWER OF WORDS - 347

[Also, the story goes that WFAA -- still used by the TV station that came along later -- stands for "Working For All Alike." Similarly, KRLD-AM, another old station (but one that clearly began after the W/K split) stands for "K Radio Labs of Dallas." Any others?}
P.S. There's a similar international code system used for aircraft tail numbers. U.S. ones are identified by tail numbers that start with "N."

--

Gary in Toronto responded to an assertion that: "I'd always heard that people with a flair for mathematics tended to have an equal flair for music."
Howard Gardner, author of the Theory of Multiple Intelligences (which I'm reading at the moment), considers the two kinds of "intelligence" (musical and mathematical) completely separate, and in fact comments that mathematical geniuses rarely have any particular gifts in other areas. - and both are separate from verbal intelligence, of course!

--

Bob in Chicago on the donut hole paradox:
When I was in grammar school, we used to sing a song to the tune "Turkey in the Straw" that went like this:

>Oh, I went to New York and I walked around the block
>And I walked right in to a donut shop.
>I picked three donuts out of the grease
>And I handed the lady a five cent piece.
>She looked at the nickel and she looked at me,
>She said this nickel's no good you see,
>There's a hole in the middle and it goes right through.
>Said I there's a hole in your donut too!

--

Mike in Brisbane commented on spoken vocabulary:
Heard on the ABC yesterday "...as the TV cameras whirred..." whirred? What kind of cameras are they using? I thought whirring went out with cine cameras. (I know it did, I was a TV producer for

years, he said parenthetically).
So that was a bit of an anachronism...which brings me to the point... (at last, they groan.) What would be the opposite of "anachronism"?

--

Jim in Philadelphia noted an irony:
Well, to quote Ronald Reagan, "This is the only country where the government department that takes care of everything that happens outside is called the Department of the Interior."

--

Mike in Brisbane commented on the "bottom" as in Ramsbottom thread:
My understanding is that these names derive from "bottom lands", which I think means low-lying paddocks, or those near the watercourse. Thus, the variations were once used to describe either where a particular piece of land was, or, later, where a person lived. In Newcastle, where I grew up, there were pubs owned by messrs Sidebottom, Longbottom and Winterbottom.
However, recently I was travelling to a conference, and was served "refreshments" on the aircraft. Along came a cup of coffee and a dinky little cello packet containing two biscuits. The biscuits were OK, but the brand name had me ROTFLMBottomO - "Emu Bottom Homestead-A Taste of Australia" the image this conjured up was too much for me.
And so to sow, or sew as the case may be. My family works on the land. My son and I sow a lot of wheat seed every year. My wife is a dressmaker. My grandfather, who lives with us, prefaces every remark with "So". In fact, you could say our family does a lot of sewing? so-ing? sowing?

--

Janet in Calgary responded to "Mooloolabah? Mike, what the heck kind of a name is that? Aboriginal?"
No, it's a French name. The translation is "There's is a public toilet for cows over there"

And Mike added:
Janet - It's actually "There's a public toilet for cows over there attached to the saloon." (Yes, it is Aboriginal)

--

Susan in Cheney, WA:
Clagary Janet has given us a marvellous typo ... (it *was* a typo, wasn't it?) where you referred to a "dick jockey?" I won't ruin it by adding ANYTHING to it, but I didn't want *anyone* to miss it, either!! I was ROFLWPS (with people staring)!!!

--

Mike in Brisbane: Lost in translation:
I was reminded of a speech the then Prime Minister of Australia made to a group of businessmen in Japan, urging closer trade links. In the course of the speech he said "So come and trade with us, we won't play silly buggers." Mr Hawke, known for his colloquial style, meant that Australia would not create bureaucratic barriers and red tape etc, but would expedite trading opportunities. There was a slight pause while the interpreters thought about his words, then they rendered "So come and trade with us, we won't jump about like insane homosexuals"...

--

Heath in San Antonio, TX quoted:
"The History of the English Language" by Owen Alun and Brendan O'Corraidhe:

In the beginning there was an island off the coast of Europe. It had no name, for the natives had no language, only a collection of grunts and gestures that roughly translated to "Hey!", "Gimme!", and "Pardon me, but would you happen to have any woad?"
Then the Romans invaded it and called it Britain, because the natives were "blue, nasty, br(u->i)tish and short." This was the start of the importance of u (and its mispronunciation) to the language. After building some roads, killing off some of the nasty little blue people and walling up the rest, the Romans left, taking the language instruction

manual with them.

The British were bored so they invited the barbarians to come over (under Hengist) and "Horsa" 'round a bit. The Angles, Saxons, and Jutes brought slightly more refined vocal noises.

All of the vocal sounds of this primitive language were onomatopoeic, being derived from the sounds of battle. Consonants were derived from the sounds of weapons striking a foe. "Sss" and "th" for example are the sounds of a draw cut, "k" is the sound of a solidly landed axe blow, "b", "d", are the sounds of a head dropping onto rock and sod respectively, and "gl" is the sound of a body splashing into a bog. Vowels (which were either gargles in the back of the throat or sharp exhalations) were derived from the sounds the foe himself made when struck.

The barbarians had so much fun that they decided to stay for postrevel. The British, finding that they had lost future use of the site, moved into the hills to the west and called themselves Welsh.

The Irish, having heard about language from Patrick, came over to investigate. When they saw the shiny vowels, they pried them loose and took them home. They then raided Wales and stole both their cattle and their vowels, so the poor Welsh had to make do with sheep and consonants. ("Old Ap Ivor hadde a farm, L Y L Y W! And on that farm he hadde somme gees. With a dd dd here and a dd dd there...")

To prevent future raids, the Welsh started calling themselves "Cymry" and gave even longer names to their villages. They figured if no one could pronounce the name of their people or the names of their towns, then no one would visit them. (The success of the tactic is demonstrated still today. How many travel agents have YOU heard suggest a visit to scenic Llyddumlmunnyddthllywddu?)

Meantime, the Irish brought all the shiny new vowels home to Erin. But of course they didn't know that there was once an instruction manual for them, so they scattered the vowels throughout the language purely as ornaments. Most of the new vowels were not pronounced, and those that were, were pronounced differently depending

on which kind of consonant they were either preceding or following.
The Danes came over and saw the pretty vowels bedecking all the Irish words. "Ooooh!" they said. They raided Ireland and brought the vowels back home with them. But the Vikings couldn't keep track of all the Irish rules so they simply pronounced all the vowels "oouuoo."
In the meantime, the French had invaded Britain, which was populated by descendants of the Germanic Angles, Saxons, and Jutes. After a generation or two, the people were speaking German with a French accent and calling it English. Then the Danes invaded again, crying "Oouuoo! Oouuoo!," burning abbeys, and trading with the townspeople.
The Britons that the Romans hadn't killed intermarried with visiting Irish and became Scots. Against the advice of their travel agents, they decided to visit Wales. (The Scots couldn't read the signposts that said, "This way to LLyddyllwwyddymmllwylldd," but they could smell sheep a league away.) The Scots took the sheep home with them and made some of them into haggis. What they made with the others we won't say, but Scots are known to this day for having hairy legs.
The former Welsh, being totally bereft, moved down out of the hills and into London. Because they were the only people in the Islands who played flutes instead of bagpipes, they were called Tooters. This made them very popular. In short order, Henry Tooter got elected King and begin popularizing ornate, unflattering clothing.
Soon, everybody was wearing ornate, unflattering clothing, playing the flute, speaking German with a French accent, pronouncing all their vowels "oouuoo" (which was fairly easy given the French accent), and making lots of money in the wool trade. Because they were rich, people smiled more (remember, at this time, "Beowulf" and "Canterbury Tales" were the only tabloids, and gave generally favorable reviews even to Danes). And since it is next to impossible to keep your vowels in the back of your throat (even if you do speak German with a French accent) while smiling and saying "oouuoo" (try it, you'll see what I mean), the Great Vowel Shift came about and transformed the

English language.

The very richest had their vowels shifted right out in front of their teeth. They settled in Manchester and later in Boston.

There were a few poor souls who, cut off from the economic prosperity of the wool trade, continued to swallow their vowels. They wandered the countryside in misery and despair until they came to the docks of London, where their dialect devolved into the incomprehensible language known as Cockney. Later, it was taken overseas and further brutalized by merging it with Dutch and Italian to create Brooklynese.

That's what happened, you can check for yourself. But I advise you to just take our word for it.

Bill in Louisville, KY had a knack for picking up on signs:
We had a sign near the elevator at work: "If out of order, call 4567"
I debated what department might have that extension:
The Medical Dept   - to cure whatever is wrong with me?
The Security Dept   - to restore order?
The Purchasing Dept - to order some more order?

Matt in Minneapolis:
All right, the 'hippy dippy weather man'!
"Tonight's forecast -- dark. Continued mostly dark tonight, followed by widely scattered light in the morning... And, if you'll look at our national map, <pause> you'll see that we don't have one...." Classic!

--

On buttons people wear, Katherine in Oakland said:
My favourite button is probably "Objectivity is in the eye of the beholder."

--

Dave in Glendale, CA said on labels:
My wife and I -- like so many others these days -- both have careers. We like to attend each other's conferences together (one of which prevented me from attending the west coast e-nic -- distinctly my loss).

One of the customs at these professional clusterings is to include an affiliation below one's name on the pin-on identification label -- Harvard or one of the Oxbridge colleges being the equivalent of wearing a cardinal's hat.

When I took an early retirement to have more time to do what I wanted to do, rather than the bureaucratic bump my post required, I used "Consultant." I soon found out that this translated to "Unemployed," as did "Independent Researcher."
Given that my attendance at Margaret's conferences was as much one of technical support as well as indulging my own interests, I thought of "Camp Follower." The thought died in earliest childhood.
Finally, I have found success; I use the term "Observer." The only problem with that one is a happy one: being occasionally asked what the prominent British newspaper might find interesting to cover at a historians' conference.

--

Alex in Adelaide mused with common sayings:
Here is a new thread that has plenty of yarn to chew on: Number phrases which tend to suggest the context without the user being fully explicit. e.g. the residents of the USA would know what we mean by:

  Taking the fifth
  Filing chapter eleven
  Citing the first
  Stole the second
  Route 66
  The 50th state

Others are:
  The eleventh hour
  The sixth sense
  Beethoven's ninth
  Ground zero
  Do a one-eighty

Alyssa in San Fransisco added:
How about "[I'll] be there in 5"?

Rich in Rindge, NH contributed few. How about:
> Zero in on
> First lady
> Second fiddle
> Three sheets to the wind
> Four on the floor
> Take five
> High five
> Seventh heaven
> She's (or he's) a ten
> Forty winks

Brian in London added:
Catch 22: If you say "one hundred and EIGHty" with the right expression, it turns into a score at darts.

And Penelope in Michigan added: dresses to the 9's
--
Kat in Rochester, NY was reminded of:
A few years ago a local store sold packages of Misfortune Cookies. They included things like "The tall, dark, handsome stranger you will meet today will steal your wallet." and "Whenever you schedule the wedding, it will rain."
--
Jim in Philadelphia:
Seven deadly sins: Happy, Grumpy, Dopey, Sleepy, >Sneezy, Bashful, and Doc
--

Richard in Rindge, NH said:
I am reminded of a TV show I'd seen many years ago called "The Newlywed Game." Some of you may recall this "game" show where young recently-marrieds would be separated to see if each spouse could guess how his or her new partner would respond to various questions. On one show, a question, asked of three blushing brides, was "Which of the Seven Dwarves would most closely resemble your husband?"
Bride number one thought about it and answered, "Sleepy, because my husband is so lazy!"
Bride number two scrunched up her face for a bit and then responded, "I guess I'd have to say Dopey, because he's so silly."
Bride number three had a kind of ditzy blank look on her face and the host had to repeat, "Which of the Seven Dwarves would most closely resemble YOUR husband?" At that her face brightened and she said, "Horny!"
Also, two real fortunes I have received in cookies:
"In case of fire, pay bill and head for nearest exit."
"Please disregard last fortune."

--

Patrick in Collegeville, MN recounted a tale about scrod, the fish:
A woman who grew up in New England and now lives in Indianapolis? Chicago? Omaha? Pokey Huddle? dotes on scrod and gets back to Boston for a plate of it whenever she can (Legal Seafood or Durgin Park), which is seldom.
It has been a long time, but she manages to fly home to indulge her passion, and does so voraciously. She barely has time to make her flight after dinner, so takes a cab to Logan airport. In the tunnel under the bay, the cabby, having noticed that she looks blissful, asks, "Have a nice time in Boston, Lady?" She answers, "Divine!
I got scrod." And he says, "Lady, I've heard just about everything in my thirty-five years of driving cab, but this is the first time I've heard the definite declarative past pluperfect of that verb."

--

Gerrt in New York had some name play in mind:
Has this list tried composing team names? For example, the Minsk Meats. Or the San Jose Canyousees. Or the Addis Abbaba Dabbados. Also, here's an interesting item from today's NY Times Magazine, in a column by Jack Rosenthal:

A colleague recently told Roger Gould, a sociologist at the University of Chicago, about a lecture, place uncertain, referring to double negatives. Every language, the lecturer observed, has a construction in which two negatives make a positive. But in English, he said, there's no construction in which two positives make a negative.
From the hall came the perfect, anonymous response: "Yeah, right."
--

John in Keele, UK related an anecdote:
Child in train asks "Are we there yet?" Mother replies "No, we're only at the outskirts".
Child waits a while, then asks "Are we at the inskirts yet?".
It's That Age!
--

Kim in Tokyo had a query from her experience:
Several of my students here in Tokyo asked me about the naming of typhoons and hurricanes. (Here, they are assigned numbers.) I explained that the U.S. uses alternating men's and women's names, in alphabetical order. At the time, we were up to Typhoon #13, Polly, which came after Oscar (#12). I explained that the next one should be a man's name that begins with a Q. (We agreed that this would be difficult, but my students came up with Quincy.) Well, #14 is Ryan, so it looks like they skipped the Q! Anyway, do any of you know more about the history of naming these storms (including who does the naming)? Are there other naming/labeling conventions used elsewhere in the world?

David in Carey, NC answered:
There are about 7 major tropical storm basins; 3 in the Northern Hemisphere Pacific, 1 in the Atlantic, 1 or 2 in the Indian Ocean. I

don't recall the rest. The naming system is different for the different basins. In the Atlantic basin, there are six sets of names that are used. They start with 'A' each season. If there's a really big system (Andrew, Hugo, Camille) it will get 'retired' and a new name put into that list. For 1996, the names will be:
Arthur Bertha Cesar Dolly Edouard Fran Gustav Hortense Isidore Josephine Klaus Lili Marco Nana Omar Paloma Rene Sally Teddy Vicky Wilfred.
They skip 'Q', 'U', 'X', 'Y' and 'Z' (I don't know why specifically, although I can guess that there aren't that many names beginning with those letters.

--

Bruce in Hobart remarked:
The sensitive poetic types amongst you should stop reading now!
> Oh to be in Sidney
> Now that spring is here
> Yet too cold for blowies
> But warm enough for beer.

--

David in Ritner, KY had a take on the pledge:
> I pledge allegiance to the faggots
> and the United Snakes of America
> and to the Republicans four witches stand
> one notion
> [under dogs]
> invisible
> with liberty and justice for owls.

The part about the dogs somehow got added later on. This happened sometime between the time when I started questioning the hypocrisy (about '51) and my open rebellion to patent untruths (about '58). Soon thereafter, this nonsense was deleted from the school schedule. Or maybe it was the politically correct "Prayer" that disappeared without a trace.

Steven in San Antonio asked:
Why do we, here in the States, anyway, have heat waves but cold snaps?

And Toni in Minnesota adeds:
Or cold spells but not heat spells?

--

Mike in Brisbane on confusing notations:
Reminds me that I heard a radio interview recently where John Cage the composer was being discussed, and he was apparently awarded an Honorary Doctorate. John Cage was famous for his composition "Four Minutes and Thirty-Three Seconds of Silence", which can be written 4'33". During the introductory speech, he was introduced as the composer of "Four feet Thirty-three Inches".

--

Pat quizzed: "Now, how did Dr. Johnson define patriotism?"
To which Caleb answered:
The "last refuge of scoundrels ..." Good for you, Pat!

--

Someone enquired about the names of all those symbols on our keyboards. So, Rollo in Adelaide set himself to the task:
OK, here it is, copied from The Telejoke Book Volume III (1990):

<>!*"#	Waka waka bang splat tick tick hash
^@'$$-	Caret at back-tick dollar dollar dash
!*'$_	Bang splat tick dollar underscore
%*<>#4	Percent splat waka waka number 4
&)../	Ampersand right-paren dot dot slash
|{--SYSTEM HALTED	
	Vertical-bar curly-bracket tilde tilde CRASH

--

On professional names, Debbie in Kalamazoo, MI:
Which reminds me of two local dentists (not partners, but perhaps they should be) by the names of Fillar and Pullum. We also have here

a chiropractor by the name of Dr. Bender.
Anybody else collect such marvels of fate?? If so, please post.

--

On the origin of words, Heath in San Antonio, TX, who still owns an Atari 2600:
I suspect the waka waka came from the resemblance to the open mouth of Pac Man, who made such a sound while devouring blips of light (waka waka waka waka waka).

--

Debbie in Kalamazoo, MI commented on:
>   Rotten's piece on malodorous pollution
>   Needle's work with intravenous drug users
>   Boring's numerous works on the history of psychology

Jim in Philadelphia followed with:
Let's see here. Around here, we've got a General Practitioner named Dr. Kwak. Also, there are two separate funeral homes, both within about five miles (8 km) of my home: the Dunn Funeral Home, and the Faust Funeral Home. Honestly, neither of these inspires me to have my wake there. (Especially the latter, although I believe I've mentioned both of 'em before on this list...) How about a barber with the last name Schearer? And a local music store is called "Loser's Music." (You wonder why I bought my drum set from Zapf's...) I'm sure there's more around here, but I'm not sure of any more right now...

Dave in Cary, NC also had a couple:
I don't really collect them, but my dentist is Dr. Grinder, and his partner is Dr. Ferri. There's a street here called Yubinaranda Circle. There's another called Escher Drive, but I'm afraid to drive down it.

And Marjorie in Boston added:
In my hometown there practices a psychiatrist named Dr. Nutt. (I kid you not!)

And Kat in Rochester added:

We used to have a couple of orthopedic surgeons (now retired) named Joynt and Payne. And there's the urologist, who specializes in vasectomies, named Dr. Stop. I am not making this up.

And Rich in Rindge, NH:

For years our veterinarian was Dr. Fox. There's a surgeon around here named Dr. Blood and another named Dr. Hacker. I used to have a whole list; I'll see if I can find it.

And Jesse in Sunnyvale, CA:

Back in upstate N.Y. I seem to recall a Dentist named Dr. Sugarmann, and his wife (and dental assistant) was named Candi.

And Frank in Ottawa:

Passed by a neat sign outside a hairdresser this morning: " Shear Heaven".

And Jane in Missouri:

I once had a wart cut off by a doctor named Cleaver. Thanks for the laugh,

And Pat in Collegeville, MN:

A local dentist is Dr. Pull. In Fort Wayne, there's an Eikenberry funeral home.

And Margie in Washington, DC:

Back in the '50s and early '60s, there was a dentist in Hermann, MO, a small, German community about 80 miles west of St. Louis, by the name of Mundmiller--German for "mouth grinder."

And Maryanne in Tallahassee, FL:

Just this morning, I read in the Tallahassee Democrat, a letter from a professor in the religion department at Florida A. & M. University whose name is Angell.

Many years when I lived in Indialantic, Florida, Dr. Addicks practiced psychiatry.

And Andy in Chichester, UK:

On the appropriate names thread, I had a dentist called Dr Fang for a while.

And John in Keele, UK:
There used to be a commercial van that ran around the Oxford area bearing the proud slogan "Aerial Erections".

--

Kat enquired about a phrase origin:
Saw this in an informal job posting discussion: "Smart-aleks need not apply."
"Smart-aleks" looks wrong somehow. Anyone know the origin of the phrase?

--

On a different tack, Janet in Calgary wondered how widespread is the use of "swivet."
Martha in Boston answered:
I have an aunt who is a reference librarian. For years she worked in the New York Public Library, answering phoned-in questions. One day, someone phoned asking her to explain the difference between a swivel and a pivot. Off she went (this was *long* before computers), searching the shelves. After a few minutes, she decided that a swivet was the state induced by trying to distinguish a swivel from a pivot. Anyway, the term is certainly used in our family too.
Mike in Brisbane claimed that:
There's also "getting oneself into a snit". Although this can also mean in a state of high dudgeon.

--

Kat in Rochester, NY had a take on collective nouns:
A Crash of Rhinoceroses: a dictionary of collective nouns Rex Collings (1993)
"This compact, illustrated dictionary offers explanations and references for the English language's most delightful collective nouns. More than just an illustrated compendium as in _An Exaltation of Larks_, this book gives explanations and sources to the names that have been given over the centuries to collections of animals, inanimate objects, people and concepts."

Sandi interjected: oohhhhhhh nnooooooo.........
Another case of self-doubt that descends upon you at the very nano-second that you click on the "send" icon. (Could there possibly be a word for that? Any ideas from this group for creating one?)

Martin in Los Angeles responded:
You are exactly right. A few months ago, the term "ohno-second" appeared in Wired to describe this phenomenon.

--

Alex in Adelaide:
Grandpa was over this weekend and in the process of conversation I discovered a great deal in common between the following sentences: Do you need your hearing aid <==> I am looking for my glasses

--

Jesse in Sunnyvale, CA:
Rich, you were not receiving an alien subliminal transmission, or if you were, I got it too. I learned this bit of nonsense a long time ago as some sort of theatre game. The way I learned it was:

One hen.
Two ducks.
Three squawking geese.
Four Limerick oysters.
Five corpulent porpoises.
Six pairs of Don Alphonso's tweezers.
Seven thousand Macedonian warriors in full battle array.
Eight brass monkeys from the ancient, sacred, crypts of Egypt.
Nine apathetic, sympathetic, diabetic, old men on roller skates, with a marked propensity towards procrastination and sloth.
Ten lyrical, spherical, diabolical denizens of the deep, who haul and stall around the quo of the qua of quay, all at the same time.

--

ANIMAL SOUNDS

Maryanne asked :
How do other languages represent the sounds that animals make?

Mike in Brisbane answered:
In Indonesia, ducks say "bebek", In Papua New Guinea toads say "rokrok", and roosters say "kakaruk"

Terrence in Bermuda asserted:
A good German cat says "schnurren" when it is contented.

Kat in Rochester commented:
With Germanic r's, I can hear the onomatopoeia, but I don't think a cat of ANY nationality has ever made the sound "schnu". For that matter, I've only known one feline who actually pronounced the M in 'mmmmew'. And has anyone met a dog that can handle the B in 'bow-wow' or the W in 'woof'? seems to me most furry companions have a lot of trouble with consonants.

--

Catie in Arlington had a dittie to share:
It's been ages since I've contributed, but found this on my quilting list, thought you all might be interested: The sender is from Sweden. (we've been having an ongoing discussion about cows - don't ask what this has to do with quilting)

information we got on our milk packages earlier this autumn. They had specified cow-language of different countries, a cow dictionary so to speak. I ordered the information from our dairy today...

    MUUU says both the swedish and the italian cow
    BOE says the dutch cow
    MEUH says the french cow
    MMMMMMMMMMM says the cow from Chile
    AMMMU says the estonian cow
    'MOOUU says the greek cow
    MOO says the english cow
    Mööö says the turkish cow

Anita in Goteborg, Sweden
Do you think they can talk to each other??? We've also had a pig dictionary, a dog dictionary, a cock dictionary and a horse dictionary on our milk packages lately... Kind of breakfast infotainment.

--

Martha in Boston on funny headlines:
Sometime around the turn of the century, the Boston subway system was extended into neighboring cities, including Cambridge. It was proposed that a subway station be built in the middle of Harvard Square. The President of Harvard felt that this would be an eyesore, and spoke fervently against it. [It was built, and is quite handsome, actually.] The Harvard Crimson_ article on the dispute had this headline: "President Eliot Fights Erection in Harvard Square"

And Susi had a goodie too:
From the Westport (Conn) News: "Women compromise 26% of town's workers."
And they comprise a lot, too.

Heath in San Antonio shared real ads found in papers:

2 female Boston Terrier puppies, 7 wks old, Perfect markings, 555-1234. Leave mess.

Lost: small apricot poodle. Reward. Neutered. Like one of the family.

A superb and inexpensive restaurant. Fine food expertly served by waitresses in appetizing forms.

Wanted: 50 girls for stripping machine operators in factory.

For Sale. Three canaries of undermined sex.

For Sale -- Eight puppies from a German Shepherd and an Alaskan Hussy.

Great Dames for sale.

Have several old dresses from grandmother in beautiful condition

Tired of cleaning yourself? Let me do it.

Dog for sale: eats anything, fond of children.

Sheer stockings. Designed for fancy dress, but so serviceable that lots of women wear nothing else.

We build bodies that last a lifetime.

For Rent: 6-room hated apartment.

Man wanted to work in dynamite factory. Must be able to travel

Christmas tag-sale. Handmade gifts for the hard-to-find person.

Modular Sofas. Only $299. For rest or fore play.

Wanted. Man to take care of cow that does not smoke or drink.

Auto Repair Service. Free pick-up and delivery. Try us once, you'll never go anywhere again.

Wanted. Widower with school-age children requires person to assume general housekeeping
 duties. Must be capable of contributing to growth of family.

Mixing bowl set designed to please a cook with round bottom for efficient beating.

Semi-Annual after-Christmas Sale.

And now, the Superstore--unequaled in size, unmatched in variety, unrivaled inconvenience.

--

Lomond in Sacramento reported:
Overheard at the convention - A naked Scotsman, although out of kilter, cannot be deceived because no one has pulled the wool over his thighs.

--

Kimberley on warning labels:
Report from Week 110, in which we asked you to come up with absurd warning labels for common products. We loved one particular entry for its wonderful idiocy: On a cardboard windshield sun shade: "Warning: Do Not Drive with Sun Shield in Place." We were going to make it a winner, until we discovered that it wasn't made up.

Fourth Runner-Up: On an infant's bathtub: "Do not throw baby out with bath water." (Gary Dawson, Arlington)

Third Runner-Up: On a package of Fisherman's Friend(R) throat lozenges: "Not meant as substitute for human companionship." (Tom Witte, Gaithersburg)

Second Runner-Up: On a Magic 8 Ball: "Not advised for use as a home pregnancy test." (Chuck Smith, Woodbridge)

First Runner-Up: On a roll of Life Savers: "Not for use as a flotation device." (Jean Sorensen, Herndon)

And the winner of the Power Ranger pinata: On a cup of McDonald's coffee: "Allow to cool before applying to groin area." (Elden Carnahan, Laurel)

Honorable Mentions:

On a Pentium chip: "If this product exhibits errors, the manufacturer will replace it for a $2 shipping and a $3 handling charge, for a total of $4.97." (Russell Beland, Springfield)

On a refrigerator: "Refrigerate after opening." (CJ. Owen, Leesburg)

On a pack of cigarettes: "WARNING - The Tobacco Institute has determined that smoking just one cigarette greatly increases your risk of heart attack by making you so incredibly sexy that gorgeous members of the opposite sex will surround you night and day, begging for sexual intercourse and wearing you into exhaustion, unless, of course, you have another couple of cigarettes to steady your nerves." (Jacob Weinstein, McLean)

On a disposable razor: "Do not use this product during an earthquake." (Jim Gaffney, Manassas)

On a handgun: "Not recommended for use as a nutcracker." (Art Grinath, Takoma Park)

On pantyhose: "Not to be used in the commission of a felony." (Judith Daniel, Washington)

On a piano: "Harmful or fatal if swallowed." (Peter Fay, Herndon)

On a can of Fix-a-Flat: "Not to be used for breast augmentation." (Jerry Robin, Gaithersburg)

On Kevorkian's suicide machine: "This product uses carbon monoxide, which has been found to cause cancer in laboratory rats." (Meg

Sullivan, Potomac)
On Lyndon LaRouche literature: "Mr. LaRouche is a serious political figure and not a paranoid lunatic, and should therefore...Hey, what are you looking at? Quit staring at me!" (Meg Sullivan, Potomac)
On work gloves: "For best results, do not leave at crime scene." (Ken Krattenmaker, Landover Hills)
On a palm sander: "Not to be used to sand palms." (Patrick, Taneytown)
On a calendar: "Use of term 'Sunday' for reference only. No meteorological warranties express or implied." (Elden Carnahan, Laurel)
On Odor Eaters: "Do not eat." (Chuck Smith, Woodbridge)
On Sen. Bob Dole: "WARNING: Contents under pressure and may explode." (Doug Keim, Schaumburg, Ill.)
On a blender: "Not for use as an aquarium." (Gary, Arlington)
On a fax machine: "WARNING! Never attempt to directly fax anyone an image of your naked buttocks. Always photocopy your buttocks and fax the photocopy." (John Kammer, Herndon)
On syrup of ipecac: "Caution - May cause vomiting." (Paul, Olney)
On a revolving door: "Passenger compartments for individual use only." (Elden Carnahan, Laurel)
On a microscope: "Objects are smaller and less alarming than they appear." (J. Calvin Smith, Laurel)
On children's alphabet blocks: "Letters may be used to construct words, phrases and sentences that may be deemed offensive." (David Handelsman, Charlottesville)
On a wet suit: "Capacity: 1." (J. Calvin Smith, Laurel)
And last...
On the Washington Post: "Do not cut up and use for blackmail note." (Joseph Romm, Washington).

--

Ann in Davis, CA was amused by what she saw:
There's a sign in my gym that says: "Towels are required to work out". There. I feel better.

Bob in Chicago:
On another subject...I recently came across an item where automobile drivers in a certain country were said to use their car horn as a "sound fender" or "aural amulet", the idea being that the horn had protective powers beyond that of an audible warning device. I was delighted with these terms and found them to be rather poetic...

Bill in Columbia, CT wanted to point out oddities in English:
The English language is "pregnant" with communication that makes no sense. After conversing with a "Drift" of superintendents who were trying to add logic to a base of illogical beginnings, I advanced an argument to the "Head of Heads" (of elite cerebral background), who told me on Monday that it was "Hot as Hell" and then told me on Tuesday it was "Cold as Hell," that he was accepting the new for the sake of new. He then responded my statement with "Slim Chance!" and then, two minutes later said, "Fat chance."

We departed with his saying that he was going to get "on" a plane. I told him to get "in" it. He said he was taking a "non-stop flight." I told him it was impossible because fuel was an issue. He retorted that I was a wise guy who was too analytical and was a threat to the English language. I told him that I appreciated that compliment of being a "wise guy" but that my cyber friends were teaching English. In any event, he told me he was taking the parkway. I responded by saying that only on Earth can someone park on a driveway and drive on a parkway.

I told the "Head of Heads" that I write on a blackboard that's white. He told me he could care less? I told him that means you have more feeling. He said, "It will fall between the cracks?" "Certainly, you jest!" I said, "That means that it is going to fall on the center of the boards. "He said, "Put your best foot forward?" I replied, " What? Do you have, three feet?" He departed in a roar, screaming (and smiling) that I needed help."

Dani in Atlanta, GA reported other amusing signs:
I once worked at a place where the restrooms were on (what we called) a "first come, first relieved" basis. We also had a 'routine offender' in the office. After several weeks of just avoiding using the particular room this offender frequented, a sign appeared over the back of the toilet tank. "We aim to please. You aim, too, please."
No one ever took credit for the sign, but it helped to solve our little problem. I think the next course of action would have been to paint a target symbol at the bottom of the bowl.

--

Katherine in Oakland recalled;
As Nancy the button-maker says, when marriage is outlawed, only outlaws will have in-laws.

--

Karen in Manchester, on the absurdities of word-by-word translations, quoted from "American Demographics" magazine:
Here is a look at how shrewd American business people translate their slogans into foreign languages:
When Braniff translated a slogan touting its upholstery, "Fly in Leather," it came out in Spanish as "Fly Naked."
Coors put its slogan, "Turn It Loose," into Spanish, where it was read as "Suffer From Diarrhea."
Chicken magnate Frank Perdue's line, "It takes a tough man to make a tender chicken," sounds much more interesting in Spanish: "It takes a sexually stimulated man to make a chicken affectionate."
When Vicks first introduce its cough drops on the German market, they were chagrined to learn that the German pronunciation of "v" is "f," which in German is the guttural equivalent of "sexual penetration."
Not to be outdone, Puffs tissues tried later to introduce its product, only to learn that "Puff" in German is a colloquial term for a whorehouse.
The Chevy Nova never sold well in Spanish speaking countries. "No Va" means "It Does Not Go" in Spanish.

When Pepsi started marketing its products in China a few years back, they translated their slogan, "Pepsi Brings You Back to Life", literally. The slogan in Chinese really meant, "Pepsi Brings Your Ancestors Back from the Grave."
"When Coca-Cola first shipped to China, they named the product something that when pronounced sounded like "Coca-Cola." The only problem was that the characters used meant "Bite the Wax Tadpole." They later changed to a set of characters that mean "Happiness In The Mouth."
A hair products company, Clairol, introduced the "Mist Stick", a curling iron, into Germany only to find out that mist is slang for manure. Not too many people had use for the manure stick.
When Gerber first started selling baby food in Africa, they used the same packaging as here in the USA--with the cute baby on the label. Later they found out that in Africa companies routinely put pictures on the label of what is inside since most people cannot read.

--

Bob in Chicago had some childhood memories:
My high school biology teacher, Father O'Malley, used to tell us boys that kissing was no good for you...that it is unsanitary. Why? Because the lips are connected to the anus, that's why. In between the two you have this long thirty-foot passage made up of the colon and the little intestine and the big intestine and the stomach, the esophagus, the throat, and finally the mouth. He said that in particular we should never kiss aggressively and that we should always remember one thing. When you kiss aggressively you are in reality sucking on a thirty-foot tube half filled with fecal matter!
Ah...those high school memories...

--

Frank in Ottawa had a new definition:
Just reminded myself of my favourite definition of a cynic: Someone who looks both ways before crossing a one-way street.

--

Katherine asked: Anybody know a good cure for nightmares?

Bob in Chicago had an answer: Oooo, Oooo, I know...how about nightstallions?

--

Gary in Sheffield UK recalled an anecdote:
I don't know why exactly but this brings back an exchange between Billy Bremner (a combative Scottish footballer who used to play for Leeds United) and a referee:

> Bremner to Ref: What would you do if I said you're a blind, half-witted git?
> Ref: I would have to send you off Billy.
> Bremner: What if I just think it?
> Ref: I can't send you off for thinking.
> Bremner: Okay, I think you're a blind, half-witted git.

--

Leigh-Anne had a collection of ditties:
These are from a local credit union's newsletter, but they did actually appear in various church bulletins.

> Don't let worry kill you -- let the church help.
> Thur night -- Potluck supper. Prayer and medication to follow.
> Remember in your prayer the many who are sick of our church and community.
> For those of you who have children and don't know it, we have a nursery downstairs.
> The rosebud on the altar this morning is to announce the birth of David Alan Belzer, the sin of Rev. and Mrs. Julius Belzer.

--

Frank in Ottawa wrote:
In a Pizza flyer delivered to the door yesterday: "Serving full coarse meals."

Mike in Brisbane retorted:
My favourite was in a deli, which offered "Sweat and Sour Pork".

--

Andrea in Atlanta compared distribution lists:

Someone said: "You know, Andrea, I noticed that about Copyediting-L myself. I got to thinking that the difference might be in that those "guys" are more anal retentive while Wordplayers have more of a scatological nature :)"

--- Wow -- just a bit of insight into my innermost self. It's a bit scary that I like frolicking with you guys more!

Martin added:

Maybe we're anal-expulsive!

--

Catie in Arlington, VA:

On the day/night thread. According to my husband, night is from whenever it gets dark, until midnight, then it is morning. To me, night is whenever it is dark. If I wake up at 3 am, to me, it is still night-time, and I'll say so.

 He'll reply: It isn't night anymore, it's morning. ARARRGGGHHH!! Yeah, yeah, I know, technically, he's right. But I would say there are two definitions of night. One is technical (until midnight) and one is ... oh, what's the word, social? when darkness is night.

Bev acquiesced:

You're on the right track, Catie. I would say that one definition of night is chronological and another is perceptual.

Bill in Columbia, CT elucidated:

"Night" is "night." The roots are as follows: "Mid" = middle and "Night" = dark (dusk to dawn). Midnight means the middle of the night. In "general parameters," 6:00 to 12:00 midnight is the first half and 12:00 midnight to 6:00 A.M. is the second half (part of the morning). Many people think that morning has to include the sun only. In general terms, in Connecticut, during the winter, we have 12 hours of night and twelve hours of light, which compose a day of 24 hours; however, in different locations night can be much longer as determined by dusk and dawn. In any event, a day equals both night and light and totals 24 hours.

Susi in Louisville, KY had a different irritation:
In Michigan there was much controversy over the colloquial "Michigander". Should it be the non-sexist Michigoose? Just one of the joys of being from a state where everyone points to their hand when asked where they're from.
Oh, well, it could've been Delaware, which doesn't exist....

Dani in Atlanta related:
People from Tampa, FL tend to refer to themselves as "Floridians" instead of as "Tampans." Too much sophomoric humor in that one.
I'm a Saskatoonian from Saskatchewan. Saskatoonians are proud of their berries. Saskatchewanian sounds really bad to me. Canadians are okay, as are North Americans. However, I think West Hemispherians is just a little too much. Earthlings are fine. Anything more than that is just hokey.

Matt in Minneapolis, MN responded with positivity:
Oh sure, Alyssa, Nyquil may make you combobulated and ruly, but I'm on some prescription cough medicine which keeps me shevelled, gruntled, and plussed. If only more postal workers were gruntled...
I would have said I was ruthful, reckful, hapful, and kempt, but my AmHer dictionary informs me that ruth, reck, hap, and kempt are words. If it says so...

Kent had a novel way of phoneticizing alphabet:
The same old standard phonetic alphabet (which you would use to describe spelling "Wilson" as "Whiskey, India, Lima, Sierra, Oscar, November") has been used by aircraft pilots, military personnel, and many others for many years now. So, I finally decided to come up with something a bit more "original" for those people who annoy me:

A Are   N Nine
B Bee   O Owe
C Cite   P Pseudonym

D Double-U	Q Queue
E Eye	R Rap
F Five	S Sea
G Genre	T Tsunami
H Hoe	U Understand?
I I	V Vie
J Junta	W Why
K Knot	X Xylophone
L Lye	Y You
M Me	Z Zero

People don't ask me to spell anything over the phone anymore.

--

Jim in Philadelphia followed up on the oddities and inconsistencies of our language:
Bill extolled some of the finer points of the English language, which is a tad too lengthy to repeat here, but I must add a few points of my own: If fire fighters fight fire, and crime fighters fight crime, what do freedom fighters fight?
Also, in the movie Clue (great camp flick!), Tim Curry (of Rocky Horror Picture Show fame) plays Wadsworth, the butler. When asked what he does (by Col. Mustard, played by Martin Mull), he responded, "I buttle, sir."

--

Phil in Salt Lake City:
I was at the grocery store the other day and looked at a can of "Fat Free" refried beans. Somehow, the phrase came across to my addled brain as "Fart Free" refried beans. Now that would really be something!

--

Raymond picked up on a historical event:
When Apollo Mission Astronaut Neil Armstrong first walked on the moon, he not only gave his famous "One Small Step for Man, One Gi-

ant Leap for Mankind" statement, but followed it by several remarks - usual COM traffic between him, the other astronauts and Mission Control. Before he re-entered the lander, he made the enigmatic remark "Good luck, Mr. Gorsky."

Many people at NASA thought it was a casual remark concerning some rival Soviet Cosmonaut. However, upon checking, there was no Gorsky in either the Russian nor American space programs.

Over the years, many people have questioned him as to what the "Good luck, Mr. Gorsky" statement meant. On July 5, in Tampa Bay, FL, while answering questions following a speech, a reporter brought up the 26-year-old question to Armstrong. He finally responded. It seems that Mr. Gorsky had died and so Armstrong felt he could answer the question. When he was a kid, Neil was playing baseball with his brother in the backyard. His brother hit a fly ball which landed in front of his neighbors' bedroom window. The neighbors were Mr. and Mrs. Gorksy. As he leaned down to pick up the ball, he heard Mrs. Gorsky shouting at Mr. Gorsky, "Oral sex? Oral sex you want? You'll get oral sex when the kid next door walks on the moon!"

--

On the origin of nicknames, Jim in Philadelphia postulated:
James in Spanish is Diego, because James and Jacob are the same – Jacques in French is one translation, and Iago for Jacob (Latin I think). Anyway, Saint James becomes Saint Jacob - Santiago - San Diego - Diego.

Catie in Arlington, VA said:
Sometimes it's very hard to determine where a nickname comes from, but I've found the study of names very interesting.

> Margaret - Marg - Mag - Meg - Peg – Peggy
> Mary - Molly – Polly
> Sarah - Sally – Sal
> John - Jack (still haven't figured out that one)
> William - Will - Bill – Billy

James -Jamie -Jemmie - Jem - Jim – Jimmy
Edward - Ed - Ted - Ned (Ted also for Theodore)

Family names are also interesting, there are basically 4 types:

Patronymic (coming from your father: Williamson, Thompson, Anderson, etc.
Place names (Rivers, Hill, Ridgeley)
Description names (Cruikshank, (can't think of any more))
Occupation names (Carter, Wainwright - (you know, that means wagon-maker), Miller, Goldsmith, etc.)

Also interesting is the same name in different languages:

John:
Juan (Spanish)
Sean (Irish)
Jan (Dutch & Scandinavian)
Jean (French)
William:
Guillermo (Spanish)
Guillaume (French)

She also added:
Technically, constructions like Jimmy for James, and Catie for Cathleen are DIMINUTIVES. Nicknames are totally different, like "Dusty" Rhodes, or "Chalky" White (to use Frank's example), or "Babe" Ruth.

On similes, Barb oversaw:
"supervising a bunch of PhD's is a lot like herding turkeys down the ditch with a stick"
Mike in Brisbane answered with:
And another nice expression is "pushing a wheelbarrow full of frogs".

Phil in Salt Lake City related:
I have also heard "...pushing a wheelbarrow full of feathers." And "...pushing a wheelbarrow full of smoke." Also: "herding cats."

--

On euphemism, Marcus observed:
RR, I think you may be the victim of a male hoax here ... could a "one-armed clarinetist" be like "going Japanese" ... a synonym, in other words, for masturbation?

--

Bruce in Sydney, AU:
Since all you good Americans have been recently enlightened as to the finer niceties of Ostrayan Kultcha and slang through the poetic power of Men At Work, perhaps one of you could reciprocate and explain what a "hoosier" is? And why should Indiana be especially proud of them (it?). Please please do tell as it has been bugging me since that film of the same name I never saw with Gene Hackman came out.
And while you're at it, why is Iowa "The Hawkeye State" and did it give "Hawkeye Pearce" from M.A.S.H. his nickname?

--

Gerry in Ottawa wondered about an overused term:
And finally, why "politically correct" anyway? Why not "socially correct?"

--

Rich in Rindge, NH recalled:
I was reminded of my aunt who, 30-some-odd years ago, decided to come out of the closet and inform the family of her sexual preference. She gathered everyone around and announced that she had decided to get married. When everyone started to congratulate her, she raised her hand to silence us and said, "Before you get too excited, there's something you ought to know about my fiancé."
After a very long pause she announced, "She's not Jewish." (true story)

--

On Mondegreens, Matt in Minneapolis offered:
Mondegreen for the day: Artist: The Police, Song: Spirits in the Material World.
Mondegreen: "There are spirits eating my Cheerios"
   Jim In Philadelphia countered:
I always knew it as "We all spit in the material world." Maybe if we kind of mixed mine and yours, it'll become a lot of fun.
My mondegreen for the day is from Tommy Shaw's Kiss Me Hello: "Would you leave this healthy mattress? Would you get yourself a gun?"
(What he's actually singing, is "Would you leave yourself defenseless?/Would you get yourself a gun?")

   Bob weighed in on the discussion on what to call people of various skin tones:
Here's something from a comedian's script:
>   When I was born, I was black.
>   When I grew up, I was black.
>   When I'm cold, I'm black.
>   When I'm hot, I'm black.
>   When I hold my breath, I'm black.
>   When I'm dead, I'll be black.
>   When you were born, you were pink.
>   When you grew up, you were white.
>   When you're cold, you're blue.
>   When your hot, your red.
>   When you hold your breath, you're purple.
>   When you die, you'll be grey.
>   And you have the nerve to call me "colored."

   Mike in Brisbane observed:
In New Guinea, the PC word was "mixed race", and the PI word was "half-caste". In some societies it went to "quarter-caste", "octoroon"

and so on. "Coloured" had this meaning in South Africa, didn't it? They used to talk of "Cape coloureds"?
Something I've been wondering about: If the Kurds come from Kurdistan, and the Afghanis come from Afghanistan, and so on, why don't we call those from Pakistan "Pakis", instead of "Pakistanis"?

--

Catie in Arlington, VA resuscitated an old thread:
OK, I went home and found the book. A while back, I posted a list of cow sounds in different languages. Here are a few others:

What a pig says:
English: Oink Oink
French: Groin Groin
German: Grunz
Japanese: Boo Boo
Russian: Khru
Swedish: Noeuf Noeuf

What a rooster says:
English: Cock-a-doodle-doo
Arabic: KooKooKoo-koo
Chinese: Koo Koo Koo
French: Cocorico
German: Kikeriki
Greek: Keekeereekoo
Hebrew: Koo-koo-ri-koo
Hindi: Kuk Ruu-kuu
Japanese: Ko Ke Kokkoh
Russian: Ku-ka-rje-ku
Swahili   KokoRikoo Koo
Swedish: Kuckeliku

What a dog says:
English: Bow wow (or ruff ruff)

German:	Wau Wau
Hebrew:	Hav Hav
Japanese:	Wan-Wan
Russian:	Gav-gav
Swahili:	Hu Hu Hu Huuu
Swedish:	Voff Voff

The title is Hear Here, Sounds Around the World_, and was compiled by Michele Slung

--

Catie also got curious about the similarities in naming a certain bodily function:

My 12-month-old has a cold and a very runny nose. Got me to wondering about the lay term for mucus (or is that mucous?). Anyway, snot. And I got to thinking about other "SN" words that had to do with the nose, and there were quite a few:

snot, sneeze, snort, snore, sniff, sniffle, snuff, snuffle, snivel, snout, snorkel

So what's the story behind all these SN words, and the nose? Is it because that is the sound one hears when one makes that noise?

13

Language Jokes

Sara in Boston related a Joke:
My sister owned a pickup truck for a while and noticed at one point that the idle was rough and it was threatening to stall out. She asked her boyfriend if he thought there was anything wrong with the truckburator. When he looked at her blankly, she explained, "Well, a car has a carburettor, so..." and couldn't understand why he was laughing so hard.

--

John in Keele, UK:
From a recent Open University broadcast [about the development of language in children]:
> Q: What do you call a blind dinosaur? A: D'youthinkysaurus.
> Q2: What do call a blind dinosaur's dog? A: D'youthinkysaurus Rex.

Of course, only the juveniles on this list will find these funny...

--

Proof again that truth is stranger than fiction:
15 actual announcements taken from church bulletins:
> 1. Don't let worry kill you -- let the church help.
> 2. Thursday night - Potluck supper. Prayer and medication to

follow.

3. Remember in prayer the many who are sick of our church and community.

4. For those of you who have children and don't know it, we have a nursery downstairs.

5. The rosebud on the alter this morning is to announce the birth of David Alan Belzer, the sin of Rev. and Mrs. Julius Belzer.

6. This evening there will be a meeting in the South and North ends of the church. Children will be baptized at both ends.

7. Tuesday at 4:00 PM there will be an ice cream social. All ladies giving milk will please come early.

8. Wednesday, the ladies Liturgy Society will meet. Mrs. Jones will sing, "Put me in My Little Bed" accompanied by the pastor.

9. Thursday at 5:00 P.M. there will be a meeting of the Little Mothers Club. All wishing to become little mothers, please see the minister in his study.

10. This being Easter Sunday, we will ask Mrs. Lewis to come forward and lay an egg on the alter.

11. The service will close with "Little Drops of Water." One of the ladies will start quietly and the rest of the congregation will join in.

12. Next Sunday a special collection will be taken to defray the cost of the new carpet. All those wishing to do something on the new carpet will come forward and do so.

13. The ladies of the church have cast off clothing of every kind and they may be seen in the church basement Friday.

14. A bean supper will be held on Tuesday evening in the church hall. Music will follow.

15. At the evening service tonight, the sermon topic will be "What is Hell?" Come early and listen to our choir practice.

Author unknown

Janet in Calgary was reminded:
Someone posted on church bulletins. A Canadian broadcaster tells the story from his childhood of his aunt finding a ladies' purse in the washroom of the church. Since it contained no identification, she asked the pastor to make an announcement. She'd never had cause to think twice about her name until the pastor announced: "If you have mislaid a purse, you can go to Helen Hunt for it"
Somebody way back on the topic of fruitcakes: A gay friend of mine tells me that they refer to the women who hang out in gay bars (hoping to cure them?) are referred to as "fruit flies"

--

From Mike in Aurora, IL:
This appeared in the HUMOR Digest - 8 Jul 1995.
Since it seemed to be on topic with what we have been talking about, I thought I would repost it, for those of us who have not yet subscribed to the HUMOR digest.
Standardized Guide to the Baseball analogy to sex and dating

> On Deck-- Having plans for a date
> Strike-Out-- Duh!!
> Walk—Kissing
> Bunt—Masturbation
> Single-- Tongue Kissing
> Double-- Breasts/chest touched, some clothes off, lots of grabbing and feeling
> Triple-- Most clothes off, genital contact, mutual masturbation
> Inside the Park Home Run-- Oral Sex
> Home Run-- SEX!!!
> Taking a long lead from second-- Would Have Sex, But No Condom
> Error-- Condom breaks during sex (Oops!)
> Banned for Life for Gambling-- Sex without condom - got AIDS

Hall of Fame-- When you ask if "Was it good for you" and they say "YES!!!"

Now that we've got the basics, let's introduce some terms to better explain all the things that can happen now a days.

Balk-- Premature ejaculation
Pine Tar-- KY jelly
Relief Pitcher-- Vibrator/Use of other hand
Rain Delay-- Parents/roommate return home unexpectedly
Box Seats—Waterbed
Seventh Inning Stretch-- Unusual positions
Minor Leagues-- Under 18
Loaded Bases-- Menage a trois
Grand Slam-- Sex four times in twelve hours
Foul Tip—VD
Three Up and Three Down—Impotency
Double Play-- Having two partners at the same time
In a pickle-- Getting caught cheating on a partner
Wild pitch-- Shooting your load across the room
Getting the signals crossed-- Moving in for the home run and ending up with a strike out
Squeeze Play-- Gripping of the genitals
Pinch Runner-- Tag-team sex with your roommate
Ground Out-- Moving for first but s/he says "Not on a first date"
Knocked out of the box-- Vaulting the hedges when her dad comes home
Fast ball-- Three strokes DONE!
Out of play-- That time of the month (her friend is in town)
Stealing home-- Telling her that she won't have to do anything she doesn't want to / Date rape
Bleacher Seats-- Roommate's view while you're going at it
Forfeit-- Date stands you up

Ejected from game-- Partner throws you off during rodeo sex
Second Opinion-- Partner has to ask roommate if it was "Good for them"
Cleared the bases-- Changed the sheets
Stranding the runner-- You orgasm before your partner
Pre-Game Warm-up-- Fore-play
Dome Stadium-- Under the sheets
Open-Air stadium-- Anywhere else
Spectator-- Peeping Tom
Scout-- Someone scoping out your partner on a date
Talent Agent—Pimp
Rookie—Virgin
Veteran—Prostitute
All Stars Game-- Doing it with your X while still going out with your present
Score Card-- Number of times you orgasm vs. number of times partner orgasms
Being Traded-- Being dumped for someone else
Free Agent-- Recently dumped, Currently unattached
Disabled list-- Done it so much can't get it up anymore
Suspended-- Partner says they need some time alone

Dean in New York followed up:
I couldn't resist a swing at America's favourite pastime:
>   Base Hit - purely sexual encounter
>   Foul Line - an indecent proposal
>   Strike Zone - the area defining a Foul Line (depends on the person receiving the pitch)
>   Thrown Out - as opposed to an Intentional Walk
>   Sacrifice Fly - in your haste, you left your underwear behind

--

Lomond in Sacramento, CA:
Talking Real Estate - A relative of mine sold his parcel of land in Scotland recently. The lake, the cattle, the hillside covered with green, pink, and yellow crystals; he sold it all - loch, stock, and beryl.

--

Alex in Adelaide:
Jane from way down under started a thread about baseball/dating game, then Mike Sladek gave us an impressive lexicon on the subject matter. While I no longer use this terminology in my circles, I still remember vividly the instance in college when a friend asked me about the state of my playing ability. My answer was: "Well, at the rate things are going I'm still in Spring training. I am still playing with members of my own team."

Mike in Brisbane:
Kristofer, you've never been to an Australian Labor Party Branch Meeting. It goes like this:
Chairman: We have a motion. Does it have a seconder?
Someone else: I second the motion.
Chairman: Allthoseinfavouragainstcarried! (This is probably the longest word in the Labor Party Lexicon)
(The Australian Labor Party, aka the ALP, _approximates_ the US Democrats.)

--

Heath in San Antonio, TX wrote:
To put some fun into "Wordplay, the List", and to celebrate the revivals of baseball and Mickey Mantle, do any of you have any Yogi Berra lines to share? He was an artful (if accidental) wordplayer.
Jim in Philadelphia came to the rescue:
Here're some of my faves (all credited to Yogi):
> "You can observe a lot by watching."
> (On why it's tough to play left field in Yankee Stadium) "It gets late early."

(On receiving a check made out to "Bearer") "How could you spell my name like that?"
"No wonder nobody ever comes here. It's too crowded."
"If you can't imitate him, don't copy him."
"Half the lies they tell me aren't true."
"Ninety nine percent of this game is half mental."

Here's a dialog bit between Yogi and Mickey...
   M.M.: What time is it?
   Y.B.: You mean right now?
And, of course the tradition lives on...
Dale Berra, on his father, Yogi: "Our similarities are different."
New York Mets broadcaster Ralph Kiner informed us, three or four years ago, that "The Mets are welding a hot bat this year." Must be aluminum... :-P

Jeff in the UK on odd names:
US placenames (from Bryson, MIA)

   Who'd a thought it, Alabama
   Eek, Alaska
   Two egg, Florida
   Rabbit hash, bug, OK, and Sugar Tit, Kentucky
   Sleepy Eye and Dinky Town, Minnesota
   Tightwad, Peculiar and Jerk tail, Missouri
   Hot Coffee, and Good Food, Mississippi
   Wynot, Nebraska
   Brainy Boro, and Cheesequake, New Jersey
   Stifflknee Knob, and Shoofly, NC
   Knockemstiff, Pee Pee, Lickskillet, and Mudsock, Ohio
   Bowlegs, Oklahoma
   East Due West, SC
   Yell, Bugscuffle, Gizzards Cove, and Zu Zu, Tennessee
   Chocolate bayou, Ding Dong, Looneyville, Jot 'em Down, and

Cut and Shoot, TX
Lick Fork, Unthanks, and Tizzle Flats, VA
Humptulips, and Shittim Gulch, Washington
Superior bottom, Weat Verginia
Embarrass, Wisconsin

(all sic), and some towns/landmarks that did once exist, but were taken off the map, for some unknown reason:

Puke, Shitbreeches Creek, Two Tits, and Delirium Tremens, California
Whiskey Dick Mountain, Washington
Dead Bastard Peak, Wyoming
Shit-House Mountain, Arizona
Fucking Creek, and Tickle Cunt Branch, VA
Coldass Creek, NC

Nipple Mountains (changed to Teton Mountains) and Tit Butte, various states. Just thought you oughtta know,

---

FC recounted:
My wife, who is a successful executive, was complaining that all of the men she worked with were wimps, so she says "I have more balls than they do!" I replied that she was getting delusions of glandure.

Mike in Brisbane recalled:
A very clever piece of graffiti, printed very small on the ceiling above one of those communal urinals. "While you are reading this, you're pissing on your boots!"

Pat in Collegeville, MN followed up:
When I was a kid, a figurative graffito often found above public urinals: Little bulls with short horns stand close--the next guy may be barefoot.

Janet in Calgary bemused:
Don't laugh - they renamed the film "The Madness of King George" because they thought that if they left it as originally titled, "The Madness of George III", American audiences might think it was the third in a series!

--

Jan in Hobart, AU had few puns up her sleeve:
Why can you only have two doors on a chicken coop? If it had four it would be a chicken sedan.
A "Frisbeterian" believes that when you die, your soul goes up on the roof, and you can't get it back down.
Photons have mass? I didn't even know they were Catholic.
Q: How do you spell "onomatopoeia"? A: The way it sounds.
I'd rather have a bottle in front of me than a frontal lobotomy.

--

Sara in Boston on Hemingway's style of writing:
I agree with Lee's assessment of Hemingway... one of the worst assignments I had in high school was reading "A Farewell to Arms." It puts me in mind of a classic Dennis Miller line: "What's with these maxi-pad commercials? To listen to them, you'd think these girls had more periods than a Hemingway novel!" None of my friends got that one; they couldn't understand why I was ROTFL.

--

Mike in Brisbane:
On the currenttnerruc thread: reminds me of the man who opened his refrigerator and saw a mouse lying back on the lettuce. "What are you doing?" asked the man. "This is a Westinghouse, isn't it?", said the mouse, "well, I'm westing."

--

Katherine in Oakland, CA:
My favorite was probably
    Knock, knock.
    Who's there?

Banana. Knock, knock.
Who's there?
Banana. Knock, knock.
Who's there?
Banana. Knock, knock.
Who's there?
Orange.
Orange who?
Orange you glad I didn't say Banana again?

Pat in Collegeville, MN followed up:
Amusing us with knock-knocks, writes:
The most ingenious, to me—and possibly the worst to many, was
> Shostakovich who?
> [sung] Shostakovich small, by a waterfall...

--

Russ in Fredericton, NB:
My granddaughter, on being handed one of our Danish-design forks (looks sort of like a spoon, with two slots, making three tines): "No, I want a fork, not a threek."

--

From Mike Down Under:
There's a brand of nuts called "Nobbys" sold in bars in Australia. Their slogan is "Nibble Nobby's Nuts". Ah well.

--

Ktherine in Oakland:
Well, I've liked "When an eel hits your eye like a big pizza pie, that's a moray..."

--

From Jim in Philadelphia:
Seven dwarves: Anger, Gluttony, Greed, Envy, Lust, Sloth, Covetous

--

Jeff in San Diego, CA:
Question: Why did the cowboy go out and by himself a dachshund?
Answer: Because everyone kept telling him: "Get a long little doggy!"

--

Bill in Lexington, KY shared a poem:

> There was a young man of St. Paul
> Who fell in a spring in the Fall
> 'Twould have been a sad thing
> Had he died in the Spring
> But he didn't, he died in the Fall.

> A tutor who tooted a flute
> Tried to tutor two tooters to toot
> Said the two to the tutor
> "Is it easier to toot, or
> To tutor two tooters to toot?"

> A canner exceedingly canny
> One morning remarked to his granny
> "A canner can can
> Anything that he can
> But a canner can't can a can, can he?"

--

Mike in Brisbane added:
Dave, after giving us an essay on the use of the radical "stand" in various combinations follows up with: "Oops. I couldn't stand it if I lost the substance of my standing because of my substandard spelling of substantial…"
Thanks Dave, you can stand down now. I assume you've been standing tall, standing fast and standing firm?

--

Kat in Rochester, NY:
"A couple of copy editors drove up north to go hunting. They saw a road sign that said BEAR LEFT. So they went home."

--

Gerry in New York:
Two brothers, Roland & Anderson lived in the same house. They wanted to get a name plate affixed to the mail box so that people would know this fact. They got a sign painter to do the job. When he returned with the name plate, they noticed a problem. Said Roland: "The space between Rol and and, and and and and, and and and And, and And and erson is not quite right"!
(That's 13 'and's in a row ... but who's counting!)

--

Mike in Brisbane responded to Rich who asked: (I thought there were more ovines than homo sapiens Down Under?)
Rich, yes, you're right. When I was in school, I was told that "There are ten sheep for every man, woman and child in Australia." I'm still looking for my ten, I think someone's nobbled them.

--

Sara in Boston responded to the contest on Abcedarian insult:
You aggravating blowhard, completely disgusting egghead, fart-blowing gross hamster-brained ingrate, jugheaded knock-kneed loose-moraled megalomaniac nincompoop, overblown pompous quite rejected stuck-up toady, underachieving violent warthog, x-out, you zipperhead!!
Don't know if I'm allowed to throw in all the hyphenated words... if not, I'll try again. (Q and X are always the toughest!)

--

Matt in Minneapolis, MN was a bona fide wordsmith:
Mike DownUnder, you asinine, bovine, colubrine, desmodontid, eusuchian, fungoid, gastropodan, hircine, ichthyic, jackaline(?), kiangine(??), limacrine, murine, novercal, oligochaetous, porcine,

THE POWER OF WORDS - 393

quisquilian, ranine, soricine, talopid, ursine, vulturine, waspish, xiphosuran, yohimbine zibeline!

Alternatively, you acephalous, borborygmous, coprophilic, dysypygal, esurient, flagitious, gnathonic, hebetudinous, ithyphallic, jumentous, kakistocratic, lubricitous, mephitic, nugatory, oligophrenial, proctalgesic, quidnunc, rebarbative, stercoraceous, thersitical, ultracrepidarian, vecordious, weasy, xanthodontous, yirning zooerast.

FM in Baltimore, MD contributed:
Here's a panalphabetic story (sorry, more than one sentence) I composed during a long and evidently boring drive recently:
Animal bones crack, deform, even fracture. Galloping hurts intensely. Just kneeling leaves marks. Nothing overcomes pain quickly. Relax! Some talented, understanding veterinarian will x-ray your zebra.

Matt in Minneapolis, MN:
On the business of a business of ferrets: Yes, business is the common collective noun, but an acceptable alternative is the bizarre 'fesnyng'. I also found another strange one: a group of capercailzies (Old World grouse) is called a tok.

Mike in Brisbane:
Thanks for all the animal collectives, they've been really interesting - didn't see one for beavers? What do you think? A confluence? An obstruction? A construction? A labor? An edifice? Also didn't see one for frogs; toads, yes, but no frogs?

Terrence in Bermuda answered:
My source gives ranine for frogs and batrachian for toads.

Matt in Minneapolis followed up:
Mike Lean asked about the frog collective. Terrence answered with the adjective ranine. I do not have anything as comprehensive as "A Crash of Rhinoceroses", but by collecting the collectives from 3 different sources, I have over 100 of them. It's an army of frogs - probably advancing as part of a coup to overthrow the Lord of the Flies. One

more interesting collective: a singular of boars. So, a singular boar means one, but a boar singular means a group.

Bill in Columbia, CT waxed creative about collectives:
It is a "murder" of crows. The crow came about from Prometheus who flew up to the sun to bring man fire and got singed and became a crow. What about this English precision?

    cattle - drove (to the market)
    geese - gaggle on ground and skein in flight
    apes - shrewdness (evolution?)
    locusts - plague (do harass)
    asses - pace (Fast?)
    chickens - peep (sound)
    eggs - clutch (Don't do that)
    peacocks - ostentation (They do show off)
    turtles - bale (All I can think of is bringing turtles home in a pail.)
    toads - knot (They do have warts)
    whales - gam (Loyalty in marriage)
    ravens - unkindness (Black is considered murderous or unkind - Why do priests dress in black?)
    leopards - leap (They do leap)
    turkeys - rafter (on perch)
    ducks - paddling (they do paddle)
    mules - barren (makes sense)
    Birds - dissimulation (They are dissimilar)
    hogs - drift (They are in lala land)
    bees - swarm (They certainly do that)
    bears - sloth (Sleep is important)
    doves - dule (Harmless identification)
    finches - charm (cute)
    horses - harass (never bothered me)
    trout - hover (over their nests)
    boars - singular (loners)

jellyfish - smack (when falling)
ponies - string (pulled along)
rhinoceroses - crash (Did you know the horn is comprised of hair – powerful crash)
foxes - skulk (they do skulk)
owls - parliament (They are wise, after all that "Blonde" Athena (Minerva) is the goddess of wisdom and the owl is her symbol)

Jesse in Sunnyvale, CA rebutted:

Bill, that doesn't sound at all familiar. Prometheus stole fire from the gods (not the Sun) and gave it to man, and for that he was punished by being chained to a big rock where birds would come each day, tear out his liver and eat it, fly off. He would grow a new liver each night. It was Daedalus and Icarus who made wings out of wax and feathers, and Icarus flew too close to the sun, melted his wax, and fell. I don't remember either legend having someone turning into a crow. Can anyone else help confirm or deny my mythological memory?

--

Katherine in Oakland. CA responded:

I don't know that one, Jesse, but I remember one that went like so:

> Mary Jane put on her skates
> Upon the ice to frisk,
> Wasn't she a silly fool
> Her little *

--

Sara in Boston asked:

Wordplay as a weapon - I can't remember the name of the author or the title (how embarrassing!), but does anyone else remember the essay about solving hunger by eating children? It was excellently written, and made to sound perfectly logical.

Pat in Collegeville, MN recalled:

Probably Dean Swift's "A Modest Proposal." Many readers still miss the irony and are appalled at the seeming author's inhumanity.

--

Rich in Rindge, NH posed:
What's the difference between a cat and a comma?
A cat has claws at the end f his paws, and a comma's a pause at the end of a clause.

Bill in Lexington, KY introduced The American Hyphen Society:
The American Hyphen Society is a community-based, not-for-profit, grass-roots, consciousness-raising/education-research alliance that seeks to help effect the across-the-board self-empowerment of wide-ranging culture-, nationality-, ethnicity-, creed-, gender-, and sexual-orientation-defined identity groups by excising all multiculturally-less-than-sensitive terminology from the English language, replacing it with counter-hegemonic, cruelty-, gender-, bias-, and, if necessary, content-free speech. The society's motto is "It became necessary to destroy the language to save it." Its headquarters is in Wilkes-Barre, Pennsylvania.
(Not original, but I don't know the source.)

--

Frank in Ottawa:
A chap enters the Olympic Stadium carrying a long pole. Security guard approaches, asks: "Are you a pole-vaulter?" "No, I'm a German, but how did you know my first name?"

--

Alex in Adelaide, AU:
In Australia these days the government is trying to boost its political and economic appeal by using and encouraging administrators to use name-phrases ending with _nation_ e.g. working nation, creative nation, productive nation, prosperous nation etc...
However, some wicked minds from the opposition party (Liberals) jumped on the occasion and came up with: halluci nation, procrasti nation, debt-o-nation, and flatulnation.
Any other such words partners?

--

Jan in Tasmania had some twisted wordplay:
To all of you langua-philes..........
The following are winners in a New York Magazine contest in which contestants were asked to take a well-known expression in a foreign language, change a single letter, and provide a definition for the new expression.

HARLEZ-VOUS FRANCAIS? - Can you drive a French motorcycle?
EX POST FUCTO - Lost in the mail
IDIOS AMIGOS - We're wild and crazy guys!
VENI, VIPI, VICI - I came; I'm a very important person; I conquered
J'Y SUIS, J'Y PESTES - I can stay for the weekend
COGITO EGGO SUM - I think; therefore, I am a waffle
RIGOR MORRIS - The cat is dead
RESPONDEZ S'IL VOUS PLAID - Honk if you're Scots
QUE SERA SERF - Life is feudal
LE ROI EST MORT. JIVE LE ROI - The King is dead. No kidding.
POSH MORTEM - Death styles of the rich and famous
PRO BOZO PUBLICO - Support your local clown
MONAGE A TROIS - I am three years old
FELIX NAVIDAD - Our cat has a boat
HASTE CUISINE - Fast French food
VENI, VIDI, VICE - I came, I saw, I partied.
QUIP PRO QUO - A fast retort
ALOHA OY - Love; greetings; farewell; from such a pain you should never know
MAZEL TON - Lots of luck
APRES MOE LE DELUGE - Larry and Curly get wet
PORTE-KOCHERE - Sacramental wine
ICH LIEBE RICH - I'm really crazy about having dough
FUI GENERIS - What's mine is mine

VISA LA FRANCE - Don't leave chateau without it
VENI VIDI VISA - I came, I saw, I bought
CA VA SANS DIRT - And that's not gossip
MERCI RIEN - Thanks for nothin'.
AMICUS PURIAE - Platonic friend
L'ETAT, C'EST MOO - I'm bossy around here
L'ETAT, C'EST MOE - All the world's a stooge

Matt in Minneapolis, MN picked up the baton:
I like the Twisted Titles. Here are a few more:
"The Lard of the Rings" (The definitive onion ring cookbook)
"The Tee Commandments" (improve your golf swing)
"Ben Hud" (escaped slave shops for affordable housing)
"The Good Garth" (Wayne's World goes to China)
"The Lord of the Rinks" (Gretzky's biography)
"Canterbury Males" (Playgirl's photoshoot in Chaucerian England)
"The Bobbit" (the adventures of Bilbo's wife, Lorena)
"Of Mice and Hen" (a touching barnyard tale of a large, dumb chicken)
"Animal Fart" (Bolshevik Russia retold with metaphor of borborygmous barnyard)
After that last one, I'd best be going.... :-}

Suad from Kuwait:
Ground Hug Day -celebrated by people afraid of flying.
Bah-Steel day -celebrated by plastics manufacturers.
Indian Penance Day -politically correct version of Columbus Day.
--
Gerry in Ottawa shared:
Someone on another net was wondering this morning about the

meaning of "deja vous" which he'd just spotted in the local press. I could only suggest that the paper had obviously bought itself a French spelling checker. But it did remind me of a restaurant in Washington, D.C. that used to call itself the Deja Vu. I never dared ask why but suspected that it must specialize in leftovers.

--

Dean said:
Finally, whenever, as a child, I would go to the barber to "get a haircut (get a hair cut)", she would ask me why I didn't get them *all* cut.

--

John in Keele, UK:
The Children's Society [formerly The Church of England Children's Society] has just sent me their latest campaign publicity material featuring the slogan "We couldn't care more!"
Just thought you'd like to know!

--

Michael in Minneapolis, MN came face to face with a pun:
Today I had a message come through my in-box. It contained the line: "A lot of what you said about servers, etc. was geek to me." Was geek to me!! It's all just geek to me!! I've been amused ever since with this wordplay. By simply dropping an 'r', the phrase is brought up to date and none of its meaning lost.

--

Har brought us some Clever Anagrams:
I found this in an old Readers Digest, I think:

> THE ANAGRAM/GRANT ME A HA!
> The Morse code/here come dots
> The countryside/no city dust here
> Clothespins/so let's pinch
> Conversation/voices rant on
> Dormitory/dirty room

Credit to Howard W. Bergerson, quoted by Rod L Evans and Irwin M. Berent.

--

Bill in Columbia, CT picked up on few ironies: Hi, Cyberholics One of my cyberjunkies e-mailed me this array of verbal humor. I thought I'd share these humorous images with you. I hope you enjoy them.

Why isn't phonetic spelled the way it sounds?
Why are there interstate highways in Hawaii?
Why are there flotation devices under plane seats instead of parachutes?
Why do bars have parking lots?
Why isn't palindrome spelled the same way backwards?
You know that little black box that is used on planes, why can't they make
the whole plane out of that substance?
Why is it so hard to remember how to spell MNEMONIC?
Why is it called a TV "set" when you only get one?
If pro is the opposite of con, is progress the opposite of congress?
Why does "cleave" mean both split apart and stick together?
Why is it called a "building" when it is already built?
Why is there an expiration date on sour cream?
How can someone "draw a blank"?
Shouldn't there be a shorter word for "monosyllabic"?
Why is the word abbreviate so long?
Why did kamikaze pilots wear helmets?
What is another word for "thesaurus"?
When they ship Styrofoam, what do they pack it in?
Why doesn't "onomatopoeia" sound like what it is?
Why do tugboats push their barges?
Why do we sing "take me out to the ball game" when we are al-

ready there?
Why are they called "stands" when they're made for sitting?

--

Jack in London:
On the Cix conferencing system where I reside, we do our best to keep "adult" material away so as not to attract the scumbag journalists of the tabloid press. This led one hacker to coin the phrase, "Beware of geeks bearing GIFs."

--

Frank in Ottawa:
Baroque. I first came across this word when reading an account of the negotiations between Michaelangelo and the then Pope when they were discussing the painting of the dome of the Sistine chapel. "OK your Holiness," said Mike, "let's go for Baroque."

--

Dani in Atlanta, GA reported:
Seen on a shirt in the "Signals" catalog: "Stop the Violins"
Katherine in Oakland, CA responded:
But medievalists are into Saxon violence...
Bill in Lexington, KY followed up:
That reminds me of the definition for "bigamist". It's an Italian fog.
And Katherine in Oakland, CA:
Which of course reminds me of the Groucho-ism (ack! my memory's slipping--I'm not sure which movie this is in!): where he says to the Margaret Dumont character that he'll marry her as well as another woman, and she says in shocked tones, "That would be bigamy!" and he replies, "Well, it would be big o' me, too, but..."

--

Mike in Brisbane:
Some of these postings will be a bit archaic, but, as the Scotsman said, "We canna have archaic and eat it too!"

--

Susi in Louisville, KY reported a sighting:
As for cultural signs, this was spotted at an IU Music School bathroom: If toilet doesn't flush, wiggle handel. Scribbled beneath: If I do, will it wiggle bach?

--

Kimberly in Fort Lauderdale, FL said:
Barb, I don't know where the term "poor house" originated, but when I was in Port St. Lucie recently, I noticed a pub called "The Pour House."

--

Jack in London:
Meanwhile back in the real world, a British newspaper often used to (perhaps still does) arrange "marriages" to make fun of names. For example, if Whoopi Goldberg married Peter Cushing.... I guess the same game is played the world over :-)

--

David in Glendale, CA:
Did I read someone refer to an awesome and horror-filled terror as being "hair-raising"? Let's not tell an expecting mother that the real thing is referred to as "heir-raising"...

Bill in Lexington, KY:
That reminds me that in one of our local hospitals the waiting room outside the delivery area was labelled "heirport".

--

David in Glendale, CA:
Mrs. Malaprop had catachresis.

--

Bill in Lexington, KY followed up:
That reminds me of something I read maybe 40 years ago:
> If an S and an I and an O and a U
> With an X at the end spell "Sioux"
> And an E and a Y and an E spell "eye",
> Say what is a poet to do?
> Then, if an S and an I and a D

With an E at the end spell "side",
There is nothing for a poor poet to do
But go commit Siouxeyeside.

Bill further said

This is a second-hand report of a radio news broadcast heard this week: "Michael Jackson has been taken to the hospital and is being treated with tranquillizers and 4 fluids, uh, wait, make that IV fluids."

--

Alex in Adelaide weighed in:
"To think is to be" Descartes
"To be is to do" – Sartre
"To do is to be" – Socrates
"Doo be doo be doo" - Sinatra

Alex further said:

Finally I offer some terms of doublespeak:

Entropy control engineer	janitor
Sex industry worker	prostitute
Civil disorder	riot
Occasional irregularity	constipation
Genuine imitation	fake
Enhanced radiation device	nuclear bomb
Therapeutic misadventure	malpractice
Negative investment increment	loss

And Bill in Lexington, KY:

That reminds me of one I saw in Playboy long ago: Sherlock Holmes and Dr. Watson are walking past a house with a roundish, yellow door. Holmes says: A lemon entry, my dear Watson.

--

And Bruce in Sydney:
As for that load on your chest, my SO swears by getting a proper fitting from a brassiere shop and not just buying off the rack.

--

Jack in London contributed:
Re heteronyms, this isn't one, but I still like it: St James St
It would also be possible to have, say, a Dr Crippen Dr, though I have never heard of such a thing, or even an Ave Maria Ave :-)

--

Jim in Philadelphia got it:
Then Frank gave us this beaut of a puzzle: "Wordplay? Ok. From my page-a-day calendar for Mensa: Unscramble the letters here to make one word. NEW DOOR"
All right. ONE WORD

--

Rich in Rindge NH:
You probably already heard about the Christmas party... Everyone was feeling merry. So Merry got disgusted and went home. Then everyone jumped for Joy.

--

Matt in Minneapolis, MN said:
Hmmm. Maybe it denotes a disparity in personalities, but I tend to include in my list of favourite quiz questions things like "How long did the Hundred Years War last?"; "Where are Panama hats manufactured?"; "What were Alexander Graham Bell's first words?"; "Do they have a Fourth of July in Great Britain?"; and "In the state of Georgia, is it legal for a man to marry his widow's sister?"

Jim in Philadelphia responded:
I've always liked, "Which would you prefer, that a lion ate you or a tiger?"

Gerry on Ottawa remarked:
On another thread altogether, someone recently suggested "Where are Panama hats made?" as an example of a question with a self-evident

answer.

Actually, I believe they're made in Ecuador. For a great in-depth account, see Tom Miller's "The Panama Hat Trail: A Journey from South America" which was published in 1986 by William Morrow and Company in New York.

--

Dan responded to Rich:

I've been to the Oarhouse on Block Island, RI. It's not a seafood place. It's more of a "high-class dive." Anyway, the walls are covered with rowboat oars that have been painted and/or decorated with the names and whatnot of customers past. When I first heard of the place, I thought I was being taken to a brothel and couldn't figure out why we were bringing that brightly painted oar with us.

Dean remarked:

In the movie "Support Your Local Sherriff", with James Garner, there was a house of ill repute that was run by Madam Oarr. It was called, of course, the Oarr House.

DK in Arkansas:

On town names: Toadsuck, Arkansas

And Hank in Philadelphia:

I don't think there's an area which can beat Pennsylvania Dutch country in eastern Pennsylvania. Within a few miles we have Bird-In-Hand, Paradise, and Intercourse. And no, if you leave Bird-In-Hand to go to Intercourse to finally find Paradise and you're stopped along the way, it's NOT coitus interruptus!

And Phil in Salt Lake City:

On place names:

In the next county we have a town called Mantua. We thought: "How nice, how cultured." until we heard the local pronunciation: "MAN-a-way".

Utah also has:

Tooele, pronounced "Too-WILL-a"
Hurricane, pronounced "HURR-a-cn"
Duchesne, pronounced "Doo-SHAYNE"

--

The Quotes of Steven Wright:

1 - I'd kill for a Nobel Peace Prize.
2 - Borrow money from pessimists -- they don't expect it back.
3 - Half the people you know are below average.
4 - 99% of lawyers give the rest a bad name.
5 - 82.7% of all statistics are made up on the spot.
6 - A conscience is what hurts when all your other parts feel so good.
7 - A clear conscience is usually the sign of a bad memory.
8 - If you want the rainbow, you got to put up with the rain.
9 - All those who believe in psycho kinesis, raise my hand.
10 - The early bird may get the worm, but the second mouse gets the cheese.
11 - I almost had a psychic girlfriend, .. But she left me before we met.
12 - OK, so what's the speed of dark?
13 - How do you tell when you're out of invisible ink?
14 - If everything seems to be going well, you have obviously overlooked something.
15 - Depression is merely anger without enthusiasm.
16 - When everything is coming your way, you're in the wrong lane.
17 - Ambition is a poor excuse for not having enough sense to be lazy.
18 - Hard work pays off in the future; laziness pays off now.
19 - I intend to live forever ... So far, so good.
20 - If Barbie is so popular, why do you have to buy her friends?
21 - Eagles may soar, but weasels don't get sucked into jet engines.
22 - What happens if you get scared half to death twice?
23 - My mechanic told me, "I couldn't repair your brakes, so I made your horn louder."
24 - Why do psychics have to ask you for your name
25 - If at first you don't succeed, destroy all evidence that you tried.

26 - A conclusion is the place where you got tired of thinking.
27 - Experience is a skill you don't get until just after you need it.
28 - The hardness of the butter is proportional to the softness of the bread.
29 - To steal ideas from one person is plagiarism; to steal from many is research.
30 - The problem with the gene pool is that there is no lifeguard.
31 - The sooner you fall behind, the more time you will have to catch up.
32 - The colder the x-ray table, the more of your body is required to be on it.
33 - Everyone has a photographic memory; some just don't have film.
34 - If at first you don't succeed, skydiving is not for you.
35 - If your car could travel at the speed of light, would your headlights work?

A linguistics professor was lecturing to his English class one day. "In English," he said, "a double negative forms a positive. In some languages, though, such as Russian, a double negative is still a negative. However, there is no language where in a double positive can form a negative." A voice from the back of the room piped up, "Yeah, right."

14

Word Games and Puzzles

Jim in Philadelphia answered Kristofer's call for: <more palindromes and anagrams, please! I like them!>

- Boston ode: Do not sob! ('Specially true for you Red Sox and Patriots fans...)
- Reviled did I live ere evil I did deliver.
- Eros? Sidney, my end is sore!
- Sit on a potato pan, Otis.
- A slut nixes sex in Tulsa.
- Star comedy by Democrats.

--

Kristofer in College Station, TX had a list of reworded sayings:
A word game for you players: Just for fun, can you figure out the familiar sayings from the following big words? You know every one of them.
1. Scintillate, scintillate, asteroid minifis.
2. Members of an avian species of identical plumage congregate.
3. Surveillance should precede salientation.
4. Pulchritude possesses solely cutaneous profundity.
5. It is fruitless to become lachrymose over precipitately departed

lacteal fluids.
6. The stylus is more potent than the claymore.
7. It is fruitless to attempt to indoctrinate a superannuated canine with innovative manoeuvres.
8. Eschew the implement of correction and vitiate the scion.
9. The temperature of the aqueous content of an unremittingly ogled saucepan does not reach 212 degrees.
10. All articles that coruscate with resplendence are not truly auriferous.
11. Where there are visible vapors in ignited carbonous materials, there is conflagration.
12. Sorting on the part of mendicants must be interdicted.
13. A plethora of individuals with expertise in culinary techniques vitiate the potable concoction produced by steeping certain comestibles.
14. Male cadavers are incapable of yielding any testimony.
15. Individuals who make their abode in vitreous edifices would be advised to refrain from catapulting petrous projectiles.
16. Neophyte's serendipity.
17. Exclusive dedication to necessitated chores without interludes of hedonist diversion renders John a hebetudinous fellow.
18. A revolving lithic conglomerate accumulates no congeries of a small green bryophytic.
19. The person presenting the ultimate cachinnation possesses the optimal cachination.
20. Abstention from any undertaking precludes a potential escalation of a lucrative nature.
21. Missiles of ligneous or petrous consistency have the potential of fracturing my osseous structure, but appellations will eternally remain innocuous.

--

Martin in Los Angeles had a stab at them:
1. Scintillate, scintillate, asteroid minifis
   Twinkle, twinkle, little star

2. Members of an avian species of identical plumage congregate.
    Birds of a feather flock (the polite word!) together
3. Surveillance should precede salientation.
    Look before you leap
4. Pulchritude possesses solely cutaneous profundity.
    Beauty is only skin deep
5. It is fruitless to become lachrymose over precipitately departed lacteal fluids.
    Don't cry over spilt milk
6. The stylus is more potent than the claymore.
    The pen is mightier than the sword (where did the "w" come from?)
7. It is fruitless to attempt to indoctrinate a superannuated canine with innovative manoeuvres.
    You can't teach an old dog new tricks
8. Eschew the implement of correction and vitiate the scion.
    Spare the rod and spoil the child
9. The temperature of the aqueous content of an unremittingly ogled saucepan does not reach 212 degrees.
    A watched pot never boils (this turns out to be true in quantum mechanics)
10. All articles that coruscate with resplendence are not truly auriferous.
    All that glitters is not gold
11. Where there are visible vapors in ignited carbonous materials, there is conflagration.
    Where there's smoke, there's fire
12. Sorting on the part of mendicants must be interdicted.
    Beggars can't be choosers (cute!)
13. A plethora of individuals with expertise in culinary techniques vitiate the potable concoction produced by steeping certain comestibles.
    Too many cooks spoil the broth

14. Male cadavers are incapable of yielding any testimony.
    Dead men tell no tales
15. Individuals who make their abode in vitreous edifices would be advised to refrain from catapulting petrous projectiles.
    People who live in glass houses shouldn't throw stones
16. Neophyte's serendipity.
    Beginner's luck
17. Exclusive dedication to necessitated chores without interludes of hedonist diversion renders John a hebetudinous fellow.
    All work and no play makes Jack a dull boy
18. A revolving lithic conglomerate accumulates no congeries of a small green bryophytic.
    A rolling stone gathers no moss
19. The person presenting the ultimate cachinnation possesses the optimal cachinnation.
    He who laughs last, laughs best
20. Abstention from any undertaking precludes a potential escalation of a lucrative nature.
    You can't win if you don't play (This is the only one that took me a while to figure out).
21. Missiles of ligneous or petrous consistency have the potential of fracturing my osseous structure, but appellations will eternally remain innocuous.
    Sticks and stones may break my bones, but names will never hurt me

--

Robert chimed in with this set:
My wife and I came up with a few of these, which she describes as a cross between "do it" lists and Tom Swifties:

> I was going to study topology, but decided it only looked good on the surface.
> I was going to study plane geometry, but it fell flat.
> I was going to be a chemist, but it wasn't the right solution.

I was going to be a proctologist, but all the clients were assholes.
I was going to be a urologist, but got pissed off ('Merkin definition).
I was going to be a geologist, but the subject matter was too hard.
I was going to be a seismologist (?), but with my lack of math I was on shaky ground.
I was going to study Anglo-Saxon history, but found I was unready.
I was going to be a Byzantinist, but it's all Greek to me.
I was going to be a flautist, but I blew it.
I was going to be a drummer, but the band told me to beat it.
I was going to be a wet nurse...oh well, no use crying over spilt milk.
I was going to be an electrician, but it didn't turn me on.

--

Michael in Mesa, AZ relayed a ditty from his chat group:
Kudos to Bryan D. Boyle, who contributed this to our bbs. What If Dr. Seuss Did Technical Training Manuals?

If a packet hits a pocket on a socket on a port,
And the bus is interrupted as a very last resort,
And the address of the memory makes your floppy disk abort,
Then the socket packet pocket has an error to report!

If your cursor finds a menu item followed by a dash,
And the double-clicking icon puts your window in the trash,
And your data is corrupted 'cause the index doesn't hash,
Then your situation's hopeless, and your system's gonna crash!

If the label on the cable on the table at your house,
Says the network is connected to the button on your mouse,
But your packets want to tunnel on another protocol,
That's repeatedly rejected by the printer down the hall,

And your screen is all distorted by the side effects of gauss
So your icons in the window are as wavy as a souse,
Then you may as well reboot and go out with a bang,
'Cause as sure as I'm a poet, the sucker's gonna hang!

When the copy of your floppy's getting sloppy on the disk,
And the microcode instructions cause unnecessary risc,
Then you have to flash your memory and you'll want to RAM your ROM.
Quickly turn off the computer and be sure to tell your mom!

--

Mike in Brisbane contributed a corollary:
Absinthe makes the fond grow harder.

--

Zeno in Minneapolis, MN was inspired:
Jan said: "PISSING ON YOUR BOOTS"--Reminded me of something I once heard a friend say about someone with no common sense: "He's so dumb; he couldn't pour piss out of a boot, even if the instructions were printed on the sole!"
This is a very old saying, no doubt, but here is the best version of it I know (William Jay Smith):

> "There are people so dumb," my father said, "That they don't know beans from an old bedstead.
> They can't tell one thing from another,
> Ella Cinders from Whistler's Mother,
> A porcupine quill from a peacock feather,
> A buffalo-flop from Florentine leather.
> They don't know their arse from a sassafras root,
> And couldn't pour piss from a cowhide boot
> With complete directions on the heel."
> That's how HE felt -- that's how I feel.

--

Michael in Mesa, AZ wrote a satire:
I once wrote a letter of resignation for a friend. It went like this:
When, in the course of business events, it becomes necessary for one employee to dissolve the fiscal bonds which have connected him to an employer, and to assume among the powers of his field, the separate but equal station to which the forces of the market and a free-market economy entitle him, a decent respect to the opinions of co-workers requires that he should declare the causes which impel him to the separation. I hold these truths to be self-evident: that not all employees are created equal; that some are endowed by their creator with certain inherent and inalienable abilities; that among these abilities are the having of a life, the taking of liberties, and the pursuit of alternative employment; that whenever any employment relationship should become destructive of these ends, it is the right of the employee to alter or abolish it, and to begin a new position, laying its ground rules on such principles and organizing its responsibilities in such form as to him shall seem most likely to affect his wealth and happiness.

--

Brian in London said:
I wanted to find an alphabet of words (like barbecue) that include the sound of the name of a letter without including that letter itself. Below is what I have come up with so far; any additions would be appreciated.

> a whey; g jeer; m empty; s decimal; y wide; b bee; h -; n men; t tea; z [easy]; c sea; i eye; o beau; u yew; d deer; j gaol; p -; v -; e bijou; k cage; q cue; w double-u; f nephew; l hell; r ah; x ecstasy

The Scots (and some others) will not like "ah" for "r": they would need "ahrrr"! And I have put "easy" for "z" for the American English speakers, but - as a British English speaker - I really need a "zed" sound.

--

On shorthand texting, someone asked:
"ROFLMAOWTIME" translation? I came in late on these and while I can figure out easy ones like LOL, I feel I'm missing something in the greater scheme of things. Could somebody post a quick user's guide to these things, and consider it the same as translating foreign sentences for the uni-literate?

To which Radmilla in Atlanta, GA was happy to oblige:
The one above means Rolling On Floor Laughing My Ass Off With Tears In My Eyes.
Some other useful ones are:

    BRB -- Be Right Back
    OIC -- Oh I See
    FLK -- Funny Looking Kid
    IPT -- In Poor Taste
    GMTA -- Great Minds Think Alike
    BTW -- By The Way
    AFK -- Away From Keyboard
    BAK -- Back At Keyboard
    IMHO -- In My Humble (NOT!) Opinion
    WTG -- Way to Go
    WB -- Welcome Back
    PWT -- Poor White Trash
    YOYO -- You're On Your Own
    SPL -- Serum Porcelain Level (i.e. a crock)
    --

Anthony in Buffalo had a puzzler:
Nothing like the pure fun and intrigue of actual good ol' Wordplay.... See if you can figure this one out...

    With thieves I consort,
    With the vilest, in short,
    I'm quite at ease in depravity;
    Yet all divines use me,
    And savants can't lose me,

For I am the center of gravity.
What am I?

Gerald in New York quickly answered: Are you a V?

Mike in Brisbane had a philosophical take on the old question WHY DID THE CHICKEN CROSS THE ROAD?
Plato: For the greater good.
Karl Marx: It was a historical inevitability.
Machiavelli: So that its subjects will view it with admiration, as a chicken which has the daring and courage to boldly cross the road, but also with fear, for whom among them has the strength to contend with such a paragon of avian virtue? In such a manner is the princely chicken's dominion maintained.
Hippocrates: Because of an excess of pink gooey stuff in its pancreas.
Jacques Derrida: Any number of contending discourses may be discovered within the act of the chicken crossing the road, and each interpretation is equally valid as the authorial intent can never be discerned, because structuralism is DEAD, DAMMIT, DEAD!
Thomas de Torquemada: Give me ten minutes with the chicken and I'll find out.
Timothy Leary: Because that's the only kind of trip the Establishment would let it take.
Douglas Adams: Forty-two.
Nietzsche: Because if you gaze too long across the Road, the Road gazes also across you.
Oliver North: National Security was at stake.
B.F. Skinner: Because the external influences which had pervaded its sensorium from birth had caused it to develop in such a fashion that it would tend to cross roads, even while believing these actions to be of its own free will.
Carl Jung: The confluence of events in the cultural gestalt necessitated that individual chickens cross roads at this historical juncture, and

therefore synchronously brought such occurrences into being.

Jean-Paul Sartre: In order to act in good faith and be true to itself, the chicken found it necessary to cross the road.

Ludwig Wittgenstein: The possibility of "crossing" was encoded into the objects "chicken" and "road," and circumstances came into being which caused the actualization of this potential occurrence.

Albert Einstein: Whether the chicken crossed the road or the road crossed the chicken depends upon your frame of reference.

Aristotle: To actualize its potential.

Buddha: If you ask this question, you deny your own chicken-nature.

Salvador Dali: The Fish.

Darwin: It was the logical next step after coming down from the trees.

Emily Dickinson: Because it could not stop for death.

Epicurus: For fun.

Ralph Waldo Emerson: It didn't cross the road; it transcended it.

Johann Friedrich von Goethe: The eternal hen-principle made it do it.

Ernest Hemingway: To die. In the rain. Alone.

Werner Heisenberg: We are not sure which side of the road the chicken was on, but it was moving very fast.

Schrodinger: Chicken? Chicken!? Where's my cat?

David Hume: Out of custom and habit.

Saddam Hussein: This was an unprovoked act of rebellion and we were quite justified in dropping 50 tons of nerve gas on it.

Jack Nicholson: 'Cause it (censored) wanted to. That's the (censored) reason.

Pyrrho the Skeptic: What road?

Frank Perdue: I breed the finest chicken I know how, and it crosses the road as part of a vigorous fitness program to raise the leanest, plumpest birds anywhere. Besides, I was chasing it with an axe at the time

Ronald Reagan: I don't recall.

John Sununu: The Air Force was only too happy to provide the transportation, so quite understandably the chicken availed himself of the opportunity.

The Sphinx: You tell me.

Mr. T: If you saw me coming you'd cross the road too!

Henry David Thoreau: To live deliberately ... and suck all the marrow out of life.

Mark Twain: The news of its crossing has been greatly exaggerated.

Molly Yard: It was a hen!

Zeno of Elea: To prove it could never reach the other side.

Howard Cosell: "It may very well have been one of the most astonishing events to grace the annals of history. An historic, unprecedented avian biped with the temerity to attempt such a herculean achievement formerly relegated to homo sapien pedestrians is truly a remarkable occurrence."

--

And Frank in Ottawa had an idea:
Why did the chicken cross the road? To show the groundhog it could be done. (Substitute your favorite road-kill if you don't have groundhogs where you are ... 'Possums in Godzone (e.g. in New Zealand).

--

Jim in Philadelphia came up with a riddle:
I've got a little puzzle I kind of stumbled across not long ago... Let's try this one out...

> A little word of doubtful number,
> A foe to rest and peaceful slumber.
> If you add an "s" to this,
> Great is the metamorphosis.
> Plural is ploral now no more,
> And sweet what bitter was before.
> What am I?

--

Hans in the Netherlands, and on self-referential sentences, asked: Can you make up a sentence which statistically describes itself?

Matt in Minneapolis, MN answered:
OK, first, a less ambitious version which I "figgered" myself.
This sentence contains sixty-four letters, eighteen syllables, and ten words.
Also: In this sentence, there are seventy-three letters, twenty-one syllables, and twelve words.
One step further: This sentence is made up of ninety-two letters, twenty-eight syllables, sixteen words, and six punctuation marks.

--

Tony was reminded of a fun game:
That brings up a word game that I was introduced to a couple years ago. The first guy that told me about it called it HINK PINK. Then last year I ran into a guy (ouch) who calls it STINKY PINKY. Basic rules:

1. Person #1 thinks up a rhyming answer
2. Person #1 declares number of syllables in rhyming answer -- One syllable = STINK PINK, Two syllables = STINKY PINKY, Three syllables = STINKEDY PINKEDY,
3. Person #1 gives a clue/definition.
4. Person #2 gives the rhyming answer that Person #1 has in mind.

Example:
Person #1: "What is a STINK PINK for the money paid to someone who runs errands?"
Person #2: PAGE WAGE

What's a STINK PINK for a bunch of Model T's? FORD HORDE
What's a STINKY PINKY for a paint salesman? SEALER DEALER
What's a STINKEDY PINKEDY for the man in the White House? RESIDENT PRESIDENT

--

Toni, in Minneapolis, MN related:
In the Minneapolis Star Tribune they run a regular feature called "Isaac Asimov's Super Quiz". I thought the one from Saturday, August 19 might be of interest here:
The four words in each set share something in common.

1. raccoon, settee, embarrass, bassoon
2. foot, eel, vacuum, Hawaii
3. select, tramp, trace, golden
4. radar, laser, scuba, snafu
5. level, redder, rotator, mom
6. irate, scatter, bath, millionaire
7. thorn, teas, shout, stew
8. horn, pommel, skirt, seat
9. tops, earth, anger, ought
10. sum, win, ring, all
11. tea, sea, are, why
12. TAX, FAIL, COURT, MIND
13. star, parts, drawer, diaper
14. rain, pure, reign, pains
15. begins, almost, chin, abhor

Jim in Philadelphia had a crack at it:
Toni Morgan gives us these puzzles:
1. raccoon, settee, embarrass, bassoon: Two pair(s?) of double letters
2. foot, eel, vacuum, Hawaii: Double vowels
3. select, tramp, trace, golden: "Behead" the word (lop of the first letter) and get a new word
4. radar, laser, scuba, snafu: Acronyms (Forgive me but I forget what radar stands for, but the others are Light Amplification by Stimulated Emission of Radiation, Self-Contained Underwater Breathing Apparatus, and Situation Normal: All F(ouled) Up
5. level, redder, rotator, mom: Reflog a golfer! Palindromes

6. irate, scatter, bath, millionaire: All of them contain the names of animals (rat, cat, bat, lion)

7. thorn, teas, shout, stew: anagrams of names of compass directions

8. horn, pommel, skirt, seat: Since a pommel is the horn of a saddle, and one definition of skirt is "the flaps on a saddle that protect a rider's legs" (Collins), I'd guess they are all parts of a saddle...

9. tops, earth, anger, ought: Take the last letter and put it on the beginning for a whole new word

10. sum, win, ring, all: portions of the names of the seasons

11. tea, sea, are, why: Words that spell out letters

12. TAX, FAIL, COURT, MIND: First and last letters are postal abbreviations for states.

13. star, parts, drawer, diaper: Backwards they're all new words

14. rain, pure, reign, pains: Anagrams of countries: Iran, Peru, Niger, Spain

15. begins, almost, chin, abhor: All letters are in alphabetical order

--

Frank from Ottawa posited:
It struck me that this could be the genesis of a new thread. Match appropriate businesses or institutions with towns, cities, states, provinces or countries.

Terrence in Bermuda answered the call. Here's a few:
> A photocopier manufacturer in Dublin
> A condom company in Bangkok (or Bangalore)
> An annoying proselytizing Eastern religious organization from Budapest
> A sandwich make in Delhi
> A doorbell chime maker in Belfast
> A school bell maker from Belgrade
> A telescope maker in Peking
> Bible-quotations-on-demand Internet service from Halifax
> Paving service in Rhode Island
> An ice-cream addiction counselling service from Copenhagen

A laxative producer from Colon
A mine-site cleanup consultant from Oregon
An industrial laundry service from Washington
A match maker from Bern
A military aircraft parts supplier from Bombay
A brassiere maker from Brest
A sweater manufacturer from New Jersey
A get-married-at-sea service from Gibraltar
An ambulance-for-transporting-mental-patients manufacturer from Madagascar
An employment agency that only offers one type of job, form Seoul, Korea
A depression counsellor from Saigon
A nom de plume suggestion service from Phnom Pehn
A refrigerator manufacturer from Chile
A real estate agent in Acre
A lion tamer from Aden
An "Oliver Twist" publisher from Samoa
An arbor maker from Ann Arbor
A MacIntosh Laptop factory in Minneapolis

Jack in Pine Bluff, AR had a few. For some swinging place/businesses, how about:
--A fox farm in Huntsville
--A tavern in Beltsville
--A pork-storage locker in Hamrick
--A all-female, horse-shoeing establishment in Ladysmith
--A cross-dressing club in Queenstown
--A military aircraft repair shop in Bombay
--A nitroglycerine factory in Bangalore
--A Halloween supply shop in Cebu
--A pastry cemetery in Bunbury
--A bootery for crows in Ravenshoe

--A males-only, outdoor, sports arena in Mansfield
--A bull-fighting stadium in Gore

Toni in Minnesota added:
An eating disorder clinic in Gainesville.

Rich in Rindge, NH:
  A nerdy bug in Antwerp
  A young horror movie actor in Babylon
  An animal farm in Barnstable
  A sauna in Bath
  A collection agency in Billings
  A well driller in Bora Bora
  A lighting designer in Brighton
  A jumping pig in Buckingham
  A bureau manufacturer in Chester
  A stock car driver in Chevy Chase
  A stove switch manufacturer in Cimarron
  A defeated general in Concord
  A fawn nursery in Dearborn
  A cave painter in Denmark
  A stereopticon producer in Dublin
  A poultry cemetery in Duxbury

And David in Pheonix, AZ.
Still more offerings for the placenames thread:
  A bakery in Bismarck
  A blacksmith in Bend
  A left handed blacksmith in South Bend
  A boil removal service in Lansing
  A brush maker in Bristol
  A catering service cleanup provider in Decatur
  A charity in Sharon

A comedy club in Blythe
A comedy club in Yuma
A consulting firm for protesters in Banning
A Democratic U.S. election committee in Hope, AR
A dentist in Plymouth
A dock manufacturer in Pierre (pron'd 'peer' in S. Dakota)
A dog leash maker in Leeds
A family planning clinic in Tucson
A fireworks factory in Sparks
A fresh-water preservation society in Fond du Lac
A Halloween costume shop in Erie
A home for emotionally challenged male offspring in Madison
A miniature toy truck maker in Minnetonka
A municipal consulting firm in Council Bluffs
A parrot aviary in Auckland
A political debate consultant in Dodge City
A royal tax collection agency in Peking
A sex therapist in Moorhead
A Slinky manufacturer in Palm Springs
A sorrowful poetry publisher in Versailles
A stunt man agency in Great Falls
A superhero's clothier in Cape Town
A sweet wine storage service in Portage
A throne maker in Chernobyl
A time management consultant in Rapid City
A travel agency in Fargo
A wordplayers support group in Whittier
An algae farm in Green Bay
An assertiveness training agency for women in Cheyenne
An elephant/walrus dentist in Tuscaloosa
An earth compacting firm in Tampa
An errand service run by a cat woman's husband in Katmandu

Someone proposed:
Here's another neologism for you all to ponder: Sleptomaniac – it means "the spouse who wakes up with all the covers".

Michael in Mesa AZ, thus answered:
Rich Hall used to bring a slew of "sniglets" to NNTN each week. The only ones I can still remember are:
Aquadexterous: having the ability to adjust the bath water temperature with one's feet.
Asprixactability: the uncanny ability, prevalent in television commercial actors, to overturn a bottle of asprin and spill the exact number of pills in the recommended dose into one's hand.
Mussquirt: the inevitable glob of thin yellow liquid that proceeds mustard out the end of a squeeze bottle.
Reminds me of Wayne's World: "If she were president, she'd be Baberaham Lincoln."

--

Zeno answered John of Palo Alto who quizzed "...what's the only word in English with three consecutive letter pairs?"
BOOKKEEPER

--

Sara in Boston answered a quiz:
Hmm... 9 letters & one vowel.. how about "strengths?"
The 7-letter with none of the five vowels: "rhythms"

--

Matt in Minneapolis MN noted:
Ken, after responding to the rhythms, asked about a 6-letter avocalic word (actually, semivocalic). One would be the penultimate word in the following sentence, which is missing a letter: Tr m spr gps szg rhthms.

--

Rich in Rindge, NH answered to Matt who puzzled: "What is the longest string of consonants latched together in an English word?"
Undoubtedly you must be referring to "laTCHSTRing."

Martin in Los Angeles quizzed us:
Here is a challenge to all you word-plunkers: Find a two-syllable, plural word which, when an "s" is added at the end, becomes a three-syllable non-plural word.

Jeff in San Diego, CA:
I think the answer is: Timelines. (two syllables). Add an "s" and it becomes: Timeliness. (three syllables)
I was thinking of this along with other words that the addition of an "s" at the end changes. Including "needles" and "needless." (although they don't necessarily meet the two to three syllable growth requirement).

Jim in Minneapolis has one:
After much consideration I finally got it just in time to post before leaving for Labor Day weekend, and then I understood his subject line: deadlines / deadliness

Stephanie in the Colorado Rockies challenged us:
A few months ago someone mentioned a song called "The Ballad of Davy Crockett". My father wrote the lyrics to the song and the screenplay for the TV show of the same name. Based on that little tidbit, I have a challenge for the agile and facile minds on this list. Try singing the lyrics to "Davy Crockett" to the tune of some other well-known song (Star Spangled Banner/God Save the Queen). Have fun.

Rich in Rindge, NH had a puzzler:
To keep my brain active while sitting at yesterday's all-day faculty workshop, I devised the following puzzle: For each of the three-letter palindromic consonant combinations (say THAT quickly four times!) listed below, can you come up with at least one English word which contains it? (Only dictionary-resident words allowed, no proper names, no plurals.) After a reasonable time, I'll post my solutions; more than one answer may be found for some, your mileage may vary.

CHC, CKC, HSH, KSK, LBL, LDL, LFL, LKL, LPL, LTL, NDN, NGN, NKN, NSN, NTN, PSP, RBR, RDR, RFR, RGR, RKR, RMR, RNR, RPR, RTR, SHS, THT, TST, WKW, WNW, WSW.

Rich gave us his solutions:
1. CHC beaCHComber, arCHConservative, witchcraft
2. CKC coCKCrow, sackcloth
3. HSH eartHSHaking, eartHSHine, rougHSHod, dachshund
4. KSK sharKSKin, buckskin
5. LBL galLBLadder, celLBLock, full-blown
6. LDL boLDLy, coldly
7. LFL haLFLife, seLFLess, wallflower
8. LKL foLKLore, chaLKLine
9. LPL heLPLess, ballplayer
10. LTL fauLTLess, guiltless
11. NDN foNDNess, eNDNote
12. NGN riNGNeck, hangnail
13. NKN baNKNote, uNKNown
14. NSN traNSNational, uNSNap, eNSNare
15. NTN viNTNer, bluNTNess
16. PSP topspin
17. RBR fingeRBReadth, undeRBRush, gingeRBRead, saueRBRaten, charbroil
18. RDR eaRDRum, boaRDRoom, waRDRobe, oveRDRive, oveRDRessed, underdressed
19. RFR hoaRFRost, oveRFResh, stiRFRy, waterfront
20. RGR undeRGRaduate, undeRGRound, undeRGRowth, oveRGRaze, ambergris
21. RKR workroom
22. RMR aRMRest
23. RNR cornrow
24. RPR fingeRPRint, undeRPRivileged, oveRPRiced, oveRPRotect, surprise

25. RTR poRTRait, heaRTRending, fortress
26. SHS waSHStand, fiSHSkin, brushstroke
27. THT baTHTub, deathtrap
28. TST hearTSTring, booTSTrap, haTSTand
29. WKW aWKWard
30. WNW doWNWind, downward
31. WSW neWSWoman, neWSWorthy, newsweekly
32. HTH dipHTHong, dipHTHeria, ichthyology
33. MPM encampment
34. RCR aiRCRaft, oveRCRowd

I haven't yet found good solutions to FTF (craFTFair is two words) or GHG, although I'm convinced there are some out there. Other combos I'm sure there should be solutions for are: DSD, HCH, HPH, LGL, LSL, MSM, PHP, RLR, WLW, and WTW. I also never found solutions to SKS, SPS, or STS that weren't trivial plurals (aSKS, liSPS, toaSTS). Any takers?

And Jim in Philadelphia added a comment:
I confess that number one had me thinking and thinking, and I finally figured it out when I heard a certain Frank Sinatra song come on the radio... (And I just thought of another one for RBR... chaRBRoil... Any special reason why all three of my answers for that one are food-related???) And I used my spell checker to make sure I spelled dachshund correctly...
By the way, Rich, you missed FTF...

And Jack in London had a go too:
horouGHGoing, higHCHair, catcHPHrase, graPHPaper, helMSMan, breaSTSroke and duSTSheet.
FTF: leftfooted and softfocus are better than craft fair, but in my opinion still not quite good enough. The coach brought on a righthanded batsman and a leftfooted kicker? Alternatively, if you can

do something artfully, why not craftfully? :-) :-)
I think most answers are likely to be two words yoked together. How acceptable they are will often be a matter of argument ... though something like breaststroke is a lot less likely to be argued about than highchair.

--

Alex in Adelaide had a riddle:
Does anyone know why a cat sitting on the beach reminds us of Christmas?

Dean in Manhattan, NY spontaneously burst with:
T'was the yule-tide, and all through the sound not a creature was stirring. Not even a [ed. sea creature that rhymes with mouse?]. When who should appear but a feline, fine sand in claws.

--

Anthony in Buffalo, NY posed a teaser:
OK, here we go. Take the word PRECARIOUSNESS. Delete one letter and rearrange the remaining letters to make another word. Now delete one letter from this new word and rearrange the remaining letters to make another new word. Keep doing this until there is only one letter left.
And yes, that last letter should be a word.

Andy in Chichester, UK answered the call:
Anthony's puzzle certainly kept me busy on the train home last night (NB: no dictionary, no anagram solver). I'm not sure whether two of the words exist, but how about:

Precariousness
Repercussions
Repercussion
Precursions
Precursion
Conspirer
Conspire
Princes

    Prince
    Ripen
    Pine
    Pin
    In
    I
Anthony provided the intended answer:
Here is the answer provided in my puzzle book:
    Precariousness
    Repercussions
    Preciousness
    Percussions
    Supersonic
    Conspires
    Princess
    Pincers
    Prince
    Price
    Pier
    Rip
    Pi
    I

--

    Mike in Brisbane contributed to an earlier offering:
Toni's list for word abuse - I hesitate to indulge in self-abuse:
    officiate - That big plate officiate made Pete sick.
    meteor - Was the dog's bone very meteor not?
    oscillate - The b osscillate it if you turn up late.
    gargoyle - I've been staring at this so long I'm gargoyle eyed.
    saxophone - You want phone parts? I got saxophone parts!
    grandiose - I hope he pays me that ten grandiose me soon.
    filibuster - Don't filibuster bursting point.

liverwurst - Or liverwurst people come from the other side of town.

acetone - This radio acetone control.

dishonesty - Our parrot's got a dishonesty. (Cocky's perch = a tee)

gingham - I think he was sin gingham, arum, "Blinded by the Light".

acoustic - Don't acoustic! Dick's as honest as the day is long!

bizarre - People who work in show bizzare usually very interesting.

carnivorous - Oi, you in the Avis office, is there a carnivourous?

argyle - We'll have to use argyle to get out of this situation.

Martin in Los Angeles added:
sanctuary - sanctuary much.

Toni in Minnesota added: Here are some of the "different" offerings from the book:
Aren't you going to introduce meteor aunt?
>   Oscillate I missed my train.
>   Betty found work in Bayonne as a cigargoyle.
>   During saxophone call is very annoying.
>   Beatrice was resigned to liverwurst years with Cecil.
>   Acetone the time will be 6:51 ... and ten seconds ...
>   Dishonesty nearest star.
>   The Catskill comic kept zing gingham.
>   Ivan got to bizarre of all Russia.
>   Argyle beat your guy any day.

Pat in Collegeville, MN:
Reminds me of the knock-knock jokes of my pubertal years, recently (but barely and briefly) revived. The first one I remember--must have been about '38--was
>   Knock, knock.
>   Who's there?

Tarzan.
Tarzan who?
Tarzan stripes forever.

--

Jim in Philadelphia:
Apple must think it's cute or something by using the following sentence to demonstrate its fonts:
How razorback jumping frogs can level six piqued gymnasts. Now I admit that this is better than the tired, cliche "The quick red fox jumps over the lazy red dog." But I thought, I can come up with something better, and a minute later, I had come up with Perhaps silver zirconias don't exactly belong in the mosque with Jake's wife.

Here's my challenge to the wordplayers on this list:
COME UP WITH MORE SENTENCES USING ALL TWENTY SIX LETTERS OF THE ALPHABET...

Matt in Minneapolis, MN answered:
I had these written down already; I cannot claim ownership, except for an 'improvement' on one.
Pack my box with five dozen liquor jugs. (32 letters)
Quick waxy bugs jump the frozen veldt. (31 letters)
Jackdaws love my big sphinx of quartz. (31 letters)
The five boxing wizards jump quickly. (31 letters)
Judges vomit; few quiz pharynx block. (30 letters)
How quickly daft jumping zebras vex. (30 letters)
Foxy nymphs grab quick-lived waltz. (29 letters)
Waltz, bad nymph, for quick jigs vex. (28 letters). [That's the one I 'improved'. The original was: Waltz, nymph, for quick jigs vex Bud.]
Brick quiz whangs jumpy veldt fox. (27 letters)
Mr. Jock, TV quiz PhD, bags few lynx. (26 letters, resorts to abbreviations Credit to Richard Lederer)
Cwm, fjord-bank glyphs vext quiz. (26 letters, but does it make any sense? Credit to Dmitri Borgmann)

Quartz glyph job vex'd cwm finks. (26 letters, if you buy "vex'd" as a word)

Mike in Brisbane enlightened us:
A sentence like this is called a pangram:
How about - "Veldt jynx grimps waqf zho" - these are all legitimate words!
--

Cindy in Montpelier, VT:
Now challenge these statements with proof.
 The shortest word with all five main vowels is EDUCATION.
 The longest word in which no letter is repeated is PURCHASING.
 Observe this longest-found sentence in which each word has one more letter than the word before it.
 I do not want drunk people selling lavender wallpaper everywhere.
 Consider this circular sequence. house-fly, fly-paper, paper-work, work-out, out-house, house-fly, fly-paper... Try to make one like that, but longer.

Observe the pattern here and duplicate it with other sets of opposites.
> right
> sight
> sigh
> sign
> sin
> sing
> swing
> wing
> wring
> wrong.

Rules.
   1. A letter can be switched with another letter in its place.

2. A letter may be added or removed.

3. Only one of the above things may be done with each transformation.

Try to write a sentence like this with each word starting with the next letter in the alphabet. Try to use fewer proper names, though.

Analysis by Concord detective Edward Frank Gregory Henderson indicated Jackson killed Larry Michaelson; nevertheless, Officer Paul Quayle remained sure the unidentified villain was Xenocrates Yannis Zaharias.

Read across the rows and down the columns in each system. Notice any similarities. Also notice how all words are verifiable with any dictionary.

Try to make larger figures like these. Oh yes, also notice that inner squares can be noticed in capital letters inside the larger figures. These can be read like separate figures.

    elks
    lONe
    kNOt
    sets

    apses
    pETAl
    sTaRe
    eAREd
    sleds

Notice how the center letter in that square is also a word.

    malice
    animal
    limped
    impose

THE POWER OF WORDS - 435

>caesar
>elders

Consider also the two-letter words in this word system and use it as a guide for how to make funny-shaped puzzles.
>aboard
>banter
>on to
>at an
>retake
>droned

Another rule to observe is that if the only usage of a word is as a proper noun, it may not be used.

Here is a more easily seen example of what in the world has been going on here.
>YES yEs yeS
>Era ERA erA
>Sad sAd saD

However, Matt in Minneapolis, MN objected:
I challenge the first statement because SEQUOIA is only seven letters long, while EDUCATION has nine.
I challenge the second statement because both DERMATOGLYPHICS [the study of fingerprints] and UNCOPYRIGHTABLE have 15 letters, while PURCHASING has only 10.

Also: "Observe this longest-found sentence in which each word has one more letter than the word before it." >>I do not want drunk people selling lavender wallpaper everywhere<<

Observe this longer-found sentence:
I do not know where family doctors acquired illegibly perplexing handwriting; nevertheless, extraordinary pharmaceutical intellectuality, counterbalancing indecipherability, transcendentalizes intercommunications' incomprehensibleness.

And: "Try to write a sentence like this with each word starting with the next letter in the alphabet. Try to use fewer proper names, though."
After boxes containing dynamite exploded furiously, generating hellish inferno jets killing laboring miners, novice operator, paralyzed, quickly refuses surgical treatment until veteran workers x-ray youth zealously.

And: "Consider this circular sequence. house-fly, fly-paper, paperwork, work-out, out-house, house-fly, fly-paper... Try to make one like that, but longer."
backboard, boardwalk, walkway, waybill, billfold, foldout, outbreak, breakdown, downplay, playback, ...

It seems that a much longer one could be made.

Terrence in Bermuda had a contribution too:
Regarding the challenge to produce acronymically abecedarian sentences:
A Bermudian contributor, Doctor Ellis, found great happiness in just killing lots (mostly nocturnal) of poor quality (relatively speaking) time, ultimately verifying wry, xeric, youthful zip.
--

Alex in Adelaide picked up on another topic:
Hank takes us back to the subject of collective nouns. Here is your chance to play groupie. Match the collections below with the animals they describe on the left. (Courtesy of Richard Lederer)

1.	a barren of	ants
2.	a bed of	bears
3.	a colony of	clams
4.	a crash of	ducks
5.	a gaggle of	fish
6.	a leap of	foxes
7.	an ostentation of	geese
8.	a paddling of	leopards
9.	a parliament of	lions
10.	a plague of	locusts
11.	a pride of	monkeys
12.	a school of	mules
13.	a skulk of	owls
14.	a sloth of	peacocks
15.	a troop of	rhinoceroses

However, I'd like to take it at a slight tangent and start a thread to which you wordplayers are welcome to contribute. Make up your own collective nouns for animals or for people using some punny connections. Examples:

    a prickle of porcupines
    an aroma of skunks
    a rash of dermatologists
    a brace of orthodontists
    a bunch of florists
    a circle of architects
    a line of fishermen
    a file of secretaries
    scores of soccer players
    a mix of chefs and chemists
    a tumult of wordplayers

Any more anyone?

Rich in Rindge, NH jumped on it:
Alex nominated the thread: "Make up your own collective nouns for animals or for people using some punny connections."
Okay...
> a snippet of mohels
> a gigabyte of geeks
> a glut of lawyers
> a delay of procrastinators
> a click of e-mailers
> a round of pregnant women

And Dean suggested: How about:
> a court of lawyers.
> a brace of dentists

David in Ritner, KY had a correction:
It is a pact of lawyers, and a pack of liars.

Mike in Brisbane: How about:
> a run of cricketers
> a flotsam of canoes
> a luxury of cats

Matt in Minneapolis, MN: How about:
A 'fabrication of politicians'? Or a 'nitpick' of copyeditors? (You're all welcome.) To be fair, I'll add a 'nerd' of engineers.

Jack in London: How about a column of journalists?
--

Jesse in Sunnyvale, CA posited:
Here is the question of the day for wordsters. What is noteworthy about the following paragraph? The answer will be provided if nobody gets it, but I'm sure someone will.

From "Minds, Brains, and Programs", by John Surl.

If you support a particular position about minds, you may try it out by asking: what follows if my mind actually works that way? I will apply this philosophy to Schank's program, using an intuition pump as follows: In our imagination, I'm shut within a room, with a big batch of writing in Mandarin. I know no Mandarin, visually or aurally; adding insult to injury, I doubt that I could distinguish Mandarin from, say, Arabic, or from random scribbling. In Mandarin writing, all I fathom is pictorial scrawl.

In conjunction with that batch (Batch A), I obtain an additional quantity of Mandarin script (Batch B), and also a compilation of instructions for associating Batch B with Batch A. That compilation of instructions is in my own idiom, Australian, and as such I can grasp it as thoroughly as any Australian. Using such instructions, I bring into conjunction two groups of formal symbols in a straightforward way (by "formal", I imply that I can distinguish speific symbols visually).

In addition, I obtain a third batch of Mandarin (Batch C), and additional instructions, again in Australian, for associating symbols from Batch C with symbols from Batch A or Batch B. Following such instructions, I can also construct strings of particular Mandarin symbols (with particular visual form), if I first obtain a string of symbols from Batch C.

Although I don't know it, a Board of Control is controlling this situation. Individuals in Control call Batch A a "script", call Batch B a "story", and call Batch C "inputs". An input is an inquiry, which calls in turn for an "output" on my part. Also, all instructions form, in unison, what is known as a "program".

Complicating things a bit, occasionally I am also shown a story in Australian, which I can grasp without difficulty. Control asks (in Australian) for information about a particular story, which I furnish, in Australian, if I can. Slowly I gain so much ability in following instructions about manipulating Mandarin symbols, and Control gains so much ability in writing such instructions, that an actual Mandarin, from China, could not distinguish my outputs from typical communication of his kin. Nobody just looking at my outputs would know that I don't know any Mandarin at all. As for my outputs in Australian: without a doubt, all such outputs look natural, as Australian is my own idiom. A bilingual jury, giving an opinion about my ability, would hold that my outputs in Mandarin look just as natural as my outputs in Australian.

But production of my Mandarin outputs, contrarily to that of my Australian outputs, consists wholly in my syntactic manipulation of formal symbols. Putting it simply, I function computationally, blindly following computational instructions. I am simply an instantiation of a formal program.

The answer is: No e's

15

Soliloquies from Michael

Michael of Milwaukee, WI was a participant in the wordplay forum for a brief period in 1995, who displayed a remarkable talent for verbosity and wordsmithing. His prolific compositions left us all in awe of his brilliant mind. Here are but a few of his brain spurts.

This posting carries out the promise (or threat) made in my August 4th letter: reportage on a Movable Feast known as either The Midwestern Melange or The Blandlanders' Rendezvous. (The Wisconsin Romp, The Madison Frolics, and The Wordplay E-caper were all wisely rejected during a plenary session of the governing board and the arbiter elegantiae, while diluting their sorrows through an equal admixture of pancakes and maple syrup at a Beltline bodega known to the initiates as Perkins'.)

The ensuing scene is, of course, beyond the capabilities of mere human faculties to describe. The loam of my imagination lies fallow in the face of such responsibility. Abulia sets in. Nevertheless, I shall gird my literary loins, tie my semantic sandals, and endeavor to depict an objective portrait, Cromwellian warts and all, of that consummation devoutly to be wished for, The First Convening of the Heartlanders' E-picnic.

For the record (and to forestall any subpoenas) let me state here that I was not privy (I simply WON'T let myself be used in that way, anymore!) to Saturday's saturnalia involving viscous inebriants and word lists.

By the time I arrived posthaste (Now THERE'S a plethora of jokes and one-liners just begging to be begot.) from an attempt to extricate my teen-aged offspring from his self-induced legal and personal imbroglio, the festivities (not to mention several revelers and a large chandelier) were in full swing. Across a squirming sea of late football-victory-celebrants was an assemblage of jaded rakes and naive innocents, a melange of unassuming ingenues and seasoned sophisticates, disporting themselves with all the vehemence and vigor that their obviously flagging energy would allow.

With nothing more than a cursorily reassuring glance at the emergency exit, I screwed up my courage (I like to use a #2 Phillips screwdriver.) and introduced myself. "Well, hell's bells, Shorty", the burly one with the endearing <<Death Before Dishonor>> tattoo and the smegma-stained bowling shirt said. "We ain't no freakin' Wordies or nuttin'. It's jest me an' da ol'lady here, we come inna town widda couple'a frien's to watch Da Game. Howabout dem Packers, ain'a? Oh yeah, I seen some Word Nuts at da odder table, ova dere," he continued, smiling and showing me the remnants of what must have been an unauthorized dental experiment that went awry and was the most likely source of the malodorous miasma that emanated from his personage. This buccal bête noire caused him to pronounce the name of the group as an amalgam of 'weirdos' and 'beer nuts'. Is this prescience? I mused.

Having barely flicked the flecks of spittle and beer off my shirt, I espied a group of my ilk, and clapped glad eyes on that covey of courteously charming wordplayers: Ken Losee & his chauffeuring mate, Connie; Pat; Jim; the affianced couple, Cindi & Ken.

The mental construct I had erected (Do not drag in Freud at this juncture.) of each of these worthy listers (Nor nautical terms.) in the park-like setting of my fancy, was not chipped, eroded or beshat by the pigeons of reality: I tremulously report that every person is EXACTLY as one imagines her or him, some even more so.

So dazzling was the banter, so disarming the quips, so astonishing the pleasantries, so blinding the bons mots, so insightful the retorts, so agreeable the waggishness, so pervasive the prankishness, so scintillating the drollery, so pungent the Attic wit, that no merely printed (or electronically phosphorescent) record would record more than a simulacrum of a representation of a shadow of a memory of an evanescence of a fleeting moment of this glorious fete.

Allow me to proceed indirectly and obliquely; on the bias, as it were. The great compilation, whom we conveniently conflate into "Homer", indulged in such deflexure when he described the beauty of Helen. Instead of giving us a similitude of her comeliness, he adumbrates her pulchritude by indirection. Here's what I mean: During the last years of this protracted fracas two old men espy Helen from the ramparts. She is so beautiful, they concede, that their nearly decade-long period of suffering, deprivation, and loss has been worth it. We are not told of what her attractiveness consists, rather what effect her gorgeousness has observers.

Let me attempt, then, to indicate the extent to which I was carried to heights of ecstasy beyond mortal limits to describe. This is what went on underneath my fevered brow, inside the dome of my brain. Imagine a dark, close vaulted span of skull. In this fertile zone are ten billion unformed intimations. Ten billion tendrils of minute bio-electrical energy strain their boundaries, groping toward embodiment. A cacophonous chorus of synapses modulates with the gibbering of a host of impulses from axon to dendrite. A connection is made. Tentatively, branch brushes tributary, and from within those myriad neural miracles something completely new emerges from the wholly familiar. The germ of invention finds easy rooting in the warm overfertilized hospitable clime of my predilections. An idea swims to the bubbling surface of consciousness. It stretches and writhes its ganglia; a thought lurches toward realization. The thought ripens and blossoms in that dim hothouse, yielding one great exotic bloom. The waxy petals droop. Sentience animates; mind to hand, hand to keyboard, keyboard to computer, computer to internet. That miniscule electro-chemical seed is grown great as Shakespeare's Globe itself; and lo! the vaunted image forms, oozing: "E-NIC!"

The rest is silence.

An apt depiction of the goings-on could be surmised if one combined The Teddy Bear's Picnic with the Marquis de Sade; or Babette's Feast with Tom Jones.

The only thing left undone is the description of the ineffable: Cindi's eyes. Were they the color of a sky pregnant with immanent rain? Was it her corn-fed wholesomeness that made them seem cerulean blue? Are they aquamarine with a minglement of bleu d'Azur or jouvance blue with a suffusion of bleu celeste? Ah, questions. They are like open doors, fresh breezes ... and Cheese Curls (tm): one leads to another....

Your wistfully-like-a-bolt-out-of-the-blue friend,
Michael

THE POWER OF WORDS - 445

Michael responds to Heath in San Antonio, TX, who asks: "I appreciate the camaraderie here, but why is the wordplay drying up?" Well, Heath, it's a function (or non-) of age, I'd guess. Have you tried ginseng, or (as Donne advises) mandrake root? Magical, that mandrake. (Also, pace yourself, my friend.)

This is known as the logoaludic effect. Concerning your querulous query, you undoubtedly have pursued & caught so many verbal nuances, that your quandam quota of quaint quotidian quips has been quelled & quashed; You, quintessential quidnunc, have been quieted. But I quip. A quintillion pardons. I quibble like a quattrocento Quixote, quaffing quarts and eating quahogs. Quelque chose; a quirk. You may quote me quinquennially. (That's queer: I quiver with quinsy-like queasiness, yet the quarrelsome "q"-words just won't queue up. I'm in a quandary. I quaver. How quizzical! Oh, if I could just quack out a few quick quality words. It must be the quinine I contracted at the quay; or the quarry. That's really a quodlibetic point though, because I have no qualms about quitting.)[[

And finally, [a smattering of sighs] for those who wanted to gut the cat thread, here's a cur or two to cure you too of your cursorily curdled courtesy -- curse it!

CATchy as the feline subject was, it seemed to be nearly CATastrophic to our usual CATholicity. We have built a CAThedral to tolerance, only to CATapult ourselves into a CAT-and-dog fracas. To a CATechumen this must appear CATaclysmic, the result of CATalepsy, or worse. I may be CATching at straws, but this is a real CATaclysm. A CATalogue of our faults shouldn't include CATty comments or CATegorical remonstrations. Such a CATouse can cause only CATchpenny quarrels and CATfights. Instead we should anchor our CATechism to the CAThead of CATullian CATchwords: facility of languge and perfection of form. Let no one accuse even one of us of being a CATso.

{This one, ya gadda look up!} When I awakened from my un-CATonian CATnap, (it was, after all, in a CAThouse) I uttered my CATalan CATchcry designed to call my CATalonian assistant (who was CATercorner from a CATalpa tree) and sometime CATamite, to accompany me to the CATacomb of the library. There, in the CATmalison, I found a veritable CATadupe of CAtalectic verse concerning CATilinarian intrigue. It convinced me: from CAThay to CATalina there was no dispute so bitter as ours. We have here a minor CATaclasm. (The last expression is a deliberate CATachresis.) Even a CATamenial cramp should not occasion such CAterwauling. Let all of us, then, CATer to the CATathetical progress of others, no matter how CATawampously they hold to their personal _CATalogues raisonnes_. Allow me to be a CATalyst towards this end: Let's put the unmentionable CATamount subject on a CATafalque and bury its nine lives. Having myself studiously avoided any direct references to c***s, I adjure you to do the same.

 Awaiting your catcalls
  & sending feliform felicitations,
    Your felid friend,

            Michael

References

Participants to the list have consulted a number of references in the process of answering queries and providing input to the debates. Below is a list of some of those references they have mentioned:

"The Harper Dictionary of Foreign Terms", 3rd ed. (NY: Harper and Row, 1987].
Eric Partridge: "A Dictionary of Slang and Unconventional English". My copy was published in 1961 ...
Eric Partridge: "A Dictionary of Catch Phrases, British and American , from the Sixteenth Century to the Present Day", published in 1977.
"The Concise Columbia Encyclopedia" is licensed from Columbia University Press. Copyright 1995 by Columbia University Press. All rights reserved.
"A Dictionary of Americanisms on Historical Principles" edited by Mitford Mathews and published in a second printing by the University of Chicago Press in 1956.
"I Hear America Talking: An Illustrated History of American Words and Phrases" by Stuart Berg Flexner. This was put out in 1976 by the Touchstone Book Division of Simon and Schuster.
Sidney Barker's "Australian Language".
"The Random House Historical Dictionary of American Slang", vol. I, A-G, 1006.
Farmer and Henley's "Dictionary of Regional and Dialectical English".
Wentworth and Flexner, "Dictionary of American Slang". (New York: Thomas Y. Crowell, 1975).
"What's the Difference?: A British American Dictionary" by Norman Moss which was published by Harper & Row in 1973.
"English English: A Descriptive Dictionary" by Norman Schur, published in 1980 by Verbatim Books of Essex, Connecticut.
"The State of the Language" edited by Leonard Michaels and Christopher Ricks. Pub: University of California Press, 1980.
H. L. Mencken's classic, and cranky, "The American Language"
Bill Bryson's "Divided by a Common Language".
"Abuse This Word", subtitled "The Art of Perverse Punning", by Patrick Cosgrove and Lawrence Hussar.
"A Crash of Rhinoceroses": a dictionary of collective nouns, Rex Collings (1993)
"The Wordsworth Book of Intriguing Words", previously published as "The Insomniac's Dictionary", ISBN 1-85326-312-5
Pier Anthony's Xanth series.
"Who Put the Butter in Butterfly - and Other Fearless Investigations into our Illog-

ical Language" by David Feldman (Harper & Row, 1989)
"The Australian Language" by Sydney J. Baker-Pub by Sun in p/b
Charles Earl Funk's "A Hog On Ice & Other Curious Expressions".
"Cambridge Encyclopedia of the English Language".
William Safire's "Political Dictionary".

About the Wordplay List

WORDPLAY was a discussion forum dealing with the usage of words and phrases in English, including vocabulary, metaphors, puns, and the fun use of language. Debates ensue around wording and phrasing of controversial nature, origins of idioms, subtleties, and nuances of verbal and written English.

Rollo, the list manager in Adelaide, summed up the list analytics:

In the beginning, Wordplay was not "digestified" - messages were sent out to all subscribers as soon as they arrived. As the number of subscribers built up, this rapidly got out of control. By 14th February, we had around 500 subscribers, with an average of 50 messages waiting for delivery to each one. The backlog of about 25000 messages almost drowned my system, and I had to put the list on hold while we re-thought our methods. We quickly moved to the current Digest format where multiple messages are sent out in one posting, which annoyed (and annoys) some people but at least keeps the load manageable.

Turnover of our subscribers has been surprisingly high; only 12 of the first hundred people to subscribe are still with us. Apparently, many people don't get what they expected from the list, although some people do, but can't cope with the volume. About 2400 people have subscribed since the beginning, but the peak number simultaneously subscribed was about 1000. The current count is 606.

Speaking of volume, and in the space of six months, we've had about 4500 messages (about 25 per day), totalling about 7 MB. The top 10 posters, by number of messages, have been:

170 (Alyssa, San Francisco)
139 (Jim, Philadelphia, PA)
129 (Bill, Lexington, KY)

126 (Pat, Collegeville, MN)
94 (Zeno, California)
81 (Ken, Victoria, Canada)
79 (Lee "I am woman", Atlanta)
77 (Dr Terrence, Bermuda)
70 (Katherine, Oakland, CA)
70 (Mike Down Under, Brisbane, AU)

The topics had certainly been wide-ranging, and not always strictly related to the use of English in wordgames. Still, the complaints about offensive language have died down. (Is this because the offensive language has died down, or are the remaining readers more thick-skinned and/or tolerant than average?) We've had discussions about the use of words in Spanish, Italian, Greek, Latin, Polish, Russian, Welsh, Portuguese, Norwegian and Danish and probably a few more, as well as some sideplay on being and/or eating Danish, Berliners, Weiners, Copenhagers, with a bit of Welsh Rarebit, French fries and the English disease. We've had anagrams and acronyms, palindromes and mondegreens, Malapropisms and Spoonerisms, acrostics and Ohrwurms. We've had speling errors and grammar complaints, its been fun to see you're advise on what to end a sentence with. [Yes, everything in that last sentence was intentional, thank you.]

Oh, and just to keep us from being too closely-focused, we've heard about weddings and resignations, baby names and housepaint colours – and Technicolor yawns. We *do* cover some wide territory, don't we?

We should all pay homage to Alex Hariz for his idea of setting up such a list; I didn't think it would take off, but I was obviously wrong. It's turned out to be popular and a lot of fun as well. Happy half-birthday, Wordplay! May the next six months be just as much fun.

Pat in Collegeville, MN responded:
And I feel no need to defend myself for posting often to the list.

Much thanks to you for so skilfully and humanely moderating and administering Wordplay. All list-members are in your debt.

And homage for sure to Alex, a man who clearly discerned a market, if a kind of crazy one, and opened it up with no expectation of material profit. That's altruism, as is your management. Hoping you will see us through the next half-year, I remain
Gratefully yours

--

And a word from the originator:
What an exciting 6 months it has been! Indeed, I am truly pleased to see so many people share my fascination with language. I set up the list to get some fun out of language and what I got back is beyond what I imagined, little did I know then that I would be in company of such well-versed people in language and culture, wordsmiths, witty wordsters, and cunning linguists!

The result was lots of fun and tons of learning. Some people have already indicated that they are hooked and that they can't imagine a day go by without their daily dose of wordplay. I thank all of you who contribute to the list, you are the ones who make it happen, and who gave the list its global appeal, we are simply the facilitators, and you are an irresistible bunch. My admiration goes also to un-lurkers who sheepishly step out into the cross-fire, only to get carried into the whirlwind.

Perhaps the least expected thing of all at the outset was the amount of behind-the-scene work and maintenance required to run a list of this magnitude, it was an oversight from my part but we were fortunate, thanks to you know whom. So fellow wordplayers keep your moral support to Rollo coming, and keep up the good stuff.
Alex in Adelaide, whose first language is French but found far more play in English.

Testimonies:

From Mike in Brisbane:
Happy half-Birthday, Wordplay and Wordplayers!
And thankyou to Rollo, our sorter-out-of-problems par excellence, and to Alex, our redoubtable list originator. It's been a great experience, I've learned a lot, and met some wonderful people - all of you. Look forward to lots more in the years to come.

--

Allan in Brandon, Manitoba insisted that he has the very distinct impression that this discussion group is drifting away from what he thought was its original intent regarding words and their usage.

Kent reassured Allan:
I find that Lomond and others have very ably addressed Allan's concerns already, so my thoughts will be repetitious. Skip past if this bores you.

Other lists I have subscribed to, as well as some I am still on, do flame a person for expressing opinions that differ from the rest of the list. Possibly you will get a few flames (I hope not). I stay on this list because for the most part, flames are not a part the community that has grown here.

Copy-Editors-L is where rules can be discussed and argued about bitterly, but I like WordPlay because this is where friends play with words.
My feeling is that I am willing to put up of non-word-play postings since most of those off-topic postings are expressing the concern that are sometimes missing in many of our "local world" environments. I find this an oasis of friendly people sharing enjoyable comments, and using words that teach me to do it better. Alyssa's descriptions of San Francisco, Mike "Down Under"'s description of a part of the world I may never visit (but would love to), Ken's beautiful descriptions of the environment he lives in, all these instruct me in how words can be used properly and well. Occasionally, they have misused or misspelled the words, and were generally corrected, but not lambasted. To each

of the people who have painted word pictures of their locality, thank you.

In addition, words are often used here as powerful conveyors of emotion, sympathy, compassion, enjoyment, pleasure, even dislike and disagreement. I don't find this combination on any of the other lists. I have learned more in the time on this list about proper word usage than I have in a long time.

This list has taught me grammar, spelling, and punning, to name a few. I have gained a list of Latin phrases (with explanations!) that has helped me tremendously. I know, I could, and have, found a similar list in the back of a dictionary, but I've never learned from it the way I have from the list posted here on WordPlay.

I have received a great insight into regionalisms (phrases, culture, and environment) through words used here that has given me an appreciation and understanding I didn't have before. I do understand your concern about seeming to drift from the stated purpose. Anytime I find that discussions of Shakespeare's grammar (whoever she was) and the finer points of gerunds to be deeper than I have a background for, I skip it and come back later to see if it makes more sense. If there isn't enough of it, I can always go to books or visit other lists to get my daily requirements.

When I talk about the sense of community I enjoy on this list, let me reassure you I am happily married, have two great girls in elementary school, work with a great bunch of people who like their job, and all give our best to the work we do (helping people solve problems on their computers), and I don't feel left out socially. But I find there is still room to enjoy more courtesy and concern for, and from, people.

I agree some of the postings could be tightened up, but I probably would pick different postings than anyone else. I hope your posting serves as a wakeup call, but I would hate to think that we might lose the sense of enjoying the wordplayer as well as the wordplay. Thanks go to our List Master, Rollo, for setting the tone and helping nudge us occasionally as needed. Many of us appreciate you, Rollo, and those who don't, well, we can talk to them off-list like a Dutch uncle in terms not appropriate to the list! <big grin>

Stay with us, Allan; bear with us; and learn with us. It's more fun with you than without you.

--

Frank in Ottawa, added:
I add my accolades to Rollo and Alex for creating the most friendly, erudite, and fun group in Cyberia. To you both, and the assembled multitude and your families, and even your bloody cats, warm wishes for the season from a cold clime. May we all keep meeting here throughout the new year.

www.ingramcontent.com/pod-product-compliance
Lightning Source LLC
Chambersburg PA
CBHW071226070526
44583CB00017B/2074